Statecrafting Monetary Authority

Statecrafting Monetary Authority

Democracy and Financial Order in Brazil

Edited by
Lourdes Sola and
Laurence Whitehead

Centre for Brazilian Studies
University of Oxford

Published by
Centre for Brazilian Studies
92 Woodstock Road
Oxford OX2 7ND

ISBN 09544070-6-7

Cover design by Kate Prentice
Typeset by Koinonia, Manchester
Printed by Lightning Source

Contents

Preface

THIS BOOK HAS had a long gestation. At first Lourdes Sola and Laurence Whitehead collaborated on the theme of democratization and central bank autonomy, taking Brazil as the principal focus of interest. In 2002 this resulted in a series of seminars at the University of Oxford's Centre for Brazilian Studies (where the Brazilian case was evaluated side by side with that of Turkey), at the 19th World Congress of the International Political Science Association (IPSA) held in Durban, South Africa (where the South African case was also considered), and at the Fundação Getulio Vargas in São Paulo. The eventual outcome was *Banco Central: autoridade politica e democratização – um equilibrio delicado* (Fundação Getulio Vargas, 2002), a book edited by Lourdes Sola, Laurence Whitehead and Eduardo Kugelmas. The situation in Brazil continued to evolve, new research became available, and in February 2004 the Centre for Brazilian Studies convened a further conference in Oxford on 'Central Banking in New Democracies: Brazil in Comparative Perspective'. The present volume represents the end product of that process. It is the first publication arising from this process to appear in English, and it constitutes a considerable development of the work previously published in Portuguese. We owe a special debt of thanks to the Centre for Brazilian Studies, and its director, Professor Leslie Bethell, for steadfast support. Funding was provided by the Centre, together with some from Nuffield College, backed of course by IPSA, the University of São Paulo, and the Fundação Getulio Vargas. Kurt von Mettenheim and Oliver Marshall both provided indispensable editorial and technical support for this publication.

Lourdes Sola and Laurence Whitehead
30 September 2005

Notes on contributors

Leslie Elliott Armijo is the author of *Financial Globalization and Democracy in Emerging Markets* (Palgrave, 1999) and *Debating the Global Financial Architecture* (SUNY Press, 2002). She is also the author of articles concerning global economic governance and/or the politics of democratization and economic reform in Brazil, Argentina and India. In 2004–5 she served as co-chair of the Organized Section on Economics and Politics of the Latin American Studies Association and a member of the American Political Science Association's Presidential Task Force on Difference and Inequality in Developing Countries.

Eduardo Kugelmas teaches political science at the University of São Paulo and is the coordinator of the politics and economics section of the Brazilian Political Science Association. His research interests include federalism, international relations and the politics of economic policy-making. He is co-editor (with Lourdes Sola and Laurence Whitehead) of *Banco Central, autoridade politica e democratização – um equilíbrio delicado* (Fundação Getulio Vargas, 2002).

Gustavo Loyola had a long career with the Central Bank of Brazil, including serving as its director of banking regulation and two periods as its president. He is now a partner with Tendências Consultoria Integrada, a consulting firm based in São Paulo.

Moisés Marques has worked in financial markets since 1984 and is currently the strategic planning manager of Nossa Caixa, one of Brazil's most important banks. A graduate of engineering and also social sciences, he is a doctoral candidate in political science, at the University of São Paulo.

Kurt E. von Mettenheim is a professor of political sociology at the Escola de Administração de Empresas de São Paulo (Fundação Getulio Vargas). He is a former lecturer in Brazilian Studies and fellow of St. Cross College at Oxford University and has held positions at universities in Brazil, Germany and the USA. His publications include *The Brazilian Voter: Mass Politics in Democratic Transition, 1974–1986* (University of Pittsburgh Press, 1995) and, as editor, *Presidential Institutions and Democratic Politics: Comparing Regional and National Contexts* (Johns Hopkins University Press, 1997) and *Deepening Democracy in Latin America* (with James M. Malloy, University of Pittsburgh Press, 1998).

Mailson da Nóbrega was Brazilian finance minister from 1988 to 1990 after a career with the Banco do Brasil and the Brazilian federal government. He has also worked with the European Brazilian Bank as deputy-manager in London (1985–87). He is now a partner with Tendências Consultoria Integrada, a consulting firm based in São Paulo.

Javier Santiso is chief economist for Latin America and emerging markets at BBVA (Banco Bilbao Vizcaya Argentaria) in Madrid. He has been professor of international political economy at Sciences Po Paris (CERI) and at Johns Hopkins University as well as senior emerging markets economist at Crédit Agricole Indosuez. Santiso's most recent books are *The Political Economy of Emerging Markets: Actors, Institutions and Financial Crises in Latin America* (Palgrave, 2003) and *Latin America's Political Economy of the Possible: Beyond Good Revolutionaries and Free Market Capitalists* (MIT Press, forthcoming, 2006).

Lourdes Sola is professor of political science at the University of São Paulo and first vice-president of the International Political Science Association. She has been a visiting fellow at Notre Dame and Oxford universities, and has held the Rio Branco Chair of Brazilian Studies at the University of California at Berkeley. Sola is co-editor of the *Journal of Political Economy* (*Revista de Economia Política*) and of the *Brazilian Review of Political Science*. Her books include *Idéias econômicas, decisões políticas – estabilidade, crescimento, populismo* (Edusp, 1994) and, as co-edited with Eduardo Kugelmas and Laurence Whitehead, *Banco Central, autoridade política e democratização – um equilíbrio delicado* (Fundação Getulio Vargas, 2002).

Matthew M. Taylor is an assistant professor of political science at the University of São Paulo. He has worked as a consultant on economic and political issues in the Southern Cone and Brazil between 1994 and 2000, and has published articles on courts, public policy, and policy reform in the *Brazilian Journal of Political Economy*, *América Latina Hoy*, *Economics of Governance*, *Bulletin of Latin American Research* and *Comparative Politics* (forthcoming), among other scholarly journals.

Laurence Whitehead is Official Fellow in Politics at Nuffield College, Oxford University, and Senior Fellow of the College. His most recent books are *Democratization: Theory and Experience* (Oxford University Press, 2002) and, as editor, *Emerging Market Democracies: East Asia/ Latin America* (Johns Hopkins University Press, 2002). His next book, *Latin America: A New Integration* is due to be published by Palgrave in December 2005.

Matthew M. Hurley is an assistant professor of [illegible] University of São Paulo. [illegible]

[illegible]

Introduction

Laurence Whitehead and Lourdes Sola

THE DOMINANT ORTHODOXY in the new democracies of the 1990s was that financial markets should be liberalized and internationalized as rapidly as possible, with political discretionality curbed or dismantled. Politicians were stereotypically viewed as rent-seekers incapable of responsible monetary conduct. When such prescriptions produced financial crises and/or severe economic contractions, the typical conclusion was that these were the transitional costs of introducing a superior economic model, or that liberalizing reforms had been too slow or too half-hearted. Brazil was commonly identified as a laggard in this respect. International opinion perceived Brazil as slow to learn, while debate within Brazil – especially after the debacle of the Collor presidency (1990–92) – revolved almost entirely around 'gradualists' and 'resisters'. The 'shock treatment' approach pursued by Argentina, Mexico, and Peru never had a significant domestic constituency in Brazil.

Indeed, even during the period of military authoritarian rule, Brazilian policymakers differed from those of neighbouring Spanish American republics in that they never embraced shock treatment or a sudden opening of the economy to international market disciplines via the law of one price. Instead, both military governments and their civilian democratic successors pursued a conflict avoidance approach to economic policy. This lay behind the military regime's heavy reliance on compensatory indexation devices to mitigate the political impact of accelerating inflation, and it also underlay the diagnosis of inflation as 'inertial' during the civilian governments that preceded the 1993–94 Real Plan. The results of President Collor's brief attempt at a more root-and-branch approach (in 1990) only reinforced this conflict avoidance reflex. This theme is further developed in Chapter 4 by Eduardo Kugelmas and Lourdes Sola.

With the benefit of a decade of hindsight we can see that the dominant orthodoxy of the 1990s was inadequate. The 2001 default in Argentina was only the most spectacular of a series of setbacks to this view. The most successful 'emerging market' of the 1990s – (communist-ruled China) – was a conspicuous deviant from neoliberal orthodoxy. Democratic Brazil was far less economically successful than China and also deviated far less from the standard western model of market liberalization, but it adopted a basically different course, as analysed in this volume. So far the results, while disappointing in many respects, have not confirmed the Cassandra-style forecast of Dombusch, and are not clearly inferior to the achievements of most liberalizers. A simple way of checking the relative standing of Brazil as compared to its neighbours is to consult the standardized cross country tabulations that are now being made available from a variety of sources (each with their own value preferences and methodological biases).

Thus, from the 'free market' perspective it is possible to track how Brazil has performed according to the United States Heritage Foundation's 'Index of Economic Freedom'. Of the 155 jurisdictions ranked from best (Hong Kong) to worst (North Korea), the Heritage Foundation placed Brazil 80th in 2004. It was thus classified as offering less economic freedom than Mexico (63rd) Peru (58th) or El Salvador (24th) and placed on a par with Albania. But it was considered more 'free' than Colombia (83rd) Paraguay (106th) and Argentina (116th). The comparison with Argentina is particularly instructive for our purposes:

	1996	*2000*	*2004*
Argentina	2.63	2.23	3.48
Brazil	3.56	3.46	3.10

Source: Index of Economic Freedom (Heritage Foundation, Washington, 2004, p. 11).

As can be seen, although Argentina was rated much more favourably than Brazil in the 1990s, it was also more volatile. By 2004 its rating had slipped below Brazil's which was registering a modest but steady advance.

From a European perspective the Bertelsmann Foundation has undertaken a parallel exercise, dealing only with 116 countries classified as 'in transition' towards market-based democracy. According to the

Foundation's 2003 'Transformation Index' Brazil rates well above Mexico, El Salvador, and Peru, and far above Argentina, both in terms of the status of the economic transformation achieved between 1998 and 2003 (22nd out of 115) and in terms of its 'management performance' (14th out of 110). In Latin America only Chile, Costa Rica, and Uruguay were rated higher in terms of their leaders' capability of governing and high degree of reliability in pursuing goals.[1]

In this book we have not tried to argue that there is only one right way to practise economic reform, and that essentially the same model is appropriate for all cases. The focus of this study has been on Brazil, a continent-sized economy with distinctive structural and institutional legacies, and with a different pattern of insertion in world markets (and a different experience of authoritarianism and its gradual replacement by democracy) from that of most new democracies. Its financial history was also highly *sui generis* as we shall see. Our basic position is that projects for financial liberalization and reform that ignore such national specificities, and that disregard the distinctive texture of political-economic interactions in Brazil, are unlikely to work, or to produce their predicted results.

The Argentine default, along with other politico-economic crises of Latin America after 2000, have understandably provoked a series of reassessments of the assumptions guiding orthodox analysis in the previous decade. The theme of 'governability' has come to the fore, and comparative economic research has begun to explore the reasons for contrasting 'policy styles' in the economic management of the main republics. However, it remains problematic how to integrate more political and national contextual variables into analytical frameworks that still remain mechanical and objectivist in conception. Such initiatives are to be welcomed for their innovativeness and open-mindedness. This book proceeds from a different starting point, but aims to contribute to a constructive dialogue on how to understand the logic and dynamics of liberalizing economic and financial reforms within a democratic political context. In this respect it parallels some of the concerns of the Bertelsmann Foundation, and opens a dialogue not only with mainstream economics, but also with much of the political science literature comparing democratization processes.

Much of the democratization literature can also be found wanting for a failure to integrate economic institution building into its analysis of political crafting and so-called 'consolidation'. Analyses of democratization that marginalize or exclude financial market pressures/dilemmas/ constraints are also unlikely to work as expected, or to deliver their predicted results. Both democracy and monetary stability can be regarded as highly valuable collective goods, and (as Leslie Armijo argues in Chapter 5) it is also possible to view them as mutually reinforcing. However, in many of the countries covered by this volume (large, peripheral, new, democracies) these desirable outcomes are still precarious. They are not yet socially embedded. Even if there is a popular consensus in favour of their persistence this may not be accompanied by a deep commitment to all the associated adaptations. The audiences for different components of the liberal democratic package may still be highly fragmented. Understanding the self-restraints and civilities implied by this type of non-coercive system of coordination may not be widespread. Extremely unequal societies with weak institutions, limited experience of citizenship, and poorly secured rights, can hardly be expected to view either democracy or the market as self-evident or natural systems of regulation. Voters and consumers have to learn how to operate within a more liberal framework, and for that purpose they require guidance from specialists and professionals. But journalists, lawyers, accountants, and bureaucrats also need to be socialized into these new 'rules of the game'. There may be no prior 'epistemic community' of democratic market facilitators, standing by to lubricate the new liberal regime. Such expertise and awareness has to be constructed through detailed practice and supervision.

Over time, with patience and good leadership and design, it may be possible to deepen social commitment to the new norms and conventions required to embed democracy and to stabilize market relations (including an overall level of price stability). But there are few short cuts. This is why we take a decade long view of the changes underway in Brazil since 1994, and why more generally we view both democratization and economic liberalization as works in progress.

This is where such key concepts as incrementalism and statecrafting make their entrance. A politically informed analysis of the construction of a stable and open monetary order has to go beyond the reductionist categories found in the existing comparative economics literatures. As recent upheavals in Argentina and Venezuela make clear, it does not suffice to measure 'central bank independence' using formal statistical and legal indicators. Nor can we continue to overlook the multiple roles occupied by central bankers in emerging democratic regimes – roles that require them to operate with both technical competence and political skill and discretionality. Some developed countries, such as New Zealand, have attempted to limit central bank function to a single objectively measurable inflation target, thus virtually eliminating discretionality. Apart from the fact that the results of these experiments remain in doubt, this approach can hardly be generalized to central banks in developing countries that are also required to participate in long-run projects of overall state reform and financial restructuring. In Brazil, as in many other countries, exchange rate intervention may generate large losses that are added to the fiscal deficit, quite apart from the potentially huge redistributive and distributive costs of bank rescue programmes.

Moreover, given all the accumulating evidence that central bankers, just like other officeholders, can lapse into committing abuses if they are not held fully and democratically accountable, we cannot endorse an absolute conception of 'insulation' without jeopardizing the legitimacy of economic reform. For all these reasons our analysis highlights a succession of historical-political categories – statecrafting, institution-building, brinkmanship, incremental reformism, muddling through and the construction of convergence between economic and political dimensions of a monetary regime – categories that all enrich standard comparative analyses.

Although we focus on Brazil, this is not purely a single country study. We believe that what we have to say is relevant to a significant number of relatively large and at least semi-developed new democracies which all face pressures to liberalize their financial markets. In at least this regard, it is fair to compare the Brazilian situation with the position in Argentina, India, Mexico, Russia, South Africa and Turkey. This volume is assertively comparative and theoretical, as well as providing a serious single country case study. We hope it will stimulate further focused case studies of other countries, and thus enrich our stock of comparative analysis. As all the above listed countries attempt to democratize their political institutions, all face highly constrained margins of fiscal and monetary discretionality, and the costs and dangers of error are clearly very real. These are not just economic costs, but political system risks as well. Even so, the experience of Brazil so far suggests that some margin of policy discretionality *does* exist, even if it is narrow and hedged by dangers. Virtuous circles of statecrafting, market stabilization, and legitimation *are* possible. There is, however, nothing automatic or unilinear about such developments. On the contrary, the Brazilian example indicates a great deal of experimentation, back-tracking, and 'learning by doing'. There were, for example, no fewer than seven failed stabilization attempts between 1986 and the eventual success of 1994. Overall the media played an important role in helping society learn constructive lessons from these misadventures. The Cardoso administrations had the merit of capitalizing on this painful sequence of lessons, and instead of continuing Collor-type attempts to shock the public into a different pattern of expectations it opted for a step-by-step pedagogic therapy, aiming to keep society more or less informed and prepared for successive incremental reforms. This worked because it was what the public had come to require, and because opinion-formers and the media broadly cooperated. Thus, comparative experience suggests that there are real strategic choices available, and the right choices can be cumulatively beneficial.

The idea of cumulative incremental reforms, in which achievable initial measures generate more favourable conditions and a broader support base for subsequent follow throughs, is not particularly new or distinctive. Hirschman referred to 'reform-mongering', and rational choice analyses refers to side-payments and the construction of minimum winning coalitions. But this is not the main neoliberal image of how liberalization comes about. Their alternative picture envisages mounting distortions and rent-seeking until the illiberal system becomes unviable and collapses. Then enlightened technocrats (probably paid, and recruited from outside the society) can sweep away all the inherited clutter of interventionist measures and institutions, creating a *tabula rasa* after which free market incentives can dictate behaviour. So on this view crises pave the way for collapse of the old and birth of the new. This is not the picture of the reform process envisaged in this study. Here the process of causation (particularly in the chapters by Lourdes Sola) proceeds according to a reverse sequence. It is not actual crises, but the looming threat of a potentially unmanageable outcome, that triggers change. Teetering on the brink of crises ('brinkmanship') induces a last minute coordinated response. To avert the worst and to save inherited practices and institutions the relevant actors are driven to engage in 'statecrafting'. They introduce new rules and tacit understandings that provide more insurance against crises. In other words potential crises create an opportunity for a creative political response within the established framework. The state emerges more effective and resourceful, instead of being dismantled. Obviously this is not a deterministic argument. It identifies a central tendency, and serves as a corrective against the 'necessary breakdown' logic of the neoliberals. But this path to cumulative incremental reforms is inherently vulnerable to setbacks, unintended consequences and reversals. The essential contention is that if the situation deteriorates under the impact of such adversities, the chance of an effective policy response increases. The assumption is that the society and economy are broad and resilient enough to absorb such strains. So far this has proved true of Brazil, although there is no guarantee that it will always prove so.

In a federal democracy, such as Brazil, incremental reforms involve protracted rounds of negotiation and compromise between an electorally constrained federal executive, a bi-cameral congress, and a variety of lower-level political actors with varying policy interests and degrees of leverage (state governors, mayors of large cities, party bosses, labour and business lobbyists, media moguls, etc.). So the reform process is strewn with potential 'veto points' and opportunities to impose delay and extract 'side payments'. All this can generate confusion and demoralization, especially among market observers anxious for clear and prompt reform outcomes. But this erratic and 'second-best' character of incremental reform has its compensations. After all these checks and filters have been surpassed, the resulting policy outcomes are solidly embedded. They are more legitimate and institutionalized than the kind of top down measures of reform-by-decree introduced elsewhere (e.g. in Menem's Argentina). Matthew Taylor's chapter takes up this general theme, and adds an important extra dimension to it. Focusing on the two Cardoso administrations, he draws attention to the prominent role played by the federal judiciary in sometimes blocking or delaying and other times legitimizing federal reforms. He provides an empirically grounded and unsentimental account of the procedures and conditions under which some key veto players may operate through the courts to obstruct certain reforms. But he also brings out the legitimating role of the courts, which can affect policy substance as well as procedural propriety. This is an important component of the 'statecrafting' of reform in democratic Brazil.

A similar approach to statecrafting as a non-deterministic process of strengthening the collective capacity to cope with economic and political shocks underlies Chapter 1 by Laurence Whitehead on what he describes as the 'delicate balance' between the requirements of monetary stability and those of democratic legitimacy. Whereas Lourdes Sola is theorizing about the contingent dynamics of reform, Whitehead focuses on the tension between two rival requirements for a stable outcome, and how they might be reconciled. His 'delicate balance' concerns the equilibrium or trade offs between two competing domestic logics: the technical requirements of economic rationality (as understood within the central bank and the associated financial community) and the political requirements of legislative and electoral consent (as filtered through emerging democratic processes).

But there is also a related tension between these domestic political and economic dynamics, on the one hand, and the pressures and expectations emanating from the international financial markets into which these liberalized economies have increasingly become integrated. Laurence Whitehead's chapter modelling the interactions between a democratic election and the reactions of the international market sketches a non-deterministic framework for analysing such dynamics. Instead of postulating one or other side of interaction as the 'dependent' variable it aims to track the causation in both directions. It emphasizes different speeds of reaction time in the two areas as the most critical feature of such dynamics. It is instructive to compare this modelling exercise with the more empirically based chapter by Javier Santiso, which presents an unusually clear and detailed analysis of one side of the relationship – how international market operators shifted their evaluations of Brazil's exchange rate prospects during the course of the 2002 election campaign. Santiso does not embrace a wholly one-sided or deterministic interpretation, but his perspective is inevitably coloured by the clarity of his evidence on the international drivers of the interaction. A counterpart study from the domestic side, with the same depth of coverage, would be a most valuable addition to this analysis.

It is also important to contextualize Santiso's evaluation of external market pressures from the international side. In Chapter 2, Eduardo Kugelmas does this by tracing the historical evolution of Washington's debates on financial liberalization from the early 1990s to the present. His interpretation draws attention to the changing historical and institutional context, and to the partly technical but also partly ideological content of the prevailing discourse. His decade-long perspective contrasts with Santiso's immediatism, and underscores both the variability of successive Washington orthodoxies, and their partial insulation from contrary evidence and analytical feedback. Given the picture he presents of a notable degree of instability and unpredictability at the centre of the world's international financial system, it would be a mistake to think in terms of tight one-way causation from the blueprint at the 'core' to the passive recipients of influence on the 'periphery'. His analysis reinforces the view espoused by this volume that substantial 'emerging market' democracies[2] such as Brazil cannot simply import financial stability by conforming to Washington-based prescriptions. There is too much instability at the centre of the system, and it has insufficient sensitivity to the complexities of financial management in large developing countries, for a single 'best practice' formula to work in all cases. What seems to follow from Kugelmas' analysis is on the one hand that emerging market democracies need to be carefully attuned to the doctrines and prescriptions currently in fashion at the centre, but they also need to preserve sufficient political autonomy and independent capacity for analysis to generate their own counter-proposals, or to modify and adapt standard blueprints, in order to fend off extremely generated instabilities, and to construct homegrown financial institutions that are both viable and locally legitimate.

Within this framework, Leslie Armijo's chapter offers a challenging suggestion. She presents mass democracy as a fundamental source of financial stability rather than as a potential threat to it. This argument also needs to be contextualized. It would not necessarily apply to the introduction of mass democracy in all circumstances, but it could be particularly relevant to those cases where democratization takes an incrementalist form, and where large complex societies would be more unstable (more prone to zero sum conflict and authoritarian regression) if the electorate were denied a responsible role. Cases such as Brazil, India, Mexico and Turkey might fit this description, although many other new democracies could be somewhat different. The point of this chapter is not to propose a 'large N' covering law, but rather to offer a time-sensitive middle range generalization that is particularly pertinent to the concerns of this volume. The methodological interest of the chapter is that, as with the Lourdes Sola chapter on statecrafting, it suggests a reversal of the usual causal arrows. Mass democracy could both be good and necessary in its own right, and also (incidentally) a promoter of financial stability in societies that have hitherto been exposed to politically motivated manipulation of monetary variables. This may only be a tendency statement, rather than an inevitability, and it may require considerable contextual infilling before the postulated relationship becomes a solid one. But it points to the potential for a positive relationship between regime change and financial order. This is a more optimistic take on democratization than the usual arguments, which stressed the need to 'insulate' technocrats from the irresponsible conduct of myopic elected politicians

In our view, therefore, the Brazilian experience runs directly counter to one of the key elements in the orthodox mantra of 1990s policy prescriptions. This was first 'put the institutions right' (meaning insulate and empower the experts with the necessary international support and technical understanding). It was not thought important to legitimize these institutional reforms, but rather it was recommended to rush them through as fast as possible (over-riding resistance and cutting legal corners if necessary). This was on the assumption that once the 'right' pro-market structures were securely in place they would generate financial confidence and economic reactivation and thus in turn would make the politics of reform more tractable. Contrary to this prescription the Brazilian reforms of the 1990s were negotiated within the inherited institutional constraints of the 1988 Constitution. As shown in Chapter 6 by Sola and Marques, the stabilization process proceeded first, thus creating the economic and political conditions favouring subsequent delegation of substantial de facto autonomy to the Central Bank. This continues even under the administration of Luiz Inácio Lula da Silva, even though the operational autonomy of the Central Bank of Brazil remains qualified and – from an orthodox standpoint – incomplete even now (a point we discuss further in the volume's Conclusion).[3]

Although most of this volume is focused on contemporary Brazil, the arguments outlined above are clearly of broader theoretical and methodological significance. Not only is Brazil an extremely important case, worthy of study in its own right. It is also an exemplary, or even 'test' case for a series of broader arguments and assertions that need to be fed into the comparative politics literature in general. If it is not possible to achieve satisfactory economic and political liberalization through incremental reforms and 'statecrafting' in Brazil, then the implications are also ominous for quite a few other 'emerging market' democracies as well. Brazil, after all, has a number of advantages that are not always so well-established elsewhere: it is outside the range of the major geo-political conflict zones; it has a large and diversified economic base with substantial segments of modernity and even in some cases best practice; its political institutions have been developed and refined over a long period, with a considerable degree of sophisticated input; its national identity and territorial integration is not in question, and the military seem no longer a real problem; and it has an unusually large and well-structured left-wing (originally trade union based) political party that has abandoned revolutionary strategies and has successfully won office through a strategy of legal political contestation within the constitution. With such favourable conditions in the background, much is riding on Brazil's capacity to construct a stable and effective financial order that rests on democratic consent. Clearly the authorities have only a narrow margin for manoeuvre, but this book rests on the assumption that (contrary to neoliberal root and branch doctrines) there is a margin of choice here. If that were not to prove to be the case, the implications for Brazilian democracy and for Brazilian economic progress would be highly troubling. Moreover, if this were not possible in Brazil, the scope for the development of broadly 'social democratic' initiatives in other emerging markets would be small indeed. In fact the scope for social reform more generally would be brought into question. Unless a poor electorate can be offered some realistic prospect of eventual social progress through democratic advance, it will not be possible to secure the consent needed for a non-coercive system of market relations. So the stakes could hardly be higher, and this volume is focused on exploring the scope for a constructive response to these challenges.

Notes

1 *Bertelsmann Transformation Index 2003*, Gütersloh: Bertelsmann Foundation, 2004, pp. 11–12.

2 The term 'emerging market' democracy refers to recently democratizing countries that have also been undergoing financial liberalization in accordance with prevailing market doctrine. It provides a convenient label for bracketing countries such as Argentina, Brazil, Chile, Korea, Mexico, Russia, South Africa and Turkey without vouching either for their economic or political success.

3 McNamara and Castro explain the worldwide diffusion of central bank independence over

the past twenty years as follows: 'it is a rational reaction to a specific transnational social environment that privileges the idea of central bank independence irrespective of its intrinsic effect on economic performance and sometimes at the expense of more effective strategies of economic policymaking.' They recommend further 'qualitative and case study' work to check this hypothesis, including investigating 'several cases of countries that are outliers in this process and have yet to adopt CBI, such as Brazil', Kathleen R. McNamara and Eduardo D. Castro, 'The diffusion of central bank independence', APSA paper, Philadelphia, August 2003, pp. 2 and 14.

Chapter 1

The political dynamics of financial crises in 'emerging market' democracies

Laurence Whitehead

SEVERE FINANCIAL CRISES (maxi-devaluations, systemic bank failures, extreme contractions, even breakdowns in the payments chain) have disrupted the economic and political routines of a large number of 'new' democracies since the end of the Cold War. Such episodes have been so frequent and recurrent in major 'emerging market' democracies over the past decade that they can no longer be dismissed as isolated, marginal or disconnected from the normal functioning of these recently liberalized politico-economic regimes. A comparative and theoretically informed analysis of their causes, rhythms, and consequences should therefore be attempted, in order to clarify their implications for the stability and quality of these democratization processes. This chapter operates on a wide canvas and raises more questions than it can answer. It aspires to set an agenda for more detailed comparative and case study research. The following questions merit collective consideration:

i. Do these financial crises share enough common features to merit investigation as a single cluster?
ii. Can they be adequately explained in terms of a purely economic analysis, or do they require a 'political economy' interpretation?
iii. Can they be satisfactorily modelled within a unitary framework, or are several (perhaps overlapping) schemas required?
iv. Can they be contained (or, better still eliminated) through the adoption of a single standard package of rational design principles or corrective measures? Or are all plausible countermeasures partial and context-specific?
v. Are these episodes merely characteristic of a 'transitional' period

within a trajectory of liberalization, which will therefore be overcome when democracy is fully consolidated and these markets have finally emerged? Or are they recurrent, endemic, features of an unequal international system?

vi. What kinds of democracy are being envisaged? Are these to be competitive electoral regimes with no significant margin of discretion over the workings of the financial markets and the operations of monetary policy? Or does democratic legitimation require some last resort authority to regulate markets that would otherwise generate disruptive financial crises? What trade-off is possible between the stabilizing benefits of depoliticization, and the democratic requirements of regulatory oversight?

vii. What international arrangements (if any) might serve to alleviate such episodes, and what scope is there for improving the global management of these crises?

The cases

Table 1 lists the major countries and episodes of financial crisis to which this chapter refers. The list is illustrative, rather than exhaustive, but it does cover the major financial crises in large 'emerging market' democracies that have demanded international attention since the end of the Cold War. Several features of the list merit attention. It records thirteen episodes over thirteen years. Nine of these episodes took place in the second half of the period. There is no evidence here to support the hypothesis that these were 'transitional' events due to fade away as liberalization proceeded. Although almost half the crises were in Latin America (six out of thirteen), all regions of the 'developing' world are represented. On the face of it we are dealing with a worldwide rather than a localized phenomenon. Two countries appear twice, with Argentina figuring prominently both at the beginning and at the end of the period. It is not self-evident that exposure to a first financial crisis inoculates any of these regimes from subsequent exposure.

Only a limited number of countries meet the various criteria for inclusion in this list. It is limited to new democracies that have sufficient economic autonomy and administrative efficiency to engage in discretionary macroeconomic management potentially capable of promoting both price stability and economic development. Only relatively diverse

Table 1.1: ***Financial crises in major 'emerging market' democracies***

Country	*Peak crisis year*	*Nearest election dates*
Argentina	1989	May 1989
India	1991	May/June 1991
Mexico	1995	Aug 1994
Bulgaria	1996	April 1997
Thailand	1997	Nov 1996
South Korea	1997	Nov 1997
Venezuela	1998	Dec 1998
Russia	1998	Dec 1999
Brazil	1999	Oct 1998
South Africa	2001	June 1999
Turkey	2001	Nov 2002
Argentina	2001	Oct 1999 /April 2003
Brazil	2002	Oct 2002

and well-structured economies and sophisticated state apparatuses can aspire to significant policy discretionality. Most new democracies fall short of this standard because they are either too vulnerable economically, or too weakly administered (or both). Even the more resilient and better-governed minority of new democracies are heavily constrained by market forces, and by proliferating obligations of international economic diplomacy (IMF agreements, WTO commitments, regional integration pledges), so that their scope for discretionary macroeconomic management is often doubted, or even denied. However, candidates competing for electoral office typically claim that they can improve economic performance (or at least do better than their rivals, who would worsen it). So the democratic process promotes the belief – or illusion – that some degree of economic policy discretionality is available and worth competing for. And some democratic governments manage to project the image that they have produced better economic results than would otherwise have been attainable, whereas others must carry the burden of blame for bad out-turns.

In countries such as Argentina, Brazil, Chile, Mexico, Poland, Spain, Turkey – and perhaps South Africa – the processes discussed in this paper occupy a central place in political debate. Some (limited) policy discretionality seems available to incoming governments and the manner in which this is exercized is a key determinant of an administration's political success or failure. Although this may only apply to a limited subset of new democracies the countries in question are large, populous, and influential. So an assessment of the scope and limitations of macroeconomic policy discretionality in such setting is of general significance.

In theoretical terms, 'democratization' acquires an enhanced significance if there is a substantial group of new democracies where the content of economic policy can be significantly altered/upgraded as a consequence of competition between alternative political projects. Were it the case that some external constraints ('globalization' or 'neoliberalism') precluded all significant economic policy alternatives then the democratic process might lose much of its justification and popular appeal.

The concepts

This chapter has so far raised a considerable number of complex and loosely worded questions. It has also invoked a series of abstract concepts (sometimes placed within inverted commas to signal the approximate nature of their significance). Without overloading the text with ponderous definitions, it may be as well to briefly comment on the following key terms in the discussions.

1. Democracy/democratization

As indicated in the third column of Table 1.1, all the episodes under consideration took place in countries that were conducting periodic competitive elections to national office around the same time. Not all these elections were equally 'democratic', but they all operated above the basic threshold required to differentiate a democratizing regime from an overtly undemocratic one (Russia was probably the closest to the borderline, but one could also express reservations about, say, Mexico, or even South Africa). This analysis does not imply a very high standard of democratic performance: the threshold is simply whether access to national office is regulated through more or less competitive elections in pre-established calendar or procedure that introduces enough uncertainty over the next government to attract attention in financial markets. The voters should also have some grounds for believing that their expression of collective preferences might elicit a significant public policy response (a macroeconomic response is particularly relevant here). Beyond these minimum threshold conditions, there is also a normative connotation to the terms democracy and democratization as used here. Whatever the immediate deficiencies of the electoral procedure, the citizenry are being encouraged to believe (or at least to plausibly hope) that over time successive elections will generate a more accountable, consensual, and rule-governed system of government. Thus, this chapter views democratization as a work-in-progress, and as a means to improve policy performance (including economic policy performance), as well as a mechanism of elite circulation.[1] An important implication of this perspective is that it is therefore harmful to democratization if the experience of democratic government comes to be associated in people's minds with an increased vulnerability to destructive financial crises.

2. *'Emerging market' democracies*

This chapter is concerned with financial crises (as defined in the introduction), episodes that can occur in many different settings. However, all the crises listed in Table 1.1 belong to a distinctive subset of events which display many common characteristics. Such crises seem particularly relevant, and perhaps particularly virulent, in the 'emerging markets' that have recently implemented the rather standardized policies of economic and financial liberalization, privatization, state shrinking, etc. that have spread around the 'developing world'. Emerging markets compete to attract transnational investments and financial flows, in part by enhancing the legal security and marketability of privately owned assets in what were formerly much more closed national economies. Not all emerging markets engage in democratization, and not all new democracies are in emerging markets. But this chapter is concerned with a subset of new democracies which (at least for a limited period in recent history) have exposed their economies to common external incentives and constraints. As a result, emerging market democracies have experienced parallel pressures and have come to learn more about each other and their common experiences. Elsewhere I have referred to this as a process of 'mutual recognition'.[2]

3. Discretionality

This is a key term, one that is open to various interpretations. From a neoliberal economic perspective political discretionality is something to be avoided, especially in the realm of macroeconomic management. On this view it is associated with statism, interventionism, rent-seeking and populism. The underlying assumption of neoliberalism is that resources can be more efficiently allocated through market mechanisms than via political processes of distribution, and that the protection of private property rights requires the curbing of previous arbitrary patterns of public policy. In the context of competitive elections this perspective works with the assumption that politicians choose their economic platforms solely on the basis of what they believe will maximize their votes, and that they are therefore highly incentivized to promise their voters immediate economic benefits (higher public spending, lower taxes, lower interest rates) regardless of the second round ('post-electoral') consequences of exercising such irresponsible discretionality. This is the 'time inconsistency' problem that still dominates the academic literature on the politics of economic reform in new democracies. This literature is discussed further in the following section. On this view 'discretionality'is an unmitigated social ill, and 'rules' are the required antidote to 'discretion'.

From an alternative democratic perspective, however it is possible to take a more critical view of some 'rules', and a more benign view of some variants of 'discretion'. One could distinguish between rules arrived at through a process of democratic deliberation, and subject to revision in accordance with constitutional procedures, and rules that are externally imposed or derived from an authoritarian heritage. The latter (including, for example, Hayekian aspects of economic guardianship imposed on Chile through the undemocratic constitution of 1980) may not always represent a disinterested public good and may not be so capable of generating collective consent as rules consultatively arrived at and subject to constitutional review.[3] Equally, a democrat could distinguish between the abusive forms of arbitrary discretionality highlighted by neoliberal discourse, and more stable, responsible, and consensual variants of discretion arising from the democratic process. To take one obvious example, the decision to allocate resources for defence (or even to go to war) must clearly be an act of discretion. It cannot be purely rule-driven. And it may have major distributive and economic consequences for the society as a whole. Here the choice is not between rules and discretion, but between legitimate and judicious versus arbitrary forms of discretion. In fact even such self-limiting decisions as the adoption of a binding rule are acts of discretionality which can be either legitimate or abusive. Democratic controls are required to adjudicate such matters.

4. Disinflation

All the countries listed in Table 1.1 have experienced double digit annual rates of inflation within the past decade. Most have suffered from much higher and more volatile financial conditions. Maxi-devaluations tend to generate severe price shocks, and if prices overshoot on the way up, it may require very painful reductions in employment and activity to bring them back down within a reasonable time frame. Problems of inflation and disinflation are therefore at the heart of the financial crises under review here.

However, if we are to model the political dynamics of such crises it is essential to distinguish between several different types of disinflation. 'Shock treatment' obeys a different political logic from 'gradualism'; and both these forms of price stabilization need to be distinguished from the long-run anchoring of the price level (e.g. through a permanently fixed exchange rate and enforcement of the 'law of one price' in a small open economy). Moreover, disinflation must be carefully distinguished from deflation – a not insignificant point when dealing with contemporary financial crises. As will be seen later in this paper, too much theorizing about financial crises is based on extrapolating from the standard circumstances of the 1970s and 1980s. Thinking more generally about the dynamics of financial crises in emerging market democracies requires consideration of a wider range of possibilities, including deflation and the return of demands for some types of economic regulation, wider democratic supervision. This will reinforce the case for flexible democratic forms of regulation as opposed to rigid and formulaic strategies of disinflation that over-insulate the policymakers from collective dialogue and feedback.

5. Development

If democratization should be viewed as a work-in-progress then so should development. None of these 'emerging market' economies can limit their ambitions to the achievement of financial stability and the security of property rights. Necessary though both these objectives may be policymakers (especially those answerable to a newly empowered mass electorate) have to attempt to go beyond them. According to the orthodoxy of the 1990s, once these economies had been stabilized and liberalized then little further political intervention would be needed. The market system would generate its own transformative dynamism, and 'take-off' into sustained growth would come about as a consequence of the depoliticization of the economy. India may provide some comfort to the advocates of this position, but most of the new democracies on our list have been experiencing no better than fitful and inadequate growth. In any case, in democratic conditions development must mean more than growth, as the burgeoning literature on 'development as freedom' and the human development index has emphasized. The case of South Africa deserves a mention here. Obviously the transition to majority rule required careful management in order to preserve economic stability and to generate international market confidence. But after forty years of apartheid democratization necessarily involves a huge project of social transformation. There is no way that a regime based on universal suffrage could limit itself to stabilizing and liberalizing the inherited status quo. Development can only be achieved over decades, and indeed generations, and it is probably best pursued through incremental reform rather than by disruptive radicalism. But in South Africa (as in most emerging market democracies), development must include far reaching measures of long-term structural change. When financial markets perceive what may be in prospect (especially at moments of electoral contestation) the risk of a crisis can suddenly become very acute.

6. Macroeconomics and the financial markets

This perspective on long-term structural change highlights questions of macroeconomic discretionality and strategic reorientation. But economic liberalization shifts the locus of economic power from the democratically elected managers of economic policy to firms, consumers, and financial operators. Short-term microeconomic rationality rules in financial markets, and the dynamics of politico-economic interaction are complicated by the extreme slowness of reaction times in the realm of national political leadership, as compared to the almost instantaneous speed of adjustment in currency and money markets. However, it is as well to recognize from the outset that this dichotomy between macro and microeconomic processes is oversimplified. Just as long-term central planners can learn to cater to market opinion (ministers even go on road shows) so even financial speculators can entertain the possibility that beyond today's trade there may be an underlying structural logic worth taking into account. In fact many of the economic issues of most interest to the parties and their voters are neither macro nor micro, but *meso*. Food security, the state of public transport, or whether VAT is levied on medicines is likely to generate more political interest than the size of the fiscal deficit, or the repo rate. Financial crises generate powerful political effects mainly because of their indirect impact on these meso-economic issues, rather than because of their more direct economic manifestations. This is just as well because it leaves scope for the democratic process to mediate what might otherwise be an unbridgeable gulf between macroeconomic strategies and financial market rationality.

7. Globalization and the 'architecture' of international finance

As early as 1995 a spokesman for the IMF referred to Mexico's so-called 'tequila crisis' as "the first financial crisis of the twenty-first century". It was a prophetic observation, and indeed the 'Asian' crisis soon followed, then Russia, then Brazil (all still in the twentieth century). But the Fund's foresight has not been matched by comparable achievements in more crucial realms of explanation, let alone prescription. Instead, the prevailing philosophy of all the Washington-based financial institutions has remained unreconstructed neoliberal. Setting aside a few details of timing and the tactics of implementation, the prescription of global economic liberalization remains unchallenged, and the only lessons to be drawn from this succession of crises is that more persistence is required in hewing to what Washington experts regard as the predetermined right course. Reference to a strengthening of the international financial 'architecture' concerns proposals to reinforce the existing structure of incentives. Although Joseph Stiglitz has stirred up controversy with his critique of prevailing assumptions, the main centres of financial power display scant inclination to re-evaluate their recommendations in the light of unanticipated results. Much of the debate is best understood in terms of blame avoidance, and a commitment to perpetuate orthodox discourse.[4]

In contrast to constructions of globalization and international financial architecture that deprive the governments of emerging markets of their autonomy of action to regulate financial crises, this paper proceeds from an alternative standpoint. The experience of successive financial crises over the past decade lends scant support to a timeless truth about an inevitable process. Instead, like the promoters of European integration, they may be the representatives of an international bureaucracy whose claims to superior knowledge about the necessary way forward greatly overstate their knowledge and their control over the forces at work. The metaphor of an 'architecture' of international financial regulation conveys a misleadingly solid image of a stable and well-constructed system of permanent authority. But the evidence suggests that they may be constantly wrong-footed by the outcomes of market processes whose dynamics are incompletely understood. Their 'architectural' solutions are in fact improvized, incomplete, and unstable. If so, the democratically elected rulers of new democracies cannot abdicate their constitutional authority in the face of technical necessity. They will need to retain enough discretionality and freedom of action to protect their citizens when international defences against financial disorder break down. And they would be well advised to build up their own counter-hegemonic expertise and capacity for collective action, in order to offer legitimate and viable alternatives to Washington-centred financial orthodoxies that may not survive the tests of experience.

The literature

Many different academic literatures have something to contribute to the political economy of financial instability in emerging market democracies. This is hardly surprising, considering the scope of the questions that have been raised earlier. This review cannot refer to more than a very select fraction of the debate. Three clusters have been selected for brief review. But the objective is not to engage with any of these rich and complex discussions in any depth. It is just to acknowledge their importance, and to position this contribution in relation to their work. Other literatures (notably the scholarly work generated within each of the countries listed in Table 1.1) may also deserve acknowledgement, but space and time limits have required extreme selectivity. The three clusters are the literatures on 'institutional choice'; on 'democratic transition and consolidation'; and on global financial 'architecture'. Under each of these three headings the objective is to clarify how far this paper builds on, (or departs from), dominant assumptions and why.

The 'institutional choice' literature draws its inspiration from the so-called 'time inconsistency' problem already mentioned above in discussion of 'discretionality'. With regard to 'emerging market' democracies, the focus has been on the potential for averting financial crises through 'pre-commitment'. The main examples of this solution are i) the adoption of a pegged exchange rate (which effectively delegates responsibility for monetary policy to an external source outside the reach of the national political establishment – usually the US Federal Reserve); and ii) the granting of central bank 'independence' (which involves insulating the direction of the central bank from pressures to loosen monetary policy for the electoral advantage of incumbent politicians). In both these cases elected politicians relinquish potential power to direct monetary policy (they 'self-limit') in order to boost market confidence and enhance their country's reputation for 'sound' money. This is expected to encourage foreign investment and reduce the risks of financial crisis. Other variants of pre-commitment can also be envisaged such as the European Union's fiscal pact in which national politicians agree to collective disciplines to limit fiscal deficits. The institutional choice literature generally takes for granted the benefits of pre-commitment, and concentrates on attempting to solve the following puzzle: why would self-interested politicians choose institutional arrangements that limit their power? A recent special issue of *International Organization* elaborated on this theme, examining, for example, whether pegged exchange rates and independent central banks were complementary or alternative forms of pre-commitment. More relevant to this chapter was the discovery that nearly all "really existing" pre-commitment arrangements are hybrid, and that in a sample of seventy-six countries approximately one quarter fell into each of the four quadrants of a two-by-two box diagram (high/low central bank independence/exchange rate fixity). The emerging market democracies in the tabulation are also widely dispersed. Moreover the researchers found no clear tendency for any one institutional choice to advance at the expense of the alternatives – for example, just as Mexico moves toward exchange rate fixity and central bank autonomy, Argentina moves away from it. My conclusion from this literature is that the factors determining such choice are much wider and more diverse than the 'time inconsistency' theorists presume, and that no option is immune from the risks of financial crisis. In fact the dominant picture appears to be the impermanence of all options, as successive crises weaken confidence first in one set of arrangements, then in another.

The democratic 'transition' and 'consolidation' literature portrays an image of heightened uncertainty and unpredictability during the first stage of the democratization process, followed by increasing routinization and institutionalization later on. While this refers primarily to elections, party system, and the procedures for decision-making at the political level, it also carries implications for the management of financial crises. On the face of it this literature would like us to expect a greater vulnerability to market instabilities (especially to politically-driven speculative attacks) in the early stages of democratization. Later on more 'consolidated' democratic regimes might be expected to inspire more market confidence, and be better equipped to manage economic shocks. As party systems become more stable and predictable, and as rival government teams alternate in office, one might expect an improved capacity to handle the 'collective action' and 'reputation' problems that could otherwise undermine market confidence. Some of the democratization literature about 'pacts', and learning through strategic interactions, certainly has the potential for extension to deal with issues of monetary policy. But the awkward fact remains that even such relatively consolidated new democracies such as Brazil continue to experience dangerous financial crises. As yet there is no evidence that this risk is diminishing as the duration of democratic institutions is extended. It remains possible that this is just about to become apparent, but if not the alternative way of rescuing the 'consolidation' argument would have to be that gains in the solidity of domestic political institutions were being offset by increasing vulnerability to shocks from the international economic system.

The literature on international financial 'architecture' concentrates on evaluating (and possibly counteracting) this possibility. As already mentioned, the metaphor of architecture conveys a reassuring image of solidity, permanence, and sound design, but from an 'emerging market' perspective this is open to question. Most of the current literature is written not from the perspective of the most vulnerable, but from the standpoint of those who wish to project reassurance and impose financial discipline without subjecting the rich industrial democracies to any additional burdens. There are certainly 'moral hazard' arguments against making it too easy for troubled debtors to repudiate their external obligations; and there are wider ideological issues about the right of international institutions to redirect resources that come ultimately from private-sector taxpayers. But the systemic imbalances in the present system of international economic regulation extend beyond these familiar reference points. They concern asymmetries and double standards that place 'emerging markets' at a marked disadvantage as compared with the old established democracies and they also concern weaknesses in the global monetary system that could pose a threat to all participants. When financial crisis strikes a new democracy, it is hit and miss how much help will be available from international financial institutions, or on what terms. Democracy does not currently appear to be much of a bankable asset, at least as compared with strategic location in the 'war on terror'.

The model

A model is a simplified account that isolates key variables and abstracts from the complexities of actual cases. In this exercise attention focuses on the timing and sequence of developments in two separate but linked realms – the democratic realm of competitive electoral struggle for national office; and the market-based realm of financial speculation in an open and liberalized economy. We are concerned here with quite short-term sequences (usually less than one year), and with the feedback between two processes with various speeds of adjustment. In democratic conditions major political readjustments require negotiation, explanation, and the observance of proper procedures, so they take weeks, if not months, or indeed years to carry through. In liberalized financial markets operators react almost instantaneously to new information. Markets initially adjust within minutes, and they fully incorporate fresh data within hours. Even the most complex of economic developments can be digested within days, and after a week market attention will be diverted to other areas of risk assessment, unless the political system generates substantial new information. Yet despite their different time scales, these two processes may be closely interlinked, certainly during financial crises that are associated with shifting market perceptions of political risk.

In the natural world the interaction of two processes operating on different time scales can be modelled precisely through some specified 'gearing' or 'feedback' mechanism. But when social processes are involved there may be no uniquely specified threshold point at which the interaction engages or disengages, and feedback may be 'fuzzy' rather than the automatic application of some fixed coefficient. This is because political actors and market operators both compete with each other in monitoring personally relevant information about the two spheres. For example, a political candidate mainly engaged in electoral strategy can hope to gain a competitive advantage by anticipating market reactions that are not so well monitored by his rivals. Similarly, a currency speculator may gain an edge over other players in his market by acquiring a superior understanding of the dynamics of an election campaign. Consequently, since social outcomes are determined by the behaviour of these actors, and since successful anticipation of interaction effects may confer an advantage on lead players, gearing and feedback will not operate mechanically, but rather in accordance with more subjective perceptions of anticipated reactions, and even opportunities to 'stampede' latecomers. Social processes with divergent reaction times may well be powerfully coordinated, but the dynamics involved will involve substantial margins of variability, contingency, and perhaps even unpredictability.

Such interactions could, in principle, be modelled in a variety of ways. Economists have elaborated a range of techniques for understanding the dynamics of financial crises: 'herding' behaviour, 'bubbles', and more structural cycles can all be invoked. This section is concerned with the *political* dynamics of a subset of such crises. So it does not focus on the internal rhythms of speculative market adjustment (or overshoot). Nor does it focus on the sequential processes of political rebalancing associated with the progress of a competitive electoral campaign. It abstracts from both these important processes, in order to highlight the mechanisms of linkage and feedback that can either harmonize or discoordinate the relations between them. The simple sequences presented below provide just one possible way to model the political dynamics that are of interest here. Alternatives should certainly be explored and, as with all social science modelling, the choice of the best framework should be guided *both* by the parsimony of the simplified account *and* by its relevance to the experiences under investigation.

The model consists of three overlapping sequences. Table 1.2 presents a stylized electoral timetable, and identifies six stages spread over 18 months, during which market interest in the political conflict may fluctuate (as in column B), and political responses to market pressures may evolve (as in column C). While a politically motivated financial crisis could erupt at any time throughout this period, the table indicates particularly high risks in the two to three months before the election, and possibly also in the early months of office of the ensuing government. Table 1.3 presents a similarly stylized timetable for a financial crisis, allowing up to six months for this to work through (although half that time is usually sufficient). Column B captures the key assumption that most politicians competing for votes are not primarily attuned to market signals, and so can be expected to react slowly and ineffectively as the crisis gathers momentum. Admittedly this assumption is an over-simplification, in that there is almost always a caretaker economic team whose main objective will be to hand over power (stage V in Table 1.2) without a crisis. So although vote-seeking politicians may be focused elsewhere, at least some of the contenders for office are likely to listen to the market warnings that are transmitted to them by those in office. So the reactions hypothesized in Table 1.3 need not express ignorance or inattention, but just the impediments to speedy collective action that arise in democracies at the height of election campaigns.

Table 1.4 offers a third overlapping timetable that could integrate the earlier two and therefore frame our understanding of the political dynamics at work. It contains an eight-stage decision tree running from long before the election to four months after it. Here we offer a stylized menu of choices that democratic politicians can make in order to manage the foreseeable risks of a financial crisis erupting around election time. Their first option is some variety of binding pre-commitment along the lines previously discussed in the literature on institutional design. Alternatives II to V cover strategic choices of the kind discussed in the literature on democratic transition and consolidation. Outcomes VI to VIII are central topics in the literature on international financial architecture. It should be noted that for simplicity each decision choice is presented dichotomously, and each 'yes' is assumed to master the risk of a financial crisis. Needless to say, this is a simplification for the sake of the model. Its plausibility should be assessed by consulting the evidence

Table 1.2: ***Stylized six-stage timetable of an election in an 'emerging market' democracy (total time 18 months)***

	A) Political calendar	*B) Markets on politics*	*C) Politics on markets*
I	Run-up to election campaign (1 year)	Fitful (moderate) interest	Low market discipline
II	Campaign in high gear (1–3 months)	Intense (speculative) interest	Polarization (tightened discipline)
III	Election day (or days)	Discontinuity	High political risk
IV	Post-elections negotiations (1 week–1 month)	Fitful (moderate) interest	Unity (market soothing)
V	New team takes office	Discontinuity	Political confidence renewed
VI	Definition of new priorities (1–3 months)	Fitful (moderate) interest	New equilibrium

Table 1.3: ***Stylized four-stage timetable of a financial crisis in an 'emerging market' democracy (maximum time 6 months)***

	A) Market perception	*B) Political reaction*
I	Anxiety threshold passed (1 month)	Playing for time
II	First big speculative attack (1 day–1 week)	Disarray
III	Peak speculative pressure (within 2 months)	Frantic Negotiations
IV	Crisis resolutions (1–3 months)	Defiance/Capitulation/ Emergency loan

of experience. It should also be noted that the final stage ('financial crisis overshoot') can take place at any time. The format of the decision tree requires this to be placed at the end of the sequence, after exhausting all the political choices that might have averted it. If there were perfect co-ordination between the political and financial realms this format would be correct. But, here again, we are dealing with a simplification for the

Table 1.4: ***Stylized eight-stage decision tree: political responses to market pressure***

	Political response	*Time line (Prior to election)*
I	binding pre-commitment	+ 1 to 10 years
	/ \ Yes No	
II	negotiated pre-insurance	+ 3 to 12 months
	/ \ Yes No	
III	campaign pact	+ 1 to 4 months
	/ \ Yes No	
IV	market-friendly election	0
	/ \ Yes No	
V	post-electoral discipline	– 1 to 4 weeks
	/ \ Yes No	
VI	capitulate to market demands	– 1 to 12 weeks
	/ \ Yes No	
VII	international rescue	– 1 to 4 months
	/ \ Yes No	
VIII	financial crisis overshoot	anytime

sake of the model. In reality a financial crisis can acquire such short-term momentum that it produces an overshoot before there has been time to attempt a political system response. Here too it is necessary to consult the evidence of experience.

In sum, this section has sought to specify the main interactions between democratic processes and financial market instabilities in large 'emerging market' democracies. Due to space limitations, it has omitted meso-economic variables, even though these may be of great significance to the electorate. It has also stylized the timetable for electoral contestation, and the rhythm of financial market speculation.

Even with the help of these simplifications it has not proved possible to specify a tight and predictable model of causal interactions. What this exercise produces is basically a checklist of probable connections, a heuristic device for interrogating the political dynamics of specific financial crises. Some social scientists will regard this as too under-specified to hold explanatory value. The alternative argument would be that these crises otherwise will be analysed in exclusively economic terms, omitting the political dynamics that are in fact integral to any realistic understanding of them. They have to be loosely specified given the contributory influence of broader contextual factors pertaining to each case, and given the fact that national crises are transformative physical reactions.

The experiences

Table 1 has identified the major financial crises of the past decade that might exemplify this model of political dynamics. Mexico in 1994/5 and the two Brazil crises seem to fit reasonably well. Precisely how well the model works in these most favourable cases are left out of the discussion here. By contrast Russia and Venezuela can most easily be understood as responses to the collapse in oil prices in 1998 – financial crises triggered by an external economic shock – even though the interactions between the markets and the political system are also important. In these cases one might conclude that the externally driven financial crises produced far-reaching electoral and political system effects, including consequences that profoundly altered the workings of the democratic system, and that also repositioned public authority in relation to the financial markets. But the two cases also produced strongly divergent effects. In Russia the personalism and deinstitutionalization of the Yeltsin government was replaced by a more disciplined and orderly (though not necessarily more democratic) administration, with a greater capacity for managing or averting financial crisis. In Venezuela the outcome was exactly the opposite. These two cases both justify the attempt to construct a model of politico-economic interactions and not to rely on a purely economic analysis of crisis. But instead of a unitary framework, overlapping schemas may be required. At any rate this paired comparison should warn us against expecting too much monocausal regularity when investigating the political dynamics of financial crises. A crisis can trigger either a 'virtuous circle' or a 'vicious circle' of subsequent reactions (Argentina and Brazil can also be paired to demonstrate the same point). The contrast between the first two cases and the second pair also indicates that even if these crises possess some common characteristics we should only expect to find loose 'family resemblances', rather than tightly determined causal regularities.

The two Argentine crises fall somewhere in between. Both in 1989 and in 2001 successive Argentine governments (both led by the Radical Party) proceeded through every stage of the decision tree set out in Table 1.4, ending with financial crisis overshoots. In both cases a strictly economic analysis of the process, leaving out the political interactions, would fail to capture much of its dynamics. However, the linkage with the electoral calendar was not quite as postulated in the model. For one thing, Argentine political timetables are not observed with the same automaticity as in most other new democracies. The May 1989 election was brought forward six months because the financial crisis had run out of control. The October 1999 election was supposed to inaugurate a four-year presidential term, but President de la Rua fled from office after only two years as the economy collapsed around him. In the first instance the IMF provided a highly controversial loan *before* the election in a thinly disguised attempt to head off a Peronist electoral victory. In the second instance it also provided a last, technically indefensible, infusion of funds in an attempt to keep President de la Rua and the fixed exchange in place. Both these unmistakably partisan international rescue efforts failed. In order to understand the political dynamics of financial crisis in Argentina it is essential to incorporate some powerful 'country specific' features of the processes at work there. The legacy of hyperinflation has been an extremely low level of financial intermediation for such an advanced economy, and a great propensity for capital flight. The legacy of Peronism has been an inability to forge stable cross-party agreements or pacts that can generate trust and predictability in the political realm. The convertibility plan was an exceptionally powerful form of pre-commitment embraced as a substitute for normal political compromise and market confidence. Its collapse (outside the electoral timetable) was therefore a particularly severe shock destabilizing both the politics and the economics of this emerging market democracy. In fact as the largest defaulter in history Argentina could equally be labelled a 'submerging' market economy.

The other experiences in Table 1.1 can also be illuminated, but again with some qualifications. In India, it was the outcome of a factional struggle within the ruling Congress Party following the assassination of Rajiv Gandhi, rather than the uncertainties of a close electoral competition with the opposition, that gave rise to the adoption of a much more liberal economic model. The exhaustion of the old interventionist model precipitated an exchange rate crisis, and that triggered a shift in the balance of forces in the ruling coalition. In Bulgaria it was the refusal of the old communists to undertake inescapable market liberalizing measures that precipitated the financial collapse, and their subsequent electoral defeat.

In Thailand and in South Korea financial crises struck what had previously been regarded as extremely successful 'emerging market' economies, run by economic managers who were highly regarded in western financial markets. The severity of the crises arose mainly from the shock discovery that these international perceptions were ill founded. Nevertheless, in these two cases the political dynamics fit reasonably well with our account. The main interaction effect was that the crisis precipitated a democratically mandated change in government, and the adoption of more orthodox liberal economic policies. But the timing of the crisis was not determined by the electoral calendar, and it was not determined by the electoral calendar, and it was not fear of a populist electoral victory that precipitated the loss of market confidence. However, significantly for believers in 'pre-commitment' and central bank autonomy, the Asian financial crisis did not generate a shift to Washington-approved institutions of monetary management. On the contrary, in Thailand, for example, the election of January 2001 installed a more free-spending government which promptly removed the orthodox Governor of the Bank of Thailand, and thus abrogated the law on central bank independence. It also switched to a 'free float' of the exchange rate. Similarly the new democracy in Indonesia first bowed to IMF pressure and passed a central bank law guaranteeing Bank of Indonesia's independence and the five-year term of the new governor. But in March 2002 that gentleman was sentenced to a three-year prison term for complicity in a banking scandal, and the current administration has modified the law to permit the government to dismiss future bank governors in mid-term, and to appoint politicians to the board of governors.

The temporary collapse of the South African rand in 2001 does not seem to have been driven mainly either by electoral or more generally political precipitants, but it may be that it fed back into the political process, reinforcing economic discipline and an inclination to pursue market orthodoxy. Perhaps that political response helps to explain the subsequent recovery of the currency (a 'virtuous' circle).

In the Turkish case, the precipitant of the crisis was not an election but an earthquake. However that may be, markets correctly observed that the existing administration was disintegrating and would eventually be swept away. As the Turkish crisis deepened, the government ran through most of the political responses to market pressure identified in Table 1.4. The election took place well after the crisis had ended, but its effect was to reinforce Turkey's commitment to undertake liberalizing reforms in order to enter the European Union, and thus secure external reinforcement of its status as an 'emerging market democracy'. As a democracy the Turkish parliament responded to public opinion by voting against United States' demands for troop transit to Iraq, even though this has meant the sacrifice of a $24 billion aid package, and the risk of further financial turbulence.

Reviewing all these experiences in the light of the model, it can be argued that they share enough common features to merit investigation as a single cluster. In all cases there is a political component to the dynamic of financial crisis that precludes reliance on purely economic modes of explanation. But it would be a mistake to impose too unitary a framework of interpretation.[5] The model presented earlier is one possible simplified heuristic device. Experience from the comparative survey indicates the potential of alternative schemas that pay less attention to the electoral calendar, and devote more space to the ways in which financial crisis may induce a regrouping of political forces around an orthodox policy consensus.

The broader implications

This chapter began by posing a series of seven questions, starting with the most specific and proceeding to the most general. The previous paragraph has provided tentative answers to the first three of these questions. The last four are not answerable in the same way, certainly not in the space available. Broader reflections that engage these issues are in order.

The most basic implication of the analysis presented above is that we should prepare ourselves for the occurrence of further financial crises in various emerging market democracies. Whatever its limitations, the modelling exercise attempted here should draw attention to political-economic interactions that are likely to be recurrent (and perhaps widespread) in the years ahead. Generalizations on the basis of comparative experience that help us to identify underlying regularities, and to integrate economic and political realms of analysis, should therefore be of prospective as well as of retrospective interest. This attempt to lay out an interpretative schema could stimulate further and better efforts, especially from political scientists in developing countries who are most sharply challenged by the phenomenon in question.

A second implication of this approach is that we are unlikely to find any unique system of institutional design that can provide a reliable protection against the occurrence of politically destabilizing financial crises. Pre-commitment, electoral pacts, and precautionary IMF-loan packages may all have something to contribute in individual cases, but none of them can provide cast-iron guarantees, and all can misfire when the context is wrong. It is sometimes assumed that the developed market democracies have put such problems behind them, and must therefore possess some blueprint or stock of accumulated wisdom that needs only to be transferred to the inexperienced new democracies. But this overlooks the severity of the crisis currently afflicting democratic Japan, and reflects a highly selective reading of the experience of other advanced democracies. In any case, there is more than one blueprint that might be exported from the OECD countries. The EU's stability and growth pact, and its rigidly insulated European Central Bank, is quite different in structure from the USA's system of congressional budgetary sovereignty, and a Federal Reserve under indirect political supervision. The New Zealand formula is different again.

A third implication, then, is that the strategy of macroeconomic management appropriate in one emerging market democracy may not entirely coincide with what works best in the next. Argentina and Brazil are unlikely to require exactly the same forms of economic regulation, given their structural and historical differences. A party of the left can win in Brazil and yet trigger an apparent 'virtuous circle' response in financial markets, whereas the victory of a centre-right party in Argentina can fail to head off the most severe of vicious circle market effects.

Looking further afield, Bulgaria and Turkey may have the option of borrowing from European institutional practice, but Mexico will have to find its way within the different framework of NAFTA. What works for India may be inapplicable to Russia. This in no way implies that these countries have wide scope in their choice of options of economic governance. On the contrary, as indicated at the outset, the constraints now bearing down on even the most resilient and autonomous of emerging markets are ever more uniform and restrictive. That is why the risk of further crises is likely to prove enduring. But within these very narrow confines, different new democracies will have to consider alternative tradeoffs. Instead of simply embracing whatever the current international orthodoxy may be, the best chance of crisis minimization may be to attend to the national context and its specificities, and to borrow only selectively from those foreign models that can be proven to be pertinent. None of this should be interpreted as licensing reckless experimentation, however. Effective defences against financial crisis require great realism, caution, and interest in international collaboration to strengthen best practices.

A fourth implication is that in a dangerous and unstable world, where no single blueprint of best practice can be relied upon to substitute for local judgement, democracy can display twin merits. It can act as an error correction mechanism, when insulated technocrats might prefer to ignore the adverse consequences of their unsuccessful strategies. And it can diffuse responsibility for the economic sacrifices that may be required in hard times, through generalizing a sense of co-responsibility and policy ownership. In undemocratic regimes, where these merits are absent, the consequences of financial crisis can be far more destructive. But it is critical to note that these merits only exist in democracies that retain a significant margin of economic policy discretionality. They cannot be expected in democracies that are purely procedural in structure having 'depoliticized' or removed from the realm of democratic public authority all powers of economic decision-making.

Finally, political scientists cannot rest content with an analysis that takes the individual nation state as its unit of analysis, leaving aside the common processes and structures that operate on all the separate countries discussed in this paper. Emerging market democracies are all entangled in an interdependent global network of relationships. Just as democratic practices are reproduced in successive countries and across large regions, so also episodes of financial crisis get rapidly transmitted from one site to the next. Conditionality and contagion operate as forcefully in the political realm as in the economic sphere, and mutual learning is as important as the drive for differentiation. The master narrative of global politics can change at great speed (for example from the liberal internationalism of the late 1990s to today's 'war on terror') and all emerging market democracies are powerfully affected by such shifts. If there are to be effective countermeasures to limit the spread and virulence of financial crises in this universe of nations, they will have to be promoted and coordinated internationally. But this would require more than just some technical fix, or the funding of a new bureaucratic programme. It would require deliberation and social construction at the international level. This would imply the reinforcement of the democratic discretionality exercized by global institutions. At present this seems a distant prospect, which is why study of the political dynamics of financial crises could well prove to be a growth industry.

Notes

1 These issues are more fully discussed in Chapter 1 of Laurence Whitehead, *Democratization: Theory and Experience*, Oxford University Press, 2002.

2 Laurence Whitehead, ed., *Emerging Market Democracies: East Asia and Latin America*, Johns Hopkins University Press, 2002.

3 In Delia Boylan's phrase they may be aimed at 'defusing democracy'. See: Delia M. Boylan, *Defusing Democracy: Central Bank Autonomy and the Transition from Authoritarian Rule*, Ann Arbor: Michigan University Press, 2001.

4 For an illuminating analysis from a constructivist perspective see Rodney Bruce Hall, 'The discursive demolition of the Asian development model', *International Studies Quarterly*, 47 (2003), 71–99.

5 This reprises the main conclusion of Laurence Whitehead, 'Political explanations of macroeconomic management: a survey', *World Development*, 18/8 (1990).

Chapter 2

Recent modifications of the international financial system

Eduardo Kugelmas

THIS CHAPTER EXAMINES recent changes in the international financial system. The primary focus is on the approach, rhetoric, and policies of the International Monetary Fund (IMF) toward developing countries and international financial structures. Preliminary interpretations of the consequences of these changes for Brazil are also presented. During the last few years, a number of scholars, policymakers, and activists have vehemently questioned IMF approaches and policies. In response, the Fund has made at least a timid attempt to change. As has been widely observed, the image of this institution was badly shaken by successive financial upheavals such as the crises in East Asia in 1997–98, Russia in 1998, Brazil in 1998–99, and Turkey in 2001. This process reached a low point with Argentina, where crisis began in 2001 and continued for three years. The IMF's approach was questioned by economists from diverse viewpoints, it became the preferred target of anti-globalization movements, and revision of it's recommendations for structural reform have been cited as an indispensable prerequisite in almost all proposals for modification of international financial structures.

The Fund has taken a select number of moderate steps towards revision (some might call it self-criticism) of its previous positions, particularly its earlier advocacy of the ample liberalization of cross-border capital flows. Review of policies applied during the sequence of crises in emerging economies was conducted and a new Independent Evaluation Office (IEO) was created outside the bureaucracy of the Fund. The intense debate over new procedures for restructuring national debts, such as the Sovereign Debt Restructuring Mechanism (SDRM), was another signal of change.

What lessons can be drawn from the international financial crises of the 1990s and the beginning of the new century? Can the role of the IMF be altered? Is it possible to reinstate measures of control over capital flows, similar to those in effect in Malaysia at the peak of the crisis? These questions have become central to policy debates and scholarship on the structure and the performance of the international financial system, occupying considerable space in the media, academic seminars, and conferences held to discuss the role and future of the multilateral organizations. It is striking how this agitation contrasts with the optimism that prevailed at the time of the IMF meeting of September 1997, held in Hong Kong. At that time, the Fund's Interim Committee affirmed the need for an institutional framework that could guarantee the freedom of capital flows. To this end, the Executive Board was requested to prepare an amendment to the Fund's *Articles of Agreement*, that is, to the founding statute of the entity. This amendment would place universal free convertibility on capital accounts of the balance of payments as one of the central goals of the institution, granting the IMF jurisdiction and control over this goal. The objective was to widen the meaning of 'monetary convertibility', in the *Articles* from current account transactions to capital account transactions as well. More than one observer noted that such an orientation would be a 180-degree turnaround from the intentions of the founders of the Fund in 1944.[1] The proponents of this proposal, who were strongly supported by the United States Treasury, viewed this initiative as the crowning of the trend of deregulating international financial flows that started in the late 1970s and in the 1980s, and gained speed in the 1990s, especially towards the developing countries. The 1997 Hong Kong meeting was the zenith of the idea that the process of international financial integration could and would be an essentially benign force, acting as a lever for economic and social progress and a fundamental mechanism for the dissemination of global development. In its more ideological versions, propounded by a sizeable part of the media and by prestigious academic economists and social scientists, the building of a new integrated world was the *leit-motif* of a new epoch to emerge in the wake of the collapse of the Soviet Union. Simplified versions of Francis Fukuyama's well known thesis about the 'end of history' were invoked to support this vision. The 1994–95 Mexican crisis, which had required a $50 billion bailout, was seen as an isolated incident that already had been solved, with no further consequences.

The disillusions of the East Asian financial crisis postponed indefinitely the most ambitious proposals to modify the *Articles*, but the emphasis on the need to lessen restraints on capital flows was still present in the official documents through 1998. However, the Hong Kong optimism was soon supplanted by a change in ideological and cultural mood, due to growing criticisms of the IMF's handling of crises and increasing doubts about the benevolent role of financial integration. These doubts were not confined to leftists, anti-capitalists or anti-globalizers. The IMF assumed a defensive stance in response to criticism by such personalities as Joseph Stiglitz, chief economist of the World Bank,[2] and George Soros, the symbol of financial speculation. Other media-savvy economists with impeccable academic credentials, such as Paul Krugman and Jeffrey Sachs, joined in. The publication of a critical article by Jagdish Bhagwati,[3] well known for his energetic stand in favour of free trade, in the prestigious journal *Foreign Affairs* caused a very strong impact. Bhagwati firmly rejected the expansion of free trade to the financial sector, insisting on the important analytical differences existing between flows of goods and services and those of money. Employing language that brought to mind expressions used by critics of globalization, Bhagwati referred ironically to the "Wall Street–Treasury complex". For Bhagwati, proposals to liberalize capital accounts were driven by the interests associated with this complex.

Thus criticism of financial globalization became a 'respectable' academic stand. Academic respectability was critical, considering the enormous importance of the epistemic community, composed of graduates of prestigious universities in the United States and elsewhere, that have been intellectually moulded by mainstream neoclassical economics. In what we might term the worldwide 'public sphere' in which questions concerning the international political economy are debated, arguments and controversies about the role of the IMF and the other multilateral entities have become an integral piece of the debate over reforms proposed for the international financial structure.[4]

These matters have been amply debated during the past years and have provoked replies and reactions from the entity itself. Criticisms directed at the IMF can be separated into four topics[5] on different levels of analysis. The topic most frequently and widely commented on in the media and political debates is the nature of the conditionalities usually attached to its programs. Critics argue that the 'packages' of fiscal austerity, monetary restraint and trade liberalization are often unsuitable to the specific conditions of the countries where they are applied.

Moreover, they will be unable to spur economic growth, tending to worsen the situation of the poorest states. The programs have also been criticized for being promoters of 'moral hazard' and for being too supportive of private lenders' interests. Another frequently mentioned topic is the matter of legitimacy and sovereignty. The IMF is often accused of subverting the internal political processes of the countries in which it operates, by the imposition of undesirable structural and institutional modifications. A third criticism is that the IMF's mission has expanded well beyond the intent of its founders, which was to promote international cooperation, monetary and exchange stability. The Fund's own *Articles of Agreement* mention the need for corrections of the inequalities of the balance of payments of the member countries "without resorting to measures destructive of national or international prosperity."[6] The fourth topic is the lack of transparency and accountability within the Fund itself. This topic brings to fore the broader question of global governance, since the IMF exerts a reasonably powerful influence (although less than conspiratorial theories suppose) without clear mechanisms of accountability to the international community. The IMF voting procedures allocate 17.5 percent of the quotas to the US, and a vote of 85 percent of all shareholders is required to amend the initial *Articles.* The suspicion that the United States exercises undue influence over the Fund through this de facto veto power casts doubts on the institution's style of governance and raises questions about its procedures.

The texts and declarations of the Group of Seven (G7) advanced industrial countries and international financial institutions at the depth of the crisis revealed that their strongest concern was over the possibility that local destabilizing threats could turn into systemic crises. The case of the hedge fund Long Term Capital Management (LTCM), in the last months of 1998, was a dramatic warning of this. As markets were traumatized by the Russian crisis and Brazil appeared in an unstable situation, the sequence and the combination of disturbing factors gave birth to what could be called near panic.[7] It was not by chance that the theme of reform of the international financial structure became at that moment a top political issue; United States President Bill Clinton himself raised it during his fight to extract from a reluctant Congress an increase of the United States quota in the Fund. Clinton even used the highly symbolic expression "a new Bretton Woods" in a speech made at the Council of Foreign Relations in September 1998. From this moment on, debates accelerated and a series of practical measures were taken within the IMF itself. The Fund innovated its dissemination of data by publicizing them on the Internet, made new arrangements of cooperation with the Bank for International Settlements (BIS), and even revised some of its prudential requirements for credit and bank loans. The G-7 and OECD expanded their mutual consultation system between national treasuries and central banks. The acute crisis of the last months of 1998 also energized academic debates. Even the prestigious Council of Foreign Relations, a politically well-connected and bipartisan think-tank in New York City, instituted a task force on the subject.

During 1999, several initiatives took place. A conference of the International Center of Monetary and Banking Studies of Geneva (CEPR), an entity sponsored by the private financial sector, recommended reorganization of the IMF to make it more independent and more accountable.[8] The Cologne meeting of the G7 in June was notable for the weight given to international financial issues. Its main results were the emphatic support given to the creation of a new forum for discussion and analysis, the Financial Stability Forum (FSF), and for the promulgation of a new initiative, the G20. This new international body brings together the national financial authorities of the G7 countries, a representative of the European Union and twelve other countries: Argentina, Australia, Brazil, Canada, China, Korea, India, Indonesia, Mexico, Saudi Arabia, South Africa, and Turkey. Directors of the IMF and of the World Bank also participated in these meetings. The *rationale* for the spawning of this entity was the search for greater political legitimacy and more transparency in the decision-making process of the international financial system through the inclusion of the economic heavyweights among the developing countries. The FSF acts in a low profile way, gathering G7 representatives, Bretton Woods' entities, and technical organs linked to the BIS, with its secretariat in Basel alongside the BIS. Its goal is to reduce the occurrence of systemic risk by exchanging information and by evaluating problems such as the treatment of offshore financial centres and hedge funds.

From about mid-1999, IMF documents reflect greater concern over systemic stability and show at least some measure of receptivity towards the criticisms levelled at its usual form of intervention and crisis management. In their annual reports for 1999, the Fund and the World Bank[9] both acknowledged the existence of deficiencies in their operations related to international financial markets. They suggested that problems had roots not exclusively in the macroeconomic and institutional maladjustments of developing countries, but also in flaws such as asymmetry of information between creditors and debtors, the use of poor lending criteria by the private sector, and moral hazard, the latter understood as the expectation of intervention by multilateral entities and G7 governments in the case of a crisis of liquidity or solvency.

Several proposals to strengthen the global financial system have been elaborated by the IMF and the World Bank in cooperation with the BIS. The adoption of codes and international patterns of 'good financial behaviour', the harmonization of control and accountability procedure, and the full adoption of SDDS – Special Data Dissemination Standard – were encouraged. It was endeavoured to strengthen the norms for banking supervision and the requirements for the minimum capital, reviewing and improving the norms of the 1988 Basel Agreement. A cautious step back was taken in relation to the thesis of capital account opening; it was still seen as desirable in the long run but as a corollary to a sequence of institutional reforms in the recipient countries' financial sectors. The provisional adoption of some capital movements control measures, as in the oft-quoted Chilean model, was admitted as an extreme solution and in very special circumstances.

The introduction of these measures, the relatively swift overcoming of the crisis caused by the Brazilian devaluation of January 1999, and above all the successful solution given to the LTCM affair lessened the urgency of the search for wider reforms. Although proposals using and abusing the 'architectural reform' metaphor abounded in academic seminars, debates, think tanks and position papers of international entities,[10] the apparent diminution of the immediate threat of systemic risks dissuaded the main protagonists from pursuing the hard work of negotiation and compromise necessary to reach consensus on concrete reforms. The loss of the sense of urgency meant that more ambitious steps would be postponed. Divergent views between the Executive Branch and Congress in the US, as well as among the other members of the G7, also rendered the concluding of concrete proposals difficult. Modifications that involved tighter controls on capital flows by governments or multilateral entities faced mistrust, not to say veto, from the private financial sector, who expressed a dogmatic, almost religious belief in the virtues of *laissez-faire*, or as critics would say, in 'market fundamentalism'.

In consequence, the drive for reform that characterized 1999 did not translate itself in bolder initiatives. The assessment of this period of change, as made by Stanley Fischer in April 2000, limited itself to underscoring the importance of the reforms already in course, insisting on the importance of more transparency and accountability.[11] As noted by some critics, such as the Canadian economist Roy Culpeper, president of the North–South Institute, the solution to the problems was once again being looked for in measures of improvement of the internal governance of countries, especially the debtors. More ambitious measures of reform were hardly mentioned, reflecting the Fund's difficulties in putting forth proposals without first achieving clear consensus in the G7.[12] Nonetheless, the retreat of the IMF from its previous posture can be seen by the mention of the necessity of caution when liberalizing capital accounts. The Fund also admitted that the controversy about the pros and cons of the various exchange regimes remained unsolved. Finally, Fischer also mentioned the need for a stronger involvement of creditors in the search for solutions of crises to allow "orderly restructuring".

Despite Fischer's diplomacy and caution, observers could clearly note that a change of attitude and wording about the international financial system was taking place. At the same time, a new managing director of the Fund, German national Horst Kohler, former president of the European Bank for Reconstruction and Development, took office. Kohler soon showed a readiness to identify himself with the change of image of the institution and with a cautious admission of past mistakes. In a speech in August 2000, Kohler admitted that calls for change in the entity were justified. He explained that errors understandably arose because of the speed of world economic changes outpacing institutional change. Referring to international transactions, he commented:

> Private capital flows are now a major source for promoting growth and productivity. But it is also a fact that they can be a source of abrupt volatility and crisis. To contain the latter and to promote the former is the issue at stake.[13]

At the same time, the academic debate about the need for wider reforms intensified, overlapping with discussions of the content and design of IMF policies in relation to the succession of crises. Under the impulse of the papers and speeches of economists such as Stiglitz and Krugman, the arguments raised by critics underscored the distance between the realities of crises during the 1990s (which were caused mostly by problems originating from capital account transactions) and the Fund's traditional model of analysis and prescriptions that focused on difficulties in the balance of payments and the current account. In the new scheme, the traditional answer, similar to a conditioned reflex, of resorting to fiscal and monetary austerity, might not always be adequate and the defense at all costs of fixed exchange rates (or semi-fixed, crawling pegs) could incur tremendous costs.[14]

This way of viewing the problems coincided with the call for deeper changes in the IMF, and reflected a theoretical and methodological cleavage in economic thinking. The Fund's critics saw the institution's clear preference for a broadly conservative and *laissez-faire* economic ideology (often termed 'neoliberalism' by its critics) as an intellectual obstruction to a more serious debate about reform. The growth of the anti-globalization movements, such as the demonstrations in Seattle in late 1999 imparted further political urgency to the debate. On the other hand, strong criticisms in more conservative sectors were being directed at Bretton Woods entities, with the extinction of the IMF and World Bank proposed.

Armijo's fourfold classification of alternative reform proposals for the international financial system is very useful for our analysis. Those individuals and organizations in her first category, that of the *laissez-faire* liberalizers, want the extinction of almost all controls on capital flows in name of the allocative efficiency. This group views the Bretton Woods institutions with mistrust and favours a reduction in the scope of their activities. For the most dogmatic adherents of this position, represented by the libertarian think tank, the Cato Institute, the best solution would be to close the IMF. Identified with this standpoint of the liberalizers (but not necessarily with its extremist wing) one can find distinguished names of the academic world, such as Nobel prize winner Milton Friedman, and members of the United States establishment, such as former Treasury Secretary George Shultz, and financier Walter Wriston, longtime chief executive officer of Citibank. The appointment of Allen Meltzer, an academic economist identified with this viewpoint, to the presidency of an advisory commission set up by the United States Congress was an indicator of the political power of the *laissez-faire* liberalizers. One also can find in this group the most active lobby of the private sector, the Institute of International Finance (IIF). Interestingly, the IIF is ambivalent about IMF rescue packages, which are energetically condemned by most liberalizers, yet have been seen as important for the IIF's private bank members.

A second approach is that labelled by Armijo as transparency advocates, who are characterized by their prudence and pragmatism. They have a moderate viewpoint, favouring reforms of the kind put forth in 1999 by the international entities described above; cooperation, consultation and accountability are the key-words of this approach. The governments of the United States and the United Kingdom, and staff of multilateral financial institutions, tend to favour this approach. While acknowledging flaws in international financial institutions during the 1990s, they support only moderate corrections and carefully avoid discussions of the international distribution of power.

A third position is that taken by the financial stabilizers, who favour deep reforms in the functioning of the IMF. They view with scepticism the attribution of intrinsic virtues to the market, see regulations as not only necessary but virtually indispensable and tend to assess the recent crises from the viewpoint of the debtor countries. They observe that the traditional solutions of the IMF repeatedly provoke recessions in the countries being 'helped'. The financial stabilizers strongly favour attempts to limit and correct the instability inherent to the liberalization of the financial flows. Members of this group have put forth various concrete proposals; some (but certainly not all) of them even favour the creation of new supranational authorities. One interesting suggestion made by Paul Davidson was the creation of an International Clearing Union.[15]

Financial-stabilizers are represented in academic circles by Joseph Stiglitz, Paul Krugman, and Dani Rodrik. It also has wide support in UN organisms, such as Economic Commission for Latin America (ECLA), United Nations Conference on Trade and Development (UNCTAD), United Nations Development Program (UNDP) and United Nations Research Institute on Social Development (UNRISD), as well as in many developing countries. It is also viewed with certain sympathy by some continental European governments.

The final category is anti-globalizers; opponents to globalization itself. This position carries some weight in the ideological debate and has received considerable political recognition. However, as it seldom submits concrete proposals for reforms, it is of limited importance in the debate we are examining now, unless considered as an alarm signal strengthening the warnings of the stabilizers about the dire consequences of inaction. This classification is not exhaustive and should be used mainly as a reference framework. The distinctions between the four positions are not always clearly drawn and several participants in the technical and academic debate can be labelled as hybrids, favouring intermediate stands between the already described positions or a combination of them. For example, the economists linked to the respected Washington-based Institute of International Economics (IIE), including Fred Bergsten, Morris Goldstein and John Williamson, tend to adopt an intermediate position between that of the transparency advocates and the financial stabilizers.[16]

During 2000, the debate about reforms and IMF policies was deeply influenced by changes in the political climate of the United States. The report of the Meltzer commission, welcomed by the Republican majority in the United States Congress, suggested a reduction of the IMF scope of activities, limiting it to operations warranting short term financial support to countries facing momentary liquidity crises. Such countries, the report argued, should obey a rigorous set of pre-conditions. Some critics of the report noted that in this scenario it would have been next to impossible to organize aid packages during the 1990s.

In this ideological ambience, some observers expected the rise of George W. Bush, an ideological conservative, to the presidency of the United States to afford a golden opportunity for the *laissez-faire* liberalizers to implement some of their preferred modifications to the global financial architecture. The new Deputy Secretary of Treasury, John Taylor, a renowned academic economist who was seen as friendly to the viewpoints defended by Meltzer, became the government spokesman for international financial matters. In mid-2001, Anne Krueger, another academic economist of impeccable conservative credentials, took over from Stanley Fischer in the key post of Deputy Managing Director of the IMF. Many expected joint action from these newly appointed holders of strategic positions. What occurred, however, was quite different. International financial aid schemes involving large sums were organized, first for Turkey, then for Brazil.

In addition – and to the surprise of those who had been following her academic career – Krueger began promoting the SDRM, a mechanism that sought to institutionalize legal solutions for the problems caused by impasses between countries and private creditors. In response, Taylor, in the name of the United States government, torpedoed the proposal and favoured joint action clauses in international loans as an alternative. The Treasury opted for an attitude closer to the one defended by representatives of the private financial sector as the IIF, who feared an eventual excessive protection for debtors. It is to be noted that some debtor countries, such as Brazil, expressed doubts about the SDRM, which they felt might deter future loans.

In spite of rhetorical differences, evidenced by the notoriously tactless United States Treasury Secretary, Paul O'Neill, there were no deep changes in the international economic policy of the United States government. What can be noted is a certain conceptual indecision on part of policy makers, who seemed to be reacting to crises rather than implementing an overall strategy. Geopolitical considerations, especially after the events of 11 September 2001, also had a role in decision-making, opening the way for an operation such as the Turkish bailout. The public disagreement between the IMF and US Treasury on the SDRM issue reflected the difficulties of defining a new and clear direction in a time of turmoil and change. One possible interpretation is that the typical unilateralism of the Bush administration restrains, or rather impedes, the undertaking of multilateral measures; the peremptory refusal to accept legal formulas that may imply an extension of the jurisdiction power of international forums is typical of the Bush doctrine. Added to a greater sensitivity toward concerns and arguments of the private sector, this attitude would explain Taylor's opposition.

In other cases, positions were inverted. With respect to the ongoing financial crisis in Argentina, the United States government apparently was more forgiving than the IMF. In September 2003, the Bush administration made a political decision to support a new financial aid package for Argentina, seeking to avoid the worsening of the internal situation of the country. The United States then had to push hard to overcome the reluctance of Executive Directors and IMF management. Thus, while the IMF and Krueger showed more flexibility on the SDRM matter than the US Treasury and Taylor, regarding Argentina they assumed the role of tough defenders of the traditional line characteristic of the Fund's performance in the 1990s.

The future of global financial reforms remains uncertain. The confident push of the dominant countries and international financial institutions for external financial liberalization during the 1990s has been replaced by more moderate approaches and policies of muddling through. These policies were tested during 2004 in Argentina and other countries emerging from financial crisis. To assess this process, we must look again at the intellectual and ideological transformations in what might be called the internal culture of the Fund itself. This change reached its peak in the presentation, in March 2003, of a report co-authored by Kenneth Rogoff, then chief of the IMF research division, evaluating the effects of financial globalization on developing countries.[17] Although cautiously written, this document concludes that there is no sound empirical confirmation linking financial liberalization and economic growth. The report admitted that higher volatility might occur in developing economies that rely more on external flows. Although the report carefully tried to avoid conclusions about the policy making process, its publication may be seen as a disguised admission of the validity of central criticisms aimed at the Fund. At an IMF forum held to discuss this report, Harvard economist Jeffrey Frankel referred ironically to an *Economist* article titled 'The cruel sea of capital', which admitted that, in some cases, capital controls might be necessary. Frankel observed that many of the former enthusiasts of international financial integration were now distancing themselves from the orthodoxy of the 1990s and no longer praised the liberalization process as being undoubtedly beneficial.[18]

In 2003, the IMF's own Independent Evaluation Office also published a report evaluating Fund policies on Brazil, Korea and Indonesia that accepted various points made by the critics of the IMF. The report made two important recommendations: policies recommended for crises of the capital account should be carefully reexamined and the Fund should be more independent of its main shareholders (in other words, the G7). The study also stressed the need for wider divulgation of the information obtained by IMF missions. In the case of the two Asian countries, the report underlined the serious underestimation of the fragility of the banking sector. In the case of Brazil, little emphasis given by the IMF in 1997 and 1998 to the problems arising from an overvaluated exchange rate was seen as a serious oversight.

As has been recently noted by Cartapanis and Hertland, a discreet but significant cognitive change seems to have occurred.[19] If one admits that the functioning of the IFS itself might be considered problematic, the way is open for a different analytic perspective, in which the causes of the crises may not be only the macroeconomic and institutional imbalances of the recipient countries. Themes like financial contagion, sudden stop, and herding became more common in academic papers and seminars, reflecting the necessity of more coherent explanations for the succession of crises. It may be an exaggeration to use the expression "Keynes' revenge", as Cartapanis and Hertland do, but the British economist's trenchant analysis of the problems of the 1930s and his well-known scepticism about the liberalization of capital flows were widely quoted.[20]

This rediscovery of Keynes left its mark in debates about reform of the international financial system. The idea of 'a return to the origins' of the present IFS has gained acceptance, as the work of Cartapanis and Hartland, and also Carvalho, show. In the 1944 discussions that gave birth to the IMF there was generalized agreement on the necessity to create an organ that could guarantee world liquidity and shield against crises of the kind of the 1920s and 1930s. Although the bold attitude of Keynes, who foresaw an organization that would be the "central bank of central banks" did not prevail, the United States negotiator, Harry Dexter White, agreed with him on many points. The instability and volatility characterizing the period between the two world wars were an example of what had to be avoided at all costs. On this point there was consensus.

Thus, a pillar of the Bretton Woods regime was the control over capital flows. As distinct as present conditions may be, thirty years after severing the link between dollars and gold by the Nixon government that marked the end of this regime, retrospective studies of texts from this epoch continues to be one of the primary intellectual bases for building of alternative approaches. The already mentioned suggestions of Paul Davidson have Keynes' 1944 plan as their basis.

In this search for models, insufficient attention has been given to the political dimension. The constitution of an international regime is a matter of power; this obvious consideration is not always taken into due account. Ruggie's classic text on embedded liberalism in the Bretton Woods regime points in this direction.[21] The vast literature on the concept of hegemonic stability is also relevant to this discussion. In Ruggie's view, embedded liberalism was a compromise between a liberal economic order of intensified trade relations and the necessary leeway for the pursuit of independent economic policies by individual countries. The end of the Bretton Woods regime in the early seventies raised not only enormous problems for policy-makers but also conceptual difficulties for analysts. For those who tended to believe that a global hegemony was necessary for systemic stability, the post-war Bretton Woods regime was basically a consequence of the political, military, and economic dominance of the United States in the aftermath of World War II. Consequently, the relative decline of United States hegemony would mean a retreat of the international economic order. For Ruggie, the 'embedded liberal' regime reflected not only hegemony, but, more importantly, a change in state–society relations and a sense of social purpose that legitimized new forms of government intervention in national economies. On the other hand, many analysts, such as Susan Strange, were sceptical of the thesis of American 'decline' that was quite widespread during the 1970s and 1980s. The most influential view on the subject was that of Robert Keohane,[22] who saw the international economic order as a regime of cooperation that, once established, did not require the presence of a hegemony in order to continue.

The collapse of the Soviet Union, the relative economic decline of Japan and the long period of economic expansion of the Clinton years seemed to have rendered irrelevant the theme of United States decline, which has now been replaced by a renewed interest in discussions of types and forms of hegemony. As a consequence, blueprints for redesign of the international financial structure that do not take into account the supremacy of the United States sound too utopian. In this way, the question of a new international financial architecture becomes part and parcel of the theme of global governance. The Club of Madrid, co-chaired by former Brazilian president Fernando Henrique Cardoso and former United States president Bill Clinton, argued emphatically that any further progress in restructuring the IFS would have to consider this issue.[23] The recent controversy on the appointment of a new managing director, the former Spanish Finance Minister Rodrigo Rato, highlighted the importance of the governance issue.[24]

The financial turbulence discussed above has tested to the utmost the resources of Brazilian economic authorities, which have had to cope with the vagaries of volatile capital flows that weaken the country's balance of payments and force economic policy changes. Chronic deficits in the current account until 2001 exemplified the extent of external vulnerability. The most dramatic moment was the abandonment of the fixed exchange rate policy on 15 January 1999. Since then, Brazil has maintained a flexible exchange rate for its currency, the real, whose parameters are defined by free market action (with periodic interventions of the monetary authorities as deemed necessary). Immediately following the decision to float, the government's inflation stabilization program, known as the Real Plan, underwent a severe test. Thereafter, it recovered, and even successfully passed the test of a change of administration in 2002.

It is worth noting that Brazil has often been seen as a probable candidate for financial turbulence, but it has managed to avoid serious and lasting damage from financial crises. This may be perhaps due to the fact that its economic policymakers throughout the 1990s – despite frequently being criticized as 'neoliberals' – were sufficiently prudent to refuse to go along all the way with the prevailing fashion for wholesale financial liberalization.[25] For instance, some mechanisms for capital controls have been maintained and others can be applied in emergencies. The former include instruments such as compulsory deposits and the possibility of taxing financial operations that may partially counter sudden international change. Another point, often forgotten, is that Brazilian authorities adamantly refused to discuss the option of establishing a currency board during the 1999 crisis, a suggestion then made by the IMF's Stanley Fischer himself.

How can Brazil maintain actively participating in debates over the international financial agenda and the new 'global financial architecture'? One of the most frequent answers given, especially by those from more traditional and orthodox viewpoints, is that Brazil must keep on 'doing its homework'. In other words, Brazil must carry out fiscal adjustment, improve its macroeconomic fundamentals, maintain its stabilization policies, and satisfactorily monitor its economy. That is, Brazil should continue its effort to adapt to the changed international context.

Our review of recent international change suggests the existence of a window of opportunity for broader reforms that could limit the disruptions caused by the international financial system. Brazil's capacity to shape the new generation of stabilizing mechanisms for the world economy – and above all to participate in their effective implementation – is of course small, but must not be entirely disregarded. In the case of countries of medium influence in the worldwide scenario, the so-called pivotal states,[26] the impact of international initiatives and the search for innovative solutions in internal economic policies can be significant, depending on both the quality of their leaders and the type of the internal policies adopted by them.[27] Populist leaders tend to see only 'external threats', 'international losses' and other negative effects in the globalization process. Ultra-liberal regimes tend to passively accept the pressure of the international financial system and to endorse it. The consequences of the first case may be strong protectionist impulses, such as attempts to close the internal market and to resurrect autarkic practices. In the second case, internal policies are likely to limit themselves to reactive attitudes, by simply trying to adapt to external imbalances at whatever cost. An illustration of the latter situation is Argentina during the mid to late 1990s, under presidents Menem and De La Rua. The depth of Argentina's subsequent crisis clearly showed the social and political limitations of this kind of orientation.

There is room, however, for external renegotiations combined with internal solutions aiming at boosting economic growth, i.e. for attempting to walk on the razor's edge. International financial crises become national crises through a complex, multifaceted process that deserves more careful study. An examination of the last few years shows that each country has its own specific reaction to the triggering process, and that facile generalizations may hinder analysis. The remarkable contrast between the different reactions of Asian and Latin American countries to the international environment deserves further comparative study. It can be said that there are several possible forms of national insertion into the process of globalization, and that some have proved more successful than others.

How can Brazil initiate a new cycle of growth and confront its immense social problems? This question is at the top of the political and intellectual agenda in Brazil today.[28] Despite its difficulties, the country has some trump cards, such as the recent signs of a domestic consensus about the inevitability of insertion into the globalization process (the present debate is really more focused on the modalities of insertion), the fact that democratic governance has become more clearly institutionalized,[29] and the strength of the real economy (for example the success of the agribusiness sector), all of which justify cautious optimism. In this context, the discussion of the redefinition of external constraints and of the eventual remodelling of the architecture of the international financial system is extremely relevant. Even the notion that a country on the periphery might have a role in this redefinition no longer sounds farfetched. Brazil has had a leading role in recent debates about how to measure public investment in infrastructure and has challenged the traditional IMF methodology for the calculation of public sector accounts. The proposed changes would give more flexibility to debtor countries.

Table 2.1: ***Brazil: review of the relationship with the IMF, 1944–2002***

Date	*Historical stages of the relationship*	*Finance Minister*
1944	IMF Constitutive Agreement, in Bretton Woods	A. da Souza Costa
1946	IMF comes into force; Brazil ratifies with some exceptions (Art. 8)	P. Correia e Castro
1954	IMF gives its endorsement to a loan from Eximbank, USA	Oswaldo Aranha
1955	IMF report recommends the exchange reform	Eugênio Gudin
1957	IMF endorses the Brazilian tariff reform	José Maria Alkmin
1959	Pres. J. Kubitschek breaks with the IMF for political reasons	Lucas Lopes
1961	Renunciation of President Jânio Quadros for political reasons	Clemente Mariani
1965–72	Successive agreements stand-by; non-politicized relationship	G. Bulhões/Delf. Netto
1967	IMF-BIRD meetings in Rio de Janeiro; creation of the DES	Delfim Netto
1971	End of the Bretton Woods system; fluctuation of currencies	Delfim Netto
1974–79	Oil crises; several commercial banking loans	M. H. Simonsen
1982	Crisis of the foreign debt in South America; adjustment programs	Delfim Netto*
1984	Interruption of agreement due to non fulfillment of goals	Delfim Netto*
1987	Moratorium of external payments; suspension of credits	Dilson Funaro
1991–92	Unsuccessful attempt at reaching an agreement; political distance	Zélia Cardoso Mello
1992	Reinitiating of contacts, yet with no agreements	Marcílio M. Moreira
1992	Brazil achieves an agreement with Club of Paris without the IMF endorsement	M. M. Moreira
4.1994	Brazil signs an agreement with private creditors without the IMF endorsement	Fernando H. Cardoso
1993–97	Discrete relationship, almost distant, but without politicizing	FHC-Pedro Malan
1998 (out)	Agreements with the IMF for a program of fiscal adjustment	Pedro S. Malan
13.11.98	Protective agreement with disbursement of up to US$41.5 billion (stand-by/SRF)	Pedro S. Malan
08.03.99	Adjustment to previous agreement as a result of exchange devaluation	Pedro S. Malan
5.4.2000	Anticipated reimbursement of the credits granted in the agreement	Pedro S. Malan
28.6.01	Draft of US$2.007 billion (DES 1.6016 bi), from the 1998 agreement	Pedro S. Malan

3.8.01	Advice of liberation of a further US$15 bi, as a preventive measure	Pedro S. Malan
23.8.01	Cancellation of the 1998 agreement and request for a new agreement	Pedro S. Malan
25.9.01	Agreement *stand-by* and SRF until 12.2002: DES 12.144 bi (US$15.650 bi)	Pedro S. Malan
25.3.2	Review of the 2001 agreement *stand-by*: liberation of a further US$5 billion	Pedro S. Malan
6.9.02	*Stand-by* until December 2003: US$30.4 billion	Pedro S. Malan
15.12.03	*Stand-by* extension for 15 months; over US$6.6 billion dollars were released	Antonio Palocci

* Minister for Planning in charge of international organisms.
Sources: Paulo Roberto de Almeida, 'O Brasil e o FMI de 1944 a 2002' *Cena Internacional*, vol. 4, no. 2, 2002 and IMF Annual Reports.

Table 2.2: ***Governance of the IMF***

Board of Governors
(Finance Ministers, Presidents of Central Banks)
↓
Executive Directors
(24 Permanent representatives of governments)
↓
Managing Director
(Traditionally European)
↓
Deputy Managing Directors
(The first deputy is traditionally American)
↙ ↘
Functional departments — Area departments

Source: IMF site – www.imf.org.

Notes

1 See J. Boughton, 'Inventing the postwar international system', *IMF Working Paper*, no. 52 (2002).
2 Stiglitz left the World Bank over dissensions with Larry Summers, at the time U.S. under-secretary of the Treasury, and a distinguished academic economist. In 2002, Stiglitz won the Nobel Prize in Economics. Although the prize was conferred for previous works, its prestige reinforced the legitimacy of his stance as a critic of the IMF and some aspects of globalization.
3 See J. Bhagwati, 'The capital myth', *Foreign Affairs*, 77/3 (1998)
4 See L. Armijo, ed., *Debating the Global Financial Architecture*, New York: SUNY Press, 2002.
5 The bibliography on this subject is substantial: here I draw mostly upon J. Stiglitz,

Globalization and its Discontents, New York: W. W. Norton, 2001, and S. Lee, 'Global monitor – the IMF', *New Political Economy*, 7/2, 2002.

6 Article I-(v). Text available at www.imf.org.

7 A detailed description may be found in P. Blustein, *The Chastening*, New York: Perseus Books, 2001.

8 See www.cepr.org.

9 See M.C. Freitas and D. Prates, 'Restructuring the international financial system', *Brazilian Journal of Political Economy*, 22/1 (2002), based on an ample set of documents from the IMF and World Bank.

10 For a critical appraisal of the metaphor, see Laurence Whitehead's article in Armij, op. cit.

11 Text available at www.imf.org.

12 See www.nsi-ins.ca.

13 *IMF Survey*, 29/16, p. 1. Available at www.imf.org/external/pubs/ft/survey/2000/081400.pdf accessed April 2005.

14 See Stiglitz, op. cit., and P. Krugman, *The Return of Depression Economics*, New York: Norton, 1999.

15 See P. Davidson, *Financial Markets, Money and the Real World*, Cheltenham: Elgar, 2002, a key exponent in the post-Keynesian current of economic thought.

16 See www.iie.com.

17 E. Prasad et al., 'Effects of financial globalization in developing countries – some empirical evidence', International Monetary Fund, March 2003 available at www.imf.org/external/np/apd/seminars/2003/newdelhi/prasad.pdf.

18 See for example, 'Economic forum – Is financial globalization harmful for developing countries?', available at: www.imf.org/External/NP/EXR/ECForums/2003/052703.htm.

19 A. Cartapanis and M. Herland, 'The reconstruction of the international financial architecture – Keynes' revenge?', *Review of International Political Economy*, 9/1 (2002).

20 F.C. Carvalho, 'The changing role and strategies of the IMF', *Brazilian Journal of Political Economy*, 20/1 (2000).

21 See J.G. Ruggie, 'International regime, transactions and change: embedded liberalism in the postwar economic order', *International Organization*, 36/2 (1982).

22 R. Keohane, *After Hegemony*, Princeton, NJ: Princeton University Press, 1984.

23 The Club of Madrid is an organization composed of 44 former heads of states or governments. Its purpose is the promotion and strengthening of democracy. See its site www.clubmadrid.org.

24 Rato's appointment in May 2004 was the result of a closed-door bargaining process between European countries and was widely criticized for its lack of transparency. See *The Economist*, 3 June 2004.

25 See: P.R. Almeida, 'O Brasil e o FMI de 1944 a 2002', *Cena Internacional*, 4/2 (2002).

26 For the concept of pivotal states, see R. Chase et al., 'Pivotal states and US strategy', *Foreign Affairs*, 75/1 (1996).

27 See Almeida, op. cit.

28 See chapter by von Mettenheim in this volume.

29 See chapter by Sola in this volume.

Chapter 3

The long and simultaneous construction of fiscal and monetary institutions

Mailson da Nóbrega and Gustavo Loyola

BRAZIL IS ONE of the rare examples of a country that constructed a reasonably complex economy without having to implement strong budget restrictions or measures to keep the currency stable. On the contrary, during most of its history, the country maintained an incestuous relationship between the monetary regime and public finances. This has conditioned generations to the idea that the state 'always has money' and in many ways still constrains the construction of a sustainable fiscal regime. This process has been extremely costly in two ways. First, it contributed to the deterioration of income distribution during the last fifty years. Second, it led to hyperinflation, whose roots were the weakness of the fiscal and monetary institutions. The first ideas for the creation of a central bank in Brazil emerged in the 1930s, when a British financial commission, led by Sir Otto Niemeyer, visited the country. Thirty-five years passed, however, before the Central Bank of Brazil became a reality, under Law no. 4.595 on December 31st, 1964.

Brazil was the last major Latin American country to create a central bank. Colombia, in 1923, Chile, in 1925, Mexico, in 1925, Argentina, in 1935 and Venezuela, in 1940 all preceded the creation of the Central Bank of Brazil by decades. Several reasons explain this delay. On one hand, there was opposition by interest groups linked to Banco do Brasil, which functions and powers would be reduced if a separate monetary authority was created. As noted by Roberto Campos, "the corporatism of Banco do Brasil always represented an almost unbeatable obstacle to the creation of a central bank".[1] But practical considerations also mattered. Even leading monetarist economists like Eugenio Gudin during the 1940s and 1950s believed that the creation of a Central Bank in the

1940s would be useless given the large public deficit and unlikelihood of balancing the budget.

The creation of the Currency and Credit Superintendence (Sumoc) at the end of the dictatorship of Getúlio Vargas, in 1945, was the solution found to please all opinions. Banco do Brasil would be maintained as the monetary authority in practice. However, Sumoc represented the creation of an embryo of the Central Bank with a relevant role in the formation of technical personnel and in the dissemination of knowledge in the monetary sector. The introduction of the Sumoc, however, was plagued with controversy. The initial project, designed by Octávio Gouvêa de Bulhões, had to be adapted to the interests of the Banco do Brasil, creating a dualism in Brazilian monetary authority that would last even after the creation of the Central Bank. It is interesting to note that the creation of Sumoc served as a template for change during the next decades with respect to the evolution of the monetary institutions in Brazil. Advances were always incremental, often the result of compromises, and frequently driven by internal bureaucratic interests.

The principal role of Banco do Brasil

It is difficult to understand the evolution of public finances and monetary policies in Brazil without studying the course of one of the most unique organizations in the public sector, the Banco do Brasil. During its three incarnations, the bank had an unparalleled role in the fiscal and financial history of the country. The first Banco do Brasil originated from the transference of the Portuguese royal family to Brazil trying to escape the threat of France. In 1807, Napoleon Bonaparte declared the removal of the Bragança royal family and invaded Portugal. The royal household left Lisbon at the end of 1807 and arrived in Rio de Janeiro in the beginning of 1808. Banco do Brasil was created in October of the same year. The organization of Banco do Brasil, the third bank in the world responsible for currency emission, was designed to resemble the Bank of Sweden and the Bank of England. The objective was to supply currency for commerce – which increased after the arrival of the royal family – and create conditions to finance the Treasury. The bank combined the typical functions of a financial institution with that of an instrument of public finance. This duality would be a characteristic during most of its life.

The Brazilian Empire emerged in 1822 under the rubric of public debt. To obtain recognition from Portugal, Brazil accepted a debt of two million pounds sterling that the Portuguese government had with the City of London. The debt was later increased with a new loan to pay off late interest. Later, the debts amassed in the country resulted in a financial crisis and the extinction of the Banco do Brasil in 1829. The second Banco do Brasil was created in 1851 by Baron of Mauá to compete with the only existing financial institution in Rio de Janeiro, Banco Comercial. In 1854, the government stipulated the merger of the two banks under the name of Banco do Brasil.

The Republic (1889) inherited inflation and financial problems, which led to consecutive financial crises. After passing through other mergers, Banco do Brasil was transformed into Banco da República do Brasil. In 1905, Banco da República turned into what is considered the third, and present, Banco do Brasil. This bank, by law, had the "functions of a Central Bank, having capital to rediscount papers from other banks and aid them in moments of financial crisis". These functions would be under the responsibility of the bank, by law and in practice, until 1988. The third Banco do Brasil consolidated itself as an institution of multiple functions: agent of the federal government, commercial bank and central bank. The first formal responsibility as a central bank was granted by law in 1921, during the introduction of the Rediscount Department, but the expressive gains started in 1930, during the revolution that deposed President Washington Luis and changed the paradigm of the role of the state. Brazil would experience a long and vast process of state intervention in the economy and society, which would result in several phases until the end of the 1970s.

The new paradigm was a result of internal pressures from the armed forces, businessmen, middle class groups and trade unions, which demanded, for different reasons, firm action to foster the Brazilian economic potential. There were enough examples to go around, such as in Europe, the authoritarian and interventionist regimes in Germany, Italy, Spain and Portugal or in the US, echoes of President Roosevelt's 'New Deal'. The idea of using protectionist measures and official stimulus to promote industrialization gained force in the São Paulo business community and in the young military leaders, which had a decisive role in the revolution that deposed Washington Luis. Their dream of a military power passed through a construction of a solid industrial base.

Banco do Brasil was in the centre of all these processes. Reforms promoted by the new government extended its functions as a central bank and gave it attributions of a development bank. In the sectors of coffee and sugar, Banco do Brasil became the main agent of several functions: financier, inventory manager and trade and export regulator. In 1936, the Agriculture and Industrial Credit Department was created, which would be responsible for more than 90 percent of the credit given to agriculture and the agro-industry. At the end of the Vargas administration (1930–45), Banco do Brasil was the most important state run organization in Brazil, with ample participation in the areas of credit, economic development and foreign exchange and trade. The bank financed the Treasury with printed money, at that time classified as being public revenue. It was not difficult to carry out this function. The bank's funding came from within, via the Rediscount Department.

Due to this unique arrangement, even offering credit at low interest rates, the bank would register amazing profits. The 'miracle' convinced politicians, businessmen and bank employees that this was due to a well-run state-owned organization interested in national development. This idea is still present among a group of trade unions members and politicians, especially in the rural regions of the country. Wages above market levels gave the bank the condition to attract the best talents in Brazil, a characteristic that was maintained at least until the 1970s. Between 1940 and 1970 the Bank was the state institution that provided, on secondment, the greatest number of staff members to the federal, state and local governments. When the Central Bank was created, in 1965, more than 90% of its staff came from Banco do Brasil. Under these circumstances it was not unusual that the bank had enormous power and influence. Its presidency was one of the most sought after positions. The board of directors was comprised of politicians of national importance. In this condition, the bank was able to block, for nearly thirty years, initiatives for the creation of a Brazilian central bank. The argument was that there would be an unnecessary duplication of efforts. The bank even worked for its transformation into a central bank, keeping its development and commercial activities. As a consequence, the bank's power hindered the creation of a strong private financial system in Brazil, which would only come to be after the 1960s.

Sumoc: the embryo of the Central Bank (1945–64)

Sumoc never became an instrument of effective monetary policy and intervention. A free market did not exist, while rediscounts were controlled by the Banco do Brasil and the high reserve requirements of the banking system increased the bank's available resources. Pedro Malan notes that "the impotence of Sumoc in effectively controlling the expansion of credit by the Banco do Brasil marked the period ... and expressed itself politically in several controversies involving finance ministers and Banco do Brasil presidents".[2] The Sumoc played an important role in the exchange rate and foreign capital areas, where it had an active participation during a period marked by a chronic lack of foreign funds. During this period, the multiple exchange rate regime and auctions of foreign exchange were particularly present. The system, scheduled to last one or two years survived until 1961, when President Jânio Quadros abolished it. It is interesting to note that the premiums collected in the auctions of foreign exchange ended up being used to finance the public sector, especially during the 'Plano de Metas' (Plan of Targets) launched by the President Juscelino Kubitschek in 1956.

Although during certain periods of time Sumoc had great visibility in the public opinion, the truth is that its influence over economic policies was very volatile during its 20 years of existence, depending much more on the personality of its leaders and of the Finance Minister than on institutional factors. The idea of having Sumoc as an embryo of the Central Bank was not fully implemented, due to the failure in the creation of instruments and monetary institutions. Banco do Brasil continued as the real monetary authority, and in the majority of cases exhibiting a greater political influence than that of Sumoc. As noted by Antônio Cláudio Sochaczewski the crucial question was not to substitute the Sumoc for the Central Bank, but to determine which would be the role of Banco do Brasil in the design and implementation of the credit and monetary policies.[3]

The Sumoc was, therefore, a toothless tiger. The executive functions of a central bank remained with the Banco do Brasil: to receive voluntary and compulsory reserve requirements from financial institutions, supervise banks, keep a monopoly of foreign exchange transactions, operate the rediscount and the money emission. In spite of this, the existence of a separate organ to establish norms and participate in the administration of monetary policies created a new environment in which emerged the perception of the explosive potential of the operations conducted by Banco do Brasil. In other words, a government run bank subject to political pressures, without any budget restrictions, except the prudence that thankfully existed among its personnel. Moreover, the Sumoc was important in the achievement and dissemination of economic studies in Brazil, particularly in the monetary area as well as in the provision of macroeconomic statistics.

Due to the work performed by the Sumoc, attempts to limit the Banco do Brasil loans, which were enormous sources of monetary expansion, started to appear. In the 1950s, a mechanism to control the bank's loan portfolio was created and dubbed Monetary Budget. The financial relationship between the Sumoc and the Banco do Brasil became simpler than the rediscount and was called 'movement account'.

The creation of the Central Bank

The first legislative bill proposing the creation of a central bank dates back to 1950. The bill was extremely radical, comprising the division of Banco do Brasil into several specialized banks: rural, mortgage, import/export, investment and industrial. The creation of a Monetary Council, as a normative body, was also proposed, leaving to the Central Bank the role of executor of the monetary policy. This bill waited fourteen years before being approved at committee stage. Several changes were proposed, the last being introduced by Federal Deputy Daniel Faraco, in 1962. Faraco simplified the original bill, keeping the idea of creating the Monetary Council and the Central Bank. As to Banco do Brasil, Faraco's bill proposed only the detachment of its agriculture department and the setting up of a rural bank. Faraco's proposals faced criticisms, made by sectors linked to the Banco do Brasil, which feared the depletion of its funds and the loss of revenues from the loans made to the Treasury. Bank employees pressured the Finance Minister, Ney Galvão, who presented a new bill transforming Banco do Brasil into the Central Bank. The end of the duality of monetary authority would take place, not by the loss of these functions by Banco do Brasil, but by the consolidation of all functions within the institution.

A debate over the bill introduced by Ney Galvão was interrupted by the presentation, in 1963, of a new one by the government, whose spirit was to reconcile the two proposals presented to Congress. The bill, named after its draftsmen, Miguel Calmon and San Tiago Dantas, proposed the creation of a National Monetary Council, leaving to the Sumoc the role of a controlling and supervising agency. After the breakdown of democracy in March 1964, the new military government found a new bill proposed by Federal Deputy Jose Maria Alkmin being discussed in the House of Representatives. Alkimin's bill was very similar to the one introduced by Ney Galvão. By now, Octavio Gouvea de Bulhoes was heading the Ministry of Finance, and the idea of creating a central bank in the traditional sense gained support. But the discussions in Congress were heated, especially coming from the opposition, linked to Banco do Brasil and the rural caucus, which insisted in the creation of a rural bank. Among the concessions made to avoid distorting the project, the government agreed to send, in ninety days, another bill aimed at institutionalizing the rural credit. Finally, in September of 1964, the House of Representatives voted the bill introduced by Federal Deputy Ulysses Guimarães, which proposed the creation of a Monetary Council, leaving the Sumoc as the executor of monetary policy. This bill was modified in the Senate, which determined the creation of a central bank and the extinction of the Sumoc. After heated negotiations with the rural caucus, the House of Representatives approved the Senate text. Sanctioned by the President of the Republic on 12/31/1964, it became Law no. 4595.

During the process of discussion and voting of the law that created the Central Bank, Banco do Brasil employees mobilized a powerful blocking coalition, comprised of politicians and the main leaders in agriculture, industry and commerce. With this mobilization, Banco do Brasil was able to include in the law a provision which would bestow the Institution a significant role as an agent of the federal government and the main instrument of the official credit policies. The newly created Monetary Council, would supply the bank with funds to meet these functions. The Central Bank would be responsible for the areas of rediscount, foreign exchange operations, banking supervision and money emission, all done in the past by Banco do Brasil. The Central Bank also became responsible for the supervision of the capital markets. The monetary budget was institutionalized.

Law no. 4595: the reform left on paper

From the time the Central Bank was created, it was independent – or, at least, that is the view of the main players who participated in its creation. "The Central Bank," said Roberto Campos, "created independently, later became a subservient organization. From a severe sheriff became a depraved money printer."[4] For Bulhões, the independence of the Central Bank would be guaranteed by the stability of its directors, who would have fixed terms. In that same line of thinking, Dênio Nogueira, the first governor of the Central Bank said, "I set up a Monetary Council through which I dominated even the minister of finance. I did not dominate fiscal policy, but indirectly, if I refused to finance the public deficit, the cost of the public debt would skyrocket. And the finance minister would have to behave himself."[5]

In reality, Law no. 4595 had already brought the embryos, which in time would bury the independence of the Central Bank craved by the economic authorities of 1964. In a regime where the president could impeach federal deputies and mandatorily retire judges, how could one expect the bank's governor to 'dominate' the finance minister? The main obstacles to building an independent central bank, such as described in Law no. 4595, were the preservation of Banco do Brasil as a monetary authority and the attribution of development functions to the Central Bank. These two distortions made it necessary to make concessions to pressure groups in order to obtain the approval of the law that created the Central Bank.[6] The preservation of Banco do Brasil as the depositary of the voluntary commercial bank reserves and the executor of decisions of the Central Bank generated the necessity for the creation of a special account to register the transactions between the two institutions. This account, which also became known as 'movement account' supposedly would be in balance every week, but this rarely happened, with Banco do Brasil becoming systematically in debt, with rising negative balances. The vices of the old system – monetary budget and the open 'movement account' – had survived.[7]

The creation of the Central Bank of Brazil, was, therefore a partial victory. Casimiro Ribeiro, who also participated in the process, is close to the truth when he says that "there are no examples, in the world, of a country which took so long to create its central bank, and much less of one which left it unfinished".[8] In reality, despite what Bulhões, Campos and Nogueira had imagined, the construction process of the Central Bank was far from finished. This would be an institution to be built gradually, through the next decades.

From Brazilian mirage to Brazilian miracle (1967–74)

During its three first years, the Central Bank was, in fact, independent. There was fiscal austerity and the bank did not face pressures to finance the Treasury. During this period, the Central Bank had a policy of strict control of the rediscount system and closed many banks which were insolvent. The Central Bank often went against the interests of, and supported pressure from, influential political groups. This brief period of independence was to end with the termination of President Castelo Branco's administration. Costa e Silva and his finance minister, Antonio Delfim Netto, were not enthusiastic with the idea of an autonomous central bank. In March of 1967, Dênio Nogueira was forced to resign.[9] The following years have been called the 'Brazilian miracle', when the country obtained high growth with monetary stability. During this period, there was an increasing sophistication of the Brazilian financial market due to the Central Bank, which introduced new instruments, such as open market operations, in 1973.

In this period of consolidation, the bank started recruiting its own staff, but was not marked by advances in relation to its autonomy. On the contrary, the monetary budget increased its importance as an instrument of public policies, being used by Banco do Brasil as a tool by which the bank got funds to finance government-backed programs. The irony of it all was that the presence of old vices, the 'movement account' and the monetary budget produced effects contrary to what was imagined. Banco do Brasil expanded its lending activities through the traditional method. This was due to an error in interpreting the law, in relation to the supply of funds to the bank. The mistaken idea was that the Monetary Council would not only be responsible for the supply of funds but also had the power to generate them. The correct interpretation would be to allocate the corresponding appropriations in the fiscal budget. The Treasury would transfer the funds to the Monetary Council, which in turn would decide how to give them to the Bank. The temporary solution became permanent and the vices survived for another 22 years.

This institutional arrangement gave Banco do Brasil its most fruitful phase in its history. The Monetary Council authorized the bank to expand its loans to agriculture, exports and agro-industry. During the second half of the 1970s the Bank was the eighth largest credit institution in the world, without having increased in any significant manner its funds and without having provoked a substantial increase in printed money. It was not a miracle. In reality, the spectacular growth of loans was possible due to an institutional distortion: the use of the public debt to supply funds for the monetary budget. In 1971, the Complementary Law no. 12, of a constitutional nature, gave powers to the Monetary Council to authorize any expansion of the public debt, "to fulfil monetary policy objectives". It is probably the only case in the world. The fiscal budget approved by Congress was balanced, but it did not include funds to subsidized credit and other benefits to agriculture, exports and the agro-industry. It also did not provide funds for the purchase of surplus coffee yields, crops supported by minimum price policies and for the export of sugar, which was a state monopoly. All these operations, of a fiscal nature, were considered as mere credit policies. The fiscal budget deficit was eliminated but reappeared in the monetary budget.

Brazil had, in practical terms, institutionalized the free budget expansion and not its constraint. The subsidies, the cheap and plentiful credit programs and consequently the increase of the public debt became dependent on the will of the finance minister, who presided over and controlled the Monetary Council, once its members in a certain manner were subordinates. In reality, the finance minister in Brazil had such a power to authorize spending that he would make a medieval king envious. The tax reform of 1965 permitted enormous gains of economic rationality and revenue collection. Because of this, the so-called institutional arrangement was strengthened. Two new taxes – tax over financial operations and export tax – were earmarked, by the Constitution, to be used as 'monetary reserves'. The corresponding revenues were transferred directly to the Central Bank, to be available for the Monetary Council. It is perhaps one of the few cases, if not the only, in which the tax collected did not go through Congress.

The 'abundance' of resources brought about another distortion. The Central Bank became a powerful development bank. It had a department in charge of refinancing loans given by the financial system to selected sectors. The development area had mechanisms similar to the Banco do Brasil's 'movement accounts'. They were the 'advances for funds and programs' included also in the monetary budget. The Monetary Council had powers to expand them as it wished. The Central Bank also negotiated loans with the World Bank and the Interamerican Development Bank to further support these programs. During a certain period, the Central Bank had teams to appraise long-term investment projects financed by this method. Despite these problems, the creation of the Central Bank had forged a new environment, which would result in its future strengthening. The staff seconded by Banco do Brasil had ten years to choose: either go back or join the Central Bank as employees. The bank began recruiting its own personnel. In the middle of the 1980s, the umbilical cord, which had linked the Sumoc and the Central Bank to the Banco do Brasil was definitely severed. The change would be fundamental for the construction of an autonomous monetary authority in the future. Nevertheless, differently than imagined, the 1964 reform had, in practice, worsened the fiscal and monetary institutions in Brazil. The system was vulnerable to social and political pressure, which grew in the wave of the loss of legitimacy of the military regime, the oil crisis, the foreign debt crisis and the exhaustion of the development model based on pervasive state intervention.

External shocks: the oil crisis and the foreign debt crisis (1974–84)

The period between 1974 and 1984 was marked by external crisis and by the increased macroeconomic disequilibrium. The Central Bank during this decade focused on the country's foreign debt, taking advantage of the strong international liquidity. With the foreign debt crisis in 1982, the Central Bank was forced to introduce severe exchange controls, while at the same time the economy had to endure a deep recession. From an inflationary point of view, it was a period of increasing instability, especially during the period of Finance Minister Delfim Netto, responsible for the premature fiscal and monetary easing, which led to an increased inflation in the first years of the 1980s, when the country was preparing to end the military regime.

The years 1974 to 1984 were also a period in which economic growth lost its momentum. Brazil experienced for the first time a decline in real GDP (1981 and 1983), which decreased the popularity of the regime. The monetary budget made it possible for a strong expansion in the development activities of Banco do Brasil and the Central Bank, but the size of these operations became unsustainable. The system did not resist its first test. With a new economic and political environment and the dependence of important sectors on the monetary budget, the pressures became too great. In the early 1980s, there were growing difficulties in 'balancing' the monetary budget. Inflation had surpassed two digits (105 percent in 1982 and 164 percent in 1983 according to the Ample Consumer Price Index – IPCA) increasing substantially the real value of subsidies, implicit in the fixed interest rates of loans to agriculture, exports and agro-industry. In 1983, there was a new and very serious development. Some of the new governors, elected directly by the people, realized that their state banks could withdraw unlimited funds from reserve accounts in Banco do Brasil. The information about negative balances took more than a month to reach the Central Bank.

The monetary budget also deteriorated. In the case of subsidized loans, the corrosion of its real value required that every year there be either an increase in debt or more money emission to preserve at least the real value of the credit. The governors had opened up a road to fiscal irresponsibility through withdrawals in state banks. They seemed to have noticed that the military government had their hands tied and could not adopt the necessary measures in this circumstance, the liquidation of these banks. The Constitution at the time had a provision by which federal intervention must take place in states where there was bad financial management. The liquidation of banks, would mean the suspension of payments, including employee wages. The corresponding chaos would require federal intervention and the removal of the elected governors, one of whom was from the opposition: Leonel Brizola, from Rio de Janeiro. The process of democratization would lose its credibility. In view of these facts, nothing was done. The state banks became autonomous sources of expanding printed money.

In the Ministry of Finance, these factors started to indicate the institutional vulnerability of the federal government finances and of the monetary policy. The democracy that was arriving required the adoption of institutional reforms to create strong budget constraints. The Treasury and the monetary policy would need to prepare themselves to deal with the natural pressures of the democratic process. Time had come to re-evaluate the institutional arrangement and eliminate the errors in the implementation of the 1965 reform. Preliminary studies, done in 1983, called for a broad overhaul of the public finances. The Monetary Council approved the study and created a special commission to propose the necessary measures. The commission would be presided over by the secretary-general of the Ministry of Finance.[10] Participating were 150 experts who involved themselves in the formulation and execution of the fiscal and monetary budgets and came from the Ministries of Finance and Planning, the Central Bank and the Banco do Brasil. During a few weeks, three foreign advisers, members of a technical assistance mission from the International Monetary Fund (IMF) helped the Commission.

In November 1984, the Commission presented its report to the Monetary Council. It was the largest blueprint ever done in public finances and monetary policy. It proposed measure of ample scope, such as:

a) elimination of the Banco do Brasil 'movement account' and the simultaneous authorization for the bank to operate in all areas permitted to commercial banks;
b) elimination of the development functions of the Central Bank and its gradual transformation into a classical monetary authority;
c) elimination of the monetary budget and the transfer of its fiscal operations, including subsidies, to the fiscal budget;
d) transfer from the National Monetary Council to Congress of the power to authorize the expansion of the public debt;
e) transfer from the Central Bank to the Ministry of Finance of the management of the public debt;
f) prohibition of the Central Bank to buy Treasury bonds in primary placements;
g) transfer from Banco do Brasil to the Ministry of Finance of the execution of the fiscal budget;
h) setting up of the Secretariat of the National Treasury to care for the execution of the fiscal budget and for the public debt management, keeping the Central Bank as an agent of the Treasury for the placement of bonds.

The Monetary Council approved the measures in December of 1984, but a decision by a federal judge in Brasília determined the suspension of the program. The action, taken by Federal Deputy Elquisson Soares, from the state of Bahia, was justified by the idea that the reforms aimed at destroying Banco do Brasil and the mechanisms to support agriculture, under recommendation of the IMF, the World Bank and the foreign banks. It was paradoxical that a member of the Congress would be against measures to devolve its natural power to decide on public finances. In reality, it was an opportunistic plot of the politician. He took advantage of the fact that Banco do Brasil employees were against the extinction of the 'account movement' to further his political career.

The damage suffered by the government was due to three factors. The first was the lack of a strategy to convince relevant social actors, especially Banco do Brasil employees. The members of the Commission, whose careers had taken off during the military governments, were not accustomed to dealing with complex social facts. It was naive to think that the reforms did not need to be discussed and that the sectors most affected by them did not need to be convinced of its benefits. The second factor was the political environment of the period – the last days of the military regime – that favoured the acceptance of conspiracy theories against government measures and reduced the stimulus of the president and his ministers in fighting for ideas. The third factor was the pressures from Banco do Brasil. Twelve federal deputies were licensed employees, including the House majority leader, who declared that President João Figueiredo was not aware and did not support such measures. In reality, the president had been informed. The president of the Federal Audit Court was against the measures, although it was expected that he would support them due to their positive institutional characteristics. Being also a bank employee, he later declared, with pride, that he was the leader of the group that pushed for the cancellation of the reform. The minister of agriculture, former president of Banco do Brasil condemned publicly the measures. The reform, therefore, was suspended. The technical studies, however, would not be lost. They would be used the following year when another opportunity arose to convince political authorities.

The period of 1974–84 was also marked by several, tumultuous interventions by the Central Bank on financial institutions. The Halles case was the most notorious and resulted in several attacks by the media on the Central Bank and its directors. The negative repercussions of these interventions influenced the manner in which the Central Bank was viewed by the political class and by part of the media from then on. During this period, the first criticism of lack of transparency by the Central Bank appeared. The criticism was led by opposition federal deputies, several of whom would be in important political positions after the democratization of Brazil. One can consider the period between 1974 and 1984 as a mark on the formation of preconceived ideas of the Central Bank by the political class. These ideas still persist today and are obstacles to the autonomy of the institution. An important institutional change during this period was the transfer of the supervision of the stock market from the Central Bank to the newly created Stock Exchange Commission (Comissão de Valores Mobiliários – CVM).

Democracy, inflation and economic heterodoxy (1985–93)

During the period between 1985 and 1993, the Brazilian economy was characterized by chronic, extremely high inflation. If the main role of a central bank is to work for the stabilization of its currency, then the work of the Central Bank of Brazil could be considered a complete disaster. In the opinion of Matos Dias and Levy, "The instability in the leadership of the Central Bank, in the banking supervision and its passive behaviour towards the inflationary process, left the institution almost demoralized."[11] Such an explanation is, however, partial. If this was a time of disasters for the Central Bank, it was also one of the richest periods for institutional construction. The Central Bank became the exclusive monetary authority in the country with the extinction of the 'movement account', its functions of development were transferred to the Treasury, the constitutional reform prohibited financing the Treasury and there was a leap forward in the development in the bank's operational instruments within the monetary and exchange markets.

The government of President José Sarney (1985–89) was marked by macroeconomic instability and by the introduction of three stabilization plans (Cruzado, Bresser and Verão), which sought to eliminate an inflation diagnosed as inertial. All the plans had a similar course of action: a brief initial success, followed by the return of inflation, stronger each following time. In terms of negative repercussions, these plans contributed toward creating legal uncertainties, due to the fact that they interfered in contracts, and created big liabilities to the government. From the Bank's point of view, the worst inheritance of the plans were that they took the Bank from its normal functions and directed it to activities related to the formulation, execution and enforcement of measures introduced by the plans. This distortion, along with the fiscal crisis, which limited the institution from renovating its staff and technologically modernizing the bank, is the genesis of the problems of banking supervision of late. The plans, however, had their positive aspects, especially to the institutional construction. Normally, the eve of a plan was when the economic bureaucracy gained some influence over the political authority, which could permit it to introduce institutional changes of great importance.[12] The extinction of the 'account movement', for example, was during a period when the Cruzado Plan was being prepared (1986), while the extinction of the development operations by the Central Bank were on the eve of the Bresser Plan in 1987.[13]

Studies about the 'account movement' remained 'dormant' in the files of the Ministry of Finance until the end of 1985, when the Cruzado Plan was being prepared. Among the measures to support the stabilization plan was a better control of the public deficit. The secretary of economic policy of the Ministry, João Batista Abreu (who later became planning minister) had been the vice-president of the 1984 Commission and showed that the solution would be to retrieve the studies from the files and get their approval. The subject returned to the Monetary Council in February of 1986 and was again approved. Federal Deputy Elquisson Soares got a new decision by the same judge to save the 'movement accounts'. Luckily for the country, the environment had changed. The new judicial decision was overruled by a superior court. The 'movement account' was extinguished, and the process of reform triggered off. A few months later, the Secretary of the National Treasury was created.

The new round of measures happened during a similar context: the preparations for a new freeze (Bresser Plan) and the necessity of improving the control of the public deficit. In June of 1987, it was decided that the development functions of the Central Bank were to be abolished. The monetary budget was also abolished and the management of the public debt was transferred to the Ministry of Finance, the latter having authorization from the Congress to expand it, if necessary. The development area of the Central Bank tried to resist, but the government stood firm. In August, the fiscal budget of 1988 was sent to Congress with all the new measures. It was the first unified budget in Brazilian history. It contained all of the revenues and all of the expenditures of the federal government. Another episode in which the Central Bank had its power reinforced happened in 1986 with the extinction of the Banco Nacional de Habitação (BNH – National Housing Bank) that acted as de facto central bank housing financing. The Central Bank began to supervise financial institutions previously monitored by the BNH. As a result, the Central Bank's capacity of supervision over the financial market greatly increased.

Of particular importance to the Central Bank was the promulgation of the Federal Constitution in 1988. It is undeniable that the Constitution represented an important step in the institutional construction of the monetary authority. It is important to note the provision prohibiting the Central Bank to financing the Treasury and non-financial institutions (Art. 164). The long held dream of absolute separation of functions between the Central Bank and the Treasury was achieved paradoxically thanks to a Constitution that is not recognized by its prudence in fiscal and financial matters. Moreover, the principles of universality of the budget were finally consecrated to a constitutional level. It was the definite burial of the monetary budget.

In the National Constituent Assembly, the Commission in charge of designing the budget rules was presided over by Federal Deputy Francisco Dornelles, former finance minister and member of the reform Commission of 1984. The rapporteur, Federal Deputy José Serra, former planning secretary of the state of São Paulo, is one of the best experts on the subject in Congress and turned out to be a politician who embraced the idea of fiscal responsibility. Serra and Dornelles invited the members of the 1984 Commission to aid in the studies. The Constituent Assembly agreed with practically all of the Commission's proposals, although it re-established the ceiling of 12 percent per year on real interest rates, which has been recently eliminated through a constitutional amendment. Provisions to prevent the return of institutional primitive behaviour were also approved. The chapter on public finances is one of the best in the Brazilian Constitution.

The introduction, in the 1988 Constitution, of the requirement of approval by the Senate for the nominations of the Central Bank directors was also positive, although its importance was lessened by the lack of a provision establishing fixed terms for those directors. As is well known, fixed terms are required so that the monetary authority can acquire the indispensable autonomy necessary to perform its functions in the monetary arena and in the banking supervision. In Brazil, particularly, the high level of turnover in the Central Bank has been a great obstacle in the process of its institutional construction. This turnover is at the root of the absence of a medium to long term planning which led to the technical weakening of the Bank in the 1980s and 1990s. In its 37 years of existence, the Central Bank has had 21 governors during 24 periods, which results in a remarkable average of only one year and ten months on the job for each one.[14]

In March 1990, President Fernando Collor de Mello launched a stabilization plan that was characterized by the harshest intervention ever attempted on financial contracts. Nearly 80 percent of all financial assets were frozen during eighteen months and the Central Bank was put naturally into the centre of the economic plan. While Collor's plan worsened the problem of the Central Bank's distorted functions, changes were introduced in the monetary and exchange markets, amongst them the inter-banking market of foreign exchange, where banks negotiated foreign currency on a freer level, despite the Central Bank's interference. The obsolete system of Central Bank controlled transactions was replaced by market-oriented negotiations. Fundamental to the success of this endeavour was the experience the Central Bank had been obtaining since the second half of the 1980s with market negotiating the price of gold and the introduction, in 1988, of a limited floating exchange regime, which began a period of liberalization of the Brazilian foreign exchange market.

The process of liberalization of the foreign exchange market and of the capital account continued throughout the Collor administration, marching parallel to the trade liberalization observed during this period. The turbulent period between 1985 and 1994 also saw a tightening circle by the monetary authorities on sources of inflationary financing of states and municipalities. Although positive results would only be observed after the introduction of the real, it is undeniable the importance of the 'education' received during that period. The tension between the Central Bank and state banks rose at the end of the 1980s and beginning of the 1990s, due to the fact that these institutions were permanent sources of financial and fiscal indiscipline. On several occasions, needing to accommodate political pressures, the norms were eased by the Central Bank. The easing of regulations was also at the root of the banking crisis of 1995 and 1996.

Nevertheless, after 1990, a tendency for the reduction of the different treatment between public institutions and private ones was observed. It is important to mention that the norms definitely eliminated loans provided by state banks to their state treasuries and required due credit forecasts for public agencies. It is also worth mentioning that the conclusion of the renegotiation of the foreign debt in 1993 with the adoption of the Brady Plan did not only conclude a painful episode but also permitted Brazil to forge ahead in its quest to separate the functions of the Central Bank and the Treasury, the latter being now directly responsible for the handling of the external debt, replacing the Central Bank as the direct borrower.[15]

Stability, banking and exchange crisis and an inflation target regime (1994–2002)

The Real Plan, launched in July of 1994, finally brought Brazil to a period of unprecedented monetary stability. The impact of the stability on the Central Bank was great. For the first time, the bank could fulfil its legal mandate: to keep price stability. Although the Central Bank faced several harsh episodes during this period, there was a tendency of its institutional strengthening, especially the creation of mechanisms to increase transparency. The banking crises of 1995 and 1996 and the adoption of the National Financial System Restructuring Program (PROER)[16] and State Banks Restructuring Program (PROES)[17] deeply marked the bank. The Central Bank successfully handled the 1995 crisis and started a process of redefining its mechanisms of intervention and banking supervision. With the 1996 crisis, the Central Bank initiated a successful program to rid the country of the risks of state banks, closing a few institutions and privatizing the rest. With the measure, a source of indiscipline of the states' finances and of the entire financial system was eliminated, leaving behind one of the darkest chapters of public finance and monetary and credit policies seen in Brazil.

Although the success of both programs was only fully recognized later, great harm was done to the image of the Central Bank, especially because it was not able to detect banking problems quickly. Banking supervisors, in any country, are subjected to this type of criticism, especially because successes are not made public as easy as failures are. The problem is that criticism affected the Central Bank during a time in which, due to the country's new monetary reality, more autonomy was desirable. Given this environment, the political conditions for such reforms turned less favourable, which may postpone once again the long process of creating a legally autonomous monetary authority in Brazil. Nevertheless, the presidency of Fernando Henrique Cardoso was characterized by a considerable improvement in fiscal and monetary institutions.

In terms of monetary policy, the gains from the Real Plan after decades of mismanagement brought ample social and political support to the currency stability, which increased in practical terms the autonomy of the Central Bank. On the other hand, there has been a substantial increase in the transparency by which the Central Bank decides and the creation of mechanism of accountability. Of great importance was the setting up, in 1996, of the Monetary Policy Committee (Copom), with the aim of institutionalizing the decision-making process. Until then, interest rates were set jointly by the area director and by the governor, with a high level of informality.[18] With Copom, the decisions are taken after discussions based on technical papers prepared by the staff. Minutes of the meetings are released a few days later, increasing the degree of transparency. Furthermore, upon the introduction, in March 1999, of a new inflation-targeting regime, there was further improvement in transparency. The good management of this regime requires that economic agents understand fully the goals and the measures taken by the Central Bank.

The Central Bank releases quarterly the Inflation Report, with analysis of the international and domestic economic scenarios, emphasizing the price situation. The report contains the inflation forecasts for the next quarters and the respective models of projections. Surveys of market forecasts and articles on economic themes, prepared by the Bank's staff are also available. All of these papers can be downloaded in both Portuguese and English from the Central Bank site on the Internet (www.bcb.gov.br). Regarding accountability, the inflation target regime introduced as a novelty the necessity of justification by the Central Bank, in a letter addressed to the finance minister, every time the target is not met, stating the reasons for the failure.

In 2000, the Fiscal Responsibility Law (LRF), which regulates a provision in the 1988 Constitution and extends its principles to the federal government, the states and the municipalities, was passed. The LRF was approved in 2000 under strong pressure from opposing governors and mayors. Its greatest ally was the support of the public opinion and media. The law is creating a revolution in public finance management and is one of the most important events in the construction of strong budget constraints. The LRF established rigid amount of personnel spending as a proportion of the public sector revenues, ceilings for debt in the three levels of government, constraints to certain outlays during the electoral period, and so on. The law considers null and void loans or supplies made to the public sector without complying with its rules. It clearly introduced risks, perceived as non-existent in the past. Financial institutions made loans to states and municipalities under the impression that the federal government would bail them out if things went wrong, which in fact happened often and gave rise to a situation of moral hazard. Many analysts were sceptical about the success of the LRF even after the establishment of the offence of fiscal irresponsibility, including prison terms and the temporary loss of political rights. The challenge to the LRF during the municipal elections of 2000 was beaten successfully. It worked.

The LRF improved the status of Brazilian public finances. In the operational level, the financial execution of the budget is conducted entirely on-line, reaching all budget units of the executive, legislative and judiciary branches. Federal deputies have passwords to access the accounts and they often lent it to journalists. Even though the passwords are confidential, the leaking of them ended up being an additional element of social control. Several times the media used the system to play its role in Brazilian society, despite a few cases where the data was used for sensationalism by certain newspapers. Treasury technicians have given technical assistance to other countries, recruited by organizations like the IMF. They have done that, for example, in the countries of the former Soviet Union.

In late 2001, the IMF recognized the quality of the Brazilian public finances. According to the Fund, "during the last few years, Brazil reached a high level of fiscal transparency, combined with important advances in the management of its public finances", thanks to "an extensive number of political initiatives and institutional reforms". The report contains several other praises. The ampleness of the fiscal targets was considered to be "uncommon and amazingly extensive"; reforms were held to have "enhanced substantially the realism and transparency of the federal budget"; mechanisms of internal control were "well developed"; statistics were "of high quality, up-to-date and rich in details". Brazil, the IMF judged, was "clearly in the leadership in the sector of electronic media of countries with similar development" not only as a source of information and public service, but also "to facilitate the control by society over governmental activities and programs".

In addition to the express improvement of the Brazilian public finances, the LRF also brought further advances to the autonomy of the Central Bank in the formulation and execution of the monetary policy. The LRF also introduced new mechanisms of responsibility, such as:

a) prohibition of bond issuances by the Central Bank, separating even further the activities as a fiscal agent and its responsibilities in the open market, with the exclusive aim of regulating liquidity;
b) explicit separation of lender of last resort from functions of solving banking crisis. A new PROER, for example, would depend on a specific law;
c) the obligation of the Central Bank to present, every semester, to Congress a report on the compliance of the monetary, credit and exchange policy targets, stating the fiscal cost of these operations;
d) determination for the Treasury to cover Central Bank's negative results, with specific appropriations in the federal budget. Before that, there was a one-way road: the transfer of positive results of the Central Bank to the Treasury.

During the last few years, the Central Bank has been leaving to other government agencies responsibilities not typical of a monetary authority. It is worth mentioning the relationship with the World Bank and other multilateral institutions – except the IMF and the Bank for International Settlements – which became the responsibility of the ministries of Finance and Planning. In the near future the responsibility for the placement of bonds in the international capital markets, now under the responsibility of the Central Bank, will be given to the Treasury.[19]

Another important advance in public finance, with repercussion at the Central Bank, was the renegotiations of debts of states and municipalities with the federal treasury. The process benefited from past failures and experiences and because of that created unprecedented conditions of compliance, including its approval by the legislative branch and the establishment of strong collaterals. These agreements have already been tested on several occasions and have resisted the pressures for the easing of the obligations. The contracts resisted even the senseless moratorium declared in the beginning of 1995 by the governor of the state of Minas Gerais. The program prohibited the placement of state bonds in the capital markets, avoiding the continuation of distortions that hindered the handling of the monetary policy and the supervision of the financial markets. The so-called 'precatório' scandal,[20] subjected to a Senate investigation in 1997, called the public opinion's attention to the chaotic situation of the debt of states and municipalities. Although the Central Bank was criticized for its supposedly lenient attitude in the process of approval of bond placements, the Senate investigations gave the Central Bank more power in the approval of loans by the financial system to states and municipalities.[21]

With the election of Luiz Inácio Lula da Silva in the 2002 presidential contest, and the Worker's Party (PT) assuming executive office in 2003, the operational autonomy of the Central Bank passed through an extremely significant test. Contrary to the historic ideas defended by the party, Lula's administration has amply assured the operational autonomy of the Central Bank, appointing to its directory members with a technical profile who are committed to the execution of responsible monetary policy. Such a strategy was surely an important component to the tremendous improvement of Brazil's macroeconomic indicators that occurred throughout 2003. Even more important was the modification of Article 192 of the Constitution, carried out by Lula's administration, which opened the way to establish fixed mandates to the CB's directory only through a single complementary legislation. Concurrent to such a reform, the government publicly committed to send to the Congress a complementary reform legislation of such a nature, be it in 2004 or 2005. If such a commitment becomes a reality, Brazil will be one more country that confirms the thesis that leftist government have more incentives to delegate autonomy to the Central Bank, much like Tony Blair demonstrated in the United Kingdom early in his administration.

Conclusion

Brazil's construction of its fiscal and monetary institutions is probably one of the longest in Latin America. It took more than seven decades for all parts of the executive branch to accept the idea of the operational autonomy of the Central Bank. It took much more time for the introduction of a series of reforms that led to the approval of the Fiscal Responsibility Law. In the case of the budget process, the perception of its institutional primitive aspects only took place in the early 1980s when the fiscal crisis took a group of bureaucrats from the Ministry of Finance to diagnose the situation and suggest the necessary reforms. The idea of the creation of the Central Bank had been present since the 1930s, boosted by suggestions of foreign missions. The Sumoc was established in 1945 with the explicit objective of preparing the creation of the Central Bank. The slowness can be explained for two reasons. In the first place, the fact that the Banco do Brasil had, for nearly all of the twentieth century, a central role in the execution of the federal budget and activities not typically reserved for central banks. Due to a lack of strong budget constraints, this situation generated an incestuous and murky relationship between the fiscal and monetary regimes. In second place, Banco do Brasil had, in practice, the power to finance, via money expansion, its credit operations, turning it into the most powerful public institution in Brazil. Its president had similar prestige as the finance minister, and normally reported to the president of the republic. The president of the Banco do Brasil, could mobilize forces against changes in the status quo.

The Banco do Brasil expanded considerably at the end of the 1930s. During this time, Banco do Brasil had clearly defined development functions, by granting credit at low rates in favour of agriculture and industry. The Agricultural and Industrial Credit Department, which mimicked the American Farm Credit System, did not count on a developed capital market to raise its funds.[22] Its funding was essentially the rediscount of its notes, which were virtually 'next door' at its Rediscount Department. With such financial power, the bank transformed itself into a great source of funds for state and municipalities, and later on, for the construction of Brasília. During the 1940s the resistance of the Banco do Brasil frustrated the attempts of creating the Central Bank and at the same time of institutional constraints on the inflationary expansion of credit for development. This was the result of a blocking coalition rarely seen in the country. It grouped together the interests of the rural and industrial businessmen, of state governors and mayors and members of Congress, whose power and prestige in large part came from the access to the decision centres at the Banco do Brasil.

Such resistance explains in large part the choice of a transition for the creation of the Central Bank and the institutional unimportance of Sumoc, which despite difficulties contributed to the dissemination of a perception of risk in this institutional arrangement and to the acceptance of the idea of the creation of the Central Bank. The resistance was broken, it must be noted, by the military regime. The concessions made in the negotiations for the approval of the bill creating the Central Bank preserved much of Banco do Brasil's previous functions. The distorted implementation of the law reproduced the institutional arrangement that put Banco do Brasil in the centre of the system. The Central Bank was born with its own development area. Twenty more years passed for a new evolution to take place. The fiscal crisis and the hyperinflationary process of the 1980s led the changes. The reforms made between 1986 and 1988 permitted, for the first time, the segregation of the fiscal and monetary regimes, ending the arrangement which allowed Banco do Brasil and the development area of the Central Bank to expand their operations via printed money and/or public debt which did not finance deficits in the fiscal budget. The execution of the federal budget was transferred from the Banco do Brasil to the Ministry of Finance. When needed, the increase of the public debt should finance exclusively the budget deficit, leaving Congress to authorize the expansion.

The new institutional structure consolidated itself during the 1990s and acquired never-seen-before levels of transparency and operational efficiency. This permitted the transfer of the experience by Brazilian technicians to other countries, including those of the former Soviet Union. The strengthening of the Central Bank and the social support to measures to improve the management of the public finances and monetary policies assured an environment for the privatization of state-owned banks, ending another autonomous source of monetary expansion, abuses and corruption. All these advances culminated in two crucial measures for the institutional construction. The first was the creation, in 1995, of the Monetary Policy Committee institutionalizing the decision-making process on interest rates and contributing to the increased autonomy of the Central Bank. In addition to the minutes of the meetings, the bank also releases a quarterly inflation report, in which it includes its forecast models. The monetary policy became more predictable.

The second measure was the Fiscal Responsibility Law (LRF) approved in 2000. The law regulates a provision in the Constitution and therefore must be followed by the federal government, states and municipalities. In addition to the creation of strong budget constraints and of rigorous rules about public debt, the LRF established limits for personnel spending and for the increase of debt during the electoral period. It also established rules to eliminate moral hazard situations in loans provided by banks to states and municipalities. Later on, offences for the non-compliance of LRF rules and provisions to suspend political rights of officials were introduced into the penal law.

The increase in the transparency and predictability of the fiscal and monetary regimes, along with the economic stability and increased sophistication of the Brazilian financial system created an entirely new situation: the submission of the economic policy to market discipline. At the same time, the transformations under way in Brazil made society increasingly intolerant to inflation, corruption and the inefficiency of the public sector. Although law has not formally established central bank operational autonomy, it is very unlikely to see a reversal in the advances made. In the fiscal area, changes for the worse would face the resistance of public opinion, which would hinder legislative support to changes, since the LRF is a type of legislation subject to qualified quorum. On the other hand, the adherence of a leftist government to the ideal of an autonomous central bank reinforces the perception that we are only one step away from its formalization through legislation reform, which will serve to crown a long and gradual process of constructing monetary and fiscal institutions in Brazil.

Notes

1 Roberto Campos, *A lanterna na popa – Memórias*, Rio de Janeiro: Topbooks, 1997.

2 Pedro S. Malan, 'Sumoc', *Dicionário histórico bibliográfico brasileiro*, Rio de Janeiro: Editora FGV, 2001 (2ª edição).

3 Antônio C. Sochaczewski, 'Sistema financeiro', *Dicionário histórico bibliográfico brasileiro*, Rio de Janeiro: Editora FGV, 2001 (2ª edição).

4 Roberto de Oliveira Campos was Minister of Planning in the first military government (1964–67), when the Central Bank was created. See Campos, op. cit.

5 Dênio Nogueira, *Depoimento*. Programa de História Oral do CPDOC/FGV, Rio de Janeiro: Editora FGV, 1993.

6 Dênio Nogueira argues that the regime accepted the creation of the function of the development of the Central Bank because, as an independent institution, it could resist the expansionist pressures better than the Ministry of Finance. Ibid.

7 In January of 1965, a work group was set up to propose, within sixty days, measures to implement the central bank and balance accounts between Banco do Brasil and the Central Bank. Without disposing of previous studies, the group faced another problem: few staff. It was summer vacation and Carnaval. Days before the deadline, it was concluded that it would be impossible to fulfill the mission. The only solution would be to delay the introduction of the new law, an idea not accepted by either the finance minister or the Superintendent of Sumoc, already chosen to be the Central Bank's first governor. A temporary solution was agreed upon to guarantee the opening of the bank in the period determined by law: that the relationship between the Central Bank and the Banco do Brasil

would take place through a *conta movimento* 'movement account'.

8 Malan, op. cit.

9 The objective of the new finance minister to substitute the governor of the Central Bank was aided by never proven accusations that there had been a leak of information in the currency devaluation of February of 1967, benefiting the economic team. At the time, the first Congressional Investigation Committee was set up, having the Central Bank as it's target. The committee was set up to investigate the supposed 'scandal of the speculation of the dollar'. The author of such a request was federal representative Mario Covas.

10 The position, later 'executive-secretary', was occupied by Mailson da Nóbrega.

11 J.L. Matos Dias and Maria B. Levy, 'Banco Central do Brasil', *Dicionário histórico bibliográfico brasileiro*, Rio de Janeiro: Editora FGV, 2001 (2ª edição).

12 During the Cruzado and Bresser plans, there was a list of legal changes prepared by the staff of the Central Bank to improve the performance of the institution and financial markets. The majority of the changes were introduced in legislation associated with the plans, although they were not directly related to the stabilization process. This technique became known within the Central Bank as 'smuggling'.

13 It is interesting to note that, in general, the idea that fiscal control was important and required institutional changes was advocated by members of the bureaucracy, while economists remained concerned about the inertial factors of inflation. On bureaucracies and advances of monetary and fiscal institutions, see: Gilda P. Gouvêa, *Burocracia e elites burocráticas no Brasil*, São Paulo: Ed. Paulicéia, 1994.

14 The Central Bank of Brazil is the heir of Sumoc which, during its twenty years of existence, had sixteen executive-directors, or a term average of a year and three months.

15 International lenders deposited funds in the Central Bank due to previous agreements.

16 PROER was launched in November 1995, its main goal being to permit the transfer of assets and liabilities from banks in financial difficulties to other institutions, avoiding losses to customers and a systemic crisis. Three of the ten biggest private banks, representing 10 percent of all banking deposits suffered intervention by the Central Bank and had their assets and liabilities transferred.

17 PROES was launched in 1996; it reduced the presence of state government credit institutions in the financial system. By February 2002, nine institutions had been privatized and five closed. Four more await privatization. Four commercial banks remain under state government control.

18 At this time the governor of the Central Bank of Brazil was Gustavo Loyola.

19 The schedule and other conditions for the gradual transference of this function to Treasury was disclosed in January 2004, by the Ministry of Finance.

20 'Precatórios' are judicial decisions that condemn the Union, states or municipalities to pay a set amount in courts. States and municipalities were then prohibited from placing new debts, except those to pay out the 'precatórios'. The scandal consisted in the creation of mechanisms by which financial institutions forged 'precatórios' with the sole objective of increasing the debt of states and municipalities. Operations involved bribes and other forms of corruption.

21 Before the Senate investigation, the Central Bank could not deny a request for bond issuance or loan, only recommend to the Senate its rejection. After the Senate investigation, the Central Bank was forced to deny any request that fell out of the norms established by the Senate, ending the so-called 'exceptionalities'.

22 Mailson F. Nóbrega, *Desafios da política agrícola*, São Paulo: Ed. Gazeta Mercantil, 1985.

Chapter 4

Crafting economic stabilization: political discretion and technical innovation in the implementation of the Real Plan

Lourdes Sola and Eduardo Kugelmas

THIS CHAPTER FOCUSES on the decision-making process that led to the adoption of the Real Plan and the reasons for its success in overcoming the threat of hyperinflation and anomie that hung over Brazil during the early 1990s. This period was a crossroads. From political and economic perspectives, this time may be represented as a critical juncture. The economic changes that made price stabilization possible are accounted for here, as is the emergence of new criteria of political legitimization in Brazilian society in tandem with the process of democratization. By starting from the decisions taken by government elites and the political class in response to the dilemmas and opportunities that characterized this crossroads, subsequent policy choices become more intelligible. Likewise, many of the dilemmas which have confronted the policy-makers and the political elite since price stability in 1994 derived from changes in the economic and political context that came together during the critical juncture of the Real Plan.

Thus, one of the major analytical challenges posed by the profound changes in Latin America during the 1980s related to the extreme economic instability created by the debt crisis is addressed. How were processes of democratization reconciled with changes of economic regime imposed by the policies of structural adjustments? To what extent did convergence between processes of democratization, stability, and economic reform depend on the implementation of solutions of a type 'one model fits all', as economic orthodoxy and Bretton Woods institutions appeared to support?

Taking these questions of general order into account, it is worthwhile to briefly introduce our position in relation to the literature that deals with the links between economic reform and democratization. This is a preliminary step to assess whether or not they apply to the Brazilian experience. The economic and political background to the Real Plan is examined in the light of some common features shared with other Latin American countries at that time. It will be followed by an analysis of the conception and implementation of the relevant stabilization policies whose analytical interest may well be represented (and anticipated) in the following manner. One is dealing with an agreed economic strategy of problem solving, which emerged in the context of extreme political uncertainty associated with acute macroeconomic instability. Its technical and political effectiveness resulted from the re-blending of institutions, practices and pre-existing political resources – which we define as a mode of recombination. Two components were key factors for the success of this re-blending: the exercising of a specific type of political discretion by the relevant leadership and the availability of a technically innovative and heterodox set of economic prescriptions, derived from a diagnosis in line with the specificity of Brazilian inflation at that time.

The literature: where do we stand and why?

One of the trade marks of pioneering political literature that deals with the transition from authoritarianism has been the caution shown in relation to the prospects of democratic consolidation, above all in economic contexts such as those of Latin America, marked by the impact of their external debt crises, by stagnation, and most importantly, by the emergence of hyperinflationary pressures.[1] Later, the post-Cold War scenario and the widening of the scope for comparison with post-communist countries, presented the opportunity for a more fertile and complex vision of the possible routes of democratization cum liberalization. The emphasis, in this case, was mirrored around the significant differences in the observed routes of various countries, based on their distinctive starting points and also on whether or not democratization coincided with economic liberalization or followed it.[2]

This more pluralistic approach to dual regime change was validated by the experiences of young Latin American democracies, given their observable diversity in technical guidelines, in timing, in the manner of presentation and sequencing by which their stabilization programs and market-oriented reforms were implemented during the 1980s and 1990s.

At the same time, the effort to redeem a common denominator as a base for generalizations could be salvaged in new terms. That is to say, there was enough accumulated evidence of convergence among countries as to the final directions of such changes, in particular those concerning the basic guidelines of government agendas: economic liberalization and adherence to the principles of representative democracy.[3]

The variety of possible routes and the multiplicity of effective results, already observable during the period of interest here (1992–94) shaped a problem that proved to be long lasting. This characteristic is due to two main factors. One, a virtue in itself, is that of having introduced the component of uncertainty into the conceptual framework. The beneficial results of the combination between economic liberalization and that of political liberalization were no longer taken for granted. Calling into question the 'final point of arrival' as uncertain was in a large part due to the observation of the experiences of adjustments observed in Latin America. These did not confirm one of the crucial optimistic assumptions of orthodox analysis – and of the prescription of the Bretton Woods institutions. These were that political liberalization and economic liberalization would mutually reinforce one another and almost automatically their elective affinities would lead the relevant countries to follow the example of the dominant democracies.

This more critical approach to economic and political transitions resisted the changes in the international economic and political scenario throughout the 1990s – giving continuity to the discussion that began in the previous decade concerning the links between democratization and the neoliberal modalities of economic transformation. It centred upon two other questions, namely: What are the costs that are incurred in terms of the quality of democracy, in situations of extreme economic uncertainty, such as those marked by debt crises? And what is the place of democratic politics during such hard times? Another dimension refers to the experiences of policymaking at those early stages of democratization. As elected politicians and the new governmental elites took power, they urgently faced a policy relevant task: How do we determine the adequate mix between economic restructuring and democratic legitimization? And which is the more adequate sequencing of prescriptions, taking into consideration the differences in the relevant countries' starting points and above all the various possible routes of economic and political development?

Questions such as the incremental character of the strategies of change, their timing and their manner of presentation have gone on to occupy the domestic political scenarios. As well as this, the adoption of adjustment policies with a neoliberal stamp introduced another distinctive characteristic of regional experiences and added yet another type of uncertainty onto the domestic scenarios. In the Bolivia of Paz Extensoro, as in the Argentine of Menem, or in the Brazil of Collor de Mello one could observe an enormous hiatus, which in itself posed an important political challenge. There was an enormous gap between the content of the economic policy acceptable to the international financial institutions and foreign creditors on the one hand, and the expectations and the political composition of the electoral coalitions that supported the recently elected civilian governments on the other. More often than not, the political parties that integrated into such coalitions, to a large part, moved in the ideological universe of the 'state centred model' that had prevailed since the 1930s. This second type of uncertainty brought to centre stage the question of governance as defined by Malloy and Cunningham: how to convert an electoral coalition into an effective governing coalition supportive of liberalizing economic policies?

One of the merits of the political literature which aimed at responding to such challenges was that it made possible a change in perspective in relation to conventional orthodox analyses and prescriptions that had prevailed up until then – of the type 'one model fits all'. It is beyond the scope of this chapter to examine the contribution of those authors. The interest here is to show, in broad terms, a simultaneous advance on three fronts. First, the assumption (frequently explicit) that the processes of democratization and of economic liberalization respond to distinct logics, each following a political dynamic of its own, which may or may not mutually reinforce each other in the short term. In other words, the initiation of a virtuous cycle was not seen as a necessary outcome. From this high level of uncertainty two other components followed which were looked upon as structural problems of dual transition. One of them is the presence or absence of the qualities of statesmanship in the elected politicians, seen as the capacity to coordinate and eventually bring together the aforementioned logics. This capacity would be required especially when the gap between the content of the economic policies needed to start (or proceed with) structural adjustments and the system of interests that make up the winning electoral coalition widened. As a consequence, one of the key questions broached by this literature may be stated as follows: Is there any space open for elected politicians to exercise political discretion when the room to manoeuvre, in terms of economic policy options, is excessively meagre?

Another related advance is the specification of the types of political discretion and the quality and the skills necessary for political leaders to manage a successful transition. The concept of *statesmanship* was rescued and adapted to these contexts. Statesmanship may be defined as the capacity to build consensus around a given set of policies and institutional framework, stabilize expectations, and reconcile economic change and democratization. Contrasting successful and unsuccessful experiences suggested that statesmanship was a necessary condition of governance. Malloy defines statesmanship as "the capacity to generate new power resources from given institutions" – that is to say, from a fragile institutional framework put into their hands at the starting off point.[4]

During the early 1990s, positive changes in the international context reinforced the necessity for a more contextual analysis. On the one hand, the resumption of financial flows and the Brady Plan in 1991 opened the way for the return of private capital to Latin America. The shift of capital towards emerging countries was encouraged by low interest rates in advanced economies. On the other hand, these benign conditions benefited Latin American countries differently, according to whether or not they had carried out economic stabilization and solved their domestic fiscal crises. In comparative terms, within this new context, Brazil revealed itself as being a loser, an atypical case of 'muddling through'. Its tardy and patchy structural adjustment deprived it of taking advantage of this opportunity at the level attained by neighbours. Unlike its experience for most of the twentieth century, Brazil seemed unable to accompany international economic change and maximize benefits from new opportunities. In short, whilst international changes improved the time horizons of Latin American policy makers, Brazilians remained prisoners of short-term tasks and calculations.

The reasons for this pattern of adjustment, by 'muddling through' are various and have been explored by us elsewhere. What is important here is to highlight one explanatory variable, of a technical order, relevant to our objectives. The distinctive characteristics of Brazilian mega-inflation – of a predominantly inertial character due to the generalized indexation of assets and of income – demanded special diagnosis and remedies. These were alien to mainstream economics and policies within the Bretton Woods institutions. At the same time, although a 'theory' of inertial inflation had been framed and had been available in Brazil since the early 1980s, the failure of several stabilization plans could be blamed, in part, on the use of heterodox mechanisms of inflation control. In this context, innovations conceived by Brazilian economists during the Real Plan can be seen as a by-product of years of experimenting. Technical innovation emerged from a learning process during the failed attempts at stabilization from 1985–93. Furthermore, whether innovations became political resources depended on the existence of 'elective affinities' between political leaders and economists.

This chapter examines select aspects of the relationships between economic liberalization and democratization seen during the Brazilian experience of stabilization. Of several justifications, one has already been mentioned: Brazil was a latecomer with respect to stabilization – one of the preliminary goals of any structural adjustment. For this reason, until mid-1994 the bonanza in the international context was under-utilized in comparison to Mexico and Argentina. Also, in comparative terms, one of the weaknesses of the Brazilian political transition was its institutional fragility – thus increasing the tenor of political uncertainty inherent in the process of dual regime change. In this context, one may mention the difficulties of consolidating the party system, a feature reinforced by a type of federalism hardly coherent with the definite solution of the fiscal crisis.[5] Also for this reason the goal of self-sustained stability would strongly depend on the manner of equating some of the major factors of political and institutional uncertainty. There is as well a further reason to examine the Brazilian experience: the manner in which the economic and political legacy of the State Centred Model reflected on the cognitive maps of the sectors of the entrepreneurial and political elite and on the aspirations of wide sectors of Brazilian society. Opposition to stability programs, to economic liberalization, and to more transparent regulatory frameworks was centred in economic and political interests entrenched within the state. Resistance to change also had to do with past successes in economic policy and a Brazilian style of problem solving. On the one hand, the model of import substitution industrialization was comparatively more successful and advanced than those of the other Latin American countries. On the other hand, the long period of generalized indexation, while accommodating acute distributive conflicts, had given to mega-inflation an inertial character that commanded rather unorthodox treatment.

The polyhedral character of veto groups in this context of institutional uncertainty, points to the centrality of political coordination. Under such circumstances, the activity of equating political and economic problems – inseparable from whatever reform strategy might be chosen – depended on repeated balancing acts by the incumbent President. This also applies to any strategy of institutional reconstruction that, over a longer period, would have as its objective routines and depersonalization of decisions, in particular, the solutions for distributive conflicts. From this perspective, the question of 'political coordination', led us to take, as part of the equation to be solved, the quality of the new political leadership in a very precise manner: in their capacity to generate new resources of power starting from existing institutions.

Our analysis of decision making during the Real Plan uses an analytical framework based on the concept of statecraft as a special mode of political discretion. The concept of statecraft applies especially to situations of exceptionality, of critical junctures; situations where the parameters that regulate political and economic decisions tend to change in a non-routine manner. The direction of change, however, is a matter of strategic policy options and not fully predictable. These coordinating capacities required in times of acute uncertainty we define as statesmanship.

It is important, therefore, to point out why and in what senses the episode under analysis may be characterized as a critical juncture for the Brazilian economy and politics. This is, without a doubt, an empirical matter. We believe it is possible to rephrase this question in the following terms: as the *expected* tasks which ought to be performed by elected politicians if statesmanship was to have been exercised in the conditions prevailing throughout Latin America during the 1990s. The problem of identifying the diverse paths through which successful stabilization and liberalization were achieved during democratization, requires that another distinction be made between the different types of coordination required under specific situations. The notion of a threshold of crisis, suggested by Laurence Whitehead is a convenient point distinguishing between two different forms of coordination. One refers to exceptionally critical circumstances and another where the principal task for policy makers consists of stabilizing expectations, both economic and political. Thus it would be possible to determine some 'threshold of crisis' above which the conventional relationships between economic and political variables are no longer applicable. It would also be possible to say that below this threshold, gradualism and the negotiation of conflicts around public policies would be the most efficient forms of reconciling political participation with economic reform. Nevertheless, beyond this threshold, it seems that more radical restructuring and greater centralization of authority must substitute incremental methods of policymaking based on consultation.[6] Our study of the Real Plan and subsequent institutional developments suggest that this latter hypothesis describes the Brazilian path to stabilization.

Uncertainty and contingency: the background to the Real Plan

Economic plans may also be approached as political instruments designed to reduce uncertainty through the way they order priorities and assumptions about policy options. More often than not, plans involve redistribution of political and material resources. This is also valid for plans for stabilizing an economy undergoing hyperinflationary pressures on their way to an explosive path. In this case, the crafting of plans confronts a double-edged problem. One is dealing with the restoration of shaken confidence, of major economic agents whose behaviour is strategic in terms of the price system, by way of a drastic reversal of inflationary expectations. Moreover, in the context of democratization, it also implies obtaining the confidence of the political players in order to carry out the crossover into the direction of a new monetary regime.

Various factors were responsible for the high level of uncertainty that preceded the 1994 stabilization experiment in Brazil known as the Real Plan. Most of these factors were shared with other countries in the region, while others were specific to the local economic and political context. These differences relate to different modalities of uncertainty, from 'normal' forms of uncertainty, such as those centred on elections, to more extreme forms such as hyperinflationary crises. The latter are disruptive of productive system and contracts. From this point of view, the key question is the following: How to exit from an explosive path in the economy, in an ordered manner, exactly when the new institutional and judicial arrangements are still precarious, since they are still under construction? This exit, among other conditions, presupposes the existence and the legitimacy of an agreed economic strategy.

One of the modes of uncertainty, shared by new Latin American democracies in the late 1980s and early 1990s was that the formulation and implementation of a minimally agreed economic strategy had been constrained by three orders of factors:

- Institutions of an effectively representative party system were not yet consolidated;
- Identities of emerging political players and organized interests remained fluid, which affected the nature of the distributive conflicts;
- Distributive conflicts were not limited to distributive questions *strictu sensu*, i.e. in terms of participation in national income; during regime change, confrontations included broader strategic calculations of future positions in the new order. Hence, the intransigency of this modality of conflict in times of political regime change.[7]

The 1982 debt crisis introduced more acute uncertainty about the state and its relations with economy and society. The abrupt interruption of foreign capital flows implied a radical change in the pattern of financing and expenditures of Latin American states. This external shock increased debt and placed countries onto a new explosive path whose principal manifestation was a dramatic change in the nature and pace of inflation.[8] The mechanisms were as follows. The political decision of governments to 'nationalize' the external debt of the private sector caused a dramatic rise in already high public debt. Debt financing came to depend exclusively on internal savings and, in particular, on the borrowing capacity of states in domestic financial markets. Such markets, comparatively restricted and vulnerable, converted themselves into referees of the capacity of the state to honour its public debt. Rolling over public debt became subject to financial markets through ever-shortening bond maturities and higher interest rates. In the absence of more profound fiscal or administrative reforms, one of the few mechanisms available to finance the fiscal gap was the inflationary tax, at ever-increasing rates.

The 1980s, then, signalled a structural change towards the acceleration of inflation and the prospect of hyperinflation. This decade also meant a change in the manageability of inflation and the starting point for change in the relationship between the economy and politics. Economic policy became more and more subject to the scrutiny of markets. Market volatility came to be linked with expectations concerning solvency (i.e. state capacity to honour public debt). Political instability came to be perceived as an economic threat. This progressive weakening of the state and its growing dependency on local financial markets was one of the distinctive characteristics of democratic transitions in most of Latin America. For comparativists, the success of economic liberalization in new democracies was attributed to the coordinating capacities inherent in strong and mature states.[9] This prerequisite was not only absent in Latin America but worse; states in the region had experienced unprecedented fiscal crises. Under these circumstances the question about policy was of a different order. Given the need to reform state finances, what restrictions could prevent the imposing explosive paths of economies?

In Brazil, the solution to the state fiscal crisis depended on a set of context specific responses, of technical as much as of political order, which further increased uncertainty. The Brazilian experience had to do with the adoption and subsequent generalization of monetary correction or indexation that began in 1964. This institution had worked as a useful tool to accommodate distributive conflicts under inflation. In the 1980s, as the debt crisis gave rise to a new inflationary regime, generalized indexation made it possible for the new governmental elites during transition from military rule to circumvent the pending threat of a hyperinflationary crisis. It also made it unnecessary to confront vested interests rooted in the state apparatus opposed to reforms or restructuring the existing pattern of state financing and expenditure. After the debt crisis, indexation in Brazil fulfilled two roles. It acted as a stabilizing mechanism for conflict management and as a conflict-minimizing device by postponing structural reforms. On the other hand, it also became an important cause of inflation – as any inflationary shock would be transmitted to the whole economy, and distributive conflicts would centre round the rate of adjustments in prices and incomes. This is why curbing mega-inflation in Brazil, more than in other countries in the region where indexation was not institutionalized, required far more than fiscal and monetary discipline. Ending high inflation required the diagnosis of inertial inflation and the difficult, complex and uncertain process of de-indexation. The diagnosis had been available since the early 1980s. But five heterodox stabilization plans before 1992 failed for different reasons. Brazil was often cited as a case of 'muddling through'. A concept favoured here, however, is that of brinkmanship, a dance on the brink of an abyss, as it captures both the economic and political reasons for postponing the hour of reckoning.

Immediately prior to the Real Plan, indexation appeared no longer efficient. The analytical and political resources of different groups and schools of economic thought also appeared to be at the end of their resources. Nonetheless, these experiments produced a cumulative learning process, intense technical debates, and the following consensus between economists, sectors of the governmental elite and the political class: First, the nature of inflation demanded de-indexation; second, this presupposed a modicum of fiscal equilibrium (since under the conditions described the state was an active factor in inflation); and third, the restoration of confidence of economic agents demanded respect for contracts and the abandonment of shock therapy, whether heterodox or orthodox.

A brief reconstruction of the process through which these conditions came to a head during the extreme uncertainty of 1992–93 suggests the complexity of challenges in Brazil. Nonetheless, agreement of economic strategy was forged, one well adapted to the Brazilian context thanks to the recombination of institutions, practices, and existing political and analytical resources. The importance of this type of recombination is two-fold. On the one hand, new power resources, starting from the given resources and institutions, were engendered. On the other hand, the coordination of these resources, under the context of extreme political and macroeconomic uncertainty, presupposed a modality of political leadership that merits attention. The concept of statesmanship, adapted from classics by Malloy and Cunningham to analyse the central Andes, seems well suited to explain the Brazilian experience. It allows for taking into account the specific mode of leadership necessary for exiting a situation where economic and political order verge on hyperinflationary crisis, as was the case in Brazil in 1992–93, toward a moment when conditions of democratic governance and price stability were restored. The concept of statesmanship also emphasizes contingency under extreme uncertainty and the capacity of leaders to exercise political discretion and pursue strategic vision able to break a vicious cycle and initiate a virtuous one.[10] While, as Gourevitch suggests, space exists for political discretion and unpredictability is inherent to all economic decision making, the experience of Latin American countries is often more extreme. A further component of contingency surrounds statesmanship, which is even more distinct and remarkable when it is most necessary, that is to say, when political leaders confront the task of exiting an explosive economic path to one toward political-economic stability.[11] New forms of integration of Latin American countries into the global economy have reduced the discretion of politicians to shape economic policy. However, the Brazilian experience confirms studies of statesmanship in the sense that the space and importance of discretion may actually increase during these moments. What does this space consist of and what factors determine these critical junctures?

In the case of the Real Plan, the task is to explain how space was created for the generation of new power resources within existing, precarious institutions and, in turn, how an agreed economic strategy was developed for the specific critical juncture. The efficacy of the Real Plan is as much political as economic. From a longer-term perspective, conditions were created for surmounting the type of brinkmanship that had prevailed since the early 1980s. This was made possible by eliminating the principal factor of inertial inflation, which originated in 1964, i.e. that of generalized indexation. As will be seen, contrary to the stabilization proposals of the type 'one model fits all', the Real Plan depended on two conditions. On the one hand, the existence of an adequate diagnosis of Brazilian inflation as being inertial and the use of technological innovation, sketched out during the years of learning by way of the fiascos of successive plans. On the other hand, we have the recombination of the 'genetic' properties of the institutions that had characterized the Brazilian political and economic system. The Real Plan created conditions to overcome a pending crisis of authority and of legitimation by means of a new institutional framework. The category of statecraft best defines the decision-making process through which price stability and improved conditions of democratic governance were made viable.

Crafting the Real Plan: a recombination of political institutions and economic practices

By 1992, the economic problems and political tensions observed during the previous decade had acquired new momentum as the result of a synergy between three factors: the fiscal crisis of the Brazilian state; a crisis of legitimation of the state centred paradigm; and the re-acceleration of inflation.[12] This brought to centre stage, in an especially sharp manner, the ineffectiveness of orthodox approaches to stabilization, originally conceived to solve short-term disequilibria in the balance of payments, in fiscal accounts, or monetary aggregates. Once economists understood the inertial nature of protracted high inflation, alternative frames and analytical tools were sought. These were developed in Brazil and Argentina through a learning process involving some eight years and intense debates among Latin American economists. This situation also prompted a change of perceptions about the technical and political constraints to stabilization. Brazilian and Argentinean economists reviewed stabilization experiments and drew lessons from successful experiences of other countries (such as Israel).[13] The failure of the first experiment at stabilization in democratizing Brazil, the Cruzado Plan (1985–87) was frequently cited as proof of the inefficiency of heterodox experiments. Nonetheless, the attempt at orthodox gradualism under Minister Marcilio Marques Moreira (May 1991–September 1992) also failed to check inflation.[14]

By the 1980s, the system of monetary correction introduced in 1965 had emerged to protect practically all forms of income and assets against inflation.[15] During the final military administration under President Figueiredo (1979–83), when inflation reached levels of 200 percent per-year, the first academic papers on the theory of inertial inflation appeared. André Lara Rezende and Pérsio Arida first discussed the need to combine whatever 'classic' procedures were required to check inflation with strong measures of de-indexation. The majority of the stabilization plans, going back to 1986 under the first civilian government to take office, through those of 1990–92, had, in fact, experienced short-term success but failed to stave off the return of inflation.[16] For the purposes of this chapter, it is enough to consider a dramatic change of perception: from the Collor Plan II (1991) onwards, well-known heterodox prescriptions were discredited in both the eyes of policy makers and elected politicians. Price freezing, as with all other forms of rupture of contractual relationships, had been experimented with but none of them had had a lasting effect in curbing inflation. By the same token, the shock therapy associated with heterodox economic packages, which initially took the economic agents by surprise, had lost their efficacy. On the contrary, after each bout of inflation agents responsible for strategic pricing tended to anticipate a probable heterodox package by marking up prices before the event – thereby neutralizing even the temporary effect of the heterodox measures. The end of 1991 reinforced this adaptation by the tendency of the judicial authorities to question the legality of the interventionist measures adopted by the executive authority. Also, to this has to be added the concern of avoiding the flight of foreign capital. These factors had turned the adoption of 'shock' measures excessively difficult and ineffective: Brazilian society tended to reject the surprise inseparable from that mode of heterodox therapy.

It is against this background that the orthodox policies adopted by Marcilio Marques Moreira (1992), Collor de Mello's finance minister, become relevant. They were geared to avoiding open hyperinflation by means of classical remedies: raising interest rates while trying to restore the country's credibility in the eyes of the international financial institutions. This policy meant the reinforcement of the indexation system, and reflected an effort to put off the moment of explosive hyperinflation. Nonetheless, during second semester 1992, political developments led to crisis and the impeachment of President Collor, effectively suspending economic management while the nation awaited installation of the Itamar Franco government.

Uncertainty became the major constraint to economic policy and brought market expectations close to paroxysm during early 1993. The spectre of hyperinflation and possible social crisis hovered over Brazil from October 1992, when Itamar Franco took over as the acting vice-president (awaiting the conclusion of the impeachment process), until the indication of Fernando Henrique Cardoso as finance minister in May 1993. The unstable personality of President Franco, his lack of commitment to the liberalizing programmes of Collor de Mello and his erratic economic policy involved the substitution of three finance ministers in a space of seven months (Gustavo Krause, Paulo Haddad and Eliseu Resende). Political and economic instability fused in a perverse synergy that reinforced both the explosive path in the economy and the disenchantment with politicians unable to agree on an economic strategy to avoid crisis. Compared to this situation, the brinkmanship and muddling through that prevailed during the 1980s seemed close to normality.

While the appointment of Fernando Henrique Cardoso as finance minister in May 1993 was not sufficient to reverse economic expectations, it reduced the level of uncertainty. This was due to his prestige as a social scientist, his experience as senator, and performance as foreign minister in the Itamar Franco government. His first step was to appoint an economic team with marked predominance of academics from the Catholic University of Rio de Janeiro (PUC–Rio), including Pedro

Malan, Edmar Bacha, Pérsio Arida, André Lara Resende, Winston Fritsch and Gustavo Franco.

International conditions became far more favourable. A new window of opportunity, absent during the 1980s, had been created although, during the politically turbulent year of 1992, the Brazilian authorities were late to perceive it as such. Starting from 1991, private capital had returned to Latin America, thus overcoming one of the principal obstacles to stabilization policies, namely the shortage of foreign reserves. Shortage of foreign reserves had prevented the adoption of a stable exchange rate as anchor for prices. As mentioned above, Latin America during the 1980s had been marked by a 'feedback' relationship between the external debt crisis and high inflation. This was especially so in Brazil where the government had depended enormously on exports by the private sector to obtain foreign exchange – which had worsened even more the poor situation of public finances. In fact, the external shock of 1983 and the debt crisis deeply affected the balance of socio-economic forces within the country. The state fiscal crisis and the need to close the external gap had made the government more and more dependent on two economic sectors which up until then had been secondary in the political scenario, namely: the domestic financial market and the export (private) sector.

A number of factors explain why the international setting improved. In 1989, the Brady Plan opened up the way to re-schedule the external debt of Latin American countries and private capital flows returned. Whilst during the decade of the 1980s the flow of foreign capital had remained below one percent of regional GDP, in the 1990s it totalled some six percent. During 1994, the inflow of capital reached US$57 billion (up from US$13.4 billion in 1990).[17] This bonanza may be explained as the result of the ongoing changes in the international financial markets: the preference of private investors towards greater geographical diversification of their portfolios and the attractiveness of higher interest rates practised in the emerging economies as compared with those in the USA. The latter was the by-product of the anti-recessive policy of the United States Federal Reserve. In Brazil, even with the threat of hyperinflation and lack of market-oriented reforms, the inflow of foreign capital resumed in 1991 and increased steadily thereafter. In sum, the steady accumulation of reserves through 1994 was one of the principal conditions that made the Real Plan economically viable. Reserves rose from US$9.4 billion year-end 1991, to US$23 billion in

1992, US$32.2 billion in 1993, and, at the launch of the new currency in July of 1994, close to US$42 billion.

Another novelty was the almost total disappearance of advocates of orthodox solutions in Brazil. In the words of an economist who was far from sympathetic towards heterodoxy and an expert on monetary theory, "the experience of the Geisel government and above all that of the Figueiredo government, left an explicit message: within a formally over-indexed economy, to combat inflation by simple monetary and fiscal recipes is to turn your back to the point of the knife." In this way, Brazil had been sacrificed by shortsightedness among both orthodox economists and the IMF.[18] Most economists gradually perceived the unique features of Brazil during this time. Given a significant reduction in the public deficit, it was the innocuous character of monetary squeezes that had become the object of consensus among experts and businessmen alike. This was because in Brazil a rare phenomenon in complex economies had occurred: an almost complete 'de-monetization' of the economy. The reason for this goes back to the fact that "the monetary base (money held by economic agents plus bank reserves kept in the Central Bank) represented a very small fraction of the GDP"; this combined with a mode of bank regulation that opened the door for an endogenous monetary expansion.[19] This situation, which now severely restricted stability, had only been possible thanks to the sophistication of the indexation mechanisms and to the degree of bank modernization. The result was a highly efficient system of deposits with balances for transactions that rendered interest; which for its part had allowed the holders of the money in Brazil to escape the direct use of currency and/or the indirect use of banking reserves.[20] One of the important social implications of this system was the creation of a privileged cast of depositors, well protected from inflation because their bank balances were indexed. Such sectors included not only the middle classes but also formal sector workers and organized interests. The result was an unprecedented social cleavage under inflation; that of being either 'protected' or 'unprotected' from accelerating inflation in bank accounts.

At this point, the analysis of Brazilian inflation as basically inertial and caused by indexation became consensual. Debate turned on what kind of policies would make de-indexation possible without falling into the traps of previous heterodox attempts. The resistance of economic agents towards price and wage freezes or other violations of contracts, as well as the opposition from and through the judiciary also came into play. While the existence of foreign exchange reserves implied new degrees of liberty, policy makers still would have to deal with the expectations mobilized by hypothetical formulas for 'dollarization' and other imitations of the 'Argentine example'.

At this point, the discussion above about the specific nature of political leadership, contingency, and statecraft gain relevance. Mega-inflation weighed over the country, generating a mixture of despair, anxiety, and demands for drastic solutions. A peculiar piece of reasoning had been circulating in the press and media about the 'cleansing' character of open hyperinflation and a desperate race to real assets and the United States dollar; only with a 'wildfire' or 'volcanic eruption' of this type would it be possible to break with the resistance of vested interests to effective anti-inflationary policies. It became common to attribute the difficulties of the situation to a political and institutional framework that produced successive impasses, to stand-offs between the main socio-political players, and paralysis of the decision-making process. This theory of governance crisis was reinforced by two political events. On the one hand, the electorate had opted to maintain the presidential system of government and defeated the option of a parliamentary government in the April 1993 plebiscite. On the other hand, revisions of the Constitution of 1988 remained stalled in Congress.[21] Both appeared as further proof of structural difficulties for governance. Perhaps never before had these themes and concepts of political science been so freely discussed in economic debate. The presence of a social scientist as finance minister boosted this tendency.

The economic and political strategy

How did the strategy of Cardoso unfold? If he and his team had gone strictly by the book, according to the evaluation of many of his colleagues in the academic world, they would have focused first on changing the institutional and political framework and/or economic institutions. For more conservative economists, who had been searching to redesign the orthodox platform, the requisite for de-indexation was to produce a definite solution to excessive expenditures and the generation of primary surpluses. For heterodox analysts, one would have established a prefixed rate of price adjustments as a soft substitute to freezing. From financial markets came an emphasis on the exchange rate as anchor, (with greater or lesser proximity to the Argentine policy), looking to maximize what appeared to be the only trump card available; the existence of strong foreign currency reserves.

The strategy that was implemented was a far cry from these approaches and suggestions for economic policy making. Instead, it consisted in combining ingredients from a number of proposals into a distinct and consistent form. The first step was to take advantage of the favourable moment for constitutional revision to negotiate, in Congress, the transfer of budgetary resources to the federal government (the Emergency Social Fund FSE). This transferred funds (three percent of GDP) earmarked for state and municipal governments under the 1988 Constitution to the federal government instead. This was of course a temporary solution, given the political difficulty of sustaining constitutional reforms that would definitely increase such a participation of the federal government in national income. The economic team opted for this way out of the fiscal constraints to stabilization. Although only provisional and patchy, as various critics justly pointed out, this initiative attended to the need to promote a reversal of the pessimistic expectations of the private sector, largely the major holders of public debt.

As to political strategy, an important component consisted in the decision of the executive to seize the opportunity offered by contingency, which weakened resistance of representatives to the transfer of state government resources by the federal government (FSE). The bargaining power of the executive had increased over Congress, whose veto powers had been seriously weakened by scandals involving the Congressional Budget Committee.[22] However, in spite of this advance, few results against inflation and delay in the preparations to see things through to the end created new difficulties for the government. The proximity of presidential elections and the almost certain candidature of Finance Minister Cardoso soldered three types of uncertainty into one. One was related to questions of governance centred on a deep popular mistrust of Congress and politicians. A second came from deep misgivings toward what appeared as another set of heterodox anti-inflationary policies. Finally, uncertainty centred on the national elections to be held in October 1994 involving for the presidency, Congress, state governors and assemblies. It is important to remember that the front-runner was Luiz Inácio Lula da Silva for the Workers' Party (PT), then favouring a radical change of economic policies and a unilateral rescheduling of foreign debt.

Understanding the economic strategy adopted under Finance Minister Cardoso must take into account how its prescriptions relied on the sophistication of indexation. One of the major causes of inertial inflation was to be converted into a key part of its solution. As is well known, inflation tends to affect, sequentially, the three basic functions of money: as a value reserve, as a counting unit, and as a means of payment. The technical innovation at the centre of the Real Plan was the creation of the URV (Real Value Unit), as a general index for measuring salaries, taxes, prices and incomes between February and July of 1994, the first stage of the plan.[23] During four months, two currencies coexisted side by side. One, the Cruzeiro Real, was expected to go on depreciating under inflation and was accepted by the Central Bank at a crawling daily parity to the URV. This debasing of an old currency against a new unit of value (URV) was described as 'laboratory hyperinflation'. Inflation in Cruzeiro Real terms reached 45 percent per month, whilst inflation in URV terms reached around 2 percent. The approximate nominal parity between the relatively stable URV and the United States dollar implied the adoption of an exchange rate anchor rather than 'dollarization' as in Argentina.

To a certain extent, one of the ideas advocated by the authors of the Real Plan was taken from the 1980s. In early debates about the inertial nature of Brazilian inflation, they had contended that policy solutions implied the co-existence of two different currencies for a determined period of time. This recognition facilitated the transition to the next phase, as it made possible for policy makers to resort to three devices. The first was an unprecedented synchrony between adjustments of prices and incomes. Second, the absence of contractual ruptures was favourable, especially after years of price and wage freezes and other shock treatments had only served to deepen mistrust among economic agents. Third, the conversion of salaries at fixed values in URVs by the average of the previous four months on the date of payment averted past losses. It must be noted that the gradualism and caution exercised during the preparation and implementation of the URV reflected a learning process and the accumulation of experience during previous heterodox stabilization plans. The difference during 1994 was that widespread indexation in Brazil was used for policies rather than set against.

The second stage of the Real Plan involved monetary reforms, a task completed only by July 1994. The new currency, the real, substituted the old (cruzeiro real) as means of payment and the URV as counting unit on

1 July 1994. This reunited the traditional functions of currency. Although price indexes for July exceeded expectations (reflecting anticipatory price adjustments in the final week of June), the Real Plan was widely perceived as successful in public opinion. It brought about a dramatic reversal of expectations among the government's creditors and the place of Cardoso, now an ex-finance minister, as presidential candidate in the polls.

Misconceptions among critics of the Real Plan and political opposition are worth noting. Neither perceived that the plan had averted the scourges normally associated with price stabilization policies that, in general, further erode the real income of popular sectors. On the contrary, the end of the 'inflationary tax' signified a notable increase in real income among these classes – a fact reflected in an increase in consumption of basic products. As expected during the preparation of the plan, the most serious problem in terms of macroeconomic equilibrium became the increase in consumption spending, not trends toward recession.[24]

The crucial element for stabilization was a well thought out strategy to recombine political and economic elements. This strategy demonstrated the limits of conventional diagnoses in political science and economics that conditioned the solution of impasses to the creation of a new government coalition and/or political reforms involving constitutional amendments and/or a change in the form of government. A more economistic vision saw success as the outcome of sustained 'good behaviour', that is to say, via monetary and fiscal discipline and the correct implementation of structural reforms along the lines recommended by the Washington Consensus. When compared to the manner in which the Real Plan was conceived and implemented, such prescriptions leave a bitter taste of deductive fundamentalism. Although the Emergency Social Fund (FSE) was far from providing a safe fiscal route to achieve self-sustained stabilization, it nonetheless made it possible to eliminate two principal veto points to stabilization. It introduced a modicum of flexibility in the rigid fiscal federalism of the 1988 Constitution, namely the importance of governors and their state delegations in Congress. Fruitful interaction between the executive and legislature was created within the existing political system, instead of seeking broad change that risked paralyzing the decision-making process. The path followed began with giving up earmarked institutional and political resources. The stabilization strategy consisted in selectively mobilizing existing institutional and political resources toward a two-fold task. First, technical innovation was to create a 'breakthrough', which in turn made it possible to revert the explosive path of the economy. Second, political effectiveness was due to the enormous improvement in governance made possible by a kind of statesmanship that may be described as the capacity to generate and extract new resources of power from existing institutions. This recombination may be described as creative bricolage.

The breakthrough strategy proved far more effective than maximalist approaches. It was based on recombining existing economic and political resources to open the way for a new economic strategy. This made it possible to generate new power resources, ones that made it politically viable to free pathways towards important economic reforms. This ran contrary to recommendations and common sense that emphasized the need for completing political and economic policy prerequisites. The success of this alternative strategy made it possible to re-concentrate power resources in the hands of the government, beginning with the reversal of the electoral prospects. The outcome of the presidential election, contrary to initial expectations, ended with the victory of the government candidate, former minister Cardoso, by majority in the first round vote. This outcome also belied theories of political cycles that suggest stabilization policies tend to be initiated at the beginning of a mandate, whereas governments abstain from imposing severe fiscal and monetary discipline during and preceding electoral campaigns.

This suggests the need to consider contingency in the analysis of economic re-structuring in young democracies. Under conditions of extreme uncertainty, Gourevitch's argument about space for economic policy makers to exercise political discretion because of uncertainty and contingency gains even greater force. At the same time, the use of political discretion to create institutional improvements toward better conditions of democratic governance – this kind of *virtù* – is a political resource not necessarily at hand when most needed. Stated in Gourevitch's terms, substantive choices by policy makers are not fully or automatically deductible from objective conditions, such as the institutional framework or the social process through which preferences are formed. This is because 'decision-makers are not passive registers' of such conditions, even when the level of uncertainty is low, as in longstanding market democracies. There is always a space of indetermination and of contingency that can be explored by the political leadership. Policies cannot be deduced directly from international or socioeconomic conditions. The capacity of leaders to evaluate and initiate a chain of cumulative solutions, as well as the existence of adequate technical knowledge, become strategic variables, even more so when a country is at a critical crossroads. We do not adopt a voluntarism that ignores constraints imposed by economic necessity and the political system. Instead, we focus on the eternal methodological problem of human sciences, i.e. that of structure versus agency, from an angle that seeks to identify critical junctures during which, for better or worse, the action of strategic agents may have profoundly transforming effects.

The politics of inflation and stabilization in neo-democracies: one model *does not* fit all

The Real Plan suggests the need to bring into theoretical frameworks the distinctive character of the interactions between political and economic change in countries where reversal of the explosive path of the economy had to be carried on during democratization, that is to say, by means of an agreed economic strategy. To judge by the popular support for the first heterodox shock, the Cruzado Plan of 1986, the stabilization of prices had already become a priority for policy makers and a valued asset for society in Brazil (and Argentina). Price stability quickly became an important source of political legitimacy and popular support during the first civilian government of President José Sarney. The proof of this was the thundering victory of his PMDB in the 1986 elections when the Cruzado Plan converted itself into the principal arm of electoral competition. But it took some time before stabilization acquired the status of a first priority 'public good'. Only after the temporary character of economic stability (whether achieved by means of heterodox or orthodox experiments) became apparent – especially so for low-income groups – was it possible that stabilization could be presented as a consensual policy goal and yield strong electoral pay-offs. This qualifies conventional political theories on inflation and stabilization in three ways.

First, regarding economic fundamentals, the Brazilian experience demonstrates that policy alternatives are context specific. This implies that policies and strategies for accelerated inflation may not be of the 'one model fits all' variety, as was thought in the political economy literature at that time, namely that of viewing stabilization as a bitter pill to swallow and a measure that consequently lacking popular support. The political science literature on structural adjustment does take into account the diversity of political and institutional conditions as being the key factor in the explanation of the different degrees of success or failure of structural adjustments. However, it nonetheless tacitly accepts the existence of a unique model for stabilization and fails to adequately conceptualize different kinds of inflationary regime. For this reason, this literature highlights the social and political costs involved in resorting to monetary and fiscal disciplines, which in fact are unavoidable, especially so in the initial stages of democratization. Whilst we agree that stabilization and economic liberalization pose difficult dilemmas for elected politicians and involve threats to democratic governance, we disagree with treating inflation in generic terms, as a single phenomenon. Inflation was not the same, for example, in post-communist countries and Latin America in the wake of the external shock of 1982. Nonetheless, Przeworski attempted to build a formal model from Eastern Europe and Latin American experiences with stabilization.[25] A similar assumption, in which economic stabilization is equated with a unique model likely to be resisted by local populations, was especially noticeable in the refusal of the IMF to accept the diagnosis and prescriptions underlying the Real Plan, dubbed by one of their major analysts as 'voodoo economics'.

Behind this position lie two postulates that do not correspond to the Brazilian reality (nor, indeed, to those of either Argentina or Bolivia where the explosive path of economies acquired momentum exactly when they had begun a change of political regime). The first postulate is the theoretical (and quite normative) assumption that, when dealing with inflation and stabilization, 'one model that fits all'. This supposition is based on a false separation between fiscal and monetary discipline that are necessarily unpopular and the logic of politicians whose behaviour and expectations are predominantly (if not exclusively) determined by electoral calculation. This disjuncture is dramatized by the metaphor of a 'bitter pill' or by citing the spectra of economic populism whenever electoral calculations enter into the picture.

On the contrary, the experience of extreme situations during hyperinflationary crisis, as in Argentina, or the risks of its occurrence, as in Brazil, may well bring about profound political and cultural changes in social preferences and voting patterns.[26] One of the most important historical changes in Brazilian society consists in the conversion of price stability into criteria of both economic performance and, simultaneously, political legitimation. Consequently it became an important condition of electoral success, especially among the social sectors least protected against inflation. This change was not exclusive to Brazil, but extends throughout Latin America. The electoral success of politicians who led successful stabilization policies, however diverse from the technical point of view and despite differences concerning its social and political costs, is indicative of a profound transformation in the political culture of the region. This change has laid the roots for a greater convergence between economic credibility and political legitimacy – away from a hyperinflationary economic context. This is alien to the conventional economic wisdom that assumes divergence between economic credibility and political legitimacy.

Thus, in a regional perspective, the election of Cardoso confirms two unprecedented developments in the history of Latin America not sufficiently integrated into the analysis of structural adjustment in the democratizing countries of the region. First, under conditions of pending hyperinflation, price stability converted itself into a public good priority. Second, economic 'populism' thereby ends as a technique of governmental action and problem-solving style, because it no longer renders electoral dividends. This came to be true, as is well known, for economies, political regimes and systems of representations as distinct as those of Bolivia, the Argentine and Brazil at that time.[27] Such political developments were dramatized by the Brazilian experience. The Real Plan represented the major political asset and the principal item in the electoral platform of the former finance minister – under circumstances of great uncertainty. After all, the 1994 elections were the first combined elections since 1950 for the presidency, state governorships, federal chamber, two thirds of the senate, and state assemblies.

It is important to note that this political and economic turnabout was reinforced by aother positive impulse in terms of the legitimacy and the popularity of the official candidate. The full redistributive impact of price stabilization in favour of the least protected against inflation was felt from July–August of 1994 onwards – exactly when the electoral competition intensified. The end of the inflationary tax reflected itself in a process of income transfers, previously appropriated by the state,

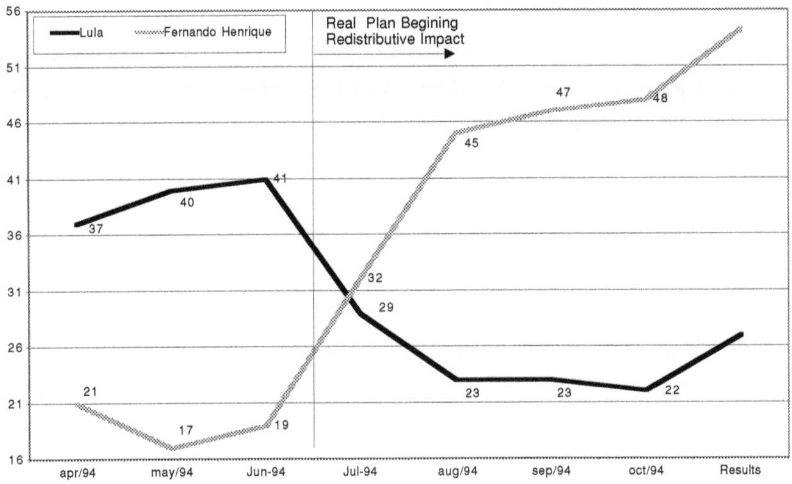

Fonte: Datafolha/TSE

Graph 4.1 ***Presidential Polls: performance of the official and of opposition candidates before and after the Real Plan***

towards society in general. This re-distribution, nevertheless, was proportionally greater for the lower popular sectors and working classes, who had not had any protection against inflation as they did not have bank accounts.

Opinion polls left little doubt concerning the motivation – and also the political and economic calculations of the electorate, above all lower-income voters. The question at stake was the continuity of the anti-inflationary experiment, which reduced monthly inflation of around 50 percent to an average of 1.8 percent during the first few months after the implementation of the Real Plan. The victory of the official candidate, Cardoso, in the first round of elections represented a dramatic reversal of the expectations registered from April until May of 1994, the period immediately prior to the introduction of the new currency, the Real. Up until then, as can be observed on Graph 4.1, opinion polls had pointed to the favourite as being the main opposition candidate, Luiz Inácio Lula da Silva, whose party, the PT (Workers Party), had already been preparing for a victory in the first round.[28]

Fernando Henrique Cardoso was elected with 54.5 percent of the total votes, the highest winning percentage in this type of election since 1945. This result, for its part, is consistent with the index of popularity of the incumbent president, Itamar Franco, of around 80 percent at the end of his government, and explains to a large extent the fact that he was the first president to secure the election of the official candidate since the elections of 1950. This was a surprising result for two different reasons. First, we are dealing with a President at the end of his term of office, and in particular, one with a short mandate of only two years. Second, this was a government that was born weak, starting with the impeachment of President Collor and that had been incapable of exercising the necessary leadership to form a stable governmental coalition.

It is worth exploring a second set of political implications. These refer to an official candidate, responsible for a government that had found itself in the middle of an anti-inflationary experiment, technically and politically different from previous heterodox experiences. The architects of the Real Plan had pledged themselves to respect contracts and avoid shock therapy or devices that would take the population by surprise. On the contrary, the trademarks of the Plan were: communicating each stage of the process in advance; taking into consideration the responses of markets; and counting upon the acquiescence of economic agents to price stabilization, that is, that strategic price makers would not mark-up their prices. The salvationalist style that had prevailed in the past and price freezes defended by opposition candidates were thereby left behind.[29] As well, it is important here to register the change both in the style and in the manner of presentation of the economic policy measures. Now the condition that would make possible the adoption of these directives was the capacity of the political leadership to detect changes in society and hence place their wager on the political viability of the innovative techniques developed by the economic team.

In sum, the Brazilian experience leads us to qualify deterministic theories that established a necessary and perverse relationship between political-electoral cycles and the capacity of governments to implement stabilizing policies. Anti-inflationary policies were not initiated by recently elected governments, while expansionist policies were not pursued at the end of a mandate.

Technical assumptions about inflation in the comparative political economy literature lead us to a third group of implications. The concept of inflation is based on a particular inflationary regime, while little discrimination is made between the different types of inflation as mentioned above. We suggest that an important change in *inflationary regime* occurred in the early 1980s brought about by the fiscal crisis of the state and, in part, the external shock of 1982.[30] This combination in Brazil is fundamental not only for an understanding of economics and policy differences but also for the political dynamics of stabilization. Without this distinction, analysis slips toward the diagnosis of the Latin American crisis established by the 'Washington Consensus', which ignored the role played by external shocks, in particular that of 1982.[31] Instead, crises were ascribed predominantly to the type of industrialization – import substitution and the state centred paradigm – an interpretation that abstained from discussing the reasons why that mode of industrialization had worked reasonably well, especially in the case of Brazil. We believe that one of the most striking shortcomings of recent research is the urgency to generalize about common denominators across experiences of structural adjustment during democratization. The outcome has been the uncritical acceptance of what Hirschman, many years ago, qualified as mono-economics, that is to say, the prevalence of a unique economic theory, independent from specification and of the form of insertion of a given country (or region) in the international scenario.

Structural adjustments and the integration of countries to the global economy involve more than price stabilization. In reality, price stability may well become a curse in disguise, if policy-makers perceive it as an end in itself. Thus, the expansion of demand and GDP growth following the Real Plan gave rise to what later on was perceived as excessive optimism. This is because during the time interval between the election and the inauguration of the new president of Brazil, i.e. October 1994 until January 1995, the Mexican crisis of December 1994 would bring to centre stage the risks – and the policy dilemma – underlying the stabilization process. While resorting to the exchange rate as a stable price anchor proved to be an efficient instrument for counteracting the threat of hyperinflation, it would also generate a deficit in the current account. This in turn would put additional strains on the balance of payments – a risk that became clearer when the first trade balance deficits were reported in November 1994, that is to say, before the inauguration of the new president. It signalled a reversal of trade surpluses for over a decade. This was seen by some as not only inevitable, but also as desirable on the assumption that international liquidity and the flow of capital to Latin America would remain stable. However, the Mexican crisis of 1994 brought to the fore the volatility of financial markets and triggered controversy in Brazil about the desirability of a fixed exchange rate as price anchor. This became the most controversial topic during Cardoso's government until January of 1999, when a speculative attack on the overvalued Real led to an exchange rate crisis. The outcome was the adoption of new exchange rate and monetary policies, ones prevailing until the present day: a floating foreign exchange rate and inflation targeting.

Conclusion

This chapter has sought to show that the Real Plan interrupted a hyperinflationary cycle at a pre-crisis situation. A number of conclusions can be drawn. One relates to the factors that explain the success of stabilization, involving both technical and political dimensions that became inseparable. The Real Plan was an ingenious economic policy innovation conceived by Brazilian economists based on theories of inertial inflation. They were able to draw analytical tools from the experiences of other countries, especially through intense exchanges with economists in Argentina and Israel. The accumulation of technical and political experience from the failure of the Cruzado Plan (1985–87) through seven failed experiments in stabilization that preceded the Real Plan also was critical. What appeared to be technical innovation was also the result of adjustment to more immediate political requisites. The final content, timing and intensity of measures were defined in accordance with the political parameters set by President Itamar Franco and Finance Minister Cardoso. Another important factor explaining the economic efficiency of the Real Plan is the reality that trade liberalization and the deregulation of the economy preceded the plan, that is to say under the administration of President Collor de Mello (1990–92). Competition from imported goods had reduced the power of domestic oligopolies to set prices.

The political strategy contained an implicit wager: that successful stabilization would generate new power resources to overcome the pending threat of social anomie that threatened under hyperinflation and disenchantment with democracy. Part of the political calculation, which proved to be correct, was that price stability would become the decisive asset in the formation of electoral alliances and governmental coalition led by the PSDB (Party of Brazilian Social Democracy), the party of the finance minister. This in turn was seen as a precondition to proceed with the economic reforms needed for the completion of the structural change – thus breaking a perverse pattern of adaptive policies in the Brazilian economy dubbed as 'muddling through'. The success of the Real Plan brought to centre stage new problems, issues, and challenges including the Herculean task of elaborating an economic model that would allow for more equitable development. A crucial element in this project became reforms designed to re-structure the financing and spending patterns of the Brazilian state. This implied a profound change in the traditional role played by the state as political actor in Brazil and Latin America.

A decade on, this problem continues, now challenging President Lula da Silva. Nevertheless, a line has been crossed which we describe as the threshold of crisis. If we were to assume the view of the critical juncture of 1993 described above, and therefore the development route already trodden, the amount of progress is incontestable. Having overcome this extreme conjuncture, space became available for addressing tasks beyond what one might call the 'dictatorship of the short run pressures'. It became possible to design, with greater clarity, an agenda of policies and reforms for challenges of medium and long term duration. The central themes have been the formulation of a development project, in tune with both central questions such as the social debt and the search for new forms of insertion of Brazil in a very unstable international system. Overcoming the threat of hyperinflation and social anomie created space for the re-arrangement of complex structural problems and re-equilibration of political forces. Looking back to 1993, the extent of change in the political and economic agenda of the country is marked. How these changes were incorporated during the presidential elections in 2002 and first years of PT coalition government are addressed separately in Chapter 9.

Notes

1 See G. O'Donnell, P. Schmitter and L. Whitehead, eds., *Transitions from Authoritarian Rule: Prospects for Democracy*, Baltimore: The Johns Hopkins University Press, 1986.

2 J.C. Torre, *El processo politico de las reformas económicas en América Latina*, Buenos Aires: Paidós, 1998; L.C. Bresser Pereira, A. Przeworski and J.M. Maravall, *Economic Reforms in New Democracies*, Cambridge, Cambridge University Press, 1991, and L. Whitehead, 'On reform of the state and regulation of the market', *World Development*, 21/8 (1993). See also S. Haggard and R. Kaufman, *The Political Economy of Democratic Transitions*, Princeton, NJ: Princeton University Press, 1995, and L. Sola, 'The state,

economic transformation and democratization in Brazil', in W. Smith, C. Acuña and E. Gamarra, eds., *Democracy, Markets and Structural Reform in Latin America*, New Brunswick, NJ: Transaction, 1994.

3 See J. Malloy and C. Conaghan, *Unsettling Statecraft – democracy and Neoliberalism in the Central Andes*, Princeton, NJ: Princeton University Press, 1995; Torre, op. cit.; L. Bruszt and D. Stark, *Pathways from State Socialism*, Cambridge: Cambridge University Press, 1998.

4 See specially Malloy and Connaghan, op. cit.

5 On Brazilian federalism, see: 'Federalisme, stabilisation monétaire et démocratization au Brésil', *Critique Internationale* no. 11 (2001), 84–99 and 'La construccion del federalismo democrático en Brasil', *ICE – Informacion Comercial Española – Revista de Economia*, no. 810 (2003), 105–22.

6 On stabilization of political and economic expectations, transparency, and institutional accountability, see Whitehead, op. cit. In these terms, the efficacy of economic policy decisions and political legitimacy intertwine.

7 See, in particular, J.C. Torre, *El proceso politico de las reformas económicas*, op. cit.

8 On the concept of an 'explosive path' advanced by Latin American analysts, see J.M. Fanelli, R. Frenkel and G. Rozenwurcel, 'Growth and structural reform in Latin America: where we stand', in W.C. Smith, C.H. Acuña and E.A. Gamarra, eds., *Latin American Political Economy in the Age of Neoliberal Reform*, Miami: North South Center, 1994; F. Giambiagi, *Finanças públicas*, Rio de Janeiro: Campus, 1999; and L.C. Bresser Pereira, *Economic Crisis and Reform of the State*, Boulder: Lynne Rienner, 1996.

9 S. Haggard and R. Kaufman, *The Political Economy of Democratic Transitions*, Princeton, NJ: Princeton University Press,1995.

10 One of the virtues of the comparative analysis between Bolivia, Peru and Ecuador, by these authors is that of having demonstrated, also from this angle, the reasons by which the experience of stabilization with democratization was highly successful only in Bolivia.

11 Peter Gourevitch, 'Democracy and economic policy: elective affinities and circumstantial conjunctures', *World Development*, 21/8 (1993), 1271–81.

12 For the crisis of the state centred paradigm see E. Kugelmas and B. Sallum Junior, 'O leviatã acorrentado', and L. Sola, 'Ajustamento estrutural como política e como história', in L. Sola, ed., *Estado, mercado, democracia. politica e economia comparada*, Rio de Janeiro: Paz e Terra, 1993.

13 J.M. Fanelli, R. Frenkell and G. Rozenwurcel, 'Growth and structural reform in Latin America: where we stand', in W.C. Smith, C.H. Acuña and E.A. Gamarra, eds., *Latin American Political Economy in the Age of Neoliberal Reform*, New Brunswick, NJ: Transaction, 1994.

14 This experiment in orthodoxy was adopted by the government, once the initial positive impact of the extremely heterodox Collor Plans I and II had passed.

15 See M.H. Simonsen, *Trinta anos de indexação*, Rio de Janeiro: FGV, 1995 and G. Franco, *O Plano Real e outros ensaios*, Rio de Janeiro, Francisco Alves, 1995, pp. 30–1.

16 See Lourdes Sola, ' Heterodox shock in Brazil. Tecnicos, politicians, democracy', *Journal of Latin American Studies*, 23/1 (1991), 163–95.

17 M. Nain, 'Latin America: the morning after', *Foreign Affairs*, 74/4 (1995).

18 M.H. Simonsen, op. cit., 6–7.

19 J. Sachs and A. Zini Jr., 'Brazilian inflation and the Real Plan', *Revista de Economia Política*, 15/2 (1995), 27.

20 Sachs and Zini, op. cit., 31.

21 Problems of governance were first raised during 1988 and 1989 when economists and political scientists in government realized that the Constitution earmarked spending and reduced executive and congressional prerogatives to approximately eleven percent of the federal government budget.

22 This episode, known as the Parliamentary Commission of Inquiry (CPI) into the

'budgetary dwarfs' led to the loss of mandate for those involved. In the wake of the impeachment of President Collor two years before, this further increased scepticism.

23 Provisional Measure no. 434 of 27/02/94.

24 We thank José Roberto Mendonça de Barros for calling our attention to this point.

25 A. Przeworski, *Democracy and the Market. Political and Economic Reforms in Eastern Europe and Latin America*, Cambridge: Cambridge University Press, pp. 162–87.

26 On the socio-economic and political roots of this transformation, see Chapter 5, by Leslie Armijo, in this volume.

27 This has not made the region immune to populism, but that populism would assume new forms at odds with the traditional description of populism in the economic literature.

28 At the time the PT committed a strategic error by opposing the Real Plan, identifying it as a purely electoral manipulation.

29 Respectively, Lula da Silva, Orestes Quercia (from the majority party in the Chamber of deputies, which though formally integrated into the government of Itamar Franco, projected and confirmed himself as an opposition candidate) and Leonel Brizola (PDT – the Democratic Workers Party).

30 The debt burden of each country before the shock also mattered. This impact was greater in Brazil because, during the 1970s under President Geisel, the import substitution model of industrialization which had proved successful in the past was pursued much farther than in other Latin American countries; this in response to the previous oil shocks of 1974 and 1978. The strategy of external borrowing to 'finance development' had to do with three factors: 1) avoiding administrative and tax reforms and confrontation with vested interests, given the new government strategy to initiate political liberalization; 2) to placate military hard-liners who were deeply committed to economic nationalism; 3) the economic ideology of Geisel advisors whose alleged 'liberalism' was balanced by commitment to 'autonomous development'.

31 For criticism of conventional economic interpretations of inflation, see: L.C. Bresser Pereira, op. cit. and Frenkel, et al., op. cit. On political science, see: Sola, op. cit. and Lourdes Sola, 'Economic reform, democratization and legal order in Brazil', Economic Commission for Latin America and the Caribbean, Reform Series of Public Policy, no. 37.

Chapter 5

Who's afraid of economic populism? Counterintuitive observations on democracy and Brazilian political economy

Leslie Elliott Armijo[1]

AN INFLUENTIAL – IF sometimes unspoken – thesis in contemporary economic thought holds that a political transition to mass democracy in poor countries often hinders subsequent macroeconomic policymaking: wider political participation generates economic populism. Brazil has been presented as a classic illustrative case. This essay offers an alternative proposition: once countries adopt near universal adult suffrage, their political leaders confront powerful electoral incentives to sustain at least rough macroeconomic balance, although a period of transitional learning may be necessary. The revisionist interpretation of Brazil's late twentieth century experiences provides answers to some nagging questions that the economic populist framework avoids.

Twentieth century Brazil: from recurrent inflation to enduring stabilization

Table 5.1 summarizes three periods in recent Brazilian economic history. (1) Brazilian inflation was recurrently high or very high for many decades, from the early 1940s through the early 1980s. Although Brazil had deflation in the early 1930s, it was arguably low, given that these were the years of the Great Depression and that Brazil's economy depended on coffee exports, for which world demand plunged. Economic growth was also strong from the 1930s through 1980. (2) Inflation accelerated wildly in the late 1980s, while growth sputtered. (3) In 1994–95, after a decade of failed attempts, Brazilian policymakers finally implemented a stabilization plan that worked. Unfortunately, in the

Table 5.1: ***Brazilian macroeconomic outcomes, three periods***

Period description and years	*Mean annual inflation*	*Mean annual growth*
Mostly high inflation, high growth		
1930–34	–3.5	3.4
1935–39	4.2	5.3
1940–44	32.4	3.5
1945–49	10.5	6.9
1950–54	15.6	6.3
1955–59	19.1	8.2
1960–64	55.7	4.9
1965–69	33.9	6.5
1970–74	22.7	11.4
1975–79	44.5	6.3
1980–84	130.0	0.8
Hyperinflation, Low Growth		
1985–89	707.4	4.5
1990–94	1100.4	1.4
Stabilization, Low Growth		
1995–99	19.1	2.2
2000–2003	9.7	1.2

Sources: 1930–84 from Marcelo de Paiva Abreu, ed., *A ordem do progresso: cem anos de política econômica republicana, 1889–1989*, Rio de Janeiro: Editora Campus, 1990, pp. 398–408; 1985–89 from Werner Baer, *The Brazilian Economy: Growth and Development*, 4th edn, New York: Praeger, 1995, pp. 383, 393; 1990–99 from Edmund Amann and Werner Baer, 'The illusion of stability: the Brazilian economy under Cardoso', *World Development*, 28/10, 2000, 1805–19; 2000–2003 from World Bank, *World Development Indicators*, accessed at: www.worldbank.org on 2 October 2004.

subsequent decade growth was also low, contributing to Brazil's historic election of a president from the political left in 2002. How do we think about these facts? What is the best mental model for this trajectory?

A dominant mental model: a weak state plus political democracy equal economic populism

Democratization implies extending political 'voice' to previously excluded classes of individuals: those lacking landed titles, wealth, the correct ethnicity, permitted political opinions, literacy or the preferred gender.[2] Newly politically incorporated social groups are likely to be economically disadvantaged (or else they would have demanded political influence before) and to have benefited relatively little from past government spending. Groups of novice voters thus enter the political arena with expectations for both greater political and enhanced economic participation – with government help. Unless incumbent democratic leaders represent a radical break from an authoritarian past, politicians will be reluctant to redistribute public spending away from existing recipients, often middle and upper income groups, or to raise taxes in order to increase the state's access to real resources. In fact, many economic and social reform efforts founder on just this rock: it is difficult to direct public spending to additional claimants without expanding total government resources. One apparent solution that may appeal to a hard-pressed chief executive in a weak state is to increase total spending for consumption and investment while temporarily expanding revenues via borrowing. Governments may borrow from their citizens or foreigners via issuing public debt – or may simply lean on the central bank to purchase public securities, thus expanding the state's resources via printing money. The latter practice may seem to political leaders like an easy solution, because it does not require withdrawing resources from any group of constituents in the short run. However, it soon yields inflation. This is economic populism.[3]

In Latin America economic populism took on an additional aspect that rendered macroeconomic imbalances chronic. An interventionist state traditionally set many prices for the private sector, ranging from the minimum wage to farm price supports to the costs of electricity and subsidized industrial inputs. In some cases the state could increase the incomes of one or another group without a direct expenditure of public revenues, simply by using the state's economic regulatory power to raise the administered prices contributing to that sector's income. Special interests of all kinds thus had an incentive to invest resources in lobbying the executive for material favours in exchange for political support. Each group, such as organized labour and business owners in a particular sector, would push for a higher nominal income sufficient to return its relative income vis-à-vis its reference groups to its previous peak. Then the reference group would respond in kind, leading to a ratcheting up of nominal incomes, with no enduring shift in relative incomes, and thus economy-wide inflation. Assertive social actors, often oligopolists in their own domains, serially prevailed on a weak central government state, in an ongoing struggle for shares.[4] The stylized story suggests that rampant economic populism would in turn put political democracy at risk. At some point the accumulated macroeconomic balances would generate inflation so explosive as to destroy investment and growth, by which stage the business community, a crucially important interest, would be willing to support radical fiscal retrenchment. Orthodox stabilization inevitably implied wage repression for urban workers; if they protested, democracy itself would be ended by a coalition of the military, desirous of public order, and capitalists, representing financial, industrial, and agribusiness interests.[5] Stop-and-go macroeconomic policies might be reflected in stop-and-go political liberalization. In sum, the literature in the Latin American economic populism tradition tends to see open political contestation as problematic. Their vision of democracy is close to what Theodore Lowi once termed "interest group liberalism": public policy is a war of attrition among narrow special interests.[6]

Under economic populism's 'tug-of-war' thesis, contending claimants succeed in serially expanding their incomes, but in such a way that the aggregate of what each group feels is its justified share is fiscally unsustainable. How might this policy problem be solved? Logically, there are two possible ways to return to macroeconomic balance: either one or more special interests can reduce its material demands quite a lot, resulting in overall balance, or all groups can cooperatively reduce their expectations a little bit each. The imposition of political authoritarianism enables stabilization on the backs of the working class, who lose previously granted political voice.[7] A rising level of crisis might also convince weaker players to yield, voluntarily accepting an agreement that requires disproportionate sacrifices of them, even in the absence of authoritarian compulsion.[8]

Alternatively, some means could be found to surmount the underlying challenge of collective action, viz.: that society as a whole would be better off without high to very high inflation, but no actor trusts the other parties to engage in voluntary, mutual restraint and sacrifice of past income peaks. Political economy theory has suggested two means of accomplishing stabilization by simultaneous joint sacrifice. The first is to terrify everyone with an acute macroeconomic crisis: when confronted with impending meltdown all major socioeconomic groups (labour, urban capital, and agro-exporters, shall we say) agree to some sort of incomes policy wherein mutual and joint sacrifices are coordinated with government by peak sectoral bargaining agents. Second, structural reforms in the overall national economic regulatory apparatus could render the state *unable* to be fiscally irresponsible, thus 'solving' the collective action problem on behalf of the citizenry as a whole. This would seem to be the import of much of the 'new political economy' literature that sees a predatory, rent-seeking state as the root cause of economic populism.[9] For example, dramatically shrinking the state's economic responsibilities and budget through neoliberal reforms such as privatization and reduced taxes on capital, or insulating critical aspects of macroeconomic policymaking from the political process (as by creating an independent central bank or a currency board) have been proposed as techniques to avoid fiscal deficits.

An alternative thesis: the expanded 'median voter' paradigm

This section presents the logic underlying an alternative political economy thesis: a functioning political system of mass democracy will inspire national leaders to pursue at least a rough and ready version of macro-economic moderation. I note that the thesis does *not* claim that every increase in political inclusion and open political contestation – which I take to be the essential elements of political democracy,[10] along with a minimum respect for civil rights and liberties – necessarily brings a proportionate jump in policymakers' ability to achieve optimal macro-economic balance. I do assert that discontinuous *increases in political democracy*, and particularly those that widen the scope of political inclusion, *impose successively narrower outer limits on the range of macroeconomic outcomes* that a rational political incumbent will be prepared to accept. In other words, the establishment of political democracy, often quite a messy and imperfect process, by no means guarantees wonderful macroeconomic policymaking. Democratization may often inaugurate new social spending and pump-priming, just as the business community often fears. Yet the internal logic of political democracy is of a system in which the chief executive ultimately is answerable to the median voter, who has a powerful interest in living in a society with sound money and steady growth. A rational democratic leader cannot stray far.

This essay's extension of the median voter proposition suggests a third means – in addition to the willingness to sacrifice generated in the face of an acute national economic crisis and dramatic institutional reform to insulate economic policymaking from political interference – of solving the societal collective action problem of fiscal and monetary policymaking common to many developing and post-communist societies. The seemingly elusive goal of achieving mutual restraint of all special interests for the goal of overall macroeconomic balance will be aided by a move to a political system of liberal democracy with near universal adult suffrage. From this perspective, mass political democracy is more solution than problem for rational and sustainable macroeconomic policymaking in poor countries.

Why? I begin with the basic rational choice assumptions that (1) most voters are concerned with pocketbook issues and will evaluate incumbents according to whether public policies are perceived to be 'good' or 'bad' for themselves, and (2) politicians desire to be re-elected, as individuals or through victory for their party and close political associates.[11] A major strand in the formal modelling literature begins from the observation that every democratic political system has a 'median voter'.[12] Where the chief executive is selected by a majority vote, he or she cannot gain office, nor hope for re-election, without appealing to the median voter. Voters are 'principals' who elect politicians as their 'agents'. Ceteris paribus, politicians desire to implement a policy mix that will please the voters, who will then return them to office. These models are described as 'opportunistic', because they assume that politicians have no fixed policy preferences. In other words, politicians, once in office, are not loyal to the preferences of the partisan coalition that elected them, but rather confront powerful incentives to move toward the 'middle', or the presumptive policy preference of the system's median voter. Thus incumbent politicians do a rough demographic survey of all voters, possibly even polling voters to ascertain their preferences. Then these politicians advocate whatever policies they think will get them elected or re-elected.

The mainstream literature on the median voter, virtually all of which takes the experiences of the advanced capitalist democracies as its empirical referent, *assumes that the median voter prefers* a macroeconomic framework of stable, non-inflationary growth (SNIG).[13] Why? The median voter, as an average citizen, cannot expect special fiscal favours from government targeted to her. Subsidies and special privileges cost resources: politicians can only use them to obtain political support if they do not go to everyone. To compete among the group of voters at large, a stable macroeconomic environment that will ensure employment and the future security of citizen's savings is best. Granted, there are many reasons that may cause the median voter to lack sufficient information to calibrate her response to the policies of the incumbent very precisely.[14] Nonetheless, we can assume that large and prolonged deviations from macroeconomic stability – perhaps annual inflation above, say, thirty percent for several years running or strongly negative per capita income growth for a similar period – will cause voters to reject incumbents.

Now let us add another public-choice-style assumption: (3) not only elected leaders in mass democracies, but all political incumbents, including hereditary monarchs and despotic generals, depend for their continued tenure on political support from some groups and individuals in that society. We may call these groups and individuals the set of 'relevant political actors' (RPA) for that political system. In a polity that is not a mass liberal democracy, the incumbent has a strong incentive to satisfy the material demands of the median relevant political actor. As we move outside the set of advanced capitalist liberal democracies and into the set of polities with limited political participation and contestation, the median 'voter' will not be the median adult resident. Instead, the median voter may be the median member of the senior military officer corps, or the median large plantation owner, or the median colonial overlord, or median member of the dominant ethnic group. The opinions of all other residents – slaves, peasants, labourers, Jews, gypsies, the urban middle class, the petite bourgeoisie, non-Christians, non-Muslims, the Chinese business community, women, foreign guest workers, 'natives', and so forth – who are not politically relevant actors in that society do not limit the choices of political incumbents.

In fact, the smaller the set of politically included residents, the weaker the political incentives for rational political incumbents to pursue economic outcomes that an outsider might judge to be beneficial for society as a whole. Recall that we have assumed, following the public choice logic, that citizens wish to protect, and where possible to augment, their incomes. But once we allow for wide variations in national political inclusion, then there always will be two possibilities through which an incumbent leader can protect the incomes of those who count. The first possibility is to *increase the size of the total pie*, allowing either a proportionate or a greater than proportionate share of the increase to fall to the set of politically included actors. If all, or nearly all, of a country's residents are included in the set of relevant political actors, then the median voter can be satisfied only insofar as the total pie increases. A second possibility is to *take wealth or income away from someone*, redistributing it toward the median voter. In a mass democracy, a rational incumbent may decide to redistribute income or wealth away from a wealthy minority, thus benefiting a poorer majority. There are, however, well known limits on such a strategy, which is sometimes understood as a variant of economic populism.[15] One constraint is that the wealthy may take their capital out of the country, thus worsening overall economic outcomes. Another deterrent to incumbents who otherwise might be tempted to pursue this strategy is that the wealthy often possess considerable political resources, which might then come to be used to topple the incumbent.

However, *if substantial numbers of residents lack political rights*, they may become easy targets for explicit or implicit taxation or confiscation. Politically excluded residents may be forced to contribute their labor without adequate compensation, or they may be subject to arbitrary confiscation by an unpredictable state. The national economic regulatory regime, taken as a whole, also may embody all manner of subtler public policy twists, including agro-export bias, urban bias, or regressive taxation and state social spending. Poor quality or non-existent public education combined with state subsidies for free university education for those who pass the entrance exam exemplifies elite bias. Under these conditions of limited political inclusion a rational leader normally should prefer to allocate the main benefits of new growth towards her relevant constituents, but will not actively seek to disadvantage other residents. However, suppose the leader's constituents demand levels of subsidies and rents that cannot be sustained, given public revenues. Or suppose the leader finds herself compelled to make large public expenditures on defense or as a result of exogenous shocks, from natural disasters to external financial contagion. The incumbent's political imperative is to protect the incomes of politically salient groups. It sometimes may be *politically rational for an incumbent to sacrifice overall macroeconomic balance* as a more or less intentional strategy. Why? The costs of inflation, prolonged stagnation, or natural resource despoliation will be spread across all residents. Meanwhile, the incumbent leader can choose to concentrate scarce government resources on providing compensating benefits and protections for the group of RPA, a favoured subset within the set of all residents. She thus retains the loyalty of those who matter.

The importance of democratic transitions thus is clear. If a country's political transition is to a regime that has competitive elections, but within which access to the vote and other measures of political voice are limited in scope, as in an elite or even a middle-sectors democracy, then we do not expect that open party competition and rule by law alone will shield the country from seriously perverse macroeconomic outcomes. However, the transition to *mass* democracy with near universal suffrage and no major exclusions of social groups (for example, of a large underclass of non-citizen immigrants), should lead rational political incumbents to seek economic policy packages that yield macroeconomic outcomes that remain roughly within advanced industrial country norms (think contemporary France or Spain) over the medium run. The hypothesis is that the median RPA's tolerance for long periods of recurrent and extreme macroeconomic outcomes will be very low under mass democracy, since possibilities for state policymakers to employ the national economic regulatory framework to compensate citizens by the redistribution of income, directly or surreptitiously, from politically excluded to politically included actors will be minimal.[16]

Brazil, 1930–85: contending visions of mid-twentieth century political economy

Mid-twentieth century Brazil had three political regimes: semi-authoritarian urban populism (1930–45), postwar democracy (1945–64), and modernizing military authoritarianism (1964–84).[17] We could interpret the political economy of these years through either mental model. First, what can we learn from the lens of *economic populism*? The 1930s and early 1940s were authoritarian, yet paradoxically also expanded the scope of Brazil's relevant political actors. On the one hand, President Getúlio Vargas, the losing candidate in the elites-only election of 1930, took power via a military coup, remaining in office for fifteen years. There were no free elections for significant national offices, and Vargas also centralized political power, replacing most state governors with federal appointees and expelling about a third of the national legislature. On the other hand, Vargas expanded the set of politically relevant groups to include not only Brazil's traditionally dominant rural landowners, but also emerging urban groups, both business elites and middle income and status groups.[18] Vargas also tried to organize key social groups outside the state, for example by creating compulsory and monopolistic corporatist syndicates for both industrial entrepreneurs and their employees.

Economic policies were classically populist, as state economic activities expanded for the dual purposes of stimulating industrialization, which Vargas and his advisors identified with national power, and creating a viable base of political support. The central government executive branch consisted of multiple bureaucracies colonized by private interests.[19] Whenever possible, political opponents were coopted with side payments. For example, following the unsuccessful 1932 secessionist rebellion by the state of São Paulo, President Vargas eased the sting of defeat by having the state-owned Banco do Brasil assume the war bonds the Paulista banks had floated to pay for the raising and arming of troops.[20] Thereafter state economic activity gradually came to favour an emerging industrial bourgeoisie. Paulista industrialists praised central government investments in steel, iron ore, and hydroelectric power, all of which stimulated private entrepreneurship. The agro-export elites who had been hegemonic before 1930 also continued to receive public subsidies, the most famous of which was the 'coffee defense' program of price supports for Brazil's most important export.[21] Vargas also left quasi-feudal rural social relations alone, allowing *fazendeiros* to continue to constitute both the sole employer and (de facto) the law in their domains. New government jobs in the civil service and state enterprises opened up for Brazil's small but politically important middle class, while the limited but novel social welfare benefits organized by Vargas' Ministry of Labour charmed the small organized industrial working class, many of whom were employed by state firms such as the railroads.

In 1945 Brazil became a competitive democracy, and public policies continued their economically populist tendencies. After the democratic Allies achieved victory in World War II, Vargas' own senior generals insisted that he step down and call elections. Though the Communist Party was disallowed, historians generally agree on the open and comparatively honest nature of Brazilian party politics during its democratic period from 1945 until the coup of early 1964. Formal political democratization from the late 1940s coincided with more public investment, social spending – and inflation. The post-war pattern of national economic governance was even more interventionist than the pre-war one, as the dominant group of Brazilian business and government elites became explicit proponents of import-substituting industrialization (ISI), especially under President Kubitschek (1956–61). Specific policy instruments included a national industrial development bank, multiple exchange rates giving preference to machinery imports, and mechanisms to woo foreign direct investment in high priority sectors such as steel and automobiles.[22]

Private industrialists received subsidies, public investment, and guaranteed markets for their goods, while the middle class and formal sector working class got good jobs. Subsidies to large-scale agriculture were also maintained, as rural elites also remained a crucial political constituency. The state relied increasingly on foreign borrowing and monetary expansion, contributing to the spike in inflation that was an immediate precipitant of the 1964 military coup. There were numerous examples of subsidies to one special interest being 'offset' by subsidies to another, the final result being profound, if partially disguised, public deficits and uncontrollable inflation. Although policymakers during the democratic years made multiple attempts at implementing orthodox stabilization programs, they all went awry.

In passing, it should be noted that there is a more upbeat version of this same story. True, Brazilian economic policymaking during the mid-century years of political opening and democracy was inflation-prone. But the structuralist analysis of Brazilian reality emphasized supply rigidities due to inherited political and social institutions – which would require a certain amount of inflation to be overcome.[23] Thus, for example, the highly concentrated nature of agricultural land ownership, combined with traditional rural elites' fears that productive innovations might bring disruptive social change, meant that a quite considerable rise in domestic food prices would be necessary in order to call forth the increased supply response that would be needed to feed an expanding urban population. The structuralists stressed Brazil's strong economic growth over decades, tending to downplay concerns over inflation.

Modernizing military authoritarianism followed. The senior officers who led the 1964 coup quite explicitly justified it as a reaction to the venality and incompetence of elected politicians. Dramatic economic reforms, including immediate tax increases and spending cuts as well as restructuring of regulatory and financial institutions, reduced inflation quickly.[24] Authoritarianism had successfully dampened economic populism.

But it did not last. Despite the successful orthodox stabilization following the mid 1960s coup, the high growth and higher inflation pattern of the 'populist' years of the 1950s had returned with a vengeance by the early 1970s. Arguably beneficial developmentalism on the part of state technocrats coexisted uneasily with profound clientelism and capture of large chunks of the state by private interests.[25] The military regime's economic policy mix, once again, featured state interventionism and overlapping subsidies to multiple interests, often cancelling one another out in the aggregate![26] To remain within the model and rescue the predicted association of economic populism and political democracy, one could point to the gradual political liberalization that began under military President Ernesto Geisel (1974–79).

Alternatively, we could recast our interpretation of mid twentieth century Brazil in terms of an *expanded median voter model*, de-emphasizing the differences in the formal political rules, but highlighting the size and composition of Brazil's set of relevant political actors (RPA) in each of the three regimes during the period of mostly high growth and high inflation. Prior to 1930, Brazil had an elite-dominated political system, in which access to national power had been determined by pre-electoral pacts among key state governors, then ratified by an election open only to propertied elites, principally large landowners. After 1930, Getúlio Vargas instituted a secret ballot for sub-national and legislative elections, although direct elections for president remained 'postponed'. Though his mostly authoritarian regime was not a democracy, in order to strengthen his hold on the presidency Vargas courted the support of the urban middle class and even the small formal sector industrial working class by offering them symbolic political dignity as Brazilian citizens, along with welfare benefits provided via state-run, monopolistic unions. As compared to the elite oligarchy that it replaced, President Vargas' urban populist polity clearly expanded political participation. It was not, however, truly a mass regime, relying instead on support from a much narrower social base.

How narrow? Column 3 of Table 5.2 reports on the maximum size of the set of RPA according to occupational groups as listed in the National Census. It sums middle class and formal sector labour occupations, then adds a generous ten percent to compensate for misallocation of elites, such as landowners and agro-export managers that the census groups with farm workers.[27] The authoritarian populist years would seem to have given incumbent leaders an incentive to care about the opinions of only about a third of the Brazilian population, skewed toward urban dwellers. By the logic of this mental model, if Vargas could keep these 'voters' happy, then he could retain his hold on power, at least so long as the basic rules of the game (that is, the political regime type) did not change.

According to this revisionist political economy framing, Brazil's post-war democracy notably enhanced the open and competitive nature

Table 5.2: ***Estimates of the size of Brazil's set of relevant political actors (RPA)***

Political regime	*Census date*	*Maximum population share of RPA* (percent)*	*National elections inclusive dates*	*Number of national elections*	*Mean votes/ voting age population (percent)*
Authoritarian populism (1930–45)	1940	31	1930–44	N.A.	N.A.
Post-war	1950	34	1945–50	3	19.1
competitive			1950–54	3	29.4
democracy	1960	37	1955–59	2	31.6
(1945–64)			1960–64	3	35.2
Military	1970	22	1965–69	1	38.4
authoritarianism			1970–74	1	42.9
(1964–84)	1980	54	1975–79	1	55.5
			1980–84	1	63.7
Mass			1985–89	2	74.9
democracy	1990	100	1990–94	2	76.7
(1985–Present)			1995–2000	2	81.0

* Maximum share of RPA calculated for 1940, 1950, 1960, and 1980 by summing middle class occupations (commerce, except food service & street vendors, military, civil service, liberal professionals, and other services, except personal services), plus formal sector labour (mining, manufacturing, public utilities, transport and communications), plus ten percent for misallocation. For 1970 only formal sector labour is excluded. For 1990 all census categories are included.

Sources: Cols. 2 and 3: Fundação Instituto Brasileiro de Geografia e Estatística (IBGE). *Estatísticas históricas do Brasil: séries econômicas, demográficas e sociasis de 1550 a 1985*, Rio de Janeiro: IBGE, 1987, p. 73; Cols 4–6: International Institute for Democracy and Electoral Assistance (IDEA), 'Voter turnout Since 1945: a global report on political participation', at www.idea.int/voter_turnout, accessed October 2004.

of politics, but did not dramatically expand the set of RPA. Congress drafted a new constitution in 1946 to replace the authoritarian and centralizing document of 1938, and also made voting compulsory – but only for literates. Moreover, the formula for representation in the legislature was deliberately biased to over-represent voters from rural, conservative states and under-represent industrial states, where workers had greater potential for militancy.[28] Column 6 of Table 5.2 gives figures showing participation in all national elections, both presidential and congressional, and suggests that the scope of Brazilian political participation expanded only very slowly. If public policies worsened overall income inequality or hardened quasi-feudal rural class relations by subsidizing large landowners, these did not translate into a loss of political support for the incumbent. However, sufficient employment in the urban centres was a politically critical outcome.

When escalating inflation became a problem for politically included elites in the early 1960s, they were willing to support a military coup to restore macroeconomic balance. The new regime insulated economic policymaking from special interests and popular oversight, and stabilized the macroeconomy. Initially, the military coup in 1964 had the goal of demobilizing and depoliticizing the industrial working class. According to the rough estimates of Table 5.2, Column 3, the RPA may have dropped to under a quarter of all adult residents. However, the conservative economic policies of 1964–67 did not last, as they were inconsistent with the preferences of the set of RPA, beginning with Brazil's business community, who sought government credits and support for rapid industrial expansion. Public deficits, both obvious and disguised, were funded via a combination of money and credit expansion and the accumulation of foreign and domestic debt. One of the key regulatory innovations of the mid 1960s period of ostensibly orthodox institutional reform was inflation indexing, which linked the nominal value of long-term financial contracts to inflation, thus reducing the lender's risk.[29] Initially applied only to treasury securities and residential mortgage bonds, by the early 1970s returning inflation had spread indexation throughout the formal economy, including to financial assets, wages and salaries, rents, and government benefits. At this point, the political incentives for incumbent leaders to maintain macroeconomic stability had become quite weak. Even after the gradual political re-incorporation of urban organized labour from the mid 1970s, most members of the set of RPA would be better off under the high growth, high inflation scenario, since the main costs of inflation were borne by those outside the implicit political compact, especially the large urban and rural underclasses, whose incomes from casual and informal sector employment were not protected by indexation.

In sum, both the theory of economic populism and the perspective of the median voter provide plausible explanations for Brazil's strong growth and recurrent inflation from the 1930s to the mid 1980s. Neither is, incidentally, a theory of the role of economic conditions as a precipitant of national political change, although feedback mechanisms from economics to politics clearly existed. The dominant perspective suggests that the periods of expansion of political participation and contestation overseen by a weak and clientelistic state generated chronic deficits and inflation: political democracy might have been normatively desirable, but it was economically disastrous. This chapter's revisionist analysis instead emphasizes the incumbent leaders' needs to please the median RPA. For presidents in middle sectors regimes incorporating only somewhere between a third to just over half of Brazil's population, this meant that the national economic regulatory framework needed to ensure economic growth and an expanding pie. However, very substantial macroeconomic distortions could occur – notably high and rising inequality and inflation – so long as their costs could be channelled to groups lacking in political rights.

Brazil, 1985–2003: the economic consequences of wide political inclusion

Which perspective makes more sense as an interpretation of the economic consequences of mass democracy in Brazil? In 1985 José Sarney became Brazil's first civilian president in twenty years, and in late 1989 Fernando Collor won Brazil's first ever presidential election contested on the basis of universal adult suffrage. For the first decade following redemocratization the macroeconomy registered ever more worrying inflation, while growth slowed to a crawl. Following six dramatic failed attempts, Presidents Itamar Franco and Fernando Henrique Cardoso ended very high inflation in 1994–95, perhaps permanently. Brazilians subsequently re-elected Cardoso, then chose leftist presidential candidate Luiz Inácio Lula da Silva in 2002, trusting his pledge to rekindle growth and improve income distribution – but without a return of inflation. In other words, the coming of mass democracy first brought a decade of crazy hyperinflation. Subsequently, Brazil has settled into an alternation of politicians of the moderate right and moderate left, and macroeconomic policies and outcomes first leaning slightly toward price stability and then slightly toward economic expansion. These are the political and economic policy norms that one might expect from one of the more volatile members of the Organization of Economic Co-operation and Development (OECD), the so-called rich country club. Despite the many challenges of economic globalization, a large inherited public debt, and world record inequality, in macroeconomic terms Brazil apparently has now become an 'ordinary' country.

The *economic populist paradigm* suggests that widening political participation gives greater political voice to lower income groups, whose policy preferences will be for greater public spending and economic expansion. They also will prefer employment to inflation-protection for their non-existent financial assets. If many persons holding these classically 'leftist' economic policy preferences enter the political arena simultaneously, as should happen when a country holds its first democratic elections in many years, then the forces of popular democracy should undermine macroeconomic stability. This scenario of 'pent-up demand' seems to be a good description of Brazil after democratization in 1985. Old claimants on public resources did not disappear, yet new urgent spending priorities arose just the same. In 1986 Brazil's Congress lowered the voting age and made voting compulsory for all adults, including illiterates. Moreover, the new, very-democratically-negotiated Constitution of 1988 enshrined numerous novel, and extremely specific, economic rights and privileges – from the minimum wage to maximum real interest rates – and also mandated the transfer of over twenty percent of federal tax receipts to the states and municipalities, in the name of democratizing decentralization, thus appreciably worsening the federal deficit.[30] Governors and mayors expanded patronage employment, while Brazil's peculiar electoral rules of open-list proportional representation encouraged federal deputies to seek election via the 'personal vote', or a small group of highly committed voters, bound to the legislator by his or her commitment to defend narrow special favours.[31] As new claimants made demands of government, annual inflation went from the low triple digits in the early 1980s to the mid quadruple digits by the close of the decade. Dramatically escalating inflation led to repeated dramatic stabilization programs, each designed to stop inflation 'dead in its tracks' by simultaneous economy-wide deindexation, a new currency, wage-price controls, and emergency measures (such as temporary taxes on middle class necessities such as gasoline or automobiles) to reduce fiscal deficits. The inflation graph of the 1980s and early 1990s resembles dragon's teeth, as huge spikes seemingly inevitably followed each brief trough of a few months of stable prices. Finally, and only after repeated spectacular failures, the Real Plan (named after the new currency, the real) of 1994–95 accomplished the job. Inflation has now hovered at around 10 percent annually for a decade, Brazil's lowest numbers since the worldwide Great Depression of the 1930s.

The level of economic crisis was such that both policymakers and societal interests eventually recognized that their own costs of continued inflation exceeded the costs to themselves of stabilization.[32] Cooperation was obtained, according to this interpretation, principally due to the looming threat of macroeconomic disaster. Consequently, the weaker social actors – usually understood to be organized labour, and perhaps the salaried middle class – caved in and moderated their demands, allowing stabilization to occur at the expense of their relative incomes. A variant on this interpretation attributes successful stabilization to the combination of an acute crisis and policy learning, as many of the same government technocrats participated in successive stabilization attempts, finally getting it right after a decade of miscues.[33]

There are two potential problems with this analysis. The first lies with the explanation of stabilization, the second with expectation for the future. Supposedly, by 1994 absolute levels of inflation had reached crisis territory, sufficient to crash the economy. Normally selfish political actors engaged in a zero-sum game of competitive lobbying of the state for favours suddenly realized that an inability to negotiate joint sacrifices for the sake of containing inflation would sink them all. This thesis is not entirely convincing. For example, unlike several of its neighbours including Argentina in the late 1980s, Brazil's economy was not heavily dollarized. The financial sector did not disappear, and economic agents continued to enter into medium and long-term contracts – with indexation either implicit or explicit. There were even modest net inflows of foreign direct investment, all of which suggests a scenario short of acute crisis. Thus in early November 1991 Economy

Minister Marcílio Marques Moreira noted that the leap from fifteen percent monthly inflation in September to 23 percent in October did not constitute "hyperinflation", but merely "super-inflation", a distinction opaque to casual foreign observers – but by no means wholly specious given Brazilian conditions.[34] The second weak point in the economic populist analysis concerns its apparent expectations for the future. Although a stable price regime now has endured for a decade, there seems to be no reason, within the logic of the model, why high and very high inflation should not return, as none of the underlying social conflicts have disappeared. Thus, for example, Brazil has had incremental market-oriented economic reform on a number of fronts,[35] but remains a country characterized by patronage-oriented political parties, powerful and headstrong state governors, and a fractious national legislature.[36] Some analysts have noted the curious fact that political candidates promising seemingly conservative economic policies ('neoliberalism') have been popular with the masses.[37] But there seems to be no good explanation, other than false consciousness on the part of the lower classes, as to why.

How well does the *median voter framework* fare instead? Can it account for ten years of near hyperinflation, followed by a decade of reasonable macroeconomic sobriety? Three types of empirical evidence might support what I have termed the expanded median voter thesis as a valid interpretation of Brazil's late twentieth century political economy. First, and most simply, we might find a clear association of mass democracy and moderate macroeconomic *outcomes*. Second, we might discover that *poorer voters prefer* candidates who stand for moderate macroeconomic policies. Third, we could observe that incumbents, whatever their pre-election orientation, have implemented moderate macroeconomic *policies* once in office, presumably because they believe that this is what will get them re-elected. I take up each type of evidence in turn.

Obviously, we do not see an unambiguous association of mass democracy and an end to high and very high inflation in Brazil. Looking at the decade following the 1985 political transition, it is hard to deny that the economic populist framework contains important elements of truth. There were new claimants on public resources associated with both democratization and decentralization, yet existing beneficiaries of government economic intervention did not want to relinquish their perks. One may, and I do, term this a period of political transition, noting that Brazil's first presidential election under conditions of mass democracy did not take place until late 1989. Rough macroeconomic stability now has endured during the subsequent decade. So we cannot make an empirical judgment about enduring patterns of political economy, then, for at least another ten years.

An argument about the preferences of poor voters fares better. The last presidential election took place in 1960, with participation from 33 percent of the voting age population. In 1989, 80 percent of adults went to the polls. It seems safe to assume that most of the illiterates enfranchised after 1986 were in the bottom third of income earners, and thus low income. There were multiple candidates in the first round. Fernando Collor de Melo, the rightist candidate, won a clear second round victory over Luiz Inácio Lula da Silva, leftist union organizer and co-founder of the Workers' Party. Not only this, but poorer voters showed a marked preference for Collor. In a poll taken before the first round of voting in November 1989, among those intending to vote for Collor the most important reason by far was his pledge to fight "corruption, bribes, and maharajahs", while the most important reason citizens favoured Lula was his "support for the working class".[38] A week before the runoff (second round) elections in December a national poll reported that, among those voters with a preference, the poorest group (earning up to five times the minimum wage) favoured Collor over Lula 56 to 44 percent. Middle-income earners (five to ten minimum wages) went for Lula by 53 percent, while high-income respondents (over ten minimum wages) favoured Lula by 61 percent. Urban and better-educated voters favoured Lula, while their more rural and less educated fellows preferred Collor.[39]

Once in office, President Collor immediately implemented Brazil's most comprehensive anti-inflation 'shock treatment' plan ever, which included an instantaneous and comprehensive wage and price freeze, deindexation, a new currency, medium term 'structural' reform provisions such as privatization, and a dramatic effort to contain monetary expansion by freezing about seventy percent of private sector (individual and corporate) savings accounts for a year and a half. Collor and his Finance Minister Zélia Cardoso de Mello managed to alienate virtually all of Brazil's organized interests simultaneously, at least partly due to an imperious style at odds with Brazil's political traditions of continuous bargaining and log-rolling among a kaleidoscope of political parties and interests. Later, credible accusations of corruption within his administration proved Collor's political undoing. He resigned to avoid impeachment by the Senate.

Vice President Itamar Franco, a long-time regional political boss in the personalist and clientelist tradition, succeeded Collor. Despite his clear initial disinclination to tackle macroeconomic reform, Franco's fifth Finance Minister in three years, Fernando Henrique Cardoso, convinced him that stabilization was essential. Cardoso's Real Plan was economically innovative. More importantly, it was politically astute, understanding that a major and lasting reorganization of the national economic regulatory framework that had grown up over decades, and which had enabled the upper and middle classes (including the financial sector!) to coexist peacefully with very high inflation, would require an extended effort in policy salesmanship among all of Brazil's myriad political parties and privileged economic interests. Cardoso and his allies, initially principally within the executive branch economic ministries, had to convince Brazil's 'haves' that more or less simultaneous joint sacrifice would leave them better off than continuing the struggle for shares.[40] In this reform effort, Cardoso had the electoral support of the population at large, including that of the 'have nots'. After polling substantially behind Lula as late as May 1994, Cardoso won a resounding first round majority even in a crowded field of candidates, clearly due to the rapid fall of monthly inflation from July onwards.[41] Four years later, Cardoso again crushed candidate Lula da Silva in the first round of voting.

What do these electoral results mean? A number of thoughtful observers have puzzled over votes of the Latin American masses, not only in Brazil, for politicians who then implement reforms these analysts characterize as pro-market, pro-business, 'neoliberal', or illustrative of the 'Washington consensus'. One popular explanation for these seemingly perverse outcomes is external pressure, which clearly has been relevant for the public policy choices of smaller economies such as Ecuador or Bolivia, but is much less so for a large country such as Brazil. Another is false consciousness, since the masses seem to have forsaken the traditional leftist parties and platforms, or post-election chicanery. By the logic of the median voter model, on the other hand, lower income voters should prefer politicians who promise, above all, a relatively predictable and unbiased macroeconomic scenario. In Brazil, the end of high inflation had immediate and progressive implications for income distribution.[42] This outcome is widely accepted in Brazilian economic policy circles today, but was not so in the mid or even late 1990s. The third and final strand of evidence in support of a median voter framework for conceptualizing Brazilian political economy since the return of democracy looks to the behaviour of incumbent politicians. Both presidents Fernando Henrique Cardoso and Lula da Silva had historic ties to labour and to the left. In office, each has supported fiscal retrenchment and social security reform, which means raising the retirement age and reducing benefits, a policy adamantly opposed by unionized, formal sector labour. In my view, this is not simply a case of caving into pressure from footloose global investors – though such pressure clearly exists and not infrequently induces needless or even counter-developmental conformity in national economic policies in developing countries.[43] The strongest pressure for at least rough macroeconomic stability – which implies *both* a permanent end to high and very high inflation and an expansion of employment and growth – comes from the average Brazilian citizen.

Comparative conclusions

Fears that political democracy in poor countries would put sound macroeconomic management at risk have by no means been limited to analysts of Latin America. There is a large literature on the need to 'insulate' national economic policymakers from popular demands for clientelistic favours or massively expensive social spending.[44] One frequent suggestion is to depoliticize as much of monetary and fiscal decision making as possible by allocating their implementation to executive branch bureaucracies managed by apolitical technical experts such as independent central bankers. For example, Bates and Krueger conclude from eight careful country studies that "economic reform implies the strengthening of the executive branch of government and, within the executive branch, the financial – as opposed to the spending – ministries".[45] Other scholars have touted the virtues of rapid, synoptic economic reform to accompany democratic transitions, fearing that otherwise economic populism will render needed pro-market reforms politically untenable.[46] In general, the consensus has been that only economic crisis will put an end to populist tendencies – and then only temporarily, unless sweeping reforms in the national economic regulatory structure are able to be implemented by dedicated teams willing to ignore popular pressures to desist.

The policy implications of this essay's analysis would seem to point in the opposite direction. Rather than recommending political insulation for economic policymakers in developing countries, we could conceptualize popular accountability to a truly broad electorate as an elegant and effective technique for avoiding the sort of highly skewed, unequal, and inefficient – *yet for long periods functional* – macroeconomic patterns that characterized Brazil during much of the twentieth century. If our reform goal is to improve national economic and financial governance by properly aligning the incentives to political incumbents assumed to be rational maximizers, then a political transition *from* a polity by, of, and for the upper and middle sectors and *toward* a mass democracy might be just the medicine a genuinely far-sighted money doctor ought to recommend.

Notes

1 The author thanks the other participants in this collaborative project for stimulating comments, while retaining responsibility for errors.

2 On political 'voice', see Albert O. Hirschman, *Exit, Voice, and Loyalty: Responses to Decline in Firms, Organizations, and States,* Cambridge, MA: Harvard University Press, 1970.

3 Rudiger Dornbusch and Sebastian Edwards, eds., *The Macroeconomics of Populism in Latin America*, Chicago: University of Chicago Press, 1991.

4 See Albert O. Hirschman, 'The social and political matrix of inflation: elaborations on the Latin American experience', in A.O. Hirschman, *Essays in Trespassing: Economics to Politics and Beyond.* Cambridge: Cambridge University Press, 1981; Werner Baer, 'Social aspects of Latin American inflation', *Quarterly Review of Economics and Finance*, 31/3, 1991, 45–57.

5 See Guillermo A. O'Donnell, *Modernization and Bureaucratic-Authoritarianism: Studies in South American Politics*, Berkeley: Institute of International Studies, University of California, 1973.

6 Theodore J. Lowi, *The End of Liberalism: The Second Republic of the United States*, New York: Norton, 1979.

7 O'Donnell, op. cit.; David Collier, ed., *The New Authoritarianism in Latin America*, Princeton, NJ: Princeton University Press, 1979.

8 Alberto Alesina and Allen Drazen, 'Why are stabilizations delayed?', *American Economic Review*, 81/5, 1991, 1170–88.

9 Gerald M. Meier, ed., *Politics and Policy Making in Developing Countries: Perspectives on the New Political Economy*, San Francisco: International Center for Economic Growth, 1991.

10 On political democracy, see Robert A. Dahl, *Polyarchy: Participation and Opposition*, New Haven: Yale University Press, 1971; Philippe C. Schmitter and Terry Lynn Karl, 'What democracy is ... and is not', in Larry Diamond and Marc F. Plattner, eds., *The Global Resurgence of Democracy*, Baltimore: The Johns Hopkins University Press, 1993.

11 The model of economic populism summarized above also builds on these assumptions.

12 For a brief introduction to theorizing abut the median voter, see Torsten Persson and Guido Tabellini, *Political Economics: Explaining Economic Policy*, Cambridge, MA: MIT Press, 2000, pp. 10–11.

13 For present purposes, SNIG may be used interchangeably with another useful acronym: NAIRU, the non-accelerating-inflation rate of unemployment. NAIRU implicitly signals that there is some degree of trade-off between the twin goals of low inflation and high unemployment.

14 In fact, most of the median voter literature developed around the experiences of the wealthy democracies asks what institutional configurations – such as a particular electoral system that somehow distorts the transmission of voter preferences to political incumbents – might cause deviations from the default expected outcome of SNIG. Here I investigate situations in which SNIG is not necessarily the default expectation.

15 I have used the term 'economic populism' to refer primarily to the struggle for income shares among organized societal interests, where a weak state does not perform the role of adjudicating among competing claimants, but instead yields sequentially to all. 'Economic populism' is also used to refer to the presumed preferences of 'labour' (in a two sector model where the social groups are 'labour' and 'capital') for high economic growth and employment, even where this choice implies accelerating inflation.

16 Arguably, one of the few such public policy options in a mass democracy is to redistribute income from future citizens to current voters, as via a large public debt or unfunded future obligations, such as public pensions (a.k.a. social security).

17 For a similar list of Brazilian political regimes, see Bolivar Lamounier, 'Brazil: inequality against democracy', in Larry Diamond, Juan J. Linz and Martin Seymour Lipset, eds., *Democracy in Developing Countries, Vol.4: Latin America*, Boulder, CO: Lynne Rienner, 1989, pp. 138–9.

18 On the periods of both authoritarian and democratic populism see Robert M. Levine, *Father of the Poor? Vargas and His Era*, Cambridge: Cambridge University Press, 1998; Kenneth Paul Erickson, 'Brazil: corporative authoritarianism, democratization, and dependency', in Howard J. Wiarda and Harvey F. Kline, eds., *Latin American Politics and Development*, 2nd edn., Boulder, CO: Westview Press, 1979; Thomas E. Skidmore, *Politics in Brazil, 1930–1964: An Experiment in Democracy*, London: Oxford University Press, 1967; and Philippe C. Schmitter, *Interest Conflict and Political Change in Brazil*, Stanford, CA: Stanford University Press, 1976.

19 Edson de Oliveira Nunes and Barbara Geddes, 'Dilemmas of state-led modernization in Brazil', in J.D. Wirth, T. Boganshields, and E. de O. Nunes, eds., *State and Society in Brazil: Continuity and Change*, Boulder, CO: Westview, 1987.

20 Skidmore, 1967, op. cit., p. 19.

21 The magnitude of coffee subsidies was enormous, and almost certainly macro-economically fortuitous during the collapse of foreign demand during the 'Great Depression'. See Celso Furtado, *The Economic Growth of Brazil: A Survey from Colonial to Modern Times*. Berkeley: University of California Press, 1971 (1959).

22 Lessa, Carlos, *Quinze Anos de Política Econômica*, mimeo, Rio de Janeiro: Centro de Desenvolvimento Econômico, CEPAL/BNDE, n.d. (c. 1963); Nathaniel H. Leff, *Economic Policy Making and Development in Brazil, 1947–1964*, New York: Wiley, 1968; Helen Shapiro, 'The public–private interface: Brazil's business–government relations in historical perspective, 1950–1990', mimeo, Harvard Business School, Fall, 1991; and Marcelo de Paiva Abreu, 'Inflação, estagnação e ruptura: 1961–1964', in M. de P. Abreu, ed., *A ordem do progresso*, op. cit.

23 On structuralist economics see Albert O. Hirschman, 'Ideologies of development in Latin America', in Albert O. Hirschman, ed., *Latin American Issues: Essays and Comments*, New York: The Twentieth Century Fund, 1961; John Sheahan, *Patterns of Development in Latin America: Poverty, Repression, and Economic Strategy*. Princeton: Princeton University Press, 1987, especially pp. 11–14; and Ricardo Bielschowsky, 'Ideology and development: Brazil, 1930–1964', *CEPAL Review*, 45, December, 1991.

24 Donald E. Syvrud, *Foundations of Brazilian Economic Growth*, Stanford, CA: Hoover Institution Press, Stanford University, 1974; Thomas E. Skidmore, 'Politics and economic

policy making in authoritarian Brazil, 1937–1971', in Alfred Stepan, *Authoritarian Brazil: Origins, Policies, and Future*, New Haven: Yale University Press, 1973; and Albert Fishlow, 'Some reflections on post-1964 economic policy', in Stepan, ed., op. cit.

25 Fernando Henrique, Cardoso, *Autoritarismo e democratização*, Rio de Janeiro: Paz e Terra, 1975; Luiz Carlos Bresser Pereira, *Development and Crisis in Brazil, 1930–1983*, Boulder, CO: Westview Press, 1984; and Peter Evans, *Dependent Development: The Alliance of Multinational, State, and Local Capital in Brazil*, Princeton: Princeton University Press, 1979.

26 William Tyler, *The Brazilian Industrial Economy*, Lexington, MA: Lexington Books, 1983; Leslie Elliott Armijo, 'Brazilian politics and patterns of financial regulation, 1950–1991', in S. Haggard, C. Lee, and S. Maxfield, eds., *The Politics of Finance in Developing Countries*, Ithaca, NY: Cornell University Press, 1993; Werner Baer, *The Brazilian Economy: Growth and Development*, 4th edn., New York: Praeger, 1995.

27 For a similar effort to understand the social basis of Brazilian populism see Luiz Carlos Bresser Pereira, *Development and Crisis in Brazil, 1930–1983*. Boulder, Colorado: Westview Press, 1984, pp. 47–65.

28 Barry Ames, *Political Survival: Politicians and Public Policy in Latin America*, Berkeley: University of California, 1987, p. 196, fn. 3.

29 Werner Baer and Paul Beckerman, 'The trouble with index-linking: reflections on the Brazilian experience', *World Development*, 8/9 (1980).

30 Lourdes Sola, 'Estado, regime fiscal e ordem monetária: qual estado?', in Lourdes Sola and Leda M.Paulani, eds., *Lições da década de 80*, São Paulo: Editora da Universidade de São Paulo (EDUSP), 1995.

31 David Samuel. 'Fiscal straightjacket: the politics of macroeconomic reform in Brazil, 1995–2002', Paper presented at the annual meeting of the Latin American Studies Association, Dallas, Texas, March 2003.

32 Luiz Carlos Bresser Pereira and Jairo Abud, 'Net and total transition cost: the timing of economic reform', *World Development*, 25/6, 1997, 905–14.

33 Rudiger Dornbusch, 'Brazil's incomplete stabilization and reform', *Brookings Papers on Economic Activity, 1997*, 1, 1997, 367–404; Edmund Amann and Werner Baer, 'The illusion of stability: the Brazilian economy under Cardoso', *World Development*, 28/10, 2000, 1805–19; Eliana Cardoso, 'Brazil's currency crisis: the shift from an exchange rate anchor to a flexible regime', in Carol Wise and Riordan Roett, eds., *Exchange Rate Policies in Latin America*, Washington, DC: Brookings, 2000.

34 'Loss of control or strategic inaction?', *Latin American Regional Report: Brazil*, 28 November 1991, p. 2.

35 Leslie Elliott Armijo and Philippe Faucher 'We have a consensus: explaining political support for market reforms in Latin America', *Latin American Politics and Society*, 44/2, 2002.

36 Barry Ames, *The Deadlock of Democracy in Brazil*, Ann Arbor: University of Michigan Press, 2001; Scott P. Mainwaring, *Rethinking Political Systems in the Third Wave of Democratization: The Case of Brazil*, Stanford, CA: Stanford University Press, 1999.

37 Kurt Weyland, 'Neoliberal populism in Latin America and Eastern Europe', *Comparative Politics*, 31/4, 1999, 379–402; Susan C. Stokes, *Mandates and Democracy: Neoliberalism by Surprise in Latin America*, Cambridge: Cambridge University Press, 2001.

38 *Folha de São Paulo*, 17 October 1989, p. B8. A 'maharajah' is an overpaid, do-nothing public employee, especially one holding multiple 'full-time' positions.

39 *Folha de São Paulo*, 8 December 1989, p. B6.

40 For a more extended analysis of the political process of Brazilian economic reform, see Leslie Elliott Armijo, Philippe Faucher and Magdalena Dembinska, 'Compared to what? Assessing Brazilian political institutions', forthcoming in *Comparative Political Studies*, September 2006.

41 James Brook, 'Taming of inflation buoys centrist in Brazil polls', *New York Times*, 14

September 1994; 'Cardoso's 34 million votes', *Gazeta Mercantil*, International Weekly Edition, 17 October 1994, p. 3.

42 Marcelo Neri and Claúdio Considera, 'Cresimento, desigualidade e pobreza: o impacto da estabilização', in Fundação Instituto de Pesquisa Econômica Aplicada (IPEA), ed., *A Economia Brasileira em Perspectiva – 1996, Vol. 1*, Rio de Janeiro: IPEA, 1996, pp. 49–82; Rossana Mostajo, 'Gasto social y distribución des ingreso: caracterización y impacto redistributivo en paises seleccionados de América Latina y el Caribe', *ECLAC Serie Reformas Económicas*, 69, Santiago, Chile: United Nations Economic Commission on Latin America and the Caribbean (ECLAC), 2000.

43 See for example Ha-Joon Chang, *Kicking Away the Ladder: Developmental Strategy in Historical Perspective*, London: Anthem Press, 2002.

44 See the discussion of state autonomy (pp. 23–4) in Stephan Haggard and Robert R. Kaufman, 'Introduction: institutions and economic adjustment', in Stephan Haggard and Robert R. Kaufman, eds., *The Politics of Economic Adjustment*, Princeton: Princeton University Press, 1992.

45 Robert H. Bates and Anne O. Krueger, 'Generalizations arising from the country studies', in Robert H. Bates and Anne O. Krueger, eds., *Political and Economic Interactions in Economic Policy Reform*, Cambridge, MA: Blackwell, 1993, p. 462.

46 See Adam Przeworski, *Democracy and the Market: Political and Economic Reforms in Eastern Europe and Latin America*, Cambridge: Cambridge University Press, 1991, chapter 4; Stephan Haggard and Steven B. Webb, 'Introduction', in *Voting for Reform: Democracy, Political Liberalization, and Economic Adjustment*, New York: Oxford University Press for the World Bank, 1994, especially pp. 6–8.

Chapter 6

Central banking, democratic governance, and the quality of democracy

Lourdes Sola and Moisés Marques

Policies of economic and financial liberalization have gained new impetus since the end of the Cold War as part of an almost irresistible trend toward the establishment of a set of global norms.[1] Simultaneously, democratization has achieved wide geographic breadth. When Robert Dahl introduced the term polyarchy thirty years ago, only 29 countries met the necessary requirements. In 2004, more than one hundred countries met (at least nominally) the necessary credentials for inclusion; and half joined the group during the 1990s. The past decade has produced, in other words, a new combination of political and economic change that is one of the distinctive characteristics of developing countries. This combination of political and economic change is central to understanding the complexities of public policy formulation, institutional reform, and the narrowing of choices available to political elites and other domestic actors. It is also at the root of two of the challenges that permeate and unify the analytical framework of this chapter.

The first challenge can be formulated as the following: it is precisely at the moment that electorates are given greater political power that national policymakers also transfer financial and economic power to global markets. In the context of this economic and financial integration of emerging market democracies, what is the role (and place) of democratic policy? In other words, what is the role for policies that meet the dual prerequisites of: first, governability and economic efficacy, including global norms that are outside the control of domestic government elites; and second, are instituted under conditions of accountability and responsiveness to voter preferences? To what extent can local political elites participate in strategic decisions? What trade-offs between these two prerequisites are viable? We argue that the process of institutional change that led to the design and management of monetary regimes in new democracies in the 1990s offers important perspectives on the interaction between economic liberalization and democratization. The choice of this subject is bolstered by the fact that in less than ten years, the central banks of at least thirty developing countries have acquired formal autonomy, more than double the rate of the previous thirty years.[2] By the same token, the spreading of financial crises from one economy to another – regardless of whether the affected country suffered from the same 'structural' flaws as the country where the crisis originated – led most emerging market democracies to adopt new monetary regimes and reform their financial sectors. This chapter focuses on Brazil's recent experience, with an eye to the experience of its Latin American neighbours, to examine the following question: what is the role of politics in the formation of a democratic financial regime, one capable of producing sustainable economic and political stability that permit the normative objective of perfecting the quality of democracies? At the heart of this research is the study of factors that contribute not only to public sector efficiency, but also to democratic accountability and transparency.

The second analytical challenge has been to adjust orthodox policies to the region. A number of criticisms can be levelled against the strict limits imposed by this analytical approach, including those who argue that the insulation of technocrats and of monetary institutions is a condition for maximizing their efficacy. This chapter is not against protecting policymakers from short-term political pressures and risks of 'economic populism'. Such protections make sense, particularly in Latin America where populist practices in the past led to high electoral dividends but exacerbated socially regressive inflationary pressures. Our points are of another order. First, the diversity of Latin America invalidates 'one type fits all' prescriptions. It is essential to distinguish between prescriptions adopted in the context of democratization from those adopted under military rule. Second, the exclusive focus on economic governability and efficacy as performance criteria has led to the treatment of democracy as a residual category. Such a focus minimizes two risks associated with the 'insulation' recommended by the orthodox prescription that can be seen recently in Latin America. Insulation increases the risk of monetary institutions being captured by particular interests. An associated risk is that of overstating technical capacity under extreme insulation. In the absence of greater controls through vertical and horizontal accountability, short-term market expectations or monetary (and fiscal) dogma tend to prevail over other policy goals legitimated by voters, such as economic development, employment, and so forth. In other words, by privileging insulation in the name of efficacy and economic governability, the orthodox prescription tends to privilege performance criteria that satisfy core constituencies of central banks, the financial market and its watchdogs (such as Wall Street's so-called 'Fed Watchers'), but does not eliminate the political risk associated with satisfying only a single constituency.

For these reasons, the first topic in this chapter is the classic question of democratic theory: who will guard the guardians? We give primacy to the structural tension observed by Dahl between autonomy and democratic control, a tension inherent to institutions such as the judiciary and central banks. But there is a further aggravator in the case of central banks, which in principle are not bound by binding long-term rules, a parameter represented by a constitution for the justice system. The rules for the Central Bank are determined solely by the current monetary (and fiscal) dogma, and by the intellectual control of the epistemic community in which policy makers and monetary reforms are embedded – an international community which cannot be held accountable and is not responsive to the electorate's preferences.

Furthermore, in addressing the question of the efficacy of central banks as guardians of the currency and as overseers and regulators of financial markets, the dominant orthodox prescription tends to view statutory autonomy as an institutional prerequisite for obtaining economic stability. In this chapter we argue that Latin America's experience offers an especially relevant test of the validity of this claim. Latin America was no exception to the dominant trend toward central bank autonomy in the 1990s, but it offers contrasting experiences of trajectories of change and, above all, of the complex relationship between institutional autonomy and democratic control. Consider the apparently polar extreme cases of Chile and Brazil. The statutory autonomy of the Chilean central bank was one of the *pièces de résistance* of the negotiated transition to democracy and arose out of the authoritarian regime's belief – a view that was shared by the leaders of Chile's 'Concertación', or political accord – that the risk of 'economic populism' is greater in democratic contexts. In Brazil, where the statutory autonomy of the Central Bank is still a goal, not a reality, the trajectory has been one of progressive and gradual evolution. It began in the context of a potentially explosive rise in inflation when the Central Bank's authority was weakened during the 1980s in tandem with external shocks and democratization. But once monetary stability was achieved, it became the primary objective of the Central Bank under both the governments of Fernando Henrique Cardoso and Luiz Inácio Lula da Silva. This chapter seeks to describe this process and analyse the conditions that explain it.

Our argument is that while the autonomy of the Central Bank of Brazil is comparatively vulnerable, since it derives from an act of temporary political delegation, dependent on presidential order (which could in principle be rescinded by fiat), it has a solid foundation domestically in terms of legitimacy, accountability and responsiveness, even as the Central Bank is operationally quite effective and has international credibility. We argue that the recuperation and assertion of the Central Bank's power as a monetary authority is a gradual process that may culminate in statutory autonomy. It is driven by a combination of three factors. First, profound changes have occurred in the criteria for legitimation by society as reflected in the electorate's preferences. Second, structural economic changes – together with the previous factor – have shifted incentives for politicians. Third, governmental elites have recognized the firepower of international financial markets and the resulting need to play the confidence game, guaranteeing, among other conditions, monetary stability.

The first part of this chapter examines how economic stability became a new criterion of political legitimation and priority 'public good'. We examine under what conditions economic stabilization, conceived both as a criterion of legitimation and of economic performance, preceded the gradual recovery of authority by the Central Bank of Brazil – an authority eroded by hyperinflationary pressures and a number of veto players. We try to demonstrate that what made possible such a 'heterodox' sequence of events and gradualist approach to financial and monetary reform viable was a series of strategic decisions by politicians and the economic team in the Cardoso government. These decisions weakened economic and political veto players. Contrary to the claims of the orthodox literature, we attempt to illustrate that a great deal of political discretion was not only exercised but also necessary to circumvent two barriers: On the one hand, the veto power of the actors who resisted the socially progressive consequences of economic stability and, on the other hand, the cognitive maps and political culture of traditional Brazilian policymaking that remained deeply hostile to granting statutory autonomy to the Central Bank of Brazil. In the second part, we adopt a broader historical and comparative perspective, starting with the institutional reforms of the monetary and banking sectors undertaken under the aegis of the Central Bank of Brazil after it recovered its power as a monetary authority.

This chapter seeks to understand the comparative resilience of Brazil's economy to abrupt currency devaluations, such as that of 1999. While currency runs and devaluations generated much greater economic hardships in East Asian countries and in Russia during the 1997–99 period, Brazil's rapid recovery is attributed to the fact that the country did not suffer from a 'risky' financial sector. The financial sector proved much more resilient because of the pre-crisis *gradual* implementation of reforms geared at the dramatic reduction of the leverage of domestic financial institutions – through the gradual elimination of a moral hazard problem. We show that this reduction in leverage was carried out in a democratic framework and under the increasingly severe scrutiny of the Congress, the opposition, and the media. The near political crisis that followed currency devaluation during 1999 is also examined in terms of the improvements it generated regarding accountability and responsiveness.

In the third and final part, we demonstrate how increased financial integration in developing countries can, under certain conditions, increase the democratic accountability of domestic monetary authorities. International rules, adapted to the Brazilian context immediately after the 1999 devaluation and a political crisis that threatened the credibility and legitimacy of the Central Bank in the eyes of the population, led to a new monetary and financial regime. This enhanced the transparency and legitimacy of the Central Bank. These rules have been preserved after 2002 under President Lula da Silva – notwithstanding his party's fierce opposition both at the time of reforms and during the 2002 campaign.

Central banking, democratic governance and political authority: crafting economic institutions

This section examines two areas. First, we argue that the study of monetary authority and central banks should be an essential item on research agendas about democratic governance in political science. To study the relationship between democratic governance and monetary authority, however, one must expand the conceptual framework used to study central banks. Specifically, analysis should shift away from an exclusive focus on how central banks gain autonomy from politics toward a study of central banks as a special mode of political authority. Second, we suggest what an empirical study of monetary authority should look like when central banks are conceptualized as a mode of political authority. Drawing upon the Brazilian case, we invert a common assumption within the study of central banks: that price stability follows from an autonomous central bank. Nearly the opposite has taken place in Brazil.

The current trend towards greater central bank statutory autonomy is a special instance of state reform. It poses problems specific to transitional societies because it brings to the fore the complexity of linkages between democratization, governance and state reform. For this reason it is crucial to approach central banking in broader terms than those adopted by economists. Economists approach central banking and monetary authority as interchangeable, often synonymous categories. We are interested in examining the political and economic conditions by which an existing central bank acquires, establishes and eventually asserts its power as a monetary authority. This shift of focus leads us to adapt and develop the notion of monetary authority as a special mode of political authority, on the assumption that such a perspective can yield insights into a specific family of Latin American neo-democracies – those that have been most exposed to protracted hyperinflationary pressures throughout their experiment in democratization, such as Argentina, Brazil and Bolivia.

As mentioned, one of the most striking developments during the 1990s was the general trend toward greater central bank statutory autonomy in both advanced capitalist democracies and neo-democracies in the global south and east. Differences between these two groups of countries should not be underestimated. In OECD countries, for example, a great deal of political capital has been expended in debates over how much discretion should be delegated from individual central banks to a new institution responsible for monetary order at a regional level. The starting point of this debate, however, was an established national monetary authority acknowledged not only by members of the financial system, but also by the political elite and relevant populations. The question of how to obtain recognition of the specific powers central banks are expected to exercise had already been settled within the territorial jurisdiction of each national state. Recent studies suggest this is a long-run outcome of a number of different and convoluted institutional histories of European central banks and of the United States Federal Reserve.[3] Diverse trajectories are also apparent in different institutional designs, but two general conditions had already been met in the dominant capitalist democracies. The first was the acknowledgment of price stability as a 'public good' by domestic populations and government elites. This condition held true, irrespective of how legitimacy was achieved, whether through an ideological and socially embedded commitment to price stability and the rule of law (as in Britain, during the struggle against mercantilism); or by way of economic and social traumas generated by hyperinflations (as in Germany). A second component of legitimation consisted of the political mechanisms and institutional devices by which central banks were made accountable to other actors.

In emerging market democracies such conditions are not easily met and are often in the making. Furthermore, global norms dictated in accordance with neoliberal prescriptions rest on one essentially debatable assumption: that one model of central bank independence fits all. Indeed, central banks are an indispensable mode of authority, a necessary condition (and signal) of an uncontested commitment to monetary order on the part of strategic sectors of the relevant societies. However, the crucial question in inflationary economies and societies is how to craft this kind of commitment once democratic transition and consolidation are underway. If we want to understand the political logic and dynamics of the process by which the exercise of monetary authority is achieved in a democratic context, the mere recognition of the highly technical nature of monetary operations and the potential dangers from particularistic pressures is not a satisfactory starting point. Instead we need to acknowledge that a key requisite of such process is an act of political delegation of authority – from politicians to other actors – which may indeed have beneficial consequences, on the condition that analysts and policy makers alike incorporate the issue of accountability and transparency into this act of delegation.

A number of other political requisites must be satisfied in order to reconcile the exercise of monetary authority with democratic governance. These are to a great (although variable) degree related to the premise of social legitimization mentioned above. Recalling the special functions and powers attributed to central banks, a first question is why, and on what grounds, economists have properly labelled central banks, or institutions performing similar functions, as monetary authorities? The answer rests with their specific functions in shaping monetary and exchange rate policies, securing financial stability, and ultimately acting as guardians of the currency. The effective performance of these tasks is closely related to the exercise of specific powers: the regulation of the financial system, monetary supervision, and maintenance of external creditworthiness. In this capacity central banks are rule-makers as much as rule-enforcers, through their capacity to enforce penalties, to generate acquiescence on the part of all members of the financial system to existing regulations, and to indirectly affect growth and employment.

This function needs to be distinguished analytically, however, as Weber reminds us, from another indirect mode of power also enjoyed by central bank institutions. This indirect power consists of providing incentives for actors in the financial markets to respond to guidelines of credit and monetary policies in a cooperative way according to different criteria: financial actors' own individual calculations of what is in their best interest. While their power derives from the fact that central banks enjoy a monopoly or quasi-monopoly over credit, and can induce (but not enforce) responses from the agents in the financial system, their capacity as rule-makers stems from their expected performance and legitimate intervention in the economy as guardians of an established monetary order. We can therefore infer that monetary authority is a special mode of political authority and of power, thus providing two reasons to approach central banks as an important chapter within the study of political economy. Notwithstanding the key role the concept of authority has for political theory – democratic or not – central banking remains a topic explored primarily by economists.[4] To the extent that insulation from the political arena is indispensable for protecting monetary authorities against particular interests, the analyst is confronted with one of the most fundamental (and oldest) challenges for democratic theory: who guards the guardians?[5] And, by implication, which set of institutions is best equipped to counteract the risks of delegating the necessary autonomy to institutions regulating monetary authority?[6] Dahl best expressed this as a trade-off between autonomy and control in a pluralist democracy. Two questions follow: to whom should central bankers be accountable, and what are the limits to transparency? The latter is complicated by the fact that secrecy, or at least non-immediate disclosure, is often an important tool for effective monetary management not only on grounds of economic efficacy, but also as a means to protect against speculative attacks.

Democratic governance and inflationary regimes: towards a typology

Orthodox economic prescriptions take for granted three assumptions that influence the legitimacy of central banks, drawing on the experience of dominant democracies. All three are related to the question of the quality of democracy. First, price stability is a 'public good'. Second, because inflation is more detrimental to those sectors of society that are less able to protect incomes from the 'inflationary tax', economic stabilization is instrumental to achieving a greater degree of equity in the long run. Third, central bank independence is a principal condition for actors and the institutions charged with price stability to act in the interests of society. In other words, the conventional approach presumes a conception of what constitutes a good government and a good society.

To what extent do the same criteria for good government hold for neo-democracies? To explore the problems associated with the establishment of a legitimate and accountable monetary authority one must first make the distinction between two families of neo-democracies. On the one hand, there are countries that experienced runaway inflation and followed an explosive path as a consequence of adjustments imposed by both external shocks and by past policy-choices.[7] These cases fall under the rubric of hyperinflationary experiences. In these cases, economic stabilization became a priority inseparable from economic restructuring and, in particular, from external shocks which led to a fiscal crisis of the state. This is because hyperinflation is synonymous with the end of any monetary regime. Hyperinflation is a term which, translated into political science parlance, is nothing less than a disruption of the existing monetary order. Hyperinflation can therefore be interpreted as a process of accelerated loss of monetary – and political – authority. It may further be interpreted as an outcome of fiscal and legitimization crises, affecting the state, its regulatory capacities, and long-term relationship with economy and society. Some Latin American countries fit this category in the past, although one can draw additional distinctions amongst the most conspicuous hyperinflationary cases – Argentina, Bolivia and Brazil. Whereas in the first two countries hyperinflationary pressures developed into an effective hyperinflationary crisis, in Brazil such pressures were kept under permanent, yet precarious, control by generalized indexation until 1993. This mode of control, as far as decision-making was concerned, verged on a praxis of systematic brinkmanship.[8]

On the other hand, there are neo-democracies for which the task of reconciling economic restructuring with democratization could be achieved in the context of a comparatively manageable rate of inflation. This was due in great part to more amenable fiscal crises, in turn a result of a comparatively reduced exposure to the 1982 external shock and debt crisis in the Latin American members of this group.

In what follows we address problems typical of the first group of countries, providing evidence primarily from the Brazilian case, supplemented on occasion with examples from Argentina and Bolivia. These neo-democracies have distinctive features. They represent extreme cases where economic restructuring and democratization took place in a context in which monetary order was a goal, not a reality. Although inflation was dramatically brought down to unprecedented low levels, the achievement of self-sustaining economic stabilization in these countries has been a long-run process dependent upon the implementation of economic and institutional reforms, and the continuance of the external bonanza. This is where the role of a central bank as a permanent guardian of the currency and of monetary order comes in.

The context in which these countries laboured imposes a number of additional conditions for effective state reform compatible with democratic governance, principally concerning the re-establishment of monetary authority in the context of a broader, and conflict-ridden, process of recreating democratic political authority. Two conditions are essential to this process. The first is the recognition of self-sustaining economic stability as a public good, with the expectation that this goal is inseparable from greater equity. The second condition is an agreed-upon strategy to initiate (or reinforce) a process of institutional reforms geared to rendering monetary authority accountable to society without its becoming prey to the political arena. For this mode of state reform to be effective, its pace, timing, guidelines and design are critical. These conditions may be referred to as a quest for embedded authority, typical of a situation in which state capacity for regulation and supervision will be dependent *inter alia* upon a changing pattern of financing and composition of its expenditures. This implies, of course, a shift in state–society relations and, above all, hard policy choices about who will pay the costs and who will benefit from economic restructuring.

Furthermore, other dilemmas should be considered if democratic governance is to be counted as a legitimate competing goal. The political dynamic of economic stabilization concentrates power, at least at its initial stage. A principal feature of neo-democracies is the re-concentration of power in institutions responsible for monetary authority – a process that implies multiple acts of delegation. These acts of delegation include politicians, experts, and on occasion whole bureaucracies. Relevant actors include politicians in the executive and/or in congress, politicians in executive posts from states in a federation, and the Judiciary as the authorized interpreter of the legal order. The other side of this game is, of course, the proliferation of veto players.[9]

The technical complexities of monetary management and reform are enhanced by another factor. When hyperinflation occurs, it also generates a fiscal crisis of the state such that central banking requires a modicum of coordination between monetary and fiscal policies. The links between fiscal and monetary policies needed for stabilization in a hyperinflationary context are beyond the scope of this chapter. However, one point about this relationship is in order. A major constraint on the delegation of power to monetary authority is the often low level of understanding of technical issues and systemic policy consequences. Stated more positively, technical expertise among politicians within a democratic framework is a precondition for establishing a new monetary and regulatory financial system.[10] This is an ideal long-run condition, one more difficult to achieve in countries where uneven development – social, economic and political – is the rule. This problem is most critical in neo-democracies under hyperinflationary stress. The question can be posed as the following: which modes of political and institutional intermediation are required in order to bridge the gap between, on the one hand, technical knowledge and expertise concentrated in the hands of a given economic team and, on the other hand, the low level of understanding of politicians with mandates and whose fiat is indispensable?

Incentives to bridge this gap quickly may come from various sources. In cases where institutions are not sufficiently flexible and effective to secure legitimacy from political representation, the incentive to bridge the gap and help check hyperinflationary disruption may come directly from change in popular preferences. Such was the case in Brazil and other Latin American countries. This is why Bolivia in 1986, Argentina during 1991–92, and Brazil during 1993–94 share a common political denominator, despite their different party systems and stabilization programs.

In all three cases, the creation of a consensual economic strategy was dependent upon three conditions. The first condition was a shift in the preferences of society toward stabilization as a first order priority. This new criteria of legitimacy owes much to the effects of hyperinflation in the wake of a sequence of failed stabilization programs in new democracies. Above all, immediate economic welfare and democracy as a goal and value in its own right are decoupled. The second condition is related to the quality of leadership, in a very precise sense: the strategic decisions of politicians who coordinate economic stabilization with the economic team. An executive must have the political capacity to propose a technically sound stabilization program while also building a political coalition in response to new anti-inflationary social coalitions.[11] A third condition also relates to the quality of leadership. To bridge the gap between technocrats and politicians in a disrupted monetary order, one must delegate a high degree of autonomy to the economic team (and therefore to the monetary authority) while, at the same time, securing the support of Congress and state or provincial executives. This condition was satisfied in Brazil under Cardoso, in Argentina under Menem and, in particular, in Bolivia under Paz Estensoro.[12] In the case of Brazil, we can speak of a paradox by which, in the absence of an institutionalized fully autonomous power of the monetary authority, the Central Bank was granted the right to proceed as if it were 'independent' in the wake of the Mexican crisis of 1994–95. The de-politicization of the Central Bank was dependent upon a political decision – a delegation that also indicated the precarious statutory autonomy of the Brazilian monetary authority.

Finally, decentralization poses a crucial problem for countries, like Brazil, that faced the need to establish credible monetary authority by means of an initial reconcentration of power and authority in the hands of the central bank – while sustaining the constitutional status of a federation. Economic and political decentralization is often considered essential for viable democratic governance, through its beneficial effects upon accountability, transparency and public sector efficiency. The literature to date on decentralization, however, has not explicitly incorporated the question of monetary authority within its analysis.

Brazil and arguments in the literature

The prevailing wisdom concerning monetary authority is basically normative. It stipulates the independence of central banks from the political arena as a precondition for achieving durable price stability. In order to uphold the economy's long-term interest in price stability, monetary authority should be delegated to a central bank independent from the political arena and in particular from short-term electoral interests.[13] The well-known study by Alesina – which finds a positive correlation between independent central banks and price stability – is interpreted as evidence of causation.[14] Economic growth and price stability therefore rests on 'getting the institutions right'. While not dismissing the potentially large role political institutions have on policy outcomes, the Brazilian case qualifies the generalizability of arguments focusing on 'getting the institutions right'. This is because, as we demonstrate, conditions for creating an increasingly autonomous central bank have only recently been generated *because* of price stability, not the other way round.

There are positive lines of research that attempt to explain the conditions under which politicians delegate monetary authority to an independent central bank from both an international and national level of analysis. Sylvia Maxfield argues that politicians delegate monetary authority to an independent central bank as a way of signalling international creditors their commitment to a policy of price stability, in order to attract investment when international credit is tight.[15] International credibility is achieved through a policy of 'tying ones' hands' – by delegating monetary authority to central bankers. However, there is still a considerable amount of 'slack' at the domestic level which Maxfield's approach cannot account for, as her own country case study of Brazil suggests.

Brazil is a case that warrants the development of a domestic level hypothesis.[16] Dispersal of monetary authority – either dependent upon the federal executive,[17] or effectively divided between levels of government – has been the rule. It remained so throughout sustained periods of tight international credit and economic stagnation such as the 1980s and 1990s.

Domestic approaches to central bank independence have primarily been developed in the OECD context and can be divided in two categories: institutional and social preference explanations.[18] It is sufficient here to recall that institutional explanations generally presume that delegating authority to a central bank is costly.[19] Such delegation would be easier to achieve in countries where corporatist structures and practices prevail. Social preference explanations treat institutions as intervening variables and focus on the preferences of dominant groups that influence economic policy-making. Central bank autonomy is therefore most likely in countries where the financial sector is relatively strong.[20]

The argument we develop for the Brazilian case study adopts a domestic level of analysis that contains elements of both a social preference and institutional explanation. Our explanation, however, varies from the above orientations in a few significant ways. On the institutional side, we agree that policy change in polities with a large number of veto points is difficult,[21] but the Brazilian case indicates how the relative bargaining position of actors occupying those veto points can change over time. A strictly institutional orientation would not have the tools necessary to examine when such change is possible, and would be unable to explain the recent centralization of monetary authority in the Central Bank of Brazil.

In order to account for the dynamic element inherent in the politics of monetary authority, the analyst must turn to the relevant actors involved. Unlike the social-preference explanations previously cited, however, we do not assume the relevant actors influencing monetary policy will be the same across countries, nor that their relative bargaining positions will remain constant. In Brazil the relevant actors disputing control over monetary authority included the federal executive, state governments, and the private financial sector. After the 1988 Constitution was promulgated, Senate and the judiciary also became part of the bargaining game, and must be included as additional veto players. The achievement of greater monetary autonomy requires, therefore, multiple balancing acts on the part of the Executive. Other countries may have very different actors bargaining over monetary policy. Furthermore, in the case of Brazil, the stalemate over monetary authority and its eventual independence is diminishing because the end of inflation reduced the relative bargaining strength of the actors opposed to a centralization of monetary authority in the central bank.

The literature on decentralization has neglected the distinctive features of monetary management, the conditions for its effectiveness, and the special dilemmas it poses for democratic control. Furthermore, it fails to make a satisfactory analytical distinction between the political logic of decentralization and that of federalism in a democratic framework. In Brazil (and to a lesser degree in Argentina) states and municipalities played an active role in the passage from high inflation to hyperinflation within the context of democratization – a process inseparable from their claims for greater autonomy.

In what follows we are principally concerned with examining monetary authority from the standpoint of the relationship between the Central Bank of Brazil and state banks. This focus is justified on three counts. Democratic governance is first predicated upon coherent control by the incumbent government over the state apparatus.[22] Second, as we will see, the creation of quasi-money by state banks has had an obvious direct impact on the expansion of the monetary base. Finally, some private financial institutions that engaged in dubious practices and in systematic non-compliance with existing rules, such as the Banco Econômico in Bahia, Bamerindus in Paraná and Banco Nacional de Minas Gerais, enjoyed a quasi-monopoly in the local financial system. This explains their informal status as regional banks and their enormous bargaining power with regards the Central Bank.

An approach that does not make *a priori* assumptions about the identity of the relevant actors, nor about their relative bargaining strengths, can shed further light on the wide empirical variation in central banking models adopted. The question of 'autonomy from whom' leads thus to a preliminary task: identifying the shifts in social interests underlying the new trend toward central bank independence. This is vital if criteria such as transparency and accountability are to be included as necessary constraints to the exercise of 'effective monetary authority'.

Brazil's quest for embedded authority: the political game prior to, and after, the *real*

Brazil achieved a dramatic reversal of its hyperinflationary pressures in 1994–95 under the aegis of the Plano Real, initiated by Fernando Henrique Cardoso, the then finance minister. In a regional perspective Brazil can be considered a latecomer regarding price stabilization because of its numerous and unsuccessful heterodox shocks in 1986, 1987, 1989 and

1990. In 1992 the government resorted to orthodox monetary and fiscal short-run policies with only partial success. As in other similar countries, recent Brazilian economic stabilization brought about a dramatic change in perspectives. Price stability came to be considered as a first order public good, reflecting a clear change in social preferences and in the criteria for political legitimization – something unprecedented in contemporary Latin American history. The experience of hyperinflation and/or hyperinflationary crisis instigated a lowering of expectations concerning the economic welfare goals of democracy. All across the region, such changes inflicted a dramatic blow to economic populism. It became clear the populist policies *and* style of problem solving would not yield e*lectoral dividends as they had in the past.* This change in the political and economic climate holds true for economic structures, political regimes and systems of representations across countries as diverse as Peru, Bolivia, Argentina, Mexico and Brazil.

Why has Brazil been one of the slowest reformers? Although answering this question thoroughly is beyond the scope of this chapter, one must highlight its importance for two reasons. First, economic stabilization is an ongoing process. As a goal it is far from consolidated, for its continued success depends upon fiscal, social security, and administrative constitutional reforms that require congressional approval. Second, some of the political constraints to managing hyperinflation are still at work and have an important impact on the difficulty of establishing an embedded monetary and fiscal authority as a specific mode of political authority. In what follows we will be concerned with two kinds of constraints. The first is long-run, and refers to how monetary authority was handled under a national and federal perspective prior to the democratization of the 1980s. This discussion will provide the background necessary to address the main question of this section: how has exercise of monetary authority changed in the wake of economic stabilization?

In regional perspective, one of the distinctive features of Brazilian policy-making, in addition to an explicit inclination toward continuous growth at all costs, has been the difficulty of establishing a single monetary authority. From this standpoint, Brazil is also a latecomer. The establishment of a single monetary authority was politically viable only under the authoritarian regime. Moreover, except for a brief interlude of 1964–67, the Central Bank since its creation in 1964 has experienced very little autonomy. One could explain the history of the eight failed attempts at stabilization throughout the populist democracy (1945–64) in terms of the political constraint posed by the protracted dispute between two rival centres of monetary authority – each subjected to different political and economic pressures. Politicization of monetary management in that period therefore prevailed under the guise of the contradictory policies made possible by the existence of two monetary authorities: Banco do Brasil and Sumoc (Superintendencia da Moeda e de Credito).

The convoluted history of Brazilian central banking since 1964 provides a wealth of insights for political analysts concerned with explaining the contrast between economic programs and ideas on the one hand and the effective results of economic policy-making on the other. For, although the intentions and the rules laid down by the architects of Central Bank reform in 1964 were clearly stated in terms establishing a central bank autonomous from the political arena, such a proposal was easily defeated three years later under a military government committed to expansionist policies.[23] It was only in 1986, and subsequently in 1988 under the first civilian government, that two reforms were implemented to establish basic mechanisms for effective monetary management and a minimum degree of transparency in national accounting.[24]

The history of monetary authority in post-war Brazil therefore has less to do with the nature of the political regime than with a commitment to economic performance cast in terms of accelerated growth at all costs.[25] International liquidity, of course, played an important role from 1974–78, as Sylvia Maxfield argues. The decision taken by General Geisel in 1974, however, to prolong the period of accelerated growth and deepen import substitution *despite* the first oil shock (which required adjustments) was a domestic political option.[26] Brazil has become one of the slowest reformers for a second reason directly related to its dual monetary authority, which emerged in tandem with democratization. This dual monetary authority is intimately linked to the federal question and decentralization, for the governors acted as centrifugal forces that pressured for fiscal decentralization and used their state banks to issue 'quasi-money',[27] thus fiercely challenging the constitutional authority of the Central Bank. An important explanation for the ability of governors to use their state banks in such a manner, and thus undermine all stabilization plans undertaken by the new civilian regime (1986, 1987, 1989, 1990 and 1991), relates to the sequence by which democracy was restored.

By the time Brazilian civilian rule was re-established in 1985–86, the strategy of political devolution adopted by the military had been under way for almost ten years. For our purposes it is sufficient to emphasize two major aspects. First, devolution at the state level occurred prior to that at the federal level. Open gubernatorial elections were re-introduced first in 1982, with the opposition party (PMDB) electing a significant number of governors committed to democratization in the most economically and politically powerful states (São Paulo, Minas Gerais, Rio de Janeiro e Rio Grande do Sul). Second, the economic strategy adopted by the military government of Ernesto Geisel (1974–78) led to a process of accelerated economic decentralization at an early stage of political liberalization. Geisel's plan radically changed the previous pattern of industrialization that focused on the already industrialized southeast.

This sequence is critical to understanding the manner in which the political drive for autonomy at the state-level translated into a centrifugal pull. Economic, and eventually democratic, devolution at the state level prior to liberalization at the federal level[28] helps explain the difficulties later faced by the federal executive in exercising a coordinated authority and implementing a strategy with the consent of governors. A political economy of federalism should take into account such a political and economic sequencing.[29]

This type of political constraint is essential to explaining the difficulty of all subsequent civilian governments in building a governing coalition. For it was this sequence that set the stage for a second type of political constraint to economic policy-making and stabilization: the new constitution promulgated in 1988. The new constitution transferred a fixed percentage of federal taxes to states and municipalities without a concurrent transfer of spending responsibilities and represents the culmination of a process of fiscal decentralization initiated in 1974. Such a constitutionally determined fiscal allocation imposes an important constraint upon economic management and the crafting of social policies.

The ability of local banks to create quasi-money through their administration of state government fiscal deficits – either through issuing state bonds or providing direct loans – has had two important consequences. First, state banks became a favourite mechanism of state governors to evade elementary requirements of transparency and accountability established by monetary and fiscal authorities at the federal level. Second, this implied a deliberate challenge to the constitutionally established monopoly over money creation at the federal level. In other words, the disruption of the monetary order in democratic Brazil since the early 1980s was closely related to the operation of centrifugal intergovernmental forces that effectively created rival centres of monetary power between levels of government. This was part and parcel of the dramatic loss of both monetary and fiscal authority, which is inseparable from hyperinflation – a process leading to the absence of any monetary and fiscal regime. In effect, Brazil's monetary disorder can be characterized as a monetary tragedy of the commons. While state governments had individual interests in using their state banks as effective creators of money in order to finance their budget deficits, one could argue the collective good of price stability was jeopardized – which is a federal, not state responsibility.

That is why when examining the extreme case of Brazil it is possible to speak of a monetary and fiscal rebellion as a process inseparable from hyperinflation.[30] The complex bargaining act required for self-sustaining economic stabilization in such a neo-democracy places additional strains on the political leadership, for it constitutes a permanent trade-off between two goals. On the one hand there is the need to check and to bring under permanent control centrifugal forces which deny central monetary authority – a need which must be first turned into a political goal by federal leaders. On the other hand the executive is faced with the need to build a consensual economic and political strategy to reshape the political order in accordance with federalist principles. The study of decentralization, at least in the Brazilian case, must incorporate the question of a coherent monetary authority as an essential requisite for the viability of a new federalist pact – in addition to reconciling decentralization with the objectives of democratic governance: accountability, transparency, a predictable rule of law, and public sector efficiency.

Monetary authority has been increasingly centralized in the central bank because the federal executive increased its bargaining power over governors following the implementation of the 1994 Real stabilization plan. The federal executive was able to centralize monetary authority in the central bank for both political and economic reasons. On the political end, both the interests and bargaining power of the federal executive changed. Not only did Cardoso's administration have an unprecedented interest in sustaining the stabilization plan, but the executive gained leverage over the legislature, and therefore over governors, due to coinciding presidential, legislative and state-wide elections in 1994. On the economic end the federal government increased its bargaining power over governors because the end of inflation substantially weakened state government finances, thus making governors dependent upon a federal bailout. Cardoso took advantage of both of these political and economic factors to condition a federal bailout upon a centralization of monetary authority in the central bank.[31]

The federal executive is the branch of government usually held electorally accountable for maintaining macroeconomic stability, therefore any federal executive would have an interest in maintaining a stabilization program. The government of Cardoso, however, differed from previous administrations in the extent of its interest in upholding a stabilization program. Fernando Henrique launched and won his bid for the presidency almost entirely based upon his role as crafting the Real stabilization program as finance minister under the outgoing Itamar Franco administration (1993–94). Whereas previous presidents could craft a stabilization program after being elected, have it fail, and still have time for a second attempt, Cardoso did not have that option because he won the presidency on a specific stabilization program – the Real Plan. His political career and reelection in 1998 were dependent upon the continued success of the real.

In addition to an unparalleled interest in sustaining the current stabilization program, the executive branch gained added leverage over the legislature and governors through the wedded presidential, legislative, and state elections of November 1994.[32] For the first time in Brazil's recent democracy, legislative and gubernatorial candidates had the potential of riding presidential coat-tails. Indeed, the successful presidential bid of Fernando Henrique Cardoso (PSDB) appears to have influenced both the legislative and gubernatorial elections.[33]

The unparalleled interest in sustaining a stabilization plan combined with a wedded election in 1994, however, did not constitute sufficient causes for a successful centralization of monetary authority. The economic impact the end of inflation had upon state government finances was also essential to this process. State governments had been running fiscal deficits for quite some time before 1994. The end of inflation, however, made those deficits unsustainable. The Real stabilization plan squeezed state finances through both a monetary and fiscal mechanism. On the monetary end state governments could no longer use the large 'floating' revenue of state banks, and on the fiscal end states could no longer use inflation to corrode real spending on items like public wages and were obligated to disburse significantly higher debt payments because of the higher interest rates.

High inflation generates winners and losers. A clear winner under high inflation in Brazil was the financial sector. Each year between 1990 and 1993, the banking sector (both public and private) generated inflationary revenue to the sum of four percent of the country's GDP – with public banks appropriating roughly two thirds of the total.[34] In fact, floating revenue became a principal reason for preventing many state banks from entering complete bankruptcy during much of the 1980s and early 1990s. While most of their credit operations (assets) were directed to the public sector in the form of long-term financing, their liabilities derived primarily from short-term deposits, or bank bonds (CDBs, etc.). Without the floating revenue, state banks faced increasing difficulties in meeting their cash requirements. When a bank does not balance its account by the end of the business day, it has two options: either to borrow the money over the 'inter-bank market' (mercado inter-bancario) at a hefty interest rate, or resort to the Central Bank's discount line (linha de redesconto). By the end of 1994, the private market was no longer accepting state bank CDBs or RDBs (bank bonds), and thus prominent state banks like Banespa and Banerj (who make up 60 percent of the financial sector) repeatedly turned to the Central Bank – providing the impetus for the Central Bank's subsequent intervention in their operations. In sum, without inflation revenue many state banks became insolvent, thus inducing central bank intervention. This placed a pinch upon state finances because state banks were essentially the managers of state government debt, and through that role subsidized state finances.

The end of inflation further deteriorated state governments' finances in two ways. First, states could no longer keep budgetary costs down by using inflation as a means to corrode away real spending on items like public payroll.[35] As a result, public payroll consumed an increasing percentage share of state budgets. Second, the end of inflation had the effect of dramatically increasing debt obligations. Much like the stabilization program in Argentina, the Real Plan was based upon a stabilization of the currency through the exchange rate. Such a stabilization plan forces the government to maintain a high interest rate in order to attract foreign capital, which consequently had the effect of increasing debt payments by state and municipal governments. State level debt mushroomed at an astonishing rate after the stabilization program was implemented. Note that the dramatic increase derives from the two categories of debt whose interest rates are not fixed; bonds and debt owed to state banks.

Before proceeding, however, two qualifications are in order. First, we do not argue the end of inflation caused the fiscal crisis many state governments are currently experiencing. The first boom of state borrowing began in the 1970s under the military government's developmental project, and during the 1980s state governments were able to roll over that debt, and contract new debt through their state banks. Rather than create the fiscal crisis, the end of inflation eliminated the mechanisms that sustained chronic state government fiscal imbalances. Second, it is important to note that the bargaining position of state governments began to weaken prior to the imposition of the real. State and municipal governments began a process of debt rescheduling during the early 1990s, and both the Senate and the Central Bank imposed more stringent limits on the ability of subnational governments to contract new debt. With each new round of state debt crisis during the 1980s and 1990s, the federal government and Central Bank gained incremental leverage over state government finances. Following the state bank crisis of 1987, for example, the Central Bank, through Decree Law 2321, gained the ability to assume temporary control over insolvent state banks. The same decree law further established more stringent rules regarding the judicial accountability of state administrators for improper banking practices. While state banks placed under federal intervention in 1987 were eventually returned to their respective state governments with no significant judicial action taken against their managers, the Central Bank gained a new tool to discipline state banks. The next round of state government financial crisis during the early 1990s placed further limits on state banks and state government finances. In 1990 the National Monetary Council imposed more stringent limits on state bank loans to the public sector,[36] and in 1992 the judicial accountability rules for public administrators in state enterprises were further tightened.[37] In addition to imposing more restrictions on the state banks, the Senate, as the branch of government responsible for setting legal debt limits for states and municipalities, further limited the ability of subnational governments to contract new debt.[38]

Thus the end of inflation in 1994 did not initiate the process through which the federal government exerted greater control over state finances – either through central bank discipline over state banks or through legislative restrictions over the permissible level of state debt. The ability of the central bank to exert discipline over state banks must be viewed as an incremental process beginning in the early 1980s that was tightened with each successive state-banking crisis. These periodic crises were induced both by the political use of such banks at the time of elections and by the various, and inevitably failed, stabilization programs which temporarily ended inflation. Each state-banking crisis has coincided with the electoral calendar (1982, 1986, and 1990) and stabilization plans (1986, 1989–90).

We argue, however, that the crisis of state banks induced by the end of inflation in 1994 differs from the previous state banking crises on two and potentially three fronts. First, as we demonstrated, the executive branch had an unparalleled interest in disciplining state banks in order to sustain the stabilization program, and second, the Real Plan has so far proven a much more sustainable stabilization plan than its predecessors. Third, the central bank had more tools at its disposal to discipline state banks in 1994 in part because of the periodic state banking crises described above. The federal government therefore took advantage of both political and economic factors that weakened the bargaining position of state governors in order to, in addition to other measures, condition a federal bailout on a centralization of monetary authority in the Central Bank.

The evaluation by the federal government that disciplining state-level financial institutions was a necessary component to making the Real Plan work was made evident by declarations of members of Cardoso's economic team soon after his electoral victory in November of 1994.[39] The government didn't lose any time. On 31 December 1994, the last day of the presiding state government administrations, the Central Bank intervened in the two largest state banks belonging, respectively, to the states of São Paulo and Rio de Janeiro: Banespa and Banerj. In addition to infusing 'national' elements into a predominant local and regional congressional election, Fernando Henrique Cardoso further took advantage of a concurrent turnover of state and federal governments.[40] By intervening on the exact date of turnover the outgoing governor was not able to mobilize his political allies against the intervention, and the incoming governor didn't have as large of an incentive. The incoming governor wouldn't be directly accountable for the intervention, and more importantly, the governor might have a financially healthy bank returned to the state halfway through the term.[41] While legislators from São Paulo and Rio fought against the stated aims of the Central Bank to eventually privatize both banks, initial opposition to the intervention might have been greater if it had taken place in the middle of a gubernatorial term.

Once the Central Bank had concluded its intervention in Banespa and Banerj, the government used all tools at its disposal to increase the effective threat of privatization – especially through slowly opening the financial market to foreign competition.[42] With new foreign competitors looking to establish themselves in the Brazilian market, new buyers made the privatization threat much more credible. In sum, the political game between the executive, legislators, and governors has substantially altered during the 1990s.

Evidence of increased central bank discipline over the monetary system

The federal government was able to condition a bailout of state finances upon a centralization of monetary authority in the central bank through two mechanisms: the rescheduling of state debt, and Central Bank bailouts of state banks. While the former is also a prerogative of the Senate, the latter is exclusively a prerogative of the Central Bank.[43] Unlike previous federal bailouts of state finances, central bank interventions and state debt rescheduling under the Cardoso government demanded greater counter-measures to control state governments. In terms of monetary authority, states have been forced to strictly adhere to existing central bank resolutions, and more importantly, to privatize or transform their state banks into development agencies. Central Bank discipline over the financial sector, however, was not limited to state government-owned financial institutions, as the rescue of private banks has been conditioned on similar measures.

As the previous sections demonstrated, Central Bank intervention in state banks was not a novelty of the 1990s. State bank crisis, and subsequent central bank rescue, coincided with Brazil's electoral calendar and its stabilization programs prior to the 1990s.[44] The central bank attempted to impose restrictions on such crises recurring, but such measures either lacked the appropriate scope or were simply ignored. At the extreme, state non-compliance with central bank resolutions took the form of blatant public defiance. In 1993, for example, a state bank from Brazil's northeast region opened six new agencies without the requisite prior approval of the Central Bank. The state bank's president was called to Brasília, and verbally sanctioned for his actions. Following the meeting the bank opened another six agencies, upon which the governor stated to a Central Bank director, "The bank is mine, and I do what I want."[45]

As the example above indicates, much of the history of Central Bank–state bank relations has been one of successive non-compliance with Central Bank regulations. The state-banking sector experienced periodic crises coinciding with Brazil's electoral calendar and economic stabilization plans. In each instance, the Central Bank provided financial relief to state banks in return for administrative and banking practice reforms that were subsequently not met. During the early 1980s the Central Bank provided conditional financial relief to state banks through two programs: the PAC (Programa de Apoio Creditício) in 1983 and PROREF (Programa de Recuperação Econômica e Financeira) in 1984.[46] Both programs conditioned financial assistance on a series of measures to reduce operating expenses, close loss-making agencies, and oblige states to recapitalize their banks. Most conditions went unheeded, as in subsequent attempts to assert monetary discipline during the banking crisis of 1986–87 and in the early 1990s.[47]

One must be careful, however, in ascribing the periodic state banking crises to mere non-compliance with sound banking regulations. Journalists and financial analysts alike often cite the high allocation of state bank credit to state governments as a direct challenge to Brazil's 1964 banking legislation, which capped the credit operations of all banking institutions to their respective controllers at ten percent.[48] Despite the fact that such limits were increased to thirty percent in the 1980s, by the late 1980s, state banks would often direct up to sixty, or even eighty, percent of their credit operations to their respective state governments. State banks were able to surpass such limits upon approval of credit operations by the Central Bank and National Monetary Council under the rubric of 'extra-limit debt'.[49]

The interventions in state banks under Cardoso differed from those of the 1980s and early 1990s on two important counts. The first pertains to adherence to Central Bank regulations. While the Central Bank began to tighten the ability of state banks to loan to their controllers (the governors) during the early 1990s, the Real Plan further tightened the controls over state banking practices. The National Monetary Council re-established limits on new loans to the public sector, including the carrying of state bonds (Resolution 1990 of 30 June 1994); prohibited the Central Bank or Treasury from intervening in state banks for the sole purpose of recapitalizing their balance sheets (Resolution 1995 of 30 June 1994); and further increased the judicial accountability of state bank administrators.

Second, and more importantly, full federal rescue has been conditioned on either an eventual privatization or transformation of the bank into a development agency (Provisional Measure 1.514). In order for the federal government to refinance the entire portion of state debt owed to the respective state bank, the state government should agree to privatize, liquidate, or transform the institution into a development agency. State governments could retain control over their banks if they were willing to accept a federal restructuring of only half their debt to the state banks. Given the acute stage of the crisis, however, the later alternative often wasn't an option.[50] In sum, the bargaining game between the federal executive, governors and the legislature shifted. While the federal government began the slow process of controlling state finances and state banks during the early 1990s, the Real Plan added great impetus to this process.

The politics of financial reform and the quality of democracy

The financial crisis in emerging markets in 1997–99 generated a growing debate within academic and policymaking circles over the benefits generated by the liberalization of international capital flows.[51] Currency crashes and the resulting capital outflows in emerging markets in Asia, Russia and Latin America have demonstrated the extent to which capital markets in emerging markets are interconnected and at serious risk from 'contagion'. The impact of contagion within emerging markets, however, has also demonstrated an equally important phenomenon: the economic repercussions of currency runs and capital outflows have varied greatly across countries.

In this section we examine two questions. What explains the comparative resilience of Brazil's economy to dramatic currency devaluation in 1999, under conditions that generated greater economic hardship in other countries? Policy analysts have increasingly come to answer that question through examining the respective country's financial sector. During the years 1997–99, currency devaluations in Thailand, Korea and Indonesia sparked a domestic economic crisis because financial markets in those countries were characterized by poorly capitalized banks with large portfolios of questionable loans, and unclear financial reporting of foreign liabilities.[52] We show that Brazil's financial sector proved much more resilient because it had already implemented a series of reforms of its banking sector that reduced the leverage of its domestic financial institutions. Such reforms were carried out during Cardoso's administration under the aegis of the Central Bank and illustrate the beneficial effects of the gradual recovery of its authority, analysed in the previous section. We argue that this was a necessary (although not sufficient) condition that explains Brazil's quick recovery: the rate of growth was positive, 0.8 percent and 4.4 percent in 1999 and 2000 respectively, and the rate of inflation was 8.5 percent. This contrasted with the predictions of analysts familiar with the East Asian and Russian experiences, which forecast a 4 percent decline in GDP and an acceleration of inflation by 50 percent.

The second question is related to the first: do integrated financial markets and decreased manoeuvrability by monetary authorities lead to a loss in the quality of democratic accountability? While such a question is relevant for any democracy, it is particularly pertinent to democracies which have not yet fully consolidated their institutions, and who are potentially much more dependent upon the international financial market. Not only are democratic controls more precarious, but also the potential responsiveness of domestic monetary authorities to international pressures is also greater. While analysts have increasingly focused upon the economic benefits and potential perils of integration, a question that merits attention is the extent to which increasingly integrated financial markets may affect the quality of democracy.

In this section we attempt to demonstrate how increased financial integration in developing countries can, in certain conditions, increase the quality of democratic accountability in domestic monetary authorities. We support this claim with a brief case study of a series of allegations of improper conduct directed against Brazil's Central Bank during the 1999 devaluation of the real. Through an analysis of the events surrounding these allegations, and the subsequent reactions of the federal executive, we show how the substantial amount of economic discretion held by monetary authorities has become more of a political burden than benefit for the government. As a result, Brazil's monetary authorities have increased the transparency of their decision-making procedures – a necessary condition for the exertion of democratic control. Such a reaction, however, was only possible in the context of an increasingly integrated financial market.[53]

Central bank reform and the moral hazard problem in Brazil

In January 1999 the Brazilian government abandoned its currency peg for the real and allowed the currency to float against the US dollar, in response, at least in part, to the pressures caused by the Russian economic meltdown and a political crisis at home.[54] While similar devaluations in Korea, Thailand, Russia and Indonesia sparked a wave of bank foreclosures and subsequent bankruptcies in the 'real' economy, the Brazilian devaluation caused economic crisis far less than many expected in January 1999: recovery began three months later. Predictions by analysts in January 1999 that a devaluation of the real would lead, once again, to high-inflation, increased unemployment, and large-scale capital flight were proved wrong. In part, Brazil's financial sector was much less prone to the 'moral hazard' problem facing financial institutions than its Asian counterparts. Not coincidentally, many of the owners of Asian financial institutions had close connections to the government and engaged in such highly leveraged operations precisely because they had the implicit safety net of an eventual government bailout. The Brazilian government, however, had already significantly reduced the moral hazard problem facing its financial sector through a series of bank-bailout packages in 1995 and 1997, which conditioned private and public sector bank bailouts upon a series of banking reforms.

In contrast to economic analysts who treat the moral hazard problem in financial sectors as a technical problem amenable to correct institutional incentives, this section begins from the premise that correcting such deficiencies is essentially a political problem. The implicit assumption is that the government will bailout financial institutions in distress often stems from perceptions of the political coalition supporting the government. Creating institutional incentives to regulate a financial sector and reduce the moral hazard problem, therefore, also entails a political problem of generating a new coalition to sustain the government. The Cardoso administration was able to reduce the moral hazard problem in the financial sector only by changing political relationships with two important actors: the private financial sector and state governors. The ability of the government to eliminate the implicit assumption of an eventual Central Bank bailout for public and private commercial banks was made possible by new series of conditions, especially the end of hyperinflation under the Real Plan that reduced the government's dependence upon these two political actors. The next section discusses further the nature of moral hazard in the financial sector and illustrates how these problems are as much political as institutional. We follow by summarizing our main hypothesis, namely: overcoming the moral hazard problem required the enactment of a series of reforms which ran contrary to the interests of governors and the private financial sector. Such reforms required the correct political conditions for the federal executive to assume high political costs.

Financial sector reform and the moral hazard problem

The importance of financial sector reform in the context of international financial deregulation has been increasingly acknowledged in policy and academic circles as essential to mitigating the negative economic repercussions of currency speculations.[55] One of the primary objectives of financial sector reform is to reduce the moral hazard problem among financial agents, that is, to introduce conditions in which borrowers have an incentive to take risks aimed at capturing potential gains under good conditions, while not losing more than the capital they have invested if conditions turn bad. In the banking sector, moral hazard arises when a bank has an incentive to undertake risky credit operations because it assumes that if the operation turns sour bank owners would lose *only* the capital initially invested. If such a perception is widespread, and financial institutions subsequently become highly leveraged, then the chances of systemic financial crisis like those in East Asia greatly increase.

One important cause of this problem stems from the perception amongst financial agents that the government will act as a lender of last resort if the institution runs into trouble. Such an implicit guarantee from governments, which arises either because the financial institution is 'too big to fail' or because it is too important politically, gives financial agents the incentive to engage in more profitable and risky credit operations. If the costs of an eventual bankruptcy are distributed amongst taxpayers at large, while the benefits accrue to the financial agent, banks averting such behaviour would be receiving the 'sucker's payoff'. Moral hazard in the financial sector therefore stems from the generalized belief that governments will bail out bank owners: This assumption makes risky credit operations worthwhile.[56]

The most straightforward solution to this problem is for governments to credibly commit not to conduct bailouts, thus persuading bank owners to avert irresponsible practices. Due to the large social and political costs of not bailing out banks, however, such a commitment is often difficult to enforce. Analysts thus agree that in order to prevent such a problem, financial regulation should develop a sound *ex-ante safety net* to reduce risks associated with moral hazard that can produce systemic crises. The literature on banking safety nets usually stresses three components: capital, monitoring, and closure.[57] Capital simply refers to assets set against liabilities and represents the interest of firm ownership. The more capital bank owners invest in their institutions, the greater their interest in monitoring that bank managers avert excessive risks. While regulations that stipulate large capital ratios tend to reduce the systemic risks associated with moral hazard, 'too much' capital can increase lending rates and impede financial deepening.

The other two components, monitoring and closure, are less straightforward and involve a number of potential regulatory measures. Monitoring refers to ongoing oversight by the Central Bank to ensure that banks maintain sound financial practices. Central bank resolutions thereby seek to foster adequate capitalization of banks, restrict insider lending, and ensure appropriate rules for asset classification and provisions against bad loans. Appropriate regulations, however, should be accompanied by assessment of financial management – a difficult task that requires competent personnel in central bank auditing teams. The third component, closure, also refers to central bank regulations but is specific to rules governing the mechanisms whereby central banks act as a lender of last resort in case of financial distress. Again, to ameliorate moral hazard it becomes necessary to design rules for closure with consistent bank-failure resolutions, intervention rules, and prompt corrective action for banks that receive assistance.

The literature on ex-ante safety nets is based on the assumption that overcoming the moral hazard problem is essentially a 'technical' problem requiring an institutional fix. We argue instead that implementing such reforms entails political costs that are often more important than developing personnel in central banks capable of monitoring financial institutions. The reason is simple: A well-designed ex-ante safety net imposes significant costs upon powerful political actors.[58]

Certain financial systems may be more prone to moral hazard problems. A key distinction is made between 'repressed' and 'deep' financial systems.[59] In contrast to the deep financial systems found in industrialized economies with well-developed capital markets, 'repressed' financial systems are those characterized by active government intervention and severe distortions in resource allocation. In Latin America, 'repressed' financial systems emerged during import substitution industrialization in response to the economic crisis of the 1930s. The allocation of credit was often dominated by governmental institutions, and even in the private sector, the government played a critical role in the regulation of savings and banking practices. Under these conditions, banks rarely failed, for a good portion of banks' portfolio assets were held as central bank reserves, treasury bonds, and low-risk credit to protected import substituting firms.[60]

The moral hazard problem surfaces only in financial systems that are in transition away from financial repression, i.e. when the government role in credit allocation declines. Most Latin America governments embarked upon a reduction in this role during the 1980s and 1990s. From a political standpoint, the timing of transitions away from financial repression could not be more pertinent. Central banks have faced the difficult task of implementing sound ex-ante safety nets precisely as countries throughout Latin America were also in transition from military to democratic rule.

The politics of reducing moral hazard in Brazil

Brazil's financial sector was characterized by severe moral hazard problems for much of the 1980s and early 1990s. Both public and private commercial banks operated under the (correct) assumption that the Central Bank of Brazil would act as a lender of last resort if they became insolvent, an assumption that was most blatant in the case of state government banks. Throughout the 1980s governors used state commercial banks to indirectly finance budget deficits,[61] and with each state banking crisis (which coincided with the electoral cycle) the central bank enacted a bailout package that, eventually, returned the failed bank to its respective state government.[62] These crises also coincided with the various stabilization programs adopted over the last two decades – given that the end of inflationary revenue (however temporary) unmasked bad banking practices, as we will see later. The Central Bank attempted to impose restrictions, but such measures either lacked the adequate scope or were simply ignored. With regard to the private financial sector the moral hazard problem was not as blatant but, as discussed below, private commercial banks were also privileged by Central Bank policies in spite of questionable banking practices.

But with the implementation of the Real Plan in 1994 and the end of hyperinflation, the Central Bank of Brazil took a number of initiatives with the explicit objective of eliminating the 'moral hazard' problem. Most of these initiatives sought to implement international banking standards adopted by the Basel Accord. In other words, the Central Bank attempted to create incentives which would prevent banking institutions from engaging in high risk credit operations which were implicitly premised upon an eventual government bailout. Such measures not only addressed rules on the closure of financial institutions, but also the two other types of measures which constitute a well developed ex-ante safety net: capital and monitoring. Again, the obstacles faced by the government were more political than institutional. In addition to the administrative difficulties of creating an adequate ex-ante safety net, the government had to be willing to incur significant political costs by distancing itself from two important political actors, governors and the private financial sector. How was this possible? In the next section, we argue that Cardoso administration was able to do so through a combination of economic and political factors that coincided after the end of hyperinflation in 1994–95. Strategic decisions by politicians in government and the correct diagnosis of problems by the economic team were critical.

The private financial sector and governors: privileged coalition partners

The emergence of the moral hazard problem during the 1980s was also due to politics rather than institutional reasons. Both governors and the private financial sector assumed that the Central Bank would provide bailouts precisely because they exerted significant influence over the political decision-making process. The influence of the private financial sector on monetary policy in Brazil increased throughout the period of military rule, especially after the Costa e Silva administration (1967–69). This is best illustrated by the composition of National Monetary Council (CMN), the board responsible for conducting monetary policy, and the country's newly created Central Bank. Under the aegis of Finance Minister Delfim Neto, the National Monetary Council increased its membership to include members from the private industrial and financial sectors. In other words, the military government established an explicit policy to include the private financial sector in the decision-making apparatus for monetary policy.[63] This became a crucial decision-making arena where negotiations between private interests and the government took place. The government accepted this arrangement because it needed funds, and in exchange it gave power to the banking system and encouraged the development of the conglomerate system. With the transition to democracy in the 1980s, the relative influence of the private financial sector did not diminish. The devolution of policy to state governments prior to liberalization at the federal level helps explain the difficulties faced later by the federal executive in exercising coordinated authority and building support from governors. Governors and privileged banks correctly assumed that the Central Bank would act as a lender of last resort in case of financial distress.

The relative decline of private finance and governors

The ability of the Central Bank to initiate reform to reduce moral hazard was due to the increased bargaining power of the federal executive over governors and the private financial sector. The unprecedented interest and leverage of Cardoso's government to implement reform, and the holding of concomitant presidential, legislative, and state elections in 1994 and 1998, were behind this increased bargaining power. Interest in sustaining stabilization and concomitant elections, however, explains neither the extent of centralization of monetary authority in the Central Bank nor financial sector reform: The impact of the end of high inflation on banks (state and private) and state government finances was also critical. As emphasized above, the end of high inflation made these deficits unsustainable. Floating revenue from inflation became the principal reason for preventing state and private banks from entering bankruptcy during much of the 1980s and early 1990s. The end of inflation unmasked difficulties to meet cash requirements.

The strategic calculation that disciplining state-level financial institutions would make the Real Plan work was evident early in the Cardoso administration. As shown in the previous section, on 31 December 1994, the last day in power of exiting state governments, the Central Bank intervened in two of the largest state banks in São Paulo and Rio de Janeiro: Banespa and Banerj. It is important to stress that the incoming governors of São Paulo, and of Rio de Janeiro belonged to the same political party as the president (PSDB).[64] The timing of the intervention was strategic: Because legislators from São Paulo and Rio opposed indications of the Central Bank to eventually privatize both banks, opposition would have been greater if attempted during the middle of gubernatorial mandates. The government used all the tools at its disposal to increase the effective threat of privatization after intervention. The gradual opening of the domestic financial market to foreign competition was a critical strategy employed by the government to create more efficient banking practices in both public and private banks. Foreign bank participation within Brazil's national financial system increased from 10 percent to nearly 25 percent between 1994 and 1999 – a policy that was vociferously criticized by members of Brazil's private financial sector, and by the major opposition party, the PT.

In sum, the political game between the executive, legislators, and governors changed substantially during the 1990s. The end of high inflation made the precarious state and private commercial banks dependent on federal financial rescue. Sub-national and private financial dependence on federal rescue, however, was combined with a marked interest on behalf of the president to preserve the Real Plan and strengthen the federal executive. Since discipline over the monetary system is a precondition for controlling inflation, President Cardoso conditioned federal rescue of state and private commercial banks to both the centralization of monetary authority in the Central Bank and financial sector reforms designed to reduce the moral hazard problem. In the next section explores evidence of this process and the extent to which it countered the interests of powerful political actors, governors and the private sector, most of whom were part and parcel of the governmental coalition.

The last bailout?

The process of creating an ex-ante safety net in Brazil began with the bailout packages designed by the Central Bank for private banks and state government banks: PROER (Programa de Estímulo à Reestruturação e ao Fortalecimento do Sistema Financeiro National) and PROES (Programa de Incentivo à Redução do Setor Público Estadual na Atividade Bancária). Both bailout packages differed significantly from previous rescue operations by the Central Bank because they imposed much more severe punishment upon majority shareholders, private financiers,[65] and governors.

The private banking sector did not exhibit the blatant moral hazard problem found in the state government commercial banking during the 1980s. However, private banks nevertheless operated under the assumption that government bailouts would be lenient. In part due to the consolidation of a 'repressed financial system', the banking sector experienced few problems during the 1970s. The private sector and markets widely believed that a few banks fit under the category of 'too big to fail', and if faced with financial distress, they would receive assistance from the Central Bank as lender of last resort. In addition, the political strength of financial institutions and owners increased under Resolution n. 1.524/88 that created the institution of the Multiple Bank.[66] As Multiple Banks, many non-bank financial institutions were able to transform themselves into banks and reap benefits from a high inflation economy. This process greatly increased the number of banking institutions and made Central Bank supervision more difficult. In other words, monetary authorities facilitated the appropriation of inflationary revenue within the private sector. The moral hazard problem was therefore latent within the national financial system during the early 1990s, and became evident to the extent there was a greater opening of the financial system beginning in the mid 1990s.

A high inflation economy generates "... profits from non-remunerated liabilities, like cash deposits and revenue in transit, which act to compensate and mask administrative inefficiencies and the concession of risky credit operations".[67] The 'inflationary float' therefore permitted banks to present consecutive healthy balance sheets and good profits. Banks lived in the 'best of both worlds'; large gains combined with inefficient banking oversight by monetary authorities. The moral hazard problem, however, was most blatant and emerged as part and parcel of the democratic transition. Gustavo Loyola – former Central Bank governor – asserts that this dynamic began with the re-introduction of gubernatorial elections in 1982.[68] Despite the fact the Central Bank acted in some instances as a complacent partner with state governments, the political weight held by governors within Brazil's transition to democracy clearly played a tremendous role in preventing any attempt by monetary authorities to eliminate the moral hazard problem within state commercial banks.[69]

Despite the intervention by the Central Bank in many state banks during the 1980s, the political conditions that created moral hazard in the sector continued.[70] Rather than liquidate bankrupt state commercial banks, the Central Bank would give them back to their majority shareholders (state governments) after assuming many of the costs associated with 'cleaning up' assets of dubious value. In sum, a critical component to the moral hazard relationship between the Central Bank and state banking institutions was how such a relationship jeopardized the Central Bank's control over the money supply. By not being able to meet their balance sheet obligations at the end of each business day, state banking institutions were forced to recur to the Central Bank's rediscount line – violating basic banking practices. Such practices were chronic because the political weight of governors led the Central Bank in one form or another to assume state commercial banking debts through their use of rediscount lines. In other words, state government fiscal deficits were transferred to the federal government through state banks, with the Central Bank compensating for this indirect expansion of the monetary base by emitting new Treasury bills.[71] The end of mega-inflation with the advent of the Real Plan in 1994 induced a banking crisis primarily because it brought an abrupt end to the inflationary revenue. With the end of inflationary revenue (20 percent of total revenue in 1994), banking institutions went into crisis. As a result the financial sector's share of GNP dropped from 15.61 percent in 1993 to only 4.7 percent in 1996.

With the implementation of the new economic plan, a number of small private and large public financial institutions suffered intervention and extra-judicial liquidation. Nonetheless, it was the intervention in Banco Econômico in August of 1995 (the 22nd intervention of a financial institution since the Real Plan began), which caused the greatest controversy. The bank was ranked 10th according to total assets in the Brazilian financial system, had 800,000 clients, and further had as president Ângelo Calmon de Sá – a former minister under President João Figueiredo and associate of Senator Antonio Carlos Magalhães, who at the time was the party leader of the PFL (alliance partner of the President's PSDB). Banco Econômico's economic difficulties therefore constituted a classic case of the moral hazard problem, given the bank owner's strong political connections, its size and regional weight – a typical financial institution 'too big to fail'.[72]

The sharp downsizing of the National Monetary Council was also instrumental for eliminating the strong influence of the private sector. The council was reduced to three members: the ministers of finance and of planning, and the president of the Central Bank. With the intervention in Banco Econômico, pressure within Congress grew to provide a rapid solution to the intervention that would not impose significant costs either to the bank's clients or to the state of Bahia. Anger from Bahian legislators intensified after a leak to the press from directors of the Central Bank indicating how the bank acted to finance electoral campaigns of many politicians – information derived from a controversial 'pink folder'[73] – which led Senator Antonio Carlos Magalhães of Bahia to label Central Bank directors "criminals". The bank ended up being sold to the Spanish group Banco Bilbao Vizcaya Argentaria.

In October 1995 the market began to suspect troubles with another private bank of significant size, Banco Nacional. The press pointed out that, "when the Banco Econômico agonized, Nacional's position in the inter-bank market was exactly the same. While solid banks like Bradesco and Itaú had less than 10 percent of inter-bank deposits, both banks held close to 50%."[74] Both because of its size and political connections, the bank also easily fit into the 'too big to fail' category.[75] A systemic threat to the financial system became a real possibility, and as a result the government launched the PROER bailout package to private banking institutions. Provisional Measure n. 1.179 and Resolution n. 2.208 of 3 November 1995 created the instrument to provide assistance to private banks, yet this line of assistance differed from previous bailout packages in one important manner: the distressed banks were required to merge with another bank in sound financial condition, as determined by the Central Bank. The PROER offered some advantages to the institutions that bought the distressed banks, but the package was conditioned upon a re-regulation of the private banking sector that had the objective of eliminating systemic risk. At the time the program was strongly denounced by the major opposition party in Congress, the PT, and in the media as "a device to protect and favour bankers" – an image which was quite irresponsibly conveyed to the population, and reiterated often during the electoral campaigns of 1998 and 2002.[76] We want to make clear, however, that while on the one hand the costs to the program were relatively high and prevented the failing of many banks, on the other hand this program had the important characteristic of changing the ownership of the distressed banks. Provisional Measure n. 1.182 of 17 November 1995 further created the legal apparatus necessary to enable monetary authorities to discipline the financial system.[77]

The PROER bailout package differed from previous rescue efforts enacted in the past because of its clear intent to reduce the moral hazard problem. The first evidence that such a concern prevailed is that none of the majority shareholders of the banks under distress were able to maintain control over their banks. Second, there was a weak correlation between political connections and adhesion to the conditions demanded by the bailout program. The case of Econômico, Nacional and Bamerindus demonstrate that despite the significant political connections of the respective majority shareholders, not one of them was able to maintain continued control of their banks.

The government further demonstrated its resolve to enact unpopular measures vis-à-vis private finance by increasing the number and participation of foreign banks within the Brazilian market. These measures were extremely unpopular among Brazilian bankers because it exposed them to greater competition. One important 'round' within this controversy took shape over the privatization of São Paulo's state commercial bank (Banespa), where Brazilian bankers and even former members of the government advocated a privatization which excluded foreign banks as potential buyers because the bank represented roughly 3.5 percent of total national banking assets as of September, 1999. Despite such opposition, the government permitted foreign bids, a decision which allowed Bank Santander to purchase Banespa.

The federal intervention in Bamerindus, one of the largest Brazilian banks, was another paradigmatic case. The bank was the fourth largest in Brazil according to total assets in December 1994, and its owner, José Eduardo Andrade Vieira,[78] left his post as agriculture minister in an attempt to rescue his bank. The bank's balance sheet of 30 June 1996 already indicated serious liquidity difficulties (large inter-finance loans),

Table 6.1 ***PROER Operations – As of April 1999 (values in million R$)***

Bank	*Loan Taken*	*Date*	*Value Paid*	**Debt Remaining*
Econômico	5,226	May and Aug/96	–	6,870
Nacional	5,898	Nov/95; Jan/96	1,100	7,612
Bamerindus	2,945	Mar & May/97	3,768	–
Banorte	476	May/96	471	36
Merc. Pernambuco	530	Jun & Aug/96	–	689
CEF**	5,037	May & Set/96	–	7,587
Pontual	125	Sept/96	180	–
Antonio de Queiroz	120	March/96	71	104

* Includes principal and interest.
** The CEF, despite being a public bank, used funds from PROER in order to buy back non-performing mortgage loans from other banks.
Source: Central Bank and Gazeta Mercantil.

a mismatch between short-term assets and long-term liabilities, and a high rate of non-performing loans.[79] It seemed like one more case where political and economic forces would ally to maintain the bank essentially intact. A federal intervention, however, was decreed in March 1997, in addition to a freeze on the personal assets of the majority shareholders. Control of the bank was transferred to HSBC, constituting the third largest operation of the PROER (see Table 6.1).

As discussed earlier, the situation of state government banks also changed after 1994. In addition to intervening in Banespa and Banerj on 30 December 1994, the Central Bank subsequently intervened in the State Bank of Alagoas, the State Bank of Mato Grosso and the State Bank of Rondônia. In August 1996 the federal government created a state government bank bailout program – the PROES (Programa de Incentivo à Redução do Setor Público Estadual na Atividade Bancária) – that constitutes the most recent rescue program for state banks. According to this package, the federal government agreed to refinance state governments' debts to their respective banks in exchange for a few conditions. As noted earlier, states were given two options: a) complete federal refinancing entailed an eventual privatization, extinction, or transformation of the bank into a development agency, or b) 50 percent federal refinancing of state debts to their respective banks in exchange for bank administrative reform and more transparent rules for the concession of loans.

More effective action by the Central Bank regarding state banks after 1994 illustrates the new relationship between monetary authorities and the national financial system: the conditions were present to resolve the moral hazard problem, a hurdle which had impeded the development of a 'deep' financial market in Brazil. There are further indications of the Central Bank's development of more efficient regulatory mechanisms during this new period. During 1995 and 1996, for example, public banks printed various losses on their balance sheets, reflecting the effective enforcement of new regulations on the classification of assets with dubious value. Administrative (payroll) costs of public banks dropped, indicating that voluntary demotion programs imposed by the Central Bank were taking effect. Finally, credit operations by state banks directed to the public sector (generally state governments) also dropped, a trend which was fruit not only of debt renegotiations included within PROES, but also of the effective enforcement of regulations enacted during the 1980s which prevented the concession of new credit lines to state governments. It must be noted, however, that the largest problem of these banks was essentially a fiscal problem, because a large share of their assets took the form of loans extended to state governments who couldn't meet their debt obligations.[80] The total level of resources dedicated toward PROES reached up to R$90 billion, or two times the cost of private bank bailouts. The opposition parties, however, did not oppose the package, given their ideological commitment to greater participation of the state in the financial sector. There was, however, a significant difference between PROES and PROER. Unlike the private sector bailout, PROER was structured as a debt-swap; the federal government swapped federal bonds for the sum of debt held by state banks. Such a swap left state governments with the responsibility of honouring those bonds, but also left the state banks solvent.

Despite advances, persistent problems remain which could generate new moral hazard problems within both the public and private banking sector, as we will show by examining the Central Bank's rescue efforts in the wake of the government's devaluation of the real in early 1999. Despite these remaining doubts, however, most private banks with financial difficulties were either liquidated or changed their respective majority shareholders, and a good number of state banks have been privatized. Such measures indicate that many of the financial practices present in Brazil's financial system since the creation of the Central

Bank of Brazil have changed significantly, not only to adapt the financial system to the end of hyperinflation, but also to ensure financial institutions are acting in accordance with international financial standards.

Toward the consolidation of an ex-ante safety net

The Central Bank adopted a series of measures to create an ex-ante safety net for the financial sector to prevent the recurrence of systemic problems and avert further bailouts. Within its bank supervision department, the Central Bank implemented a Consolidated General Inspection (IGC) approach that replaced compartmentalized with 'global' oversight – a method utilizing market criteria for the risk evaluation of liquidity, credit, and asset quality. Furthermore, the Central Bank implemented independent audit boards (through Provisional decree n. 1.334 of March 1996), created a Credit Risk Board (Central de Risco de Crédito; Resolução n. 2.930 of June 97), and implemented greater control over money laundering. Financial regulation has become much more prudential, as good bank supervision stipulates, and the Central Bank has been able to implement a regulatory structure which can better prevent banking crisis. All of these measures have contributed to increased credibility within the financial system and contributed to greater responsibility by directors and majority shareholders, including the establishment of better mechanisms for evaluating technical expertise. As a rough estimate of the extent to which the Central Bank has been active in disciplining banking institutions, it is worth noting that between the Real Plan in 1994 and 1997, forty-three banks suffered intervention or extrajudicial liquidation, with eighty percent of them in the private sector. In all, there was a twenty percent reduction in the number of total financial institutions between December of 1993 and June of 1999.

During this period monetary authorities also created the Credit Guarantee Fund (FGC), which covers deposits and credit operations of up to R$20 thousand per person, and in accordance with Resolution n. 2.212 of 16 November 1995 and the Basel Accord, further increased the minimum capital required to create a new bank. New standards were also adopted to better evaluate the financial credibility of potential bank owners, and the government also eliminated the differences in capital standards required of foreigners and domestic citizens opening banks. With Resolution n. 2.682 (passed at the end of 1999), banks had to alter their method of classifying credit and non-performing loans by adopting risk criteria using techniques such as credit scoring, credit behaviour and ratings. Current debate suggests that the Central Bank will most likely adopt standards similar to those employed by the US Federal Reserve to supervise Brazilian banks and classify assets according to risk and existing controls. In sum, a variety of measures have contributed to increasing the soundness of financial institutions in the market.

The National Monetary Council also passed Resolution n. 2.685 in January 2000 to discipline bank use of rediscount lines at the Central Bank for liquidity. After an established period, such operations will only be accepted with the approval of the Directorate of the Central Bank, and institutions who make use of the discount line will have to both "demonstrate financial necessity" and "a restructuring program with the objective to capitalize or sell operational control of the bank, signed by the majority shareholder, and to be implemented in the time period prescribed". The rediscount interest rate was further delegated to the COPOM (Comitê de Política Monetária), such that monetary authorities can have the ability to punish frequent uses of the rediscount line with higher interest rates. With the restructuring of the national monetary system, it appears there no longer will be leeway for systematic abuse of the rediscount line.

Over the last five years, Brazil's financial system has undergone a transformation that has significantly reduced the risks of a systemic crisis due to unsound banking practices. Banking failures and the implicit assumption of a government bailout are always a risk, but the recent implementation of a more effective ex-ante safety net has reduced such risks in the Brazilian case. Even though the moral hazard problem has not been fully resolved in Brazil, the set of reforms described here have led to a 'silent revolution' in the financial system that, according to some analysts, has begun to transition into a 'deep' financial system. It is essential to stress the positive, distinctive features of the PROER and PROES as compared with similar bailouts carried on in other Latin American countries. In the first place the government was able to absorb its financial costs. Second and most important, it was *an ex ante package* – which prevented instead of followed a systemic crisis in the financial system, whose social costs would be tremendous, as seen in the cases of Chile, Mexico, Argentina and Venezuela.

Financial integration and accountability: a case of convergence between international rules and democratic control[81]

Economic stabilization and 'first generation' reforms of liberalization (trade, tax and fiscal, social security, deregulation and privatization) tend to generate demands for greater transparency and accountability to voters. Tolerance for insulation and lack of democratic controls over monetary authority has significantly decreased as a result of the unexpectedly high costs paid by populations during the external shocks that afflicted emerging markets beginning in 1994–95. How has this new environment affected the process of crafting monetary authority while improving the conditions for legitimation of this specific mode of political authority? To address this question, we examine the series of allegations directed against the Central Bank of Brazil during currency devaluation after January 1999. Allegations of misconduct arose when the central bank provided relief to two Brazilian financial institutions who bet against devaluation in futures markets (Bolsa de Mercadorias & Futuros – BM&F): Banco Marka and Banco FonteCindam.[82] The Central Bank prevented both institutions from going bankrupt by selling dollars to them at a rate set within the pre-devaluation exchange rate band, and justified such an action by alleging it was necessary to prevent a systemic crisis in Brazil's financial system. Independent of its validity, this explanation was largely rejected as improbable by the press, with most political commentators interpreting such actions as unjustifiable financial relief.[83] In part due to a number of details about the circumstances of the Central Bank's bailout that came to light over the following months, the Brazilian Senate established a Parliamentary Investigative Committee (CPI) to examine any potential misconduct by the Central Bank.

Such a political scandal provides a privileged vantage point from which to examine democratic accountability over monetary authorities in the context of financial integration. The scandal not only makes 'visible' the interests of the federal executive, the legislature, and groups in civil society with regard to the conduct of monetary authorities, but it also illustrates how democratic pressures are mediated under an increasingly integrated financial market. As this section will attempt to demonstrate, an important strategy of the federal executive branch in attempting to reduce the potential political costs associated with a Central Bank scandal was to accelerate the adoption of international rules of banking supervision, in order to make the Central Bank's conduct more transparent and less susceptible to allegations of misconduct. Brazilian monetary authorities were able to kill two birds with one stone: they alleviated domestic allegations of misconduct and also strengthened the solidity of the country's financial and monetary systems.[84]

Brazilian monetary authorities traditionally retained a high degree of discretion and lacked transparency. Since the creation of Brazil's Central Bank in 1964 – an institution only created after the 1964 military coup – the decision-making process within the monetary authorities has for the most part been outside public or legislative scrutiny. The lack of transparency which characterized Brazil's monetary authorities for well over two decades stems from a clear political objective of the military regime: to transfer power from the legislature to the federal executive. Unlike other Latin American authoritarian regimes, Brazil's military retained a degree of commitment to elections, however limited, to legitimize their power. In order for the military to strip the legislature of any effective power, Brazil's military government not only took away from the Congress all formal powers to legislate over financial matters,[85] but also transferred many of its fiscal powers to monetary authorities. The latter objective was attained through creating the Monetary Budget, which was approved by the National Monetary Council (CMN)[86] without any interference from the legislature.[87] As is common with many 'repressed' financial systems, the Central Bank of Brazil therefore came to adopt many programs which are essentially fiscal in nature and traditionally conducted by the legislature; such as the concession of credit to specific segments of industry or agriculture, and establishing specific regulations over non-financial segments of the market.[88]

Another reason for a lack of transparency among Brazilian monetary authorities stems from institutional multiplicity. Despite the creation of the Central Bank of Brazil in 1964, effective control over the money supply was divided between the Banco do Brasil (BB) and the Central Bank during military rule. Due to the Banco do Brasil's strong ties to agrarian interests (and the rural political elite), Brazil's largest commercial bank retained an automatic overdraft protection with the Central Bank – which for all intents and purposes gave the Banco do Brasil an indirect means to increase the country's money supply.[89] Even though the military created a National Monetary Council (CMN) with powers to approve the Monetary Budget and establish which regulations the Central Bank of Brazil should enforce, the effective division of powers between the Central Bank and the Banco do Brasil considerably weakened the very ability of the CMN to monitor how resources were spent. In addition to an effective division of control over the monetary supply, the monetary budget further included a number of federally owned financial institutions, each with its own development or financing objectives, which constituted a significant share of Brazil's financial system.[90] Such an institutional arrangement, however, is only incoherent if the objective of the government is to closely monitor spending. Since the military government made a decision, in effect, to privilege growth over fiscal austerity, however, such a plethora of institutions capable of extending credit was coherent with the regimes' overall political objectives.

With the transition to democracy and a fiscal crisis of the state in the early 1980s, however, the discretion accorded to monetary authorities began to slowly diminish. The government not only needed to closely monitor its spending in order to meet IMF obligations subsequent to the 1982 debt crisis, but with the transition to democracy the legislature pressured to curtail the enormous discretionary powers held by monetary authorities. As a result of both pressures, the Federal Executive gradually transferred functions held by the Monetary Budget to the fiscal budget (Orçamento Geral da União) throughout the 1980s, and the legislature formally abolished the Monetary Budget in the 1988 Federal Constitution.[91] In addition, the government created an organ to oversee all federal state-owned enterprises in 1980 (SEST), and created the Secretaria do Tesouro Nacional (STN) in 1986 in an attempt to unify previously decentralized budgets. Further significant reforms include the abolition of the Banco do Brasil's overdraft clause,[92] and the end of the Central Bank of Brazil's Development Department.[93]

Despite such advances, however, Brazilian monetary authorities continued to retain a large degree of discretion. One reason stems from the fact that federal financial institutions still represent a significant share of Brazil's financial system. Not only do monetary authorities determine financial regulatory policy, but they also represent roughly forty percent of the sector, with no clear mechanisms with which to make federal financial institutions accountable to either the legislature or the public at large.[94] Furthermore, and also directly relevant to our brief case study, monetary authorities have not explicitly laid out the criteria adopted by the Central Bank to intervene in financial institutions under financial duress. The Central Bank intervened in a number of financial institutions between its inception in 1964 and the re-introduction of democracy in the 1980s. Yet it did so without clear and transparent criteria of how it diagnosed what was meant by an 'unsound' financial institution worthy of intervention.

Case study of the banking CPI (Parliamentary Investigative Committee)

International pressures in January 1999 led to a rapid reduction in Brazilian foreign currency reserves and endangered economic stabilization premised upon a crawling peg exchange rate and minimum level of reserves. On 15 January, the government could no longer sustain an intermediate exchange rate system and the Central Bank allowed the real to freely float against the dollar. In the next few days the real was traded above R$2 to the dollar. The Central Bank's bailout of Marka and FonteCindam took place in the context of this foreign exchange rate instability. A Parliamentary Investigative Committee (CPI) in Brazil's Congress was called because of the Central Bank's poor explanation of policy, aggravated by the revelation of the extraordinary profits many financial institutions made in January 1999 by anticipating devaluation. In contrast, both Marka and FonteCindam bet against devaluation in the days preceding January 15 and thus were long on the real in the futures market (BM&F) against the vast majority of financial institutions. These seemingly 'irrational' expectations by Marka and FonteCindam, were odd, and observers became suspicious of malfeasance when Marka's owner, Salvatore Cacciola, was reported by the weekly news magazine *Veja* to have told friends that his bank had access to privileged information. This led analysts to become increasingly suspicious of the Central Bank's actions and triggered off a vociferous attack by the major opposition party in Congress.

On 14 January, the BM&F had established a R$1.25 ceiling on transactions on the future's market, but no one risked selling dollars at this price. In order to prevent Marka and FonteCindam from going bankrupt (also on 14 January), the Central Bank sold futures contracts on the commercial dollar to FonteCindam at R$1.322 and to Marka at R$1.2750. While both contracts were within the "endogenous diagonal" currency band established by newly named Central Bank head Francisco Lopes and his team, on that same day the market was pressuring the upper limit of the band and was already quoting the dollar at R$1.55. The situation of both banks couldn't have been more serious, and the Central Bank justified such a bailout on the grounds that it would prevent a systemic banking crisis.[95] Independent of whether there existed a real risk of a systemic banking crisis, political analysts in the press remained sceptical about whether the financial difficulties exhibited by both institutions could have led to such a crisis. Both institutions were seen as relatively obscure outside their specific markets, and thus unable to jeopardize the credibility of the financial system.[96] The Central Bank's operation drew even more suspicions after it became clear in the following days that, in the case of FonteCindam, the contracts sold to the bank not only recovered financial losses incurred by the bank, but also losses incurred by its clients who invested in the bank's derivatives fund. On January 19, by which point the real was freely floating against the dollar, Marka's owner sought help from the Central Bank alleging that investment funds administered by the bank would also be unprotected, at which point the Central Bank sold an additional 3,700 exchange rate contracts to the bank at R$1.56.[97] The press reported the cost of all these operations to the Central Bank at R$1.6 billion. Analysts were further perplexed by the very fact the Central Bank was operating in the currency futures market, which was to bring it substantial losses. The brief and failed experiment of a controlled devaluation, led to Francisco Lopes being replaced as Central Bank president by Armínio Fraga.[98]

Such actions by the Central Bank not only demonstrated a substantial degree of discretion, but also unclear criteria over which institutions it provides assistance to. Following these events, members of the press and investors began to investigate the circumstances surrounding these operations. Two pieces of information raised further suspicion among the press and analysts who followed the case. First, it was revealed that after the devaluation, Marka's owner, Salvatore Cacciola, had gone to Brasília to petition the Central Bank for help, accompanied by a close personal friend of Francisco Lopes, then its acting president. It was never proven that Francisco Lopes and Salvatore Cacciola had actually spoken personally, but suspicions over inappropriate action by the Central Bank increased substantially. Second, Cacciola sent US$17 million to a personal account outside the country only one day after the Central

Bank's bailout. Faced with these revelations, on 14 April the Congress chose to investigate, opening a Parliamentary Investigative Committee (CPI) to look into the events surrounding the case. Ironically, this CPI was sponsored by Senator Jáder Barbalho (PMDB), a party leader of one of the most important parties that sustained President Fernando Henrique Cardoso (PSDB) in the Congress.[99] Opposition deputy Aloízio Mercadante (PT) also attempted to launch a similar investigation in the lower house, but this attempt was pre-empted by the leader of the Chamber of Deputies, Michel Temer (also from Jáder Barbalho's PMDB).

In addition to the Central Bank's bailout of the aforementioned banks, the CPI investigated two other events: the extraordinary profits earned by some financial institutions during the month of the devaluation, and the government bailout program directed toward private banking institutions – PROER (Programa de Estímulo à Reestruturação e ao Fortalecimento do Sistema Financeiro Nacional).[100] Despite its roar, it appeared the PMDB never had the intention of conducting a full-fledged investigation, and was instead more concerned with gaining bargaining leverage over the Executive. The CPI took a life of its own, however, in part because of parallel investigations being conducted by the independent Public Prosecution, the Federal Police, and the Central Bank itself, which together began to create a whirlwind of information that had strong repercussions on the CPI proceedings.

The actual Parliamentary Investigative Committee also had investigative powers of its own. The Committee opened the confidential banking and telephone records of all the parties involved, including the Central Bank president, and brought twenty-eight individuals to testify before the Committee. The investigation conducted by the independent Public Prosecution, however, proved most critical. After obtaining a court order, prosecutors were able to apprehend a large amount of personal and business documents at the workplace and homes of Cacciola, Luiz Gonçalves (owner of FonteCindam), and Francisco Lopes. Some revealing documents were further leaked to the press and the CPI,[101] and became a source of political embarrassment and concern to the Federal Executive. After reading the apprehended documents, senator and chair of the CPI, João Alberto (PMDB-MA) declared, "the pillars of the nation will be shaken", and that, "horrible, terrible things", had been found. The CPI, which seemed to have been created to be a mere 'show', had gotten out of the hands of its creators.[102] At the end of April the executive tried to coordinate with party leaders in Congress in order to control the political costs associated with the investigation.

Political heat felt by the federal executive, however, became more intense when Francisco Lopes testified before the Committee. Following the advice of his lawyers, the former Central Bank head refused to testify, on the grounds that his testimony could incriminate him in a court of law, at which point the visibly upset Senators ordered his immediate, but illegal imprisonment. The CPI had reached its apex, and the ongoing investigation had begun to damage the public's perception of monetary authorities and reinforced the idea that Brazil's financial system suffered from another serious moral hazard problem. The federal executive's own credibility had begun to suffer to the extent the press began to question the motives behind Francisco Lopes' rapid demotion from the Central Bank presidency. During the month of May analysts and some members of the Congress began to suggest that Finance Minister Pedro Malan testify before the CPI. The CPI failed to document abuse or violation of law, in part because of the low technical qualifications of its members. At the end of April a separate Central Bank investigation found no evidence of improper conduct by employees. In mid-May the Senators disagreed over whether their CPI report should find the bailout illegal or merely improper.[103] The final CPI report in November 1999 requested that Public Prosecutors investigate Central Bank conduct during the private bank-bailout program (PROER) and in foreign currency futures markets. With regard to the specific case of Marka and FonteCindam, the report concluded there were problems within the Central Bank directorate, but allegations of selling privileged information were discarded. Legislators were unanimous in arguing that monetary authorities were having difficulties monitoring, and more importantly, preventing troubles in the financial system.

The central bank and government strategy to 'tie its hands' by adopting international bank supervision standards

How does the political scandal described above shed light upon the relationship between international financial integration and democratic accountability? Since their creation in 1964, Brazil's monetary authorities have primarily been characterized as having a large range of discretionary powers that have not been privy to legislative or public scrutiny.

The CPI conducted in the Senate, however, was the result of a gradual process underway since the transition to democracy that has begun to strip away at the monetary authorities' discretionary powers and attempted to make them more accountable to the legislature. We contend, however, that monetary authorities responded to such political pressures – and the CPI specifically – by adopting internationally recommended bank supervision standards in order to make their decision-making process more transparent and less susceptible to allegations of misconduct. In other words, an internationally integrated financial market facilitated the adoption of more transparent (and therefore more democratic) decision-making procedures.

In order to understand the Central Bank's response to the CPI, we must explain the danger the Committee posed to Brazilian monetary authorities. In addition to being politically costly to the Cardoso government, monetary authorities feared the ongoing investigation would lead legislators to reverse the Central Bank's operational autonomy, which had been effective since the implementation of the Real Plan.[104] In a number of instances during the CPI, senators threatened to enact mechanisms of greater political control over the conduct of Central Bank policy that, if enacted, could have jeopardized the viability of the Real Plan. Senate President Antonio Carlo Magalhães, for example, who had a few years earlier ardently defended a failed bank (Econômico) in his home state, expressed his displeasure over the conduct of Brazil's monetary authorities. Responding to the series of revelations brought forth during the CPI, Senator Magalhães stated, "all this demonstrates that despite all the scandals which the Central Bank has undergone in the past, like the cases of Nacional, Bamerindus, and others, the Central Bank hasn't done anything to improve its bank supervision standards", and further expressed his dislike by stating, "when there are economic meetings, they isolate the politicians, so the politicians won't talk about what transpired".[105] Shortly after the CPI was concluded, the Committee of Justice and Constitutionality in the Senate revealed that it was studying how the legislature could dismiss Central Bank directors.[106]

In order to pre-empt any proposals from the legislature for greater control over monetary policymaking, the Central Bank sought to establish greater transparency in its conduct by adopting international standards of bank supervision. The adoption of such standards, on the one hand, diminished the Bank's discretionary powers. But on the other hand, it more firmly established an 'ex-ante safety net' that seeks to prevent financial institutions from experiencing financial difficulties to begin with – thus reducing the need for Central Bank assistance. After adopting these standards monetary authorities are less prone to suffer accusations of misconduct on two fronts. Not only are the rules for providing assistance to financial institutions clear to all actors involved, but with a stronger ex-ante safety net the chances a financial institution will need assistance in the first place are also smaller.

The government's strategy to 'tie its hands' through adopting international bank supervision standards, however, was only made possible because of a specific international and domestic political context. Since 1988 the Bank of International Settlements (BIS), through the Basel Committee, has been emphasizing to central banks the need to adopt international standards of solvency and liquidity. These standards require monetary authorities to demand that financial institutions disclose details about the risk of their assets, establish capital and liquidity limits, adopt leverage ceilings, and implement more stringent criteria for opening and operating new financial institutions. These measures were implemented in Brazil through Central Bank Resolution n. 2.099 in 1994. In light of increasing difficulties faced by many financial systems across the globe, in the second half of the 1990s the BIS sought to establish tougher standards of bank supervision. In 1997 it detailed 25 principles for efficient bank supervision, the most important of which established new criteria over the licensing of institutions, minimal capital requirements, quality in banking assets, systems of internal information, the monitoring of incurred and potential risks, standardized internal systems of control, and policies based on the 'know your customer' principle. In September 1998 – during the Russian crisis – the Central Bank promulgated Resolution n. 2.554, mandating the implementation of internal control systems that are consistent with international criteria for risk analysis.[107]

Since the adoption of the IMF package (which took into account the extent to which Brazil adhered to the Basel Principles) the government sought monetary, exchange rate, and fiscal policy reforms, all with the objective of consolidating the stabilization program. Despite such reforms, the Central Bank bailout of Marka and FonteCindam indicates that monetary authorities still operated under a substantial degree of discretion. The CPI and the resulting political scandal, however, considerably pressured monetary authorities to accelerate ongoing reforms in monetary policy and bank supervision recommended by multilateral finance agencies and other domestic actors who were in favour of greater transparency within monetary authorities. As a measure of good faith, for example, the Central Bank adopted on its own balance books the same criteria for asset classification that it was demanding of bank. As a result of these new standards, the Central Bank presented a R$13 billion loss for the 1999 fiscal year. Furthermore, since March of that year the Central Bank has adhered to the IMF's demand to no longer trade in the dollar futures market. Central Bank President Arminio Fraga, Lopes' successor, further suggested hiring an external auditing agency[108] arguing that, "society should accompany the work of the organization".[109]

The adoption of inflationary targeting by the Central Bank constitutes a second item of reform that increased the transparency of monetary authorities. Rather than rely upon a crawling peg exchange rate policy to stabilize prices, since July 1999 the Central Bank has adopted an inflation targeting policy to stabilize inflationary expectations and also generate greater predictability in monetary policy. The government publicly announces both the inflation targets and its reasons for why the targets were or were not met. One week after the monetary authorities' monthly decision on the interbank rate of interest, the minutes justifying the decision enable the market, the press, and politicians to closely scrutinize and discuss the relevant decision. In addition, policies enacted by Brazil's monetary authorities came to be monitored by the IMF on a quarterly basis.

The Law of Fiscal Responsibility (Lei de Responsabilidade Fiscal) approved by the Congress in the beginning of 2000 further had an impact over the workings of monetary authorities. The law imposes limits on public spending on all three levels of government, in addition to establishing a series of penalties for potential violations. With regard to the conduct of monetary authorities, the law requires the Central Bank to make periodic reports which detail the costs incurred in its operations – including its participation in the exchange rate market. Brazil's stock and futures market was further regulated, and required larger guarantees for financial operations, thus diminishing the risks of another episode like Marka and FonteCindam.

The Central Bank's bank supervision department, which was severely criticized during the CPI, was reformulated. The existing department was divided between São Paulo and Brasília and between direct and indirect bank supervision. New departments were created to combat illicit exchange and financial transactions, and to supervise temporary Central Bank interventions of other financial institutions. The Central Bank further adopted a new bank supervision method, the Consolidated General Inspection (IGC), described earlier. This type of supervision replaces the previous modular method and has many phases which culminate in a multidisciplinary Central Bank team that works directly within the financial institution to evaluate the operation of disparate areas such as: treasury, general efficiency, the management of other firms held in the respective institution's portfolio, international transactions, credit operations and other assets and liabilities.

Finally, a number of measures were adopted in order to create a more sound ex-ante safety net in Brazil's financial system which include: new methods to classify credit and market risk (which had long been recommended by BIS), new criteria to classify potential losses, more rigid rules for access to the Central Bank's liquidity assistance, new procedures to designate directors of financial institutions, accountability to independent auditors, and rigid criteria over credit operations with the public sector. In addition, other important regulations were imposed on the market that increased its disclosure requirements, whether it be by divulging financial statements on the Internet that were previously only accessible to a restricted banking sector,[110] or through divulging the credit risk rating of that institution. The credit risk rating also applies to non-financial institutions that are controlled by the bank – a common cause for the bankruptcy of institutions that were once considered 'too big to fail'. The trend toward transparency has further been solidified by the Central Bank through public hearings drafting regulations that will impact the financial market, and more recently, in elaborating alternative strategies for federal financial institutions.

Conclusion

The changing function and jurisdiction of central banks in response to globalization and regional integration is an important dimension of state reform and economic restructuring in both longstanding and neo-democracies. International factors such as the liquidity crisis of the 1980s and the acute need to attract investments in Latin America, Africa,

East Europe, and South Asia, have provided important incentives to improve international creditworthiness. This international background of the global trend towards greater central bank statutory autonomy during the 1990s is important. However, the problems addressed in this chapter lead us to adopt a different analytical focus. In order to establish the links between democratization, the construction of monetary authority, and governance, we approach central banks as a specific mode of political authority. This challenges the notion of a single model for effective central banking in all countries. Categories such as peripheral economic systems and neo-democracies also appear too broad to capture the dilemmas posed by the need to reconcile the tasks (ideally) performed by central banks as 'rule-makers' and, on the other hand, the imperatives of democratic governance. Empirical evidence from Latin American experiences with hyperinflationary pressures suggests that the process of legitimization by which economic stability becomes a first order public good is especially convoluted under hyperinflation; but legitimization is a *conditio sine qua non* for achieving stability. Extreme cases provide powerful examples of the issues at stake in the construction of a new monetary order.

The recent centralization of monetary authority in the Central Bank yields a valuable analytical lesson. The Central Bank of Brazil has been able to impose increasing discipline over the monetary and financial systems in part *because* of the economic stabilization plan – not the other way around, as the conventional wisdom would predict. The key lesson is that economic stabilization has less to do with 'getting the institutions right', and is more a consequence of a dynamic bargaining game between the federal executive, legislators, and subnational governments. When studying monetary authority and central bank institutions, analysts should identify the relevant actors, their interests, and how economic and political circumstances can shift the relevant bargaining position of these actors.

Increased financial integration undoubtedly has led to substantial change in terms of how democracies can exert political accountability on behalf of their domestic monetary authorities. This chapter shows that while financial integration has diminished the options of monetary authorities, it may have facilitated the adoption of strategic decisions by politicians in government to increase the transparency of their decision-making procedures. The ability of Brazil's monetary authorities to 'tie their hands' to international banking standards presupposes that such standards are already an internationally agreed-upon standard to begin with. These specific findings confirm the general view of Hagopian that the low quality of Brazilian democracy is improving in terms of the standards of accountability and responsiveness.[111]

Notes

1 This chapter updates material published in the *Revista de Economia Política* and presented at the 18th World Congress of the International Political Association (Québec, 2000), the latter written with Christopher Garman. Research was funded by the Fundação de Amparo à Pesquisa do Estado de São Paulo (FAPESP). The Conselho Nacional de Pesquisa Científica (CNPQ) also provided a grant to the coordinator.

2 Maxfield, S., *Gatekeepers of Growth: The International Political Economy of Central Banking in Developing Countries,* Princeton, NJ: Princeton University Press, 1997.

3 Laurence Whitehead, 'On monetary authority' (chapter 6), *Democratization: Theory and Experience*, Oxford: Oxford University Press, 2002, pp. 136–64.

4 This does not mean that economists have neglected to explore political dimensions to central banking. Much theorizing about the role of central banks has focused predominantly on two dimensions of politics: the impact of their actions upon growth, employment, and other developmental issues; and the requisite political conditions for a central bank to perform its expected *economic* functions – a dimension simultaneously technical and normative.

5 This question, as is well known, also applies to the judiciary, as guardian of the law.

6 Moreover, to the extent that effective autonomy in practice has been accompanied by the exercise of a veto power by central banks over fiscal policy, there is no question regarding the specific problems raised for democratic governance and for the impact on the balance of power between winners and losers.

7 On the notion of an explosive path as a consequence of the economic adjustments imposed by the external shock of 1982 and past policy choices, see: J. Fanelli, R. Frenkel and G. Rozenwurcell, 'Growth and structural reform in Latin America. Where do we stand', in W. Smith, C. Acunã and E. Gamarra, *Latin American Political Economy in the Age of Neo-Liberal Reform*, New Brunswick, NJ: Transaction, 1994. On the case of Brazil, see: L. Sola, 'State, structural reform, and democratization', in Smith, Acunã and Gamarra, op. cit.

8 See L. Sola and E. Kugelmas, 'Crafting economic stabilization', in this volume.

9 This is more so in cases like that of Brazil where a very new and minutely detailed constitution opens multiple fronts for divergent interpretations, not to speak of the infra-constitutional legislation which is still dependent on congressional approval.

10 We are assuming that deregulation of the financial system does not preclude regulation at another level on behalf not only of monetary order but also of transparency, accountability and predictability (the rule of law) pending infra-constitutional legislation.

11 We are following Albert Hirschman in his assumption that at a certain point inflation generates a new social coalition in favour of stabilization. Our point, however, is that political intermediation and the quality of leadership are additional conditions which may be met or not but are also relevant in the choice of effective policies in the sense that they are adequate to the social profile of that coalition. This implies, of course, the choice of the economic team.

12 For the Bolivian experiment, see especially J.M. Malloy and C. Conaghan, *Unsettling Statecraft, Democracy and Liberalism in the Central Andes*, Pittsburgh: Pittsburgh University Press, 1996. For the Brazilian case, see Sola and Kugelmas and Armijo, in this volume.

13 Central bank governors should have fixed mandates not coinciding with an electoral calendar, and more generally their appointment should follow predominantly technical criteria.
14 A. Alesina, 'Macroeconomics and Politics', in S. Fischer, ed., *NBER Macroeconomics Annual*, Cambridge: Cambridge University Press, 1988; see also V. Grilli, D. Masciandaro and G. Tabellini, 'Political monetary institutions and public financial policies in the industrial countries', *Economic Policy: A European Economic Forum*, 13 (October), 342–92; for use of such arguments in Brazil see Roberto Campos, *Lanterna na Popa*, Rio de Janeiro: Topbooks, 1995.
15 S. Maxfield, op. cit. Her argument is especially relevant in a context of a growing internationalization of securities markets in the 1990s.
16 Maxfield's country case studies don't focus exclusively on the need to obtain credit. In most of her cases she blends international with national level variables, yet we contend that her general theoretical orientation is ill suited for explaining the Brazilian case.
17 Not only dependent upon the federal executive, but also divided between two federal organs: the SUMOC and the Banco do Brasil prior to 1964, and the Central Bank and the Banco do Brasil after the military coup. The exception was the short interim period during Brazil's first military government of Castello Branco (1964–67).
18 P.A. Hall, 'Central bank independence and coordinated wage bargaining: their interaction in Germany and Europe', *German Politics and Society*, 31 (Spring 1994), 1–23.
19 See S. Lohmann, 'Federalism and central bank autonomy: the politics of German monetary policy, 1957–1992', Department of Political Science, UCLA, October 1994; K. Banaian, L.O. Laney and T.D. Willett, 'Central bank independence: an international comparison', in E.F. Toma and M. Toma, eds., *Central Bankers, Bureaucratic Incentives, and Monetary Policy*, Boston: Academic Publishers, 1986, pp. 199–219. A large number of veto points hinders institutional change, thus federal countries without an independent central bank would be the slowest to implement those institutions.
20 J.B. Goodman, *Monetary Sovereignty: The Politics of Central Banking in Western Europe*, Ithaca, NY: Cornell University Press, 1992; J.T. Woolley, *Monetary Politics*, Cambridge: Cambridge University Press, 1985.
21 Stepan and Linz make this type of argument for federal countries, see J. Linz and A. Stepan, *Problems of Transition and Democratic Consolidation*, Princeton, NJ: Princeton University Press, 1996.
22 Malloy and Connaghan, op. cit., succintly make this point.
23 See R. Campos, *A Lanterna na Popa*, op. cit.
24 The separation between monetary and fiscal budgets introduced by the economic team under the first civilian government in 1986 made it possible to eliminate one of the black boxes created by Antonio Delfim Neto. The non-discrimination between these two budgets reduced executive accountability.
25 For stabilization plans under the populist democracy, see L. Sola, *Idéias econômicas, decisões políticas. Desenvolvimento, Estabilidade Populismo*, São Paulo: EDUSP, 1998.
26 Two reasons explain this. First, continuous growth may have appeared necessary to the military in order to cement a political coalition they wished to create in support of a strategy of gradual and controlled political liberalization. Second, the choice of growth at the expense of inflation and an exchange rate crisis was always taken by previous Brazilian governmental elites.
27 State banks were able to issue debt with great liquidity, in essence enabling them to expand the money supply, even if they did not actually print currency.
28 We are referring here to the federal executive. Congressional elections were held during most of the military period.
29 Stepan makes this argument in connection to the electoral sequencing.
30 See Sola, 'The state, structural reform and democratization', op. cit. While beyond the scope of this paper, monetary and fiscal rebellion occurred in the private and public sector

alike. Public and private actors often financed their investments by evading tax payments and delaying the collection of social security contributions. Under high inflation, such practices became a source of long-term finance.

31 In addition to centralizing monetary authority in the central bank, the federal government has made state bailouts conditioned on non-monetary measures (future revenue, administrative reform, and privatization of state-owned enterprises).

32 The Brazilian transition to democracy was marked not only by the re-introduction of direct elections for governor *prior* to the presidential elections, but also by concurrent gubernatorial and national legislative elections in 1982, 1986 and 1990. Direct presidential elections were only re-introduced in 1989 – an 'off' election year. Legislative candidates therefore benefited from riding 'gubernatorial coat-tails'. On the importance of electoral calendars, see: Linz and Stepan, op. cit.; F.L. Abrucio, *Os barões da federação: o poder dos governadores no Brasil pós autoritário*, São Paulo: Hucitec, 1998; C. Garman, S. Haggard and S. Willis, 'Decentralization in Latin America', paper presented at APSA, 1996. On the timing of elections, see M.S. Shugart and J.M. Carey, *Presidents and Assemblies: Constitutional Design and Electoral Dynamics*, Cambridge: Cambridge University Press, 1992.

33 The PSDB increased its representation in the Chamber of Deputies from 38 to 62 seats (out of 513), in the Senate from one to nine (out of 54), and maybe more importantly, its gubernatorial posts from one to six (out of twenty-seven), including the most prominent states of São Paulo, Rio de Janeiro and Minas Gerais.

34 IBGE/Andima, *Sistema financeiro: uma análise a partir das contas nacionais – 1990–95*, Rio de Janeiro, 1996.

35 Spending on payroll often followed an electoral calendar. Governors and mayors would swell the public sector with political appointments prior to elections to help elect successors while, once in office, governments would reduce spending on payroll by allowing inflation to corrode real wages.

36 CMN Resolution 1718 of 5/29/90, CMN Resolution 1775 of 12/26.

37 Lei da Improbidade – Código Penal – Law 8429 of 6/2/92.

38 Senate Resolution n. 94, of 12/15/89; Senate Resolution no. 58 of 12/13/90; and Senate Resolution n. 36 of 6/32/92. In 1993 a Constitutional Amendment (no. 3, 3/17/93), was further passed which prohibited the issuance of any new state bonds except for the payment of principal. See E. Guardia, 'A crise fiscal dos estados', Caderno PUC Economia, 3 (1995), 65–87; and G.C. Santos, 'Contingenciamento do crédito e finanças estaduais', in *Programa de formação de técnicos do Banco Central – Curso de formação superior*, 1993.

39 In the Senate confirmation hearing for the President of the Central Bank, Persio Arida, for example, declared he was in favour of privatizing state banks in order to sustain price stability. *Jornal do Brasil*, 14 December 1994.

40 Since prior to 1997 governors and presidents were not permitted to run for re-election, an election, by definition, constituted a turnover in government.

41 Central Bank intervention of both banks was also helped by the fact both incoming governors Mario Covas of São Paulo, and Marcelo Alencar of Rio de Janeiro belong to the same political party as the president (PSDB). The fact that both belong to the same party, however, could influence the outcome in either way. One could equally expect the governor to reduce a state 'rebellion' against the federal government, as one would expect the federal government to give the governor favourable treatment.

42 The purchase of Bamerindus by HSBC is a case in point.

43 As will become clear, the two cannot be separated in practice. Because state banks have been the administrators of state government debts, negotiation over state banks by the central bank often must be made *in tandem* with a restructuring of the state government debt – a Senate prerogative.

44 Brazil's gubernatorial elections first occurred in 1982, with subsequent elections for the governor's office held every four years, 1986, 1990, and 1994. The first Central Bank

bailout of state banks occurred in 1983, followed by a series of interventions in 1987 and 1991. These crises, however, also coincided with the various stabilization programs adopted. See Loyola, G.J.L., *Os bancos públicos estaduais*, Brasília: Banco Central, 1992; W.W. Buchi, 'Banespa: uma visão realista', *Folha de São Paulo*, 17 September 1995.

45 *Estado de São Paulo*, 17 January 1993.

46 CMN – Conselho Monetário Nacional, vote 233 of 7/20/83 for PAC and CMN Vote 446 of 4/4/ 84 for PROREF.

47 For an analysis of how state banks repeatedly ignored central bank stipulations established in those packages see Andrade, E.C., *Os bancos comerciais estaduais no Brasil: do final dos anos 1960 à crise dos anos 1980*, Master's Thesis, Rio de Janeiro: PUC, 1992. See also, Loyola, 'Os Bancos Públicos Estaduais', op. cit.; Paes, op. cit.; Lopreato, F.L. Crise de Financiamento dos Governos Estaduais (1980/88). Doctoral Dissertation. Campinas: IE/Unicamp, 1992; Ogasavara, R. and J. Vasconcelos, 'Análise Economica-Financeira dos bancos estaduais', Documento de Política, n. 7 (1992), IPEA: Rio de Janeiro and World Bank, *Brazil: The Dilemma of Brazil's State Banking System: An Analysis and Suggestions for Reform – 27/02/1990*, Washington, DC: The World Bank, 1990.

48 Law no. 4595 of 12/31/1964.

49 The category of extra-limit debt was created under the 1975 Central Bank Resolution 446, which interestingly coincides with the military government's decision to slowly liberalize the political sphere. For a direct analysis of how the military government's decision to permit state and municipal debt through the state banks served the government's political interests, see Christopher Garman's forthcoming University of California, San Diego, doctoral dissertation.

50 Medida Provisoria n. 1514, 8/7/1996.

51 For a summary of this debate, and also for discussion of whether a new international financial architecture is needed, see L.E. Armijo and D. Felix, 'Reform of the global financial architecture: who wants what and why?', paper presented at the Annual Meeting of the American Political Science Association: Atlanta, 1999.

52 Financial institutions were highly leveraged on foreign currencies, and thus with a devaluation their respective domestic debtors could not meet their payments in local currencies, resulting in a wave of bankruptcies in the banking and industrial sector. While analysts have provided persuasive, and extensive, accounts over the reasons behind Brazil's relative resilience to the 1999 currency devaluation, one factor is evident: Brazil didn't suffer from a 'risky' financial sector.

53 A second condition should be stated: the learning process by which the técnicos accused of improper conduct by the opposition and the media (wrongly in our view) came to advocate two principles: 1) it would be in their own interest to have shared responsibility with Congress and/or other institutions eventually in charge of control; 2) central bank operational autonomy should be institutionalized only and only if part of an agreed strategy – which led them to favour a very gradual approach to that reform and much political deliberation. Interviews with ex-President of Brazilian Central Bank, Gustavo Loyola, and ex-Minister of Economy, Mailson da Nóbrega.

54 Most notably the declaration by Governor Itamar Franco from the state of Minas Gerais that he would no longer pay its debt to the federal government.

55 See chapter three in S.J. Burki and G.E. Perry, *Beyond the Washington Consensus: Institutions Matter*, Washington, DC: The World Bank, 1998.

56 Critical toward generating the problem of a moral hazard, however, is the perception amongst financial agents that an eventual government bailout in times of financial crisis will entail a loss to bank owners *only* equal to the sum they originally invested. The relevant question therefore is not whether the government will, or will not, act as a lender of last resort in case of a run on financial institutions, but whether financial agents believe an eventual government bailout will also incur costs to bank owners greater than the sum they originally invested.

57 A sound ex-ante safety net can be generated through government regulation *and* through spontaneous self-enforcement within the financial sector (such as the emergence of credit bureaus and internal monitoring within financial institutions). We focus on how the government can aid in the creation of an ex-ante safety net. For analysis over banking safety nets, see C.W. Calomiris, *The Postmodern Bank Safety Net: Lessons from Developed and Developing Economies*, Washington, DC: AEI Press, 1997; L. Rojas-Suárez, *Safe and Sound Financial Systems: What Works for Latin America*, Washington, DC: Inter-American Development Bank, 1997; and S.J. Burki and G.E. Perry, op. cit.

58 "Closing down or stringently disciplining a bank is inherently a political act in all countries." P.M. Garber, 'The transition to a functional financial safety net', in L. Rojas-Suárez, ed., op. cit., p. 184.

59 R.I. McKinnon, *Money and Capital in Economic Development*, Washington, DC: Brookings Institution, 1973.

60 Burki and Perry, op. cit., p. 48.

61 While in some cases state commercial banks did conduct direct loans to state governments, state commercial banks played a more important indirect role through financing state government SOE (State Owned Enterprises), holding state government bonds which were not absorbed by the private market, and in more stark cases, providing Revenue Anticipation Grants (Antecipação de Receita Orçamentária).

62 Brazil's gubernatorial elections took place in 1982, 1986, 1990, 1994 and 1998. Central Bank bailouts of state banks occurred in 1983, followed by a series of interventions in 1987 and 1991. See Banco Central do Brasil, *Bancos estaduais: experiências e perspectivas*, Seminário Internacional, Brasília, 1992, and J.P.P. Paes, 'Bancos estaduais, "criação" de moeda e ciclo político', Master's dissertation, EAESP/ FGV, São Paulo, 1996. For an analysis which focuses on the impact of stabilization, see Buchi, op. cit.. The structural problems of democratic federalism in connection with the reconcentration of power in central bank institutions, in E. Kugelmas and L. Sola, 'Recentralização/ descentralização – a dinâmica política do regime federativo no Brasil dos anos 1990', in L. Sola, E. Kugelmas and L. Whitehead, *Banco Central, autoridade política e democratização. Um equilíbrio delicado*, Rio de Janeiro: FGV, 2002.

63 Campos, op. cit.; W.J. Barker, *Banks and Industry in Contemporary Brazil; Their Organization, Relationship and Leaders*, New Haven: Yale University, 1990.

64 This situation could have influenced the outcome in either way; one could equally expect the governor to reduce a state 'rebellion' against the federal government, as one would expect the federal government to give the governor favourable treatment.

65 The treatment given by the Cardoso administration to the private financial sector requires particular note considering that donations by members of the private financial sector to the President's campaign represented roughly 20 percent of all donations – as estimated by Superior Electoral Tribunal (STE). *O Estado de São Paulo*, 29 December 1995.

66 The creation of the multiple bank had the purpose of facilitating bank fiscalization on behalf of monetary authorities. Juridic persons could declare their multiple financial statements under one single entity – under the multiple bank. Many brokers, however, took advantage of this legislative breach to become a bank and reap inflationary revenue. With the advent of the Plano Real many of these so called 'banks' went bankrupt.

67 Central Bank document on PROER – January 1999, p. 1.

68 The group of governors who neared the end of their mandates, most of whom were of the same party of the official party, attempted to elect successors. State banks were instrumental to win elections. The heterodox manipulation of their banks for political ends, however, didn't restrict itself to electoral ends.

69 For an analysis of the political strength of governors subsequent to 1982, see F. Abrucio, *Os barões da federação*, op. cit., F. Abrucio and D. Samuels, 'The new politics of the governors: subnational politics and the Brazilian transition to democracy', *Comparative Politics*, 1997; and Kugelmas and Sola, 2002, op. cit..

70 For a description of the relevant measures, see Loyola, 1999, pp. 21 and 23.
71 The state banks of Rio de Janeiro and São Paulo (Banerj and Banespa) suffered an intervention in 31 December 1994.
72 It is also important to note that the bank was one of the oldest private banks in the country, with its home office in the state of Bahia – a critical state which provided electoral support to the government.
73 For a description of the episode and its implications see L. Sola, C. Garman and M. Marques, 'Central banking, democratic governance and political authority: the case of Brazil in a comparative perspective', in *Revista de Economia Política*, 18/2 (1998), 106–31.
74 See *O Estado de São Paulo*, 29 December 1995. Banco Nacional not only was the sixth largest Brazilian bank in terms of assets, but its owners belonged to a traditional family from the state of Minas Gerais whose patriarch and governor of the state, Magalhães Pinto had supported the military coup. It must be noted, however, that in the case of Banco Nacional, there was a great misuse of resources through conceding fictitious loans to previous bank debtors, and non-performing loans, who evidently had no knowledge of the operation.
75 In the case of Banco Nacional, political connections were especially strong. Director Magalhães Pinto not only had served as minister and participated in the President's campaign, but his daughter was married to the president's son.
76 In fact there were judicial rulings that temporarily suspended the program, but the Central Bank was able to overturn them.
77 Legislation extended 'solidarity' responsibility of majority shareholders to institutions under intervention or extra-judicial liquidation, facilitating the appropriation of assets from institutions in distress or in violation of central bank regulations.
78 Senator Andrade Vieira (PTB-PR), from a party within the government's coalition, had collaborated actively in the campaign of Cardoso in 1994 and donated funds to the campaign.
79 *Estado de São Paulo*, 25 December 1996, indicated the bank drew upon the interbank market at an average rate of R$2.6 billion a day.
80 J.R. Mendonça de Barros, G. Loyola and J. Bogdanski, *Reestruturação do setor financeiro*, Minstry of Finance, memo, January 1998. p. 10: "In reality, the problems faced by state banks are primarily fiscal rather than banking, but its dimensions do not permit any other type of solutions."
81 This part draws heavily on Moisés S. Marques, 'Conjunturas críticas e reformas liberalizantes – o papel dos fatores domésticos e internacionais – a experiência do Brasil', Doctoral dissertation, Department of Political Science, Universidade de São Paulo, 2004.
82 We would like to thank Mailson da Nóbrega and Gustavo Loyola for the substantial insights and details they provided to the authors about the financial operations conducted by the Central Bank.
83 As the following sections show, future investigations found very little evidence of any illegal conduct on behalf of the Central Bank. The primary objective of this paper, however, is not to determine whether the Central Bank acted in an unjustifiable, or even illegal, fashion. We are more concerned with the political consequences generated by such allegations of improper conduct. As a result, this paper will focus on how the press portrayed these events rather than conduct an analysis over the merits of the Central Bank's actions.
84 The latter, of course, also has the benefit of increasing the country's credit rating to international investors.
85 Lei Complementar n. 12, 1970. The law effectively transferred approval of all credit operations away from the legislature. All credit operations conducted by the National Treasury could be carried out at the criteria of the National Monetary Council (CMN) without having to register revenues and expenditures in the Orçamento Geral da União (OGU). Due to this measure, the OGU became a merely formal instrument.
86 Members from the National Monetary Council have varied across administrations, but

they are primarily drawn from the Federal Executive – which include the president of the Central Bank and other government ministers.

87 The Monetary Budget became so large during military rule that it became larger and more significant than the country's fiscal budget approved by the Congress. See World Bank, *Brazil: Financial Systems Review*, Washington, DC: World Bank, 1984.

88 I. Mas, 'Central bank independence: a critical view from a developing country perspective', *World Development*, 23/10 (1995), 1639–52.

89 This mechanism came to be known as the "conta-movimento" and was created March 29, 1965. Such an operation was meant to be a transitory instrument to make up for the incipient infrastructure and assets of the Central Bank. The Banco do Brasil was supposed to pay all debts incurred with the CB each week, with interest rates of one percent. Such a liquidity demand, however, was gradually relaxed, and the BB used such account extensively to finance a number of development projects which didn't show up on public accounts.

90 The most important of which include: the National Development Bank (BNDE), the Federal Savings and Loan Bank (Caixa Econômica Federal, CEF), the National Housing Bank (Banco Nacional de Habitação).

91 For details over the set of reforms concerning the monetary budget, see Guardia, E.. *Orçamento público e política fiscal: aspectos institucionais e a experiência recente – 1985/1991*, Instituto de Economia. Campinas: Universidade Estadual de Campinas, 1992.

92 CMN Vote n. 045, January, 1986.

93 In 1987 the government abolished the 'Área de Fomento do Banco Central', which throughout military rule played an important role as a financing agent to rural sectors. See M. Nóbrega, *O Brasil em transformação*, São Paulo, Editora Gente, 2000.

94 The five largest federal financial institutions include: the Banco do Brasil, the Federal Saving Bank (Caixa Econômica Federal), the Banco Nacional de Desenvolvimento Econômico e Social (BNDES), the Banco do Nordeste and the Banco da Amazônia. The assets of those five financial institutions represent 40% of all assets in Brazil's financial system. A report by Booz-Allen and Hamilton analysing all five institutions highlighted the lack of transparency over how all five spend public resources. See Booz-Allen and Hamilton – Fipe (Consórcio). *Instituições financeiras públicas federais – alternativas para a reorientação estratégica*, Public Hearing. Brasília, June 2000.

95 At the time some Central Bank directors stated that relief to both banks were in order to, "compensate for the losses incurred by both institutions, stop the bankruptcy of the BM and F and reduce the risk of a systemic crisis at the time of the devaluation". *O Estado de São Paulo*, 16 April 1999.

96 One must keep in mind that such decisions were made in an extremely volatile context where the costs of the inevitable devaluation to the Brazilian economy were of paramount concern..

97 *O Estado de São Paulo*, 16 April 1999.

98 According to an official statement by the government, "The dismissal of Francisco Lopes as President of the Central Bank was motivated exclusively by the failed dual band exchange rate implemented in January which anticipated the free floating of the exchange rate that culminated in the devaluation of the Real." *O Estado de São Paulo*, 15 April 1999.

99 There are indications, however, the PMDB never intended a full investigation to occur.

100 The bailout program lent a total of R$21 billion to private banking institutions in between the years of 1995 and 1997.

101 One of these documents includes a note from Cacciola to Lopes, handed over by an assistant, which was a petition for help written in a manner suggesting a degree of personal intimacy. *O Estado de São Paulo*, 24 April 1999. Another document revealed that Lopes held a bank account outside Brazil totaling US$1.6 million, whose deposit had been made by an ex-partner, the brother of Luiz Bragança, Sérgio. The ex-president appeared to have a web of 'dangerous' relations, and at the minimum, they reveal a case of tax evasion.

102 According to *O Estado de São Paulo*, 26 April 1999, the leadership of the CPI had come to the conclusion that, "... the conduct of the investigations over the relationship between the Central Bank and the financial market, and specifically the still unclear involvement of the ex-president of the Central Bank Francisco Lopes, has gone beyond the limits of good common sense."

103 It is interesting to note that at certain points the CPI could be construed to have gone beyond its delegated powers and infringe upon the Judiciary's jurisdiction.

104 By operational autonomy we mean autonomy over how to conduct objectives established by the federal executive. The Central Bank of Brazil, however, remains dependent upon the federal executive to the extent the President of the Republic nominates the president of the Bank, which must be ratified in the Senate, and can also dismiss the president of the Bank at his or her discretion.

105 *O Estado de São Paulo*, 26 April 1999.

106 *O Estado de São Paulo*, 3 December 1999.

107 This measure was popularly known in the financial market as the 'Compliance' Resolution.

108 The Central Bank of Brazil can be audited by the Federal Accounting Office (Tribunal de Contas da União) and the Federal Control Secretariat (Secretaria Federal de Controle).

109 *Folha de São Paulo*, 31 February 2000.

110 For example, credit fees and monthly balance sheet data were previously only accessible through Sisbacen.

111 Hagopian, F. 'The (too-low but) rising qualilty of democracy in Brazil and Chile: effective or representative democracies?', in L. Diamond and L. Morlino, *The Quality of Democracy*, Johns Hopkins University Press, forthcoming, 2005.

Chapter 7

Courts, policy contestation, and the legitimation of economic reform under Cardoso

Matthew M. Taylor

BRAZILIAN COURTS PLAYED an important role in integrating the nation into global markets and deepening constitutional democracy during the 1990s. This chapter focuses on the Brazilian judiciary during the two-term reformist Cardoso presidency, a presidency marked by 'neoliberal' reforms which drew explicitly or implicitly on key tenets of the 'Washington Consensus'. Many issues impinging directly on monetary policy were contested in the courts during this period: rules on public borrowing and debt, the restructuring of financial institutions, and the regulation of financial markets among them.[1] So too, were a number of other elements of the Cardoso reform program that had a significant interaction with Brazil's monetary policy choices between 1995 and 2002, through their influence on confidence in the political, balance of payments, and fiscal foundations of the Cardoso reform program.[2]

Because of the popularity and success of Cardoso's economic stabilization plan, the Real Plan, and in light of the not insignificant threats generated by a string of external financial crises, the Cardoso government was repeatedly able to craft majoritarian and super-majoritarian coalitions to pass critical reform legislation. Yet despite considerable legislative majorities, once approved, these reforms frequently faced significant contestation in the Brazilian judiciary. Even as reforms promised to yield either political or market dividends, or both, courts allowed these dividends to be contested or reapportioned. Court decisions not infrequently contributed to abrupt changes in the perceptions of market strategists about the prospects for reform in Brazil.

During the eight years of Cardoso's presidency, federal courts were called upon in some fashion to question almost all of the major reforms implemented by the administration, including social security reform, privatization, civil service reform, and various tax and fiscal measures. In many cases, judicial debate was merely a continuation of debates taking place elsewhere in the political system. The 1988 Constitution, with its statist approach to governance, provided a key justification for many legal challenges, as well as providing the institutional framework within which court challenges took place. The courts' strong commitment to the Constitution and the existing legal framework at times led them into significant conflicts with the Cardoso government. By the end of Cardoso's presidency, relations had reached a point where it was not startling to hear significant criticism of the courts from the executive branch: Cardoso's embattled attorney general went so far as to label the courts a "judicial madhouse".[3]

The judiciary served a dual function during the Cardoso presidency. First, despite its rocky relations with the executive branch, it provided legitimizing justifications for important changes to the 1988 Constitution, providing a legal defence for many of the reforms implemented by Cardoso. Second, however, it provided select opposition groups with an institutional locus from which to alter reform, thus changing the strategic considerations of the Cardoso administration in crafting reform and occasionally providing the opposition with a veto point from which to reverse key reforms.

The remainder of this chapter proceeds in three sections. The first section focuses on the relationship between the Cardoso government and three key constituencies that played a major role in the course of reform: financial markets, the broad electorate, and organized corporatist actors. The second section details the role of the judiciary, arguing that the manner in which policy reform was carried out, combined with the characteristics of the judiciary as an institution, led to predictable patterns of conflict within the court system. Finally, the conclusion suggests that the use of the courts to contest Cardoso's reforms led to a type of contentiousness in the judicialization of policy that frequently placed the three constituencies at rhetorical loggerheads, even as both government and opposition sought the courts' important legitimation of their claims.

Three constituencies influencing reform

Three constituencies were particularly important to Cardoso's reform platform: the broad electorate, financial markets, and finally, organized corporatist actors and their allies in political parties. This section briefly explains the basic logic of the Real Plan, which was at the heart of all of Cardoso's reform initiatives, within the context of these three constituencies' goals and expectations.

Fernando Henrique Cardoso was named as finance minister in May 1993; given the limited ambitions of the Itamar Franco presidency until that point, he came into office facing relatively low expectations. But Cardoso was able to array an impressive group of economists, many of whom had worked on previous economic stabilization plans and thought they could beat their bad luck the second time around, if given enough political insulation and fiscal power. The resulting Real Plan was innovative in many ways, but perhaps most important was the decision to make many necessary fiscal sacrifices up-front, so as to avoid the boom-and-bust cycle that had plagued many preceding plans.[4] Beyond these fiscal measures, the second 'anchor' for the Real Plan was the exchange rate. A strengthened currency combined with falling tariffs boosted imports to unprecedented levels, which would keep domestic prices down, albeit with the inconvenient side effect of a current account deficit that required strong and sustained capital inflows. This would later prove to be a key deficiency in the Real Plan,[5] but for the moment, it led to an enormous burst of purchasing power and a strong inflow of previously unimaginable imported goods.

Cardoso stepped down from the Ministry of Finance to run for president in April 1994, by which time his name was firmly associated with the Real Plan. Inflation fell rapidly to single digits by August 1994, and a consumption boom was well in stride by the October elections. Meanwhile, Cardoso's PSDB had reached an alliance of convenience with centre-right parties that enabled Cardoso to reach a broad mass of voters. The result was an impressive victory in the election contest against the Workers' Party (PT) and its candidate, Luiz Inácio Lula da Silva, who Cardoso came from behind to beat with a solid majority of the vote. President Cardoso was thus inaugurated in January 1995 with a clear platform of economic stabilization and liberalization.

The broad electorate was clearly at the forefront of Cardoso's reformist platform. In seeking to implement a lasting stabilization program, Cardoso sought to slay the dragon of chronic inflation in Brazil and prepare the way to genuine and lasting economic and social development that would benefit the population at large. But as the question of the timing of the post-stabilization consumption boom illustrates, this goal was also political: from the outset, the logic of the Real Plan was not merely economic, but aimed at creating a long-term political support structure that would enable the election and re-election of Cardoso, as well as constrain future presidents in their policy choices, restricting both populist and nationalist options in the national policy agenda.

While it is difficult to summarize the diverse goals of the broad electorate, the quest for a 'silver bullet' that would kill the hyperinflation that had plagued Brazil throughout the late 1980s and early 1990s was broadly consensual and explains a great deal of Cardoso's electoral success.[6] Inflation plans had played a major role in shaping the politics of post-military presidencies, with Sarney's presidency ending in pessimism over the failure of the Cruzado Plan, and Collor's ending with impeachment after the disappointing unravelling of two similar stabilization plans. Meanwhile, in part because of its effects on the government's ability to control its own fiscal and monetary equilibrium and hence, inflation, much of the post-transition period has been devoted to 'unwriting' the statist and decentralizing 1988 Constitution.[7]

While the specific tasks that lay behind this revamping of the national constitution were seldom fully consensual, when framed as part of a broader strategy of stabilization, Cardoso was able to claim the support of the broad electorate for his reforms. Indeed, this support was critical to forming the super-majoritarian coalitions needed to pass important constitutional amendments in Congress, including the re-election amendment, various fiscal packages, and social security and administrative reforms aimed at curtailing the privileges of the highly organized and vocal civil service.

The second constituency Cardoso faced in his reform program was a loose alliance formed between leftist political parties, such as the PT and Communist Party of Brazil (PCdoB); civil servants in federal and state governments and public companies; and corporatist groups like trade unions, the Brazilian bar association (OAB), and other groups with a corporate interest in blocking reform. Relations with this constituency – which have been grouped together here under the inexact title of organized corporatist actors – would prove to be contentious and far more complicated than their hydra-headed nature and minority status would suggest. In part because of the need to pass constitutional amendments if the government wished to cement lasting and long-term reform – and the inherent difficulty of passing such reform[8] – small but organized opposition groups were able to play a major role in the reform process, especially when they acted in concert across many different institutional venues.

Cardoso's reforms placed a large burden on many of the members of this constituency, with civil service and social security reform as well as privatization threatening many of the privileges they had gained in the 1988 Constitution and over the course of Brazilian history. These privileges, however, gave the Cardoso administration even more impetus to tackle this particular constituency. Following the passage of the 1988 Constitution, spending on federal public administration had risen in one year from roughly 30 percent of the budget (excluding debt payments) to almost 68 percent the following year, and stood at over 50 percent as Cardoso took office.[9] Spending on the social security system likewise grew from less than 9 percent in 1988 to account for almost 28 percent of total spending in 1999, with pensions for civil servants representing a significant portion of this total.[10] Members of this second constituency were thus a clear target of Cardoso's reform proposals, while they had significant personal and collective incentives to oppose reform in all possible venues.

The third constituency facing Cardoso were national and international financial markets, which would have the most significant effect on the evolution of the Cardoso presidency. Because of the need to guarantee capital inflows that would sustain the pegged exchange rate, especially in the first term, the acquiescence and confidence of national and international financial markets was essential to the Real Plan, and hence to Cardoso's own political fortunes.

Financial markets – especially stock and foreign exchange markets – are by nature binary, concerned with the short-term up-and-down performance of assets, and putting much less stock in the longer-term political and social ramifications of reform, or the processes surrounding it. As a result, given the critical importance of financial market confidence in the real, Cardoso's first term legislative agenda was targeted in no small measure at meeting this constituency's goals. Reforms of social policy and the political system were discussed, but largely discarded as secondary, with the hope that they could be addressed in a second term once the hard sacrifices required by markets had been undertaken. Inasmuch as stabilization provided clear economic and social benefits, there was some clear overlap between the goals of the broad electorate and the financial markets. But more substantial social policies that might require significant new fiscal expenditures were largely sidelined during the Cardoso presidency, with the emphasis remaining on policies that would reinforce the real's fiscal anchor and ensure strong capital inflows.

Cardoso's focus thus pivoted around economic issues. In addition to cementing the fiscal foundations of the Real Plan, the first term policy agenda laid the legislative groundwork for economic liberalization, focusing on constitutional amendments to the so-called 'economic order' articles of the Constitution, which ended discrimination against foreign capital in the telecommunications, shipping, mining, gas, and petroleum industries. Even more ambitiously, Cardoso also sought constitutional reforms to the social security system, civil service, and the fiscal and tax systems, all enormous projects with embedded anti-reform constituencies. Cardoso succeeded with the economic order reforms by the end of 1995, and passed an extension of the Social Emergency Fund (despite the name, a plan for withholding fiscal transfers to states and municipalities) in 1996. On the larger reforms the Cardoso administration was less successful: tax reform largely died in committee,[11] and neither social security nor civil service reform were approved during Cardoso's first term.[12]

Cardoso's largest political coup was to push through a constitutional amendment in 1997 that allowed federal, state, and municipal executives to run for re-election to a second term. The possibility of re-election prevented Cardoso from falling into political irrelevancy as early in his presidential term as some of his predecessors; it also gave him enormous leverage over the incumbent Congress, allowing for some degree of policy continuity. Thus, even as Cardoso was running for re-election in 1997, Congress was still actively considering social security and civil service reforms, rather than drifting, as it had toward the end of previous presidencies. Markets reacted favourably to this sequence of reforms.

In the non-legislative arena, the first term Cardoso presidency proved agile, if not always lucky. The government was able to contain the impact of the first of many international financial crises it would confront – the Mexican peso crisis early in 1995 – by resorting to a slight, one-off, currency devaluation, a sharp interest rate hike, and further fiscal containment, including tax increases. Using various comprehensive fiscal controls, and considerable political strong-arming, the Cardoso government was also able to wrestle state spending more effectively under control.[13] Although it proved politically costly, state banks – the bugbear of monetary policy, given their ability to expand the money supply by unrestricted lending to state governments – also were constrained, and most were eventually sold off with federal assistance. The government also moved rapidly on privatization of federal firms, selling thirty companies at a total value just shy of US$73 billion.[14]

Despite a string of such successes during Cardoso's first term, the two anchors of Brazil's Real Plan – a pegged, overvalued exchange rate and a credible commitment to fiscal containment – continued to influence financial markets' views of the sustainability of Cardoso's reforms. Without strong capital inflows, the exchange rate anchor for inflationary expectations would not be sustainable against contagion from foreign crises; without a strong fiscal commitment (even if it constrained growth), fears of state borrowing and monetary laxity would persist. Market confidence was thus fundamental to Cardoso's continued success.

The effects of the Mexican peso crisis had passed relatively easily, but proved a harbinger of things to come. As Cardoso headed into his reelection campaign against Lula da Silva, the PT's perennial candidate, Brazil was buffeted by the emerging Asian crisis, which threatened capital inflows – essential to balancing the large current account deficit – and raised questions about the government's pre-electoral commitment to both fiscal and monetary stringency. In November 1997, the government played on fears of crisis to approve a new version of the contentious civil service reform bill in the Chamber (which received final approval in the Senate in June 1998), easing tenure guarantees for public servants, capping wages, and eliminating privileged career tracks in the civil service. Despite the electoral season, the Cardoso administration also initially played by the austerity rule book, sharply tightening monetary policy, cutting spending, and raising taxes. Growth slowed, but both consumer and financial market confidence in the Real Plan remained largely intact, with inflation continuing below one percent a month throughout the crisis.

Electoral pressures proved too much, however, and by early 1998 the government had eased monetary policy and abandoned its recent commitments to austerity. Failure to meet these commitments proved a big mistake as a second financial maelstrom, the Russian crisis, began to shake emerging markets in May 1998. Initially, the Cardoso economic team held off on compensatory measures, but by late August – when the Russian moratorium was declared – it was clear that Brazil had become the next emerging market domino, with market attention focused on the government's commitment to its fiscal and exchange rate anchors. Monetary and fiscal policies were again tightened, with the key government interest rate hiked from 19 percent to an incredible 50 percent in September, while Cardoso promised a new fiscal adjustment program for 1999–2001. Most amazingly, as the election approached, Brazil began talks with the IMF for the first time since the early 1990s.

Ironically, the crisis may have helped Cardoso win re-election, by allowing him to pose as the only candidate possessed of the technocratic skill needed to preserve the Real Plan; certainly, the PT's erratic and pessimistic policy prescriptions did little to help Lula da Silva's cause during this election. The final tally was a resounding victory for Cardoso. But in retrospect, it is clear that Cardoso entered his second term a weaker president, hurt by the distractions to his policy agenda engendered by crisis; the doubts surrounding the viability of the Real Plan; and by the fact that he was now in his final term, with only two years to go before the start of a highly uncertain presidential campaign, in which it was unclear who would carry the mantle of the Real Plan.[15]

Cardoso would be further weakened by the sequence of events following his second inauguration in January 1999, which included a devaluation, a perceptible slowdown in the pace of reform, and a highly damaging electricity shortage. Because the interest here is in the effect of the courts, this is not the place for a detailed account of the second term, in large part because it was in many ways a continuation of the reform program laid out in the first. Meanwhile, policy change and policy contestation during this second term followed similar patterns, with the three constituencies vying for their primary goals. Financial markets were concerned about the sustainability of the Real Plan and its binary effect on market performance. The broad electorate was somewhat anxious about the sustainability of the Real Plan but also increasingly sceptical about the Cardoso administration's commitment to capable and honest governance, as well as to fundamental social policy reform. Organized corporate actors saw in the devaluation and the various crises of the second term an opportunity to overturn some of the reforms that had targeted them, or at the very least, to gain some leverage over the pace and content of new reforms.

Reform and the courts

The description above offers a conventional view of the reform process under Cardoso, ignoring the role of the courts. By excluding the judiciary from the process, it provides an incomplete but rather common account of the reform process. But it ignores a crucial fact: as Table 7.1 illustrates, most of the key reforms passed into law by the Cardoso administration were subsequently challenged in the Brazilian federal court system. In more than half the cases, some portion of the challenged law was stayed or overturned by the Supreme Federal Tribunal (Supremo Tribunal Federal, or STF), which by virtue of the breadth of the 1988 Constitution is the country's senior court in function, if not formally.[16]

Despite this clear evidence of courts' effect on policy, financial markets were frequently blindsided by the judiciary's role, which has generally been excluded from most executive-centric accounts of the political and economic policymaking processes. This frequently led to

Table 7.1: ***Cardoso's reforms and the courts***

Reform	*Challenged in high or low courts?*	*Any portion of reform delayed/ overturned in STF?*
Emergency Social Fund	Yes	No
Real Plan	Yes	Yes
Economic Order Reforms	Yes	No
National Privatization Program	Yes	Yes
Fiscal Stabilization Fund	Yes	No
CPMF Tax	Yes	Yes
Civil Service Reform	Yes	Yes
Social Security Reform	Yes	Yes
Civil Service Pension Tax	Yes	Yes
Electricity Rationing	Yes	Yes

abrupt changes in the perceptions of market strategists, whether it was driven by a temporary delay in a privatization auction; a reversal on a concrete reform, such as social security reform; or the discovery of some fiscal 'skeleton' that might emerge for the government to pay if courts were to uphold broad challenges to policy. Market surprise and dismay at instances of court 'interference' in policy is well captured by the newspaper headlines that led some contemporaneous press reports on the courts' action:

"Banks see judicial insecurity";[17]
"STF is once again the center of attention";[18]
"STF decision drives down shares of state-owned companies";[19]
"Uncertainty leads to valuation of dollar";[20]
"BNDES accompanies judicial battle with pessimism";[21]
"Social security vote provokes judicial battle";[22]
"The potential fiscal threat [of a court decision]";[23]
"Brazil shares close lower, off sharp lows as impact of govt defeat eases";[24]
"Brazil's efforts on budget imperiled by court rulings".[25]

Key members of the market constituency made their views of the courts' influence well known publicly, either through public statements, or by voting with their money. Quotes from contemporaneous news reports in this vein include:

"'[This court decision] makes me wonder about Brazil's ability to get serious,' said [a bank economist]."[26]

"'[This court decision] shows that one branch of the Government is more concerned with preserving the privileges ... rather than insuring the long-term health of the economy,' said [a bank economist]."[27]

"Traders said ... the market is expecting the government's response [to a court decision] early next week, but warned that a delay will not be accepted."[28]

"The [court] decision had immediate repercussions in the São Paulo stock market."

"Discouraged by the impasse that is leading to ever more delays on the sale of the bank, investors began to sell their shares. As a result, the bank's shares fell 6.37 percent yesterday alone. This week, the share price has already fallen 16.81 percent."[29]

As these examples suggest, market actors were frequently surprised and dismayed by the judiciary's role in the political process, and by its potential impact on financial markets. But perhaps the most delectable example of this latent belief that the judiciary should act according to the logic of market reform came from the IMF's chief representative in its talks with Brazil. Tereza Ter-Minassian, the IMF economist, went on the record in April 2000 to say that, "I think that the STF will be cautious" in a decision on the monetary correction of FGTS employment compensation accounts, given its enormous potential fiscal cost.[30] Whether this was an appropriate intervention by the IMF's senior representative can be left to history; regardless, her hopes were spectacularly dashed by the STF's decision shortly thereafter, which suggested once again that the judiciary paid little heed to the market or the IMF's fiscal concerns in reaching decisions about the cases before it.

These anecdotal examples illustrate that the Brazilian federal judiciary is an influential institution in terms of its political weight, its impact on policy, and the resulting implications for both financial markets and the political actors in society at large. Institutionally, there are good reasons for it to play an important role: Brazil's judiciary is the one of the best funded court systems in the hemisphere, it is highly independent of other branches of government, and the executive and legislative branches have routinely complied with its decisions.[31]

The Brazilian courts' role is also not surprising in a global context: worldwide, there has been a growing 'judicialization' of politics since World War II.[32] Courts have intervened in politics to an extent that forces governments to take judicial reactions into account when formulating policy.[33] Brazil is no exception to this trend, with courts taking an increasingly active role in policy decisions, especially since the adoption of the 1988 Constitution. Anticipating such judicial action, Brazilian governments have consulted with judges before implementing policy, tested proposals with lawyers, and altered the deliberative justifications behind policy choices with the judiciary in mind.

As a result of the Brazilian courts' institutional makeup, and of the courts' evident impact on reform, it is clear that the judiciary needs to be brought more fully into our analysis of the policy process, and its effects on fiscal and monetary policies need to be modelled more carefully. The experience of Cardoso's reforms is used below to make two related claims about the role of the Brazilian judiciary as a locus for opposition to policy. Both relate to the 'raw material' that reaches the courts, and help to explain the importance of the courts during the Cardoso administration:

1) The characteristics of a policy help to determine whether a particular policy will rise to judicial consideration, long before any decision is made by a judge. Certain types of policies, in other words, are more likely to be contested in the courts than others;
2) The institutional rules and structure of the judiciary determine how and where specific policy issues will be raised within the judiciary. Institutional arrangements that determine who is given access to the judiciary, and where in the judiciary this access is granted, are essential to determining who can challenge policy, and may also affect their chances for doing so effectively.

These two claims help to explain why it was that the three constituencies described in the previous section saw differential effects from judicial action. Financial markets – whose members seldom participated in judicial actions against policy – were frequently surprised by the continuation of policy debates in the courts, and by the effectiveness of the courts in thwarting some aspects of reform. In large part this was because market analyses ignored the potential use of the courts as a veto point on policy. Such 'surprises' played a role in shaping market confidence in the continuation of reform, and hence, influenced market expectations regarding fiscal and monetary policies. The broad electorate had recourse to the courts only on a very individual level, with individuals' suits against policies exerting little influence on the broad course of policy except in the aggregate. Organized corporatist actors, for reasons described below, were able to use the courts as one more venue from which to challenge reforms, gaining significant leverage from their privileged access to the judiciary and in the process influencing market perceptions of the Cardoso government's success on reform.

Reforms and policy contestation

Not all reforms have been equally judicialized. As Ferejohn notes, judicial politics follows legislation.[34] Policies that are not enacted through concrete legislation tend not to be heavily contested in the courts. This suggests, for example, that some non-legislative actions, like budget implementation, may be harder to contest in the courts than reforms that were entirely legislative, such as the annual budget bill.[35] Under Brazil's civil law system, given the importance of abstract forms of constitutional review at the STF,[36] concrete legislation can be more easily contested than non-legislative policy initiatives. Yet, even among the policies that have a clear legislative footprint, certain topics have been much more hotly contested than others. Drawing on the work of Lowi and Wilson, it is argued here that policies that have highly concentrated costs that hurt a specific, organized (or organizable) constituency are much more likely to be contested in the courts than other policies.

Lowi's influential assertion that "policy determines politics",[37] suggested that the nature of the political debate surrounding a given policy may be determined by some overarching characteristics of the general policy type. Rather than study the politics of banking regulation, of social security, or of health care, Lowi suggested instead that policies could be grouped into three or four major types of policy, each of which would lead to their own particular brand of political negotiation.[38] Building on this notion, Wilson greatly improved the specificity and generalzability of the typology by suggesting that the politics surrounding a policy might be determined by the distribution of the costs and benefits of the policy at hand, generating four different types of politics: concentrated benefits with concentrated costs; concentrated benefits with distributed costs; distributed benefits with concentrated costs; and distributed benefits with distributed costs.[39]

There is not room here for a more detailed evaluation of the politics that surround each of the policy types,[40] suffice to note that many of Cardoso's most important 'market-friendly' economic reforms are best characterized as policies with distributed benefits and highly concentrated costs. More so than many of its social programs, the Cardoso administration's economic reforms – from the sale of state banks to civil service reform – challenged a well-organized and mobilized opposition. As Wilson noted, such policies are often difficult to implement because they generate intense opposition during the deliberative process.

Policies of this type place an onus on one easily defined group, which is likely to feel its burdens keenly, with a strong incentive to organize. Implementing such a policy will be difficult since the burdened group will have a much easier time organizing when all members of the group feel threatened by the concentrated costs, thus overcoming potential collective action problems. It may, however, be possible to implement such policies at moments of crisis, or if a policy entrepreneur is able to make appeals against the 'self-serving' nature of the previous policy for the burdened group. Cardoso was extraordinarily successful at using both of these strategies to generate the impetus for reform, whether it was by drawing on Collor's rhetorical flourishes about the unfairness of a system of civil service 'maharajahs' or playing up the need for sacrifice in the face of continued international market instability.

Court use is often an extension of the political process seen in the executive and legislative branches. It is not surprising, therefore, that policies across such disparate issues as social security reform, civil service reform, privatization, judicial salaries, and labour reform – all of which fit into this rubric of distributed benefits with concentrated costs – tended to lead to a much higher volume of court cases than other policies that fit more neatly into other rubrics, such as agrarian reform (concentrated costs and benefits), automotive industry policy (concentrated benefits with distributed costs), or the laws surrounding electricity rationing (distributed benefits with distributed costs). Furthermore, the elements of these other policy types that have been most contested in the courts are the elements with distributed benefits and concentrated costs. Thus, in agrarian reform, lawyers contested a particular portion of the reform legislation that placed caps on their earnings; in automotive policy, the IPI tax on imports and import tariffs which hurt a concentrated group of producers were the most heavily contested elements of the policy.

Analysis of the use of one particular constitutional review mechanism which was frequently used to contest federal policy choices, the Ação Direta de Inconstitucionalidade (ADIN), shows that during the Cardoso government the most hotly contested policies during the Cardoso government were those with concentrated costs and diffuse benefits. In over half of the more than five hundred ADINs during this period, the target was a policy with concentrated costs and distributed benefits, on topics that ranged from civil service and civil service pension reform to changes in social security and the regulation of individual industries. But even in policies such as taxation and labour policy, which fit less clearly into this policy rubric, the patterns of contestation frequently followed the same rule: the most heavily challenged elements of these policies were those with concentrated costs and distributed benefits.

The notion that certain policies may be more likely to lead to court action is not a startlingly radical discovery. After all, one of the key roles of the judiciary in democratic theory as espoused by thinkers as diverse as Montesquieu, Locke and Rosseau is the protection of minority interests against either the majority or the state. And certainly many neoliberal reform policies enacted in Latin America during the 1990s were explicitly designed to be prejudicial to minority interests. But where this analysis becomes particularly interesting is in the insight that by virtue of the types of reforms Cardoso was pushing, especially in the areas markets were most sensitive to, it was no mistake that the judiciary was intensely used by opponents of reform to contest many of his policies. More importantly, under the rules governing the judiciary, these opponents frequently had relatively privileged access to the courts, as is argued below. That is, not only were these policies more likely to be contested in the courts, but the constituency most hurt by the reforms – organized corporatist actors – had special standing in the courts that made it likely that judicial mechanisms would be used to contest policy. Failure to recognize the relevance of the courts as a significant venue for policy opposition by potential veto players led to the frequent surprise and frustration of financial market players with the judicial system.

Courts and veto players

Not all plaintiffs are created equal. Some plaintiffs have been much more likely, and are frequently much more able, to contest policy in the courts than others. The motivations for plaintiffs to use the courts to contest policy choices are diverse: the decision to contest policy may be driven by genuine legal considerations, such as a belief that the Constitution has been flaunted in the process of passing reforms in Congress; by political actors' belief that their particular interests have been hurt by reform, and that legal challenges offer one more extension of the political process; or by strategic political concerns, such as a desire to delay, disable, or discredit the executive's policy initiatives, regardless of how the court case itself plays out. But whatever the motivations for bringing court cases, the institutional structure of the courts plays an important role in determining how policy is challenged, and who is able to effectively challenge policies.

Plaintiff decisions to use the courts to contest policy may also be driven by strategic considerations about the institutional mechanisms available to them. Applying veto player theory to the Brazilian courts, specific veto points within the judiciary offer an institutional locus for political actors to veto reform. Furthermore, these veto points may empower particular groups that would otherwise have little influence in the policy process.[41] There are two important findings here: analytically, our failure to identify key veto points or veto players may weaken our ability to predict policy change; and practically, failure to do so may explain the surprise felt by members of financial markets and the government itself when faced with recurring reversals to reform in the judicial 'madhouse'. This section briefly explains the concept of veto players and veto points before applying it directly to the question of reform and the courts under Cardoso.

The 'veto player' literature attempts to explain how superficially similar political systems may experience sharply different political processes, leading to very different policy outcomes. Simplifying for the sake of brevity, the key insight of veto player theory is that the more political actors whose 'agreement is required to enact policy change' exist (veto players), and the greater the distance between their preferences, the more difficult it becomes to change the status quo.[42] As more veto players with discrete preferences are added to a political system, the opportunities for finding a consensus in favour of change shrink; that is, the potential 'winset' in favour of a change in the status quo shrinks. In the context of the reforms that swept Latin America during the 1990s, veto player theory offers an interesting comparative perspective on why it is that countries with superficially similar political systems saw substantially different reform outcomes. Brazil offers a particularly interesting comparative case in this regard because it has more veto players than its peers in the region,[43] suggesting that the difficulty of reform in Brazil may be tied directly to the number of actors who had an influence over the reform process.

But a second conceptual insight needs to be addressed, which is that the institutional opportunities for the exercise of a veto matter as well. These veto points can be defined as institutional loci for political actors to exercise vetoes of legislation or policies. The concept of veto points is subsidiary to veto player theory, but it is important because of the insight it provides: namely, that institutional arrangements may result in very condition-specific opportunities for veto playing. Without the specific institutional or procedural opportunities for voicing their opposition – a congressional committee vote, a presidential decree authority, or a judicial hearing, for example – political actors may have no chance to exercise their veto, and hence, may not be able to act as veto players at all. At its most banal, this would suggest that if the judicial branch were shut down, or if the courts were always subservient to the executive, there would be no judicial veto point that could be utilized by potential veto players in the political system. In such a system, a veto player who relied solely on the courts because they had no access to the executive or legislative branches would be entirely shut out of the political system, unable to exercise any kind of veto over policy. Going a step further, this suggests that depending on the institutional structure and rules of the game, veto points may have a significant influence on how different constituencies are able to express their policy preferences and behave as veto players, or indeed, to exist as veto players at all.

The veto player and veto point frameworks have seldom been extended to courts,[44] and when they have, the courts are generally portrayed as a single veto player within the larger political system.[45] The principal architect of veto player theory, George Tsebelis, argues that the judiciary is not a veto player when performing statutory interpretations (because it can be overruled) but is a veto player with respect to constitutional interpretation. He softens this, however, by arguing that most of the time, courts are 'absorbed' by other political veto players;[46] when they are not, the 'black box' of decision-making by the judiciary makes it impossible to allocate judicial decisions to veto player policy positions.[47] These reasons for ignoring the role of the courts as veto players in their own right seem largely reasonable. But as has been argued above, there is another reason to apply veto player theory to the courts: namely, that the manner in which the Brazilian courts are structured provides an institutional environment in which veto players from outside the court system may emerge; oftentimes, these are veto players who are also not immediately evident in studies of the executive and legislative branches. While the Brazilian judiciary may only rarely act as a veto player in its own right, its more important impact on policy comes from the veto points it offers to other policy actors seeking to prevent change in the status quo.

Two aspects of the Brazilian court system enable its use by veto players, and not infrequently, provide such veto players with veto points that are constitutive of their veto 'playerhood' in ways that are not available to their peers in comparable federal systems, for example, in Argentina or Mexico. The first is the extreme congestion of the lower courts. The second is the 1988 Constitution's expansion – to a wide but nonetheless limited gamut of policy players – of the right to file constitutional review cases. The first aspect – lower court congestion – is driven by a number of factors, including the extreme independence of judges from each other, the absence of binding precedent, the possibility of repeated appeals, heavy use of the courts by the government, and problems in filling judgeships. In the aggregate, these factors mean that a typical court case, going from the courts of first instance to the STF, can take from eight to ten years for resolution. It also leads to what Arantes terms the "atomization of justice",[48] with different judges offering different judgements on similar cases across the full court system. Together, the slow and atomized nature of the courts tends to give greater weight to injunctions that can be obtained and served almost immediately in lower courts, temporarily delaying policy implementation.

Legal strategies based on broad-based pursuit of injunctions were heavily used by many opponents of the Cardoso regime. In the case of privatization, for example, the opposition frequently resorted to filing suits across as many lower courts as possible to obtain injunctions, strategies which if nothing else demonstrated to their constituencies their firm opposition to the sales. But in the process, the injunctions also frequently delayed privatization, and generated a great deal of market uncertainty about the government's ability to implement its stated goals of selling off key state-owned companies. The same occurred with the electricity rationing program, which led to hundreds of injunction requests across the lower courts, complicating the process of policy implementation, and throwing the efficacy of government policy initiatives into doubt. Broad-based action in the lower courts was useful to political actors not only because it created more of a political repercussion than any single court case on its own, but also because it involved a numbers game: in the absence of binding precedent, suits in individual lower courts offer good chances of hitting on a judge who will uphold some aspects of a challenge that might not withstand scrutiny in the high courts; and while some lower court judges might be known to be more sympathetic to the opposition's goals, the only way to hit on such judges was by spreading cases as widely as possible.[49]

The second aspect of the court system that determined how policy was challenged emerges from the first. Extreme congestion and delay in the lower courts means that the privilege of bringing constitutional review cases at the Supreme Federal Tribunal (STF) offers an expedited means of challenging policy for those groups included in the constitutional text on the subject. Over the past decade and a half, policy opponents have frequently used the ADIN (Ação Direta de Inconstitucionalidade – Direct Action of Unconstitutionality) mechanism[50] to 'jump the queue' of cases in the lower courts: by using ADINs, policy opponents have been able to obtain more rapid and binding rulings directly in Brazil's highest court. This recourse to the ADIN is an outcome of the judiciary's congestion: the sooner a case can be heard in the STF, the more rapidly the constitutionality of the policy will be definitively resolved.

Cardoso's policies were contested via ADIN over five hundred times, by a number of veto players who had little voice or only a minority vote in the legislative debate over policy implementation. The rules governing who is able to bring such cases are very important to explaining who ultimately contests policy. Under the Constitution, an ADIN can be proposed by either the president, the federal Senate leadership ('mesa'),

Figure 7.1: ADINs filed against Cardoso policies by political actor

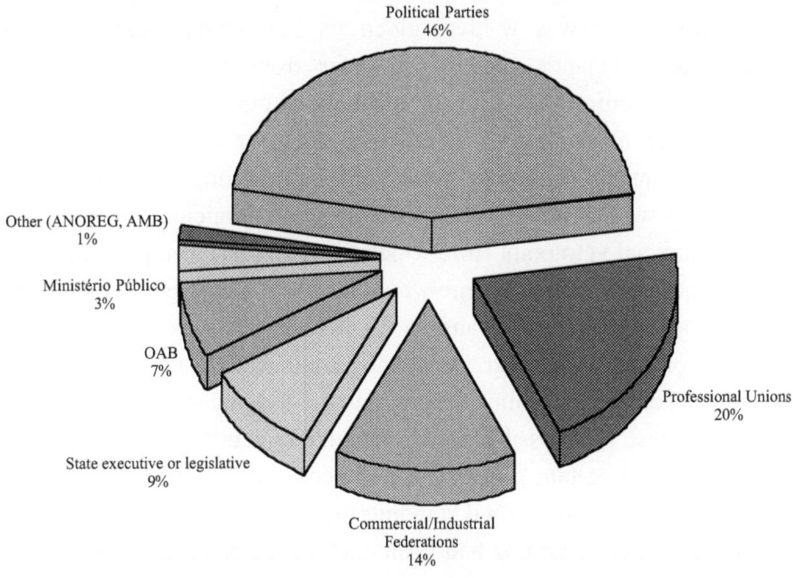

the Chamber of Deputies leadership, state governors, the head of the Ministério Público (the prosecutor-general), the Brazilian bar association (OAB), a political party with congressional representation, or by a union or 'class association' with national representation.[51] As Figure 7.1 illustrates, though, the bulk of ADINs against Cardoso policies were brought by those political actors who were not in the majority: opposition political parties, labour unions, industrial federations, and the OAB were among the most active plaintiffs. In most cases, the plaintiffs in these suits were not well represented in Congress: all of the cases filed by political parties were filed by parties outside the Cardoso coalition; and of the cases filed by professional unions, nearly three out of five were filed by unions with clear public sector ties, often affiliated with the civil service and opposition parties.

The rules governing who has the standing to bring ADINs are therefore essential to understanding who has been enabled to act as a veto player on reform. Although Brazil has perhaps the broadest standing of all countries which allow abstract constitutional review by high courts, it does limit many groups from filing ADINs, with crucial policy implications. The policy process and final policy outcomes might have been very different if Brazil's mayors were permitted to bring constitutional review cases, as Mexico's mayors can. As one example, the Fiscal Stabilization Fund – which was at the heart of the Cardoso government's strategy for combating inflation – would have been practically impossible to approve as it was written, given its 'temporary' suspension of constitutionally mandated revenue transfers from the federal to state and municipal governments. As it was, negotiation of this Fund, of tax reform, and of social security reform all required extensive bargaining with state governors, many of whom were representing important municipal interests as well. But if the nearly six thousand municipalities had been given a judicial veto point from which to wield their own potential veto of legislation, the policy picture would no doubt likely look far different than it does today, either because of the effect of such a veto threat on the leverage of mayors in congressional negotiations of the Fund, or because of the impact of suits against the law actually filed by mayors in the STF.

In contrast, it is possible also to imagine how different policy might have been had certain groups not had access to the institutional veto point provided by the formal standing they were granted in the STF. If corporatist interest groups had been excluded, a number of successful challenges that resulted in major policy implications might never have been filed. These include the bar association's challenge to Cardoso's agrarian reform;[52] judges' and prosecutors' associations' challenges to the broad privileges given to the bar association in the statute law governing lawyers;[53] the national industrial federation's challenge to social security reform[54] and a host of tax programs;[55] and labour unions' challenges to various labour policies.[56]

The veto players who are enabled by their representation in the STF face few impediments to filing ADINs, but some veto players are clearly more successful in the courts than others, with the Brazilian bar association (OAB), for example, more than 1.6 times as likely to succeed in obtaining an injunction in an ADIN case as any other group, ceteris paribus.[57] Meanwhile, despite considerable variability in the success of the various plaintiffs who challenged Cardoso policies, the chances of derailing policy via an ADIN were fairly good: historically, there has been a nearly one in five chance that the STF would grant a positive injunction or decision on the merits in any given ADIN filing.[58] These are not long odds, especially for groups that have been shut out of earlier phases of the political process, and faced few costs for filing such suits.

Institutional rules governing interest mediation in the courts strongly influenced the patterns of court involvement in conflicts over the Cardoso reform agenda. First, in its role as a constitutionally mandated defender of broadly defined constitutional rights, the judiciary was frequently called upon to rule on reforms at loggerheads with the generally statist direction of the Constitution. The prevalence within the Cardoso reform agenda of policies that challenged small groups of well-organized interests who had little representation in the congressional process meant that the courts often became the site of further policy debate. Second, the loose judicial hierarchy permitted some political actors to adopt judicial strategies that took advantage of the atomization of judicial power across many different courts, using such strategies to obtain quick, and most often temporary but nonetheless politically salient victories against key Cardoso reforms. The waves of injunctions filed against various privatization auctions and the electric rationing program are prime examples of the use of this strategy. Third, as a result of the possibility of direct appeal of some cases at the STF, the constitutionality of reform legislation was frequently contested in an expedited fashion by organized policy groups granted standing in the STF by the

1988 Constitution, who happened to be opponents of reform. In several high-profile cases, ranging from social security reform to agrarian reform, this led to the quick suspension or reversal of important legislation after major political capital had been expended in its approval by Congress. Market consternation at such decisions was considerable, leading not infrequently to abrupt changes in market perceptions of the short and medium term economic and political outlook.

Legitimacy and courts

There are many existing views of the legitimating role of courts. As many political scientists have noted, both the substantive and procedural legitimacy of policy are essential components of systemic democratic legitimacy: courts play an essential role in this regard by confirming the substantive legitimacy of policy and in so doing confirm its procedural legitimacy as well.[59] Weber laid the foundation for this claim in his classic discussion of rational, traditional, and charismatic claims to legitimacy. Rational claims to legitimacy – essential to modern bureaucratic administration – are founded implicitly on process: the "law" governing group members is an "impersonal order" that is above any single person in authority, and therefore, while the law may be "imposed", if imposed, there must be grounds of expedience or value-rationality associated with that imposition. While modern critics assail the normative neutrality of Weber's assertion, there is little doubt that the process of law-making and law-finding by courts contribute to imparting an impersonal nature to law in modern democracies.[60] As Waltman and Holland state, "[t]he legitimacy of the state cannot be disconnected from law, for law is what connects people to government both substantively and symbolically. It provides a frame of reference for the conduct of ordinary citizens as well as linking the state with a moral order."[61] More recent works have emphasized that deliberation contributes to the legitimacy of decisions made under scarcity. Given that most public policy decisions are choices under conditions of scarcity, and that courts are an important site for deliberation on priorities, courts may therefore play an important role in legitimating policy choices.[62]

The role played by the Brazilian courts during the 1990s contributed significantly to the widespread legitimation of the reform process, even though the courts were themselves seldom full-fledged supporters of change. During Cardoso's reformist presidency, the judiciary played an important role as an actor in, and a locus for, policy debate. As noted in the previous section, the judiciary was used by other policy players as an important check on an otherwise powerful executive branch, forcing the Cardoso administration to revise proposals in a range of policy areas to fit the constitutional framework as it was interpreted by the courts. Furthermore, the court system frequently represented the last step in the process of negotiation surrounding reform: following bargaining in the executive and legislative branches, reform frequently crossed the square dividing the Congress, presidential offices and STF for another round of discussion in the high court.

The role of the courts in challenging Cardoso policies was perhaps more astonishing to Brazil's market constituency than it was to either of the other constituencies discussed here: the Brazilian electorate at large and organized corporatist actors within the Brazilian political system. Brazil's geographical location may have played a role in shaping market expectations: while it is not shocking, in North American and European contexts, to assert that courts influence the course of public policy,[63] the same claim in Latin America may be more startling to those who would bundle the region's judiciaries together in a sack of equal irrelevance. The experience of Cardoso's Argentine peer is illuminating from this perspective. Unlike the remarkably independent Brazilian judiciary, the Argentine judiciary was browbeaten into submission under Alfonsín and in an even more pronounced fashion under Menem. As a result, no major reform undertaken by Menem was ever overturned by the High Court,[64] in sharp contrast to Cardoso's much more tortured experience in passing and upholding similar neoliberal reforms.

To its credit, the Cardoso government preserved judicial independence and acquiesced to judicial decisions, even as it sought to influence the legal process as a plaintiff, proposed a number of judicial reforms, complained repeatedly about the judiciary's actions, and nominated high court judges believed to be friendly to its goals. Meanwhile, courts were often very helpful to the government, providing definite backing for some key policies as robustly as they criticized and overturned others. Recognizing that the plural of anecdote is not data, a few positive headlines illustrating the government's reliance on the courts may nonetheless provide an important contrast with the kind of negative headlines listed earlier:

"Government will ask STF to manifest itself on CPMF tax";[65]
"Tactical defeat: Yesterday's STF decision, partially recognizing federal government's right to retain revenue transfers to Alagoas, was a [shock] to opposition governors";[66]
"[Opposition governor] Itamar [Franco] is defeated in the Supreme Federal Tribunal";[67]
"[Minister] will try to overturn suit in STF";[68]
"Federal court overturns injunctions against CESP auction".[69]

Courts have been called upon in Brazil to legitimate policy substance, as well as to guarantee procedural legitimacy. They have done so with considerable zeal, and while they have overturned many aspects of important reforms, they have upheld the grand majority, thus imparting a degree of legitimacy that might not exist were it not for their judgements. In addition, Brazilian courts have served as a site for further discussion of policy priorities, giving opposition groups an opportunity to express their disagreement in ways that have not always been available elsewhere in the policy process. The cumulative effect of these deliberative and procedural interventions by the courts has been a positive one for the political system as a whole, providing contentious policies with a degree of legitimacy that would not exist without their intervention, and providing greater legitimacy to a policy process that is notoriously executive-centric. In this manner, courts helped to cultivate a longer-term legitimacy for the Cardoso reforms, even as they occasionally dealt financial markets a short-term setback.

That said, the impact of the Brazilian courts in cultivating legitimacy shows some bare spots. While courts were very involved in contesting contentious policies implemented under the banner of neoliberal reform by the Cardoso government, and they acted in this field with a great deal of independence and a substantial regard for constitutionality and legality, their performance raises some important questions about their legitimizing function and role in a transitioning democracy.

The fundamental question posed by the Brazilian experience is the extent to which courts are in fact helpful in generating legitimacy, and/or whether they perpetuate power in predictable and reform-constraining ways. Three important issues are raised by Cardoso's reform experience. First, it is clear that – as in other legal systems the world over – Brazilian courts tend to represent the interests of some groups better than others.[70]

Not all policy players have been on equal footing in the judicial playing field, giving some greater power over policy than others. Brazil's courts are notoriously slow and inefficient in defending and advancing individual citizens' rights. The glacial pace of lower court challenges tends to improve the odds for legal actors who benefit from delay – often the government itself – and increase the value of access to the high court for those privileged with such access. In the framework provided by this essay, for example, it is clear that the broader electorate of individuals was on the whole more poorly served in the courts than organized corporatist actors or the government itself when questioning key policy reforms.

Second, court structure provided a veto point to specific organized corporatist actors that enabled them to more effectively parlay their opposition to reform into a veto on change than many other constituencies in the Brazilian reform process. Access to the ADIN mechanism in the STF, for example, is a veto point that provides judicial power to some organized group actors – such as the bar association, trade unions, and industrial federations – in a fashion that increases their leverage in other political arenas such as Congress. In this manner, despite strong counter-pressures arising under the aegis of neoliberal reform, corporatist structures that existed in the pre-1988 legal framework, and were written into the 1988 Constitution, have been perpetuated by the distribution of legal power. The 'remarkable resistance' of Brazilian corporatism to change, especially as it is embedded in the legal framework, in large part explains the patterns of judicial conflict over Cardoso's neoliberal agenda.[71]

Finally, while deliberation is fundamental to democratic legitimacy, too often we ignore the fact that certain groups are given a greater voice within some institutional venues, and we often confound voice with deliberation. Voice, as Dahl noted, does not always carry with it the intent to make concessions that is inherent to the concept of deliberation. Indeed, political voice may often be no more than an attempt to impose costs on the parties that refuse to listen to opposition.[72] This would often seem to be the case with the pursuit of injunctions against policy reforms in the lower courts, and frequently seems to be the case in other forms of legal opposition by political parties and other members of the opposition to the Cardoso administration. By imposing delays and instilling doubt, the opposition did not seek true deliberation on the ends of policy, but rather sought primarily to impose costs on the Cardoso government and its supporters while winning points with its own supporters and allies. The result, not infrequently, was success in creating temporary judicial uncertainty that shook financial market confidence without a corresponding gain in political or democratic legitimacy.

Conclusion

The reforms of the Cardoso period required the government to meet the concerns of three key constituencies, financial markets, the broad electorate, and organized corporate groups. Cardoso inherited a system in which reforms were both overdue and necessary, given the exhaustion of the statist economic model and the consequent need to stabilize and liberalize the Brazilian economy. To justify his approach to reform, Cardoso appealed to voters' sense of fairness and their clamour for greater governmental efficiency and performance, and used the urgency engendered by repeated international financial crises to bolster reform coalitions. In so doing, Cardoso was largely able to meet the concerns of international markets, but also raised the hackles of a highly organized opposition, composed of what have been termed here organized corporatist actors.

The role of the courts in this process has been dramatically misinterpreted in the rhetorical debate surrounding Cardoso's reforms, as well as overlooked in much of the academic literature. In the picture painted by some of the press and financial market participants, the judiciary was merely an obstacle to reform, wilfully intervening to veto policies that it disagreed with or which hurt its interests. In the picture painted by the political opposition, the courts served the markets through their overall conservatism and subservience to centre-right governments running from Sarney through Cardoso. In academic circles, perhaps more justifiably, study of the courts' impact on reform has taken a back burner, seen as providing only marginally important gains after the much larger marginal gains seen in studying the presidential and legislative institutions.

The reality of court intervention in reform is complex. While courts indeed threw obstacles in the path of numerous reforms, and on occasion sent policymakers back to the policy drawing board, they also played a crucial role in providing a degree of legitimacy to otherwise contentious policies. The courts provided a locus for democratic opposition by minority groups whose participation was restricted elsewhere in the policy process, but also implicitly ratified the policy direction undertaken on the reforms they did not reject. In sum, while judicial structure in Brazil may sometimes resemble a black box to external observers, and individual judges occasionally went to some lengths to thwart reform policies advanced by the Cardoso government, overall the federal judiciary provided an institutional locus for continuation of a constructive debate over how to accommodate the neoliberal reform package to Brazil's constitutional framework. Although the structure of the judiciary tended to privilege organized, corporatist groups over individual citizens, thereby perpetuating long-standing forms of political organization and occasionally giving markets a fright, within the limitations of this structure, the judiciary played a constructive role in providing a locus for policy contestation, and for legitimating some of the more contentious elements of the Cardoso neoliberal reforms. In this manner, despite the short-term costs the judiciary sometimes imposed on markets and the government, the courts contributed to ensuring the longer-term sustainability of Cardoso's reform project in Brazil.

Notes

1 As examples of cases directly impinging on monetary policy in the high court alone, see Direct Actions of Unconstitutionality 1307, 1376, 1394, 1398, 1454, 1495, 1527, 1667, 1715, 1716, 1720, 1763, 1976, 1992, 2150, 2193, 2194, 2252, and 2259.

2 By focusing on the Cardoso presidency, my goal is to highlight the role of the judiciary in a single reform project, constraining the variance in independent variables that may influence court action over time.

3 'Advogado-geral divulga nota explicando frase', *Folha de São Paulo*, 21 November 2001.

4 The so-called Emergency Social Fund (Fundo Social de Emergência, or FSE) was a key element of this strategy, limiting constitutional transfers to states and municipalities, restraining constitutional earmarking of revenues, and increasing taxes.

5 Eliana Cardoso, for example, notes that there was a 'missing exit strategy' regarding the exchange rate anchor, which directly contributed to Brazil's susceptibility to later crises. Cardoso, Eliana, 'Brazil's currency crisis: the shift from an exchange rate anchor to a flexible regime', in Carol Wise and Riordan Roett, eds., *Exchange Rate Politics in Latin America*, Washington, DC: Brookings Institution Press, 2000.

6 Ironically, it may also explain his failures later in his second term, as the focus of the broad electorate shifted away from stabilization – which began to be taken for granted – and back to growth, concerns with corruption, and social policy.

7 A point forcefully argued in Timothy J. Power, 'Political institutions in democratic Brazil: politics as a permanent constitutional convention', in Peter R. Kingstone and Timothy J. Power, eds., *Democratic Brazil: Actors, Institutions and Processes*, Pittsburgh: University of Pittsburgh Press, 2000, p. 34.

8 Constitutional reforms required approval in several separate committee votes, as well as two votes of 60 percent support in each house of Congress.

9 Matthew M. Taylor, 'Activating judges: courts, institutional structure, and the judicialization of policy reform in Brazil, 1988–2002', PhD dissertation, Georgetown University, 2004, p. 84.

10 Civil servants, even after much reform, continue to benefit disproportionately from the pension system. In 2002, Brazil spent 11.5 percent of GDP on its social security system, against an average of 8.9 percent in the OECD countries. But more than two-fifths of this went to civil servants: 4.7 percent of GDP is spent on civil service pensions, versus an average of 1.7 percent in the OECD. David Fleischer, 'Expenditures on social security', *Brazil Focus Weekly Report*, 19–25 July 2003.

11 This was in part because the Cardoso administration saw broad tax reform as a non-starter: it was likely to lead to strong opposition from state governors that would halt all other legislative initiatives. Furthermore, small changes in key taxes proved sufficient in the short-term to cover the government's fiscal necessities. See Matthew M. Taylor, *Brazil 1999: Country Forecast Report*, London: Business Monitor International Ltd., 1999, 29–46.

12 In fact, the government was dealt an enormous defeat on civil service reform, as the Chamber refused in June 1996 to approve changes in civil servants' benefits, after the bill had been approved in the Senate.

13 See, especially, David Samuels, 'Fiscal straightjacket: the politics of macroeconomic reform in Brazil, 1995–2002', *Journal of Latin American Studies*, 35 (2003): 553.

14 Área de Desestatização e Reestruturação, Banco Nacional de Desenvolvimento Econômico e Social. *Privatização No Brasil, 1990–94; 1995–2002*, Rio de Janeiro: BNDES, 2002.

15 The most likely candidate to receive Fernando Henrique Cardoso's blessing as a successor, Chamber president Luís Eduardo Magalhães, died in 1998, leaving a major question mark around the presidential succession as well as increasing market concern with the potential economic impact of political events.

16 Brazil has five high courts: the Superior Justice Tribunal (STJ), the Supreme Federal Tribunal (STF), the Superior Labour Tribunal (TST), the Superior Electoral Tribunal (TSE), and the Superior Military Tribunal (TSM). The STF is supposedly for use only in constitutional cases, and a few select case types. However, by virtue of the broad constitution, this means little in practice, and most cases are appealed to the STF on constitutional grounds, making it in practice the highest court. Included here are all cases in which either an injunction or a decision on the merits of a legal case in the STF overturned or halted implementation of the policy in question.

17 *Folha de São Paulo*, 23 February 1997.

18 Luiz Antonio Cintra, 'STF volta a ser o centro das atenções', *Folha de São Paulo*, 21 February 1997.

19 Ibid.

20 Ney Hayashi da Cruz, 'Incertezas puxam valorização do dólar', *Folha de São Paulo*, 3 August 2000.

21 'BNDES acompanha guerra jurídica com pessimismo', *Folha de São Paulo*, 1 May 1997.

22 Marta Salomon and Vivaldo de Sousa, 'Votação da Previdência provoca batalha jurídica', *Folha de São Paulo*, 8 May 1998.

23 Celso Pinto, 'A ameaça fiscal potencial', *Folha de São Paulo*, 26 June 1999.

24 'Brazil shares close lower, off sharp lows as impact of govt defeat eases', *AFX News*, 1 October 1999.

25 Simon Romero, 'Brazil's efforts on budget imperiled by court rulings', *New York Times*, 1 October 1999.

26 Ibid.

27 Ibid.

28 'Brazil shares close lower, off sharp lows as impact of govt defeat eases', *AFX News*, 1 October 1999.

29 Silvana Freitas, 'STF mantém parada a venda do Banespa', *Folha de São Paulo*, 14 July 2000.

30 'Para Tereza, STF terá cautela', *Folha de São Paulo*, 16 April 2000.

31 In comparison with other federally-organized systems in the western hemisphere, Brazil has the highest federal judicial budget. Using purchasing power parity-adjusted dollars, in 2000, Brazil spent $3.81 million per 100,000 inhabitants, versus $3.46 million in Argentina, $2.65 million in Mexico, and a 'worldwide' average of $2.04 million. World Bank, 'Worldwide legal and judicial indicators'. The federal judiciary's 2003 budget, at US$4.7 billion, is comparable to that of the United States federal court system, which had a US$4.9 billion budget in fiscal year 2003, even though Brazil has a population roughly three-fifths that of the U.S. Data from National Treasury, 'Relatorio Resumido da Execução Orçamentária do Governo Federal e Outros Demonstrativos', available at http://www.tesouro.fazenda.gov.br, accessed 5 March 2004; and Administrative Office of the U.S. Courts, 'The FY 2003 budget and the federal courts', available at: www.uscourts.gov/ttb/mar03ttb/budget.html, accessed 5 March 2004.

32 It is commonplace today to affirm both that courts affect public policy (H.W. Ehrmann, *Comparative Legal Cultures*, Englewood Cliffs, NJ: Prentice-Hall, 1976; C. Neal Tate, 'Comparative judicial review and public policy: concepts and overview', in *Comparative Judicial Review and Public Policy*, Donald W. Jackson and C. Neal Tate, eds., Westport, CT: Greenwood Press, 1992, 3–13; Martin Shapiro and Alec Stone Sweet, *On Law, Politics, and Judicialization*, Oxford: Oxford University Press, 2002) and that courts worldwide have become increasingly influential in politics (C. Neal Tate and Torbjörn Vallinder, 'The global expansion of judicial power: the judicialization of politics', in *The Global Expansion of Judicial Power*, C.N. Tate and T. Vallinder, eds., New York: New York University Press, 1995). These assertions, grouped together under the category 'judicialization of politics', have also been amply applied to Brazil (Rogério Bastos Arantes, *Judiciário e política no Brasil*, São Paulo: IDESP, 1997; Marcus Faro de Castro, 'The courts, law, and democracy in Brazil', *International Social Science Journal*, 49/152 (1997), 241–52; Marcus Faro de Castro, 'O supremo tribunal federal e a judicialização da política', *Revista Brasileira de Ciências Sociais*, 12/34 (1997), 147–56; Oscar Vilhena Vieira, *Supremo tribunal federal: Jurisprudência política*, 2nd edn., São Paulo: Malheiros, 2002; and Luiz Werneck Vianna, et al., *A judicialização da política e das relações sociais no Brasil*, Rio de Janeiro: Editora Revan, 1999.

33 John A. Ferejohn, 'Judicializing politics, politicizing law', *Law and Contemporary Problems*, 65/3 (2002), 41–69.

34 Ibid.

35 Although it is possible to file suit for 'omission', or failure to carry out policies required by the constitution, in practice such suits are seldom brought; these suits represent only a small minority of all ADINs.

36 Brazil has a 'hybrid system' of constitutional review, with both abstract and concrete forms of review. See especially, Arantes, *Judiciário e política no Brasil*, op. cit.

Abstract constitutional review is review that does not require an actual case or controversy for a court to challenge constitutionality; the law can be challenged in the abstract. Constitutional adjudication under the Brazilian system is hybrid: the direct action of unconstitutionality (ADIN) mechanism and the direct action of constitutionality (ADC) mechanism provide for the abstract review of laws without the need for a concrete case being brought to trigger such consideration. But the STF is also a court of appeal for cases that are brought in the lower courts using other legal instruments, most often by plaintiffs who do not have the standing to bring an ADIN, and in this sense consideration of constitutional cases can also be concrete.

37 Theodore J. Lowi, 'American business, public policy, case-studies, and political science', *World Politics*, 16 (July 1964), 677–715.

38 Much effort has been spent assessing the categories Lowi created. To his original three types of policy (distribution, regulation, and redistribution), Lowi himself later added

'constituent policy' as a fourth category, in Theodore J. Lowi, 'Four systems of policy, politics, and choice', *Public Administration Review*, 33 (July 1972–Aug 1972), 298–310. The categories were distinguished by the applicability of coercion (in individual settings or the overall 'environment of conduct') and the likelihood of coercion (either remote or immediate). Ripley and Franklin add a second set of policy types, related to foreign and defense policy: structural, strategic, and crisis policy. Randall Ripley and Grace Franklin, *Congress, the Bureaucracy, and Public Policy*, 4th edn., Chicago: Dorsey Press, 1987. Wilson criticized the original approach as too limiting: a single policy might fit into all three categories. James Q. Wilson, *Political Organizations*, New York: Basic Books, 1973.

39 Wilson uses the terms majoritarian, entrepreneurial, client, and interest group to describe the categories that result from the allocation of costs and benefits. See Wilson, *Political Organizations*.

40 For a broader discussion, see Matthew M. Taylor, 'Activating judges: courts, institutional structure, and the judicialization of policy reform in Brazil, 1988–2002', PhD dissertation, Georgetown University, 2004.

41 An extended discussion of this argument can be found in Matthew M. Taylor, 'Veto and voice in the courts: policy implications of institutional design in Brazil', *Comparative Politics*, forthcoming.

42 Josephine T. Andrews and Gabriella R. Montinola, 'Veto players and the rule of law in emerging democracies', *Comparative Political Studies*, 37/1 (2004), 55–87. This follows the definitions offered by other scholars: George Tsebelis, *Veto Players: How Political Institutions Work*, Princeton, NJ: Princeton University Press, 2002, p. 2; Steffen Ganghof, 'Promises and pitfalls of veto player analysis', *Swiss Political Science Review*, 9 (2003), 1–25; Stephan Haggard and Mathew D. McCubbins, *Presidents, Parliaments, and Policy*, Cambridge: Cambridge University Press, 2001, p. 5, fn. 10.

43 Barry Ames, *The Deadlock of Democracy in Brazil*, Ann Arbor: University of Michigan Press, 2001, p. 16.

44 Despite the importance and depth of their works, Ames and Haggard and McCubbins discuss veto players and the role of institutions, but exclude the legal system from their analyses. As Mainwaring notes, this oversight may be important: "Even if institutions fully determine the extent to which policy is decisive or resolute and public – or private-regarding, some institutions that are not in their analysis have a major impact on decisiveness ... The efficacy of the legal system affects whether policy is public – or private-regarding; with an ineffectual legal system, there are no sanctions against even patently corrupt private-regarding policies." Scott Mainwaring, 'Book review: *Presidents, Parliaments, and Policy*', *American Political Science Review*, 96 (Dec 2002), 853. The application of the veto player literature to Brazilian courts is relatively new. In the Brazilian case, Ames suggests in a footnote that courts may act as veto players through judicial review of legislation. Ames, *The Deadlock of Democracy in Brazil*, op. cit., p. 15, fn. 25. Writing prior to Tsebelis' substantive work on veto players, Sadek and Arantes argue that the Brazilian political system is one of "multi-vetos" across the branches of power. Within this system, the judiciary is able to exercise veto power: "... [the judiciary's] decentralized and de facto federalized structure allows it to paralyze policies, offer decisions in a non-uniform fashion and thus suspend, even if only temporarily, measures with national impact." Maria Tereza Sadek and Rogério B. Arantes, 'A crise do judiciário e a visão dos juízes', *Revista USP*, 21 (1994), 37.

45 Andrews and Montinola; Nicos C. Alivizatos, 'Judges as veto players', in Herbert Doring, ed., *Parliaments and Majority Rule in Western Europe*, New York: St. Martin's, 1995, pp. 566–91.

46 "Absorption" occurs when a new veto player is added within the "unanimity core of any set of previously existing veto players." If Player Y's preferences are the same, or within the same area of preferences, as the preferences of Player X, Player Y is 'absorbed' by Player X. Player Y will thus have no influence on policy stability in that particular policy

context, since Player Y's preferences are fully incorporated in Player X's already extant preference set. See Tsebelis, op. cit., pp. 19–37.

47 Tsebelis, op. cit., pp. 226–34.

48 Arantes, *Judiciário e política no Brasil*, op. cit., p. 33.

49 For more detail on the legal and political strategies used by opposition political parties in the courts, see Matthew M. Taylor, 'El Partido de los Trabajadores y el uso político del judiciario en Brasil', América Latina Hoy, 36 (August 2004).

50 The ADIN is only one of a number of mechanisms of direct constitutional challenge in the STF. However, it is by far the most widely and intensely used.

51 Article 103, *Constituição da República Federativa do Brasil*, Brasília: Centro Gráfico do Senado Federal, 1988.

52 ADIN No. 2332.

53 ADINs No. 1127 and 1194, among others.

54 ADIN No. 1659.

55 ADINs No. 1417, 2178, and 2556.

56 ADINs No. 1361, 1675, 1849, and 1861, among others.

57 Taylor, 'Veto and voice in the courts', op. cit.

58 Taylor, 'Veto and voice in the courts', op. cit.

59 See for example, B. Guy Peters, *American Public Policy: Promise and Performance*, New York: Chatham House, 1999.

60 Max Weber, *Economy and Society: An Outline of Interpretive Sociology*, Guenther Roth and Claus Wittich, eds., Berkeley: University of California Press, 1978, pp. 212–26. Dogan has highlighted the 'ethical neutrality' and datedness of Weber's concepts of legitimacy. In Dogan's view, even rational-legal legitimacy contains very heterogeneous forms of government, ranging from democracy to totalitarianism; charismatic claims used to be religious; and traditional claims are rapidly disappearing. Mattei Dogan, 'Testing the concepts of legitimacy and trust', in H.E. Chehabi and Alfred Stepan, eds., *Politics, Society, and Democracy: Comparative Studies*, Boulder, CO: Westview Press, 1995. Habermas goes further, claiming "The democratic procedure for the production of law evidently forms the only postmetaphysical source of legitimacy." Jürgen Habermas, *Between Facts and Norms: Contributions to a Discourse Theory of Law and Democracy*, Cambridge: MIT Press, 1998, p. 448.

61 Jerold L. Waltman and Kenneth M. Holland, *The Political Role of Law Courts in Modern Democracies*, London: Macmillan, 1988.

62 See, for example, Amy Gutmann and Dennis Thompson, *Democracy and Disagreement*, Cambridge: Belknap Press, 1996.

63 As Shapiro and Stone Sweet note, in the U.S., the 'political jurisprudence' school of the 1960s was characterized by this assertion of the importance of courts: "an open, childlike, acknowledgement of the obvious, or at least of what was obvious to all except those with a vested interest in denying it: that American courts were significant actors in American politics." Martin Shapiro and Alec Stone Sweet, *On Law, Politics, and Judicialization*, Oxford: Oxford University Press, 2002, p. 4.

64 William C. Prillaman, *The Judiciary and Democratic Decay in Latin America: Declining Confidence in the Rule of Law*, Westport: Praeger, 2000.

65 "Governo vai pedir que STF se manifeste sobre CPMF", *Folha de São Paulo*, 9 July 1999.

66 "Painel", *Folha de São Paulo*, 10 February 1999.

67 Silvana de Freitas, 'Itamar é derrotado no Supremo', *Folha de São Paulo*, 10 February 1999.

68 "Jungmann tenta derrubar ação no Supremo", *Folha de São Paulo*, 16 October 2000.

69 *Brazilian Financial Wire*, 27 July 1999.

70 Examples of this argument can be found in Robert A. Dahl, 'Decision-making in a democracy: the Supreme Court as a national policy-maker', *Journal of Public Law*, 6 (July 1957), 279–95; Marc Galanter, 'How the "haves" come out ahead: speculations on the limits

of legal change', *Law and Society Review*, 9 (Fall 1974), 95–160; Gerald N. Rosenberg, *The Hollow Hope: Can Courts Bring About Social Change?* Chicago: University of Chicago Press, 1991, p. 338.

71 Timothy J. Power and Mahrukh Doctor, 'Another century of corporatism? Continuity and change in Brazilian corporatist structures', in *Authoritarianism and Corporatism in Latin America, Revisited*, Howard J. Wiarda, ed., Gainesville: University Press of Florida, 2004.

72 I am grateful to Gerry Mara for suggesting this distinction. Robert A. Dahl, *A Preface to Democratic Theory*, Chicago: Chicago University Press, 1956, p. 145.

Chapter 8

Financial credibility, legitimacy and political discretion: the Lula da Silva government

Lourdes Sola

ONE OF THE distinctive features of emerging market democracies is that they are part and parcel of a global 'recombination' of economic and political change. Economic integration into global markets goes hand in hand with local populations opting for constitutional democracy. Elected politicians and government elites face unprecedented new challenges when confronted with the task of striking a balance between two distinct 'constituencies' and two different sets of policy goals. They are forced to govern with one eye on the changing moods and expectations of the market and the other on perceptions and demands of the electorate. There are also longer-term challenges of democratization: crafting institutions that are better adapted to new realities while generating a modicum of consensus around new institutional frameworks.

In principle and in the long term, policy goals geared towards securing credibility in global markets and the support of the electorate do not conflict with each other. Building the confidence of domestic and foreign investors is crucial to promoting sustainable economic growth and to improving social welfare. To the extent that these goals are also aspirations associated with democracy by the local population, it should follow that liberalizing policies and institutional reforms geared to improving 'credibility' may also yield political dividends for self-regarding democratic politicians. By the same token, economic stability and political stability are also potentially convergent goals, within the new context of global mass transitions towards democracy and economic integration into international markets. While economic stability is regarded as a necessary condition for improving financial credibility and access to global markets, it has also become a criterion for government performance and for political legitimization in the eyes of societies that had been traditionally exposed to protracted inflationary pressures and populist practices. Political stability, meanwhile, was a major aspiration of populations who experienced dictatorships of various kinds and has been rightly noted as a major pressure behind their preference for liberal constitutional democracies. As Claus Offe points out, political stability is therefore part of a normative dimension attached to that preference. The achievements of rights and liberties also include an expectation related to "the drawing of a clear demarcation line between what can be contingent upon the outcome of the political process and the conflicts of interest enter into, and what can not be the object of such conflict because it is constitutionally entrenched".[1] In principle, therefore, the pressure behind the "civilizing potential"[2] of constitutional democracy comes also from the expectations associated with that specific mode of political stability. In other words, the value attached to economic stability and representative democracy in most emergent market societies is the outcome of a deep change in the criteria of political legitimization. This was certainly the case in Latin American countries such as Brazil and Argentina.

Recent experience, however, shows that goals such as market credibility and political legitimacy may conflict with each other a great deal before convergence between them is achieved and a virtuous circle transpires. Short-term pressures emerging in either realm often place major constraints on the evolution of the desired normative sequence by which integration into global markets and democratization can reinforce each other. On the one hand, more often than not, market volatility and waves of both optimism and pessimism follow logics of their own, determined as much by the shifting perceptions and expectations of investors as by objective factors. These variables are well beyond the control of domestic politicians, even those with a high degree of political legitimacy, which enables them to play the confidence game and to pay its costs. Short term political aims, in particular those inherent in electoral competition, may also stand in the way of more strategic calculations geared towards securing stable conditions of fiscal and monetary discipline, as well as growth and institutional change. Thus the criteria markets and the Bretton Woods institutions consider essential for economic performance ('fundamentals') may not be achieved at the pace and the scale required to attract investment and to ignite growth.

This framework becomes more complex and more difficult to administer when one introduces the political and electoral risks created by abrupt changes in the perceptions of market strategists, whose effect can be almost instantaneous in terms of a re-direction of capital. Under conditions of extreme volatility, the pressures on government elites to change the direction of a 'well behaved' economic policy increase substantially. The internal cohesion of the policymaking team is put to the test, as is the unity of the political coalition that sustains the government. Inversely, a bullish market can ignore danger signals, ignoring the cumulative effects of government decisions that put at risk not only monetary and fiscal regulations but also the prospects for growth. Under these conditions an opposite political dynamic may result. The government sees the efficiency of its economic policy (if it is behaving well) being positively sanctioned by the markets, and then attempts to portray international liquidity conditions as durable, when in reality these are partially outside of their control. Under such circumstances, short-term political calculations can interfere heavily in the formation of economic policy. Access to markets becomes a decisive factor for attending to the demands of the electorate for growth, employment and higher income, consequently resulting in good electoral dividends. For this reason access to markets may well convert itself into a crucial political resource under conditions of electoral rivalry, largely at the disposition of incumbents and of government elites. One can expect that elected politicians may well project the facilities of market access as being more stable than they are, conditioning the sustainability of capital flows to their own performance at the polls. Their critics and opposition forces are easily neutralized by the incontestable assertion that foreign capital inflows substantially increase the chances of meeting the electorate's long-term demands.

Under the conditions of inherent instability caused by the post Bretton Woods international arrangement, the combination of financial integration and transitions towards mass democracies on an unprecedented scale raises a number of general questions. Will there be space for elected politicians to manoeuver to reconcile objectives that may conflict with market fluctuations beyond their control? What scope is there to exercise political discretionality – indispensable to building institutions that are sufficiently flexible to absorb external shocks without crumbling – and at the same time adhere to the principles of accountability and democratic control? What are the acceptable trade-offs between the criteria of legitimization associated with democracy, such as sustained growth and a higher standard of living on the one hand, and economic and political stability on the other? In what ways can the convergence between credibility, sustained growth and stability be promoted without incurring the twin risks of economic populism and authoritarianism, both of which are fatal for democracy?

Brazil offers important insights into the scope of possible political discretionality under conditions of extreme macroeconomic instability, as seen in the experience of the elected president, Luiz Inácio Lula da Silva and his Workers' Party (PT). We focus on the process by which Lula da Silva's enormous credibility deficit was reversed, and the limits on the extent of this reversal. The challenge of building a consensus regarding the autonomy of the Central Bank was expected to play a key role in this story. To better understand the unfolding process, we adopt a broad perspective that incorporates changes in the political and economic context that affect the perceptions and the expectations of the relevant players in the formation of consensus.

Political discretionality and the credibility gap

The period just before and just after the inauguration of the government of Lula da Silva lends itself to an analysis of political discretionality in two very different moments of political and economic uncertainty in Brazil. The electoral cycle beginning in 2001 and running through the second half of 2002 was a typical situation of financial crisis coinciding with elections. The second moment roughly coincides with the first year of Lula's administration, whose agenda was directed towards correcting the credibility gap through the intensive mobilization of an orthodox macroeconomic policy and a reform offensive centred on restructuring the social security system.

During the months before the October 2002 Lula's election, markets and various sectors of the population saw the potential for a financial crisis associated with the likelihood that a candidate whose party was seen as breaking with past policies would win. Despite these fears, the opposition's criticism and proposal to discontinue with the Cardoso government's policies greatly benefited opposition candidates, in particular Lula da Silva. There was a definite demand for change from the lower income sectors, from various middle class sectors, and in particular from the industrial sector.

The electoral performance of Lula da Silva (52,793,364 votes, or 61.27 percent of valid votes) and of his party in the congressional elections[3] was atypical in terms of the initial conditions for governance. The new government at its outset was characterized by a gap unprecedented in recent Brazilian history between an enormous 'credibility deficit' as far as the markets were concerned and a surplus of 'political legitimacy' without historical precedent as far as the electorate was concerned.[4] Administering this imbalance was the major challenge facing the government in its first year of office. In order to evaluate the PT's performance and the place of economic policy during this process, we trace the reasons for the electoral uncertainty of 2002 and the manner by which the possibility of financial crisis was reversed.

From confidence crisis to consensus

Macroeconomic instability associated with electoral uncertainty was related to the specific characteristics of the domestic scenario, some of which are clearly contingent, while others are more 'structural'. Among the contingent characteristics, the most relevant from our perspective regards the process which culminated in the estrangement of two main political parties – the PSDB (Party of Brazilian Social Democracy) and the PFL (Liberal Front Party) – that had been a part of the governmental coalition of the Fernando Henrique Cardoso government for eight years. Electoral competition began prematurely back in October/November of 2001 – a year ahead of the election – with the strong showing of Roseana Sarney (PFL), the governor of the state of Maranhão, in opinion polls taken well before she was officially launched as her party's candidate for the presidency. This had two decisive effects in raising the level of electoral uncertainty.[5] On the one hand, it highlighted the internal competition within the PSDB and forced the early launching of Senator José Serra's campaign as the official government candidate in March, and not in June or July as had been anticipated. Second, media reports of evidence that Roseana Sarney's husband had been involved in corruption brought her rise in the polls to an abrupt halt, and led to the PFL's rupture with the government, which culminated in allegations that the incident had been generated by allies of Senator José Serra.

Faced with the decline of a candidate who had presented herself as a mix between continuity and change, and whose rise had not depended on attacks on the government's political policies, the electorate shifted its preferences to Ciro Gomes, governor of the state of Ceará and a recent convert to the small PPS (Popular Socialist Party).[6] In spite of the radical tone of Ciro Gomes' criticisms towards the government's economic policy, his strategy also consisted in projecting a dressed up image of continuity and change. As finance minister during a decisive phase in the success of the Real Plan, Gomes had represented continuity and a commitment to stability. But in his new guise as a radical critic of 'neoliberal' economic policy, of the financial sector and of the privileged class, he presented himself as the proponent of a new collective project for the country, attracting support from the business sector and the middle class without ever launching strong appeals for the correction of social inequalities. He emerged as a competitive candidate, and at times appeared to have a chance of reaching the second electoral round, but ultimately proved to be ill-equipped in articulating party political alliances and addressing contradictions in his own record.

Two points should be highlighted about this experience. First, there was a common denominator between these two initially competitive pre-candidates. Both were attractive to the majority of the electorate exactly because they responded to the preference for a mix of continuity and change (albeit in somewhat different fashions). Opinion polls showed that economic stability continued to be an important criterion for the population, but it was now ceding space to other priorities, such as growth and employment. Second, for the majority of the electorate, Lula da Silva and the PT did not represent a first choice exactly because they still projected an image of breaking away from the existing 'model', though less radically than in previous presidential elections. The importance of this first stage of electoral competition comes from the fact that it signalled an electoral preference for change, but change without a large degree of commotion and without any significant rupture. A nebulous space had been created that could, in principle, have been occupied just as well by the government's official candidate, José Serra, one of the traditional internal critics of the economic policy of President Cardoso.

The uncertainty and possibility of a break with current economic policy were perceived as much more likely under the PT and its candidate, Lula da Silva. This was true in the eyes of the middle class electorate, of voters in the smallest and poorest municipalities, as well as among the business community in the productive sector, all of which were discontent with the Cardoso government. The possibility of a clear break with the Cardoso administration's policies was much greater and 'structural' for the PT candidacy than it was in the mix offered by Roseana Sarney or Ciro Gomes, both of whom were perceived as offering a more moderate mix of change than the PT, by both elites and the poor (who showed signs of fearing change, especially among lower-income women).

The PT leadership attempted and managed to move politically to the right, by changing its previous strategy to attract the centre and the centre-right of the electorate. This change was accompanied by an effort to widen the scope of alliances with a specific mix of continuity and change. It is worth emphasizing that this move took place relatively late in the electoral campaign: the party's conversion dated back to mid June 2002 and expressed itself in the 'Carta aos Brasileiros' ['Letter to the Brazilian people']. This shifting of gears would reveal it to be comparatively effective in the eyes of the electorate, but highly suspect in terms of the credibility ascribed to it by the market. Market scepticism was driven by short and long-term factors that had contributed to the consolidation of the PT's image as the chief proponent of 'rupture'.

The image and the tradition of the PT and Lula da Silva as being too radical was a key component in the extreme uncertainty that characterized the electoral cycle between June and September 2002. Two circumstances contributed to the consolidation of this image, one of long standing, and the other highlighted in December 2001 and April 2002. The first has to do with the tradition of the PT regarding the question of economic stability: the hostility demonstrated by the party and by its presidential candidate in response to all the stabilization programs undertaken during the post-military period, from the Cruzado Plan (1985) to the Real Plan (1994). The PT, however, adopted an attitude that, for a popular political party, was irrational in terms of electoral calculations, given the plans' widespread support. In the same fashion, the party also was slow to sense the dramatic shift in the criteria of political legitimization, above all among the least protected classes of society, who converted economic stability into a 'public good'. By 2000–2001 the credibility of Lula's party in the eyes of the market was further jeopardized by a signature-gathering campaign that called for a plebiscite on the re-structuring of Brazil's external debt. The campaign had support from the upper levels of the Catholic Church, and counted on PT leaders who were considered moderates, such as José Dirceu, the party president.

The second circumstance was created by the decisions taken at the national PT conference in December 2001, when the PFL candidate, Roseana Sarney, had started rising in the polls. The 'Recife Declaration' which emerged from the conference, would sound too radical for the financial markets. To make matters worse, on 10 April the Declaration was presented virtually unchanged to an annual financial market seminar attended by market analysts, representatives of major financial concerns and the media. In its basic form, the Recife Declaration had postulated "a new development model" which would centre on the "social question", with the intention of addressing issues of social equality and social inclusion. The document described a "necessary rupture", which was explained in the following terms: "The implementation of the program will break with the opening up and the radical de-regulating of the economy", so as to "avoid the dynamic subordination of the Brazilian economy to the interests of global financial capital". Part of the analysis addressed two important topics that were at the core of perceptions of the PT and therefore were important to the formation of market expectations:

1) Economic stability sacrificed economic growth, employment, the solidity of public finances, and the solidity of the country's external accounts;
2) As a reply to the distortions generated by the need for external financing, the "struggle against dependency" included four central pillars that were extremely sensitive for the formation of market expectations: as well as expanding and improving the level of exports, the document pledged to (a) regulate the entrance of speculative capital, directing foreign investment towards exports and towards import substitution; (b) deepen import substitution by revising tariff barriers and creating non-tariff protection for strategic activities; and (c) denounce the agreement with the IMF and lead an international movement for auditing countries' external debts (with Mexico and Argentina).

The perception that the PT stood a good chance of victory at the polls emerged with more clarity beginning in May 2002. This was the origin of a strategic turnabout commanded by leading party managers under the command of José Dirceu, the PT's president. Condensed within the "Letter to the Brazilian people", its content was in stark contrast to the commitments assumed in the Recife Declaration, which dealt with ideological orientation: the Letter included explicit commitments to economic stability, with fiscal and monetary responsibilities, and in particular addressed the scope of political alliances, which had previously been rejected by the PT. The agenda for the future government was less clear.

The PT's new strategy, put together from June 2002, was developed along various fronts. In speeches, the rhetoric of "rupture" was abandoned, as was the mantra of "political intent" as a means of overcoming Brazilian problems. In the same manner, economic pharmacopoeia with a foundation in strong normative theory was substituted by a mix that incorporated the principles of economic efficiency and of respect for contracts, making it more market friendly. Among the more radical changes, the scope for political alliances stood out. In this case, the pragmatism of Lula da Silva prevailed, which in part explains the wide arc of electoral coalitions, which covered not only traditional party alliances of the left, but also centrist and even right wing parties.

This about-face was consolidated by two other decisive proposals, one directed towards the electorate, the other towards domestic and international markets. An additional token of Lula´s pragmatism, and a sign of the abrupt change imposed on the PT, was the hiring of Duda Mendonça, a political strategist and market guru who had made his reputation working with Paulo Maluf, one of the most unsavoury figures of Brazilian political right. The strategy of political communication and marketing focused on winning over various resistant groups in the electorate. First, there was a concerted effort to build the candidate's image as sympathetic and kindly, summed up in the phrase "Lula – Peace and Love", along with efforts to communicate his political competence, and neutralize resistance to his lack not only of a formal education but also of either executive or parliamentary experience. Furthermore, the PT put considerable emphasis on the experience of the party's mayors, governors, intellectuals and militants as evidence of the availability of groups with technical expertise. In terms of calming markets, two successive events took place. Internationally, José Dirceu and other PT leaders travelled to financial centres in the United States and Europe, cooperating with the Cardoso administration's economic team. At home, contacts were intensified between the PT's campaign coordinator, Antonio Palocci, and financial market leaders, giving rise to a relationship that would be maintained long after the elections.

The reversal of expectations resulting from this strategy was successful only among the electorate: the market continued to project a credibility gap. Nevertheless, it is worth noting that the credibility gap associated with electoral uncertainty did not result solely from the lack of consistency between the PT's image and tradition or on its electoral strategy. It was also associated with the electoral campaign, since the other opposition candidates were also adopting a market-hostile discourse. As a result, all opposition candidates concentrated their criticism on Serra, the candidate of continuity. Electoral uncertainty, enhanced by Argentina's default on its debt, was therefore at the root of a sudden decline in the flow of capital, amounting to 6 percent of the GDP; an exchange rate depreciation of nearly 50 percent; and a substantial increase in Brazilian borrowing costs – taking the form of a typical financial crisis cum election scenario.

The deterioration in Brazilian market conditions had much to do with the perception of existing economic vulnerabilities. These would require the continuity of macroeconomic adjustments both in the fiscal accounts and the balance of payments, as well as economic and institutional reforms, all of which involved high political and social costs. The prevailing assumption in financial markets was that, given its long-term history, the leading opposition party would not be prepared to pay the high cost of such reforms. These doubts were not dispelled automatically by the change in the PT's political strategy – on the contrary, this change was accompanied by a high degree of scepticism, more so because both adjustments had been under way as part of IMF–Brazil agreements dating back to 1998. Between 1998 and 2003, fiscal adjustment amounted to 4.5 percent of the GDP. The external adjustment corresponded to 7 percent of GDP at current prices and real wages were greatly affected by the depreciated exchange rate. The financial *cum* election crisis caused a 4 percent decrease in domestic absorption (consumption and investment).[7]

The Brazil–IMF agreement and its aftermath

It is against this background that the full economic and political relevance of a new agreement with the IMF, attained in September 2002, becomes clear. The program financing was back-loaded, i.e. $24 billion out of a total of $30 billion was scheduled to be made available after the new government took office. The agreement has political relevance both from the point of view of the conditionalities attached to the package and in light of the manner by which it was brought forward and presented to the general public. It resulted in an informal political compact – coordinated by President Cardoso and the IMF's Deputy Managing Director, Anne Krueger – to which all four presidential candidates, three of whom were in the opposition, pledged their support.

Here, the Brazil–IMF agreement is extremely pertinent. It offers a body of evidence concerning the workings and breadth of political discretion of a group of players, in a multilateral cooperative game, which revealed itself as being crucial to building consensus at the peak of a gathering crisis. There are three relevant aspects to the agreement. First, its content, which was minimal. The conditions attached to the package were reduced to the minimum necessary and included few details, limited to a promise of achieving a 3.75 percent primary surplus (total revenue expenditure excluding interest payments); maintaining an inflation-targeting regime; and respect for existing contracts and for the floating exchange rate regime. Second, there was the fact that all of the candidates saw themselves obliged to participate in a ritual of adherence to the package, with each of them in turn holding a private meeting with President Cardoso and two members of his economic team. The intense press coverage for the entrance and exit of each of the candidates guaranteed that their assumed commitment would gain enormous –visibility. Third, due to the manner of the presentation itself, whether it was the episode itself or the political arguments associated with the endorsement of the IMF. The public justification of the agreement emphasized that it was aimed at securing a smooth transition and reducing the risks to democratic continuity, while also acknowledging that it would be instrumental in the reduction of economic uncertainty. Finally, the intense coverage by the media, which publicized the terms of the agreement and led to intense discussions of the agreement's economic implications, had a double pedagogical effect: it familiarized the general public with the technicalities involved and permitted access to one of the least transparent spheres in the economic decision-making process. However, the agreement with the IMF did not guarantee the complete elimination of economic uncertainty. Market volatility was unavoidable and the risk premium remained high. Nor could one predict the future rise in the price of C-Bonds, the most widely traded Brazilian government bond issue in foreign markets.[8]

In the post-electoral context two major initiatives stand out for providing better conditions of economic and political stability. Both of them correspond to the 'transition phase', that is, the October to January interlude between elections and the inauguration of the new government. Both are additional instances of multilateral cooperation between the new and the old government teams, and federal deputies, especially those from the new opposition parties (PSDB and PFL). Both are relevant as evidence of the room for political discretion in the construction of a consensus, once the painful phase of financial *cum* elections crisis had passed, without which the risk of volatility would not have been eliminated.

The first of these comes from what is conventionally called political transition, and it was in reality the most visible part. It consisted of President Cardoso's decision to open the door to a transition team nominated by the PT that participated on a daily basis in the decision-making process during the final two months of his government. In this manner two advances were obtained. On the one hand, there was a reduction in the learning curve of the incoming team, allowing them to become familiar with the technical and political dimensions of now being in command of the federal government – an additional factor in economic and political uncertainty. On the other hand, by publicly elevating the level of tolerance between political adversaries, there was a transfer to the opposing party of the onus for initiating a game of aggressions and recriminations.

The second event in the course of constructing a consensus concerns the nomination by the PT of the future president of the Central Bank of Brazil and of Senate approval. The choice as Central Bank of a PSDB federal deputy who had been a president of the Bank of Boston, showed the measure of importance that the PT attributed to the need to reverse market expectations, and to widen the scope of credibility. It also revealed a dramatic change in the PT's leadership, which ran contrary to the expectations of its activities and of its constituencies, old and new. It also reflected the pragmatic outlook of incoming president, Lula da Silva.[9] Members of the outgoing Central Bank team, such as Ilan Goldfajn, were invited to stay, thus offering a compromise in favour of the continuation of economic policy. The approval of the Central Bank president's nomination by the Senate – involving the cooperation of political parties that would become a part of the opposition, the PSDB and PFL – on 20 December 2002, ten days before the start of the new government, completed the electoral cycle and marked the beginning of the PT's participation in the confidence game.

The building of partial consensus in hybrid government: major challenges and performance

A major problem arises in defining what is meant by a multi-party coalition in a government that is formed around a dominant left-wing party, such as the PT.[10] The difficulty resides less in the fact of its being a multi-party coalition government – one of the distinctive characteristics of the Brazilian presidential system – and more from the distinctiveness of the dominant party within the government, the PT, as well as Lula da Silva's leadership. A discussion on the question of the social composition and the trajectory of the president's party is beyond the scope of this chapter. Nevertheless, it can be indirectly dealt with through an analysis of the first year of the PT government, which helps to answer the question on the horizon of the current debate: what might one expect from the PT government in the near future, especially when faced with two types of potential difficulties? First, what are the social and political costs facing a popular leftist party, such as the PT, in the short and medium term, in light of the costs of undertaking an orthodox economic policy in the pursuit of credibility? In particular, what are the costs of engaging in reforms against which the party had mobilized all of its political resources when it was in opposition? Second, to what extent might adverse changes in the international climate lead to a change in direction on macroeconomic policy and reforms that might be less market friendly? Simply put, what factors might inhibit the process of economic and financial integration that began in the 1990s? The question of the international context is decisive, especially in light of the fact that it has been highly favourable to date once credibility had been conquered among financial market participants.

These issues have converged into a debate that is both domestic and international and has been taking place within both academic and business circles around the question of what are the probabilities of the Lula da Silva government ceding to populist tendencies that threaten the fiscal and monetary disciplines adopted up until now – and consequently the solvency of the country? To put it another way, will current economic policy be continued under circumstances that are less favourable?

For social scientists, the democratic question associated with the last question brings to centre stage an extremely thorny conceptual problem. While there is unanimity as to the commitment of the PT and of Lula towards the formal procedures of representative democracy, if they were to adopt less formal criteria of performance, the debate would turn to the current government's frequent recourse to methods and to a style of leadership that are closer to a plebiscitarian model of democracy. Although it is beyond the scope of this chapter, the perspective adopted here – focused on the scope of possible political discretion during the first year of the new government, may well provide empirical elements that contribute to the debate.

In keeping with the argument so far, it is fitting to rephrase the question: to what extent will the intensive use of the resources of power, of symbolic resources and of political communication – all of which have been extremely efficient in generating consensus around an economic policy directed towards the conquest of financial credibility – be sustainable in the short and long terms? This question is pertinent given its relevance to both macroeconomic policy and to the legitimacy of the Lula da Silva government, which will depend to a large degree on Lula's capacity to deliver growth and the reduction of social inequalities.[11] In order to answer this question of sustainability, we analyze here how the new government has been responding to the main challenges that it has confronted.

The PT government: major challenges and lines of defense – 2003

The Lula da Silva administration faced four distinctive and unprecedented types of challenges. First, as already noted above, the new government was characterized by an enormous imbalance between a deficit of credibility and of accomplishments in the eyes of the markets on the one hand, and on the other by a surplus of legitimacy for President Lula da Silva and his party in the eyes of the majority of the electorate. This situation was at the root of the macroeconomic agenda and of the political strategy undertaken by the President and by his principle strategists, directed primarily at the conquest of credibility in the eyes of the markets. From the outset, these priorities have included coordination between the fiscal, monetary and exchange policies of the finance minister, Antonio Palocci, and a reformist offensive centred on the reconstruction of state finances and state spending (social welfare reform and tax reform).

The path taken by the government in 2003 and 2004 has been based on an economic policy wager. The government sought to kick-start a virtuous cycle through confidence building policies, while at the same time ameliorating the political and social costs of these policies through the intense mobilization of political resources, with the expectation that growth policies could be undertaken beginning in 2004. This can be seen in the choice of key members of the economic team, who originated in an epistemic community with a liberal orientation. Clearly the viability of a virtuous cycle of this nature was conditioned to a modicum of growth, and therefore to the recovery of investment capacity. Given the government's agreement to generate a budget surplus of 4.75 percent of GDP, the onus for investment would fall heavily upon the private sector.

This agenda occupied the government's political energies during its first year, with the intensive mobilization of two of the main resources available to it. These include the legitimacy and charisma of President Lula da Silva and the capacity of the 'hard-core' of the government to promote party discipline within the PT's ranks regarding macro-economic policy and reform initiatives within Congress.

The second challenge has a lot to do with distinctive characteristics of the PT that increased the degree of uncertainty toward a government in which it was the leading party in the government coalition. There was – and is – a lack of consistency between the content of the economic policy regarded as necessary to meet both the restrictions imposed by market forces and the perceptions and expectations of the political and social bases of the party (and its left-wing allies). There is a wide gap between the tasks and trade-offs of governance on economic policy, and the party's traditional electoral base – workers' unions, employees, social movements and rural workers – on the other. The latter consolidated themselves on the Brazilian scenario thanks to a strategy of confrontation and a political discourse of change regarding the economic model of the previous government. Nevertheless, upon entering government, the party saw itself obliged to follow the basic guidelines of this very same model. This task demanded an elevated degree of control by the party leadership over its political supporters and over the other left wing parties that are its allies, especially the PCB, PDT and PPS.

The weak linkages between the content of economic policy and the political and social bases of the government added uncertainty to the task of converting an electoral coalition into a governmental coalition.

Although this gap has been a familiar one within the Latin American scenario ever since the structural adjustments in the 1980s began, it may well be even greater in the current Brazilian case.[12] The program and ideological re-conversion of the PT and of its left wing allies is in progress.

This also broadens the space available to party leaders to exercise political discretion in the building of internal consensuses formed around economic policy. This implies greater dependence on contingent decision-making as well as on more constitutive political resources available to the dominant party. In the Brazilian case, this construction has depended on three political resources, namely:

1) The popularity of President Lula da Silva, his relationship with public opinion and with the majority of the electorate, which has more or less direct repercussions on the capacity of the PT to ensure support within Congress;
2) The singular capacity of the PT to impose internal discipline on its members – which allows it to make use of electoral mechanisms comparatively efficient in order to promote lasting loyalty. Indeed, the PT is the only party within the Brazilian political spectrum that can operate on a closed list; and
3) Control of the social movements and of the unions identified with the leaders of the PT, whose interests are affected by macroeconomic policy and by social security reform.

The third challenge and factor of uncertainty is related to the composition of the government alliance, which is much more heterogeneous than that of the previous government, which included small parties of the centre and the right that had a reputation for clientelist and corrupt practices. This could affect stability through its effects on the president's relations with the congressional base, or through its effects on the speed of the reform process. There are two reasons. The current congressional alliance consists of eleven parties who represented 45 percent of the Chamber of Deputies before the formal affiliation of the PMDB. This contrasts with the coalition created during the Cardoso government, which held 75 percent of Congress, despite being made up of only four parties. The second point has to do with the traditional governing formula of presidentialism based on multi-party coalitions ('presidencialismo de coalição'). From the outset, Lula da Silva's administration was made up of a vast majority of PT members, selected independently of their electoral performance. Many of those defeated at the polls were housed in the upper levels of the executive branch. In the same way, the filling of the highest positions in the bureaucracy, in state companies, and in federal banks followed the same criteria – with the exception of the BNDES state development bank. In short, from the very outset the government's composition reflected a typical 'winner take all' strategy. This policy was premised on the excellent performance of Lula da Silva, as well as the PT's performance in the congressional elections.

The fourth challenge that could negatively affect the conditions of governance is the challenge created by the potential congestion of decision-making processes, in light of pressures that flow towards the presidency. This is a structural problem within Brazil's multi-party presidential regime, and it was made worse at the outset by the PT's management. The unprecedented concentration of power in the hands of the Ministry of Civil Affairs (Ministério da Casa Civil) was a direct contradiction to the enshrined solution of traditional Brazilian politics for getting around this problem, which is to divide the presidential management role in two. This traditional division of labour clearly defines two functions in the coordination of the presidency's structure, exercised by two different ministers. It has proven more effective in the past, with one minister coordinating the performance of his peers in the executive and the second exercising the functions of political coordination in Congress and society as a whole.

Politics, policies and the economy in the first two years of the Lula da Silva government

For reasons already described in the discussion of the government's heavy deficit of credibility, the first year of the government was given over to establishing continuity in macroeconomic policy and to a reformist offensive centred around changes to the social welfare system. For this reason the centre stage was to be occupied by the finance minister, Antonio Palocci, and his team, as well as by the minister of civil affairs, José Dirceu, who was in charge of political negotiations with Congress and the PT itself.

Taking into account the challenges that have been mentioned, and the continuity that it established in relation to the former model, several questions arise. How was the government able to build a consensus around an agenda of this type, and what political resources were mobilized in order to achieve success in this regard during the administration's first year in office? To what extent (and at what cost) did the government set the groundwork for achieving its political and economic objectives in 2004, a year which brought municipal elections crucial to Lula and the PT's political strategy? What is the likelihood that the convergence between financial market credibility and political legitimacy will be deepened? To put it another way, what are the possible trade-offs between perpetuating the financial market credibility achieved over the course of the past two years and the political legitimacy of the PT government and of President Lula da Silva?

One of the most striking results of the first year was the reversal in the deficit of credibility, with the market favourably rating the government, and without any dramatic decline in the popularity of President Lula da Silva or in the evaluation of the government. The high cost of orthodox monetary and fiscal policies – in terms of growth rates, of real income and of employment – had very little effect on the positive expectations of the general public in relation to the government's future performance. The contrast between the governments of Cardoso and Lula during their first few months deserves mention. While the popularity of the two presidents was comparable, Cardoso's support may well be justified in terms of economic performance at the time, which included a 30 percent rise in the average real income during his first year of government. President Lula da Silva's high popularity indices and the positive evaluation of his government were maintained despite a fall in real income of approximately 13 percent, an increase in unemployment, and stagnant GNP growth – a signal of the social expectations associated with his campaign and victory.

Consensus building around economic policy was created through the use of a combination of five types of specific political resources, some of them unprecedented. First, resources derived from the surplus of legitimacy of the new government and of the PT, and especially the intense popularity of the charismatic Lula. Second, the resources derived from the traditional methods of accommodating those who would make up a support base, by distributing important positions in the state bureaucracy and in public enterprise as well as federal banks. Third, resources obtained by placing PT members (the majority of them from unions) not only in government positions, but above all in the executive management of state companies, federal banks and regulatory agencies – in a clear politicization of these spheres of public administration. Fourth, resources obtained through attempts to attract members of the opposition parties into the right-wing, clientelistic parties, a goal aimed at draining opposition parties and building a government coalition, by exploring to its most an inherent distortion of the Brazilian system. Finally, the formation of an Economic and Social Development Board, largely made up of entrepreneurs, union leaders, and members of civil society, as a forum for debating public policies. This board had nebulous functions, but was defined as "an advisory organ for the President" meant to broaden the scope of participation by these sectors in the decision-making process. The government's discretionary powers in promoting its agenda allowed it to focus on the formation of economic policy, guided by the strategy of obtaining credibility and insulating some areas from political pressures. The Ministry of Finance and subordinate organs, especially the Central Bank, remained preserved from the pressures of competitive politics, above all from party politics. Two pieces of evidence are worth highlighting. On the one hand, the de facto autonomy of the Central Bank in the formation of monetary policy was preserved. On the other hand, the Executive branch took the initiative of clearing away the constitutional barriers to the bank's statutory autonomy[13] by sending Congress a project for a constitutional amendment (PEC 40) to Article 192 of the Constitution.

Contrary to conventional wisdom, the insulation of the decision-making arenas of economic policy is an eminently political decision. Such insulation becomes especially visible under conditions of acute uncertainty.[14] In the Brazilian case, its distinctiveness is related to the lines of defence adopted and to the nature of the mobilized political resources. The most important line of defence can be defined as having been oriented towards the management of the population's expectations. The political communication strategy (a dimension on which the PT has always been very efficient) had multiple vectors. The main one consisted of maximizing the legitimacy of President Lula da Silva as a key player in two distinct moments. During the initial phase, Lula provided the justification for a recessive economic policy and its costs. Therein lay the imputation of the crisis of credibility to a 'malignant legacy' from the previous government. The president reiterated the importance of patience and in his rhetoric looked to extend the horizon of hope, or that is to say, of growth of social welfare and social justice. When the risk premium fell to surprising levels and the price of the main Brazilian debt bonds rose above 100 percent in the second half of 2003, the president and the PT were able to link themselves politically to this result, justifying the agenda of 2004 and its focus around growth. The intense recourse to rhetoric focused on social policies, where the iconic policy was the Zero Hunger Program (despite evidence that government performance in the program was lacklustre). The efficiency of this public opinion strategy is measurable. Opinion poll research revealed a dramatic change in the time horizon that the population was disposed to concede to the Lula da Silva administration to comply with its promises: from six months in the first quarter of 2003, the expectations jumped to two and a half years during the second half of the year.

A second line of defence, just as important as the first one, was the building of a congressional base and of an axis of federal support centered around state governors. In both cases, in addition to guaranteeing support for the macroeconomic policy, the government articulated support for welfare system reform and for a constitutional change that would clear away the main obstacles to the legal autonomy of the Central Bank.

Various factors contributed to assuring the relative success of these initiatives. There was the control exercised by the leadership of the PT over its congressional base, as well as the abundance of positions still available within the public administration, in state companies and banks, which facilitated the allocation of posts to party allies. Finally, there was the important political capacity to maximize the opportunities for support under different circumstances. On the one hand, in the face of the reformist proposals previously mentioned, the opposition parties (PSDB and PFL) saw themselves obliged to participate in a game of cooperation, since these reforms had been a part of their own agenda while they were in government, and a part of their own political identity. On the other hand, even though it held only two governorships, the PT managed to coordinate the support of a majority of governors – including those represented by the opposition – because of the states' eagerness for the improvements in state finances that were expected as benefits from the welfare reform.

The mixed results of the government in 2004 can be ascribed to both political and socioeconomic causes. While the government's credibility with the market remained strong and was even strengthened during the second half of the year, there was a downsizing of expectations in terms of political legitimacy and the reform agenda among the most vocal members of the electorate and among the government's core supporters. The net results for 2004 can be summarized as follows. A new export drive led to renewed growth, of approximately 5 percent of GDP. This was to become one of two anchors for government legitimacy, although it only had a substantive political effect as of the second half of the year, when growth began to translate into improved employment rates and the growth of average real incomes. The second anchor, the president's ability as a political communicator, had to be activated often during the first half of the year, in light of the erosion of the PT's political legitimacy, high unemployment and informality rates, and the slow rise in average real incomes. Neither of these two anchors, however, was able to prevent the PT from performing worse than it had hoped in the 2004 nationwide municipal elections. Nor did Lula's direct participation in the electoral campaign (which the electoral courts judged illegal in some cases, such as in São Paulo) lead to a significant increase in votes for his candidates. Lula's falling polls and the declining ratings of the government are a sign of the weakness of this strategy.

Understanding the importance of the municipal elections in the government's core political strategy – set out by the PT's core leadership when it came to power – is helpful to understanding the new balance between market credibility and political legitimacy in the Lula da Silva government. The PT's strategy aimed not only at reelecting Lula in 2006, but also at a longer-term project for holding power, with a strong plebiscitary conception of democracy.[15] The PT's initial gamble – based on its strong electoral performance in 2002, the president's ability as a communicator, and its media support – was that the negative effects of orthodox economic policies (which increased the primary fiscal surplus above the levels set in the IMF agreement) would be easily absorbed, with GDP, employment, and income levels recovering in 2004, in time to ensure a smashing electoral success in the 2004 municipal elections.[16]

The electoral results, however, revealed a more pluralist preference by the electorate, with a redistribution of party strength that will force a rethinking of electoral strategies for 2006, given the importance of mayors in the electoral machine in majoritarian elections. Opposition parties came out of the elections much more reinvigorated than their lackluster performance in Congress and gubernatorial mansions during 2003 might have suggested. The PT and PSDB were confirmed as the

Table 8.1: ***2004 Election – votes by party and number of mayorships***

The division of power in Brazil

Second round			*First round*		
Party	*Total Vote*	*Number of Mayorships*	*Party*	*Total Vote*	*Number of Mayorships*
PT	6,912,038	11	PT	16,321,808	400
PSDB	6,433,902	9	PSDB	15,705,068	861
PMDB	1,629,969	6	PMDB	14,249,488	1,047
PDT	1,625,800	5	PDT	5,558,931	297
PFL	1,047,510	0	PFL	11,219,396	786
PSB	885,291	3	PSB	4,475,086	172
PPS	780,250	4	PPS	4,925,866	300
PTB	669,469	2	PTB	5,252,310	42
PP	329,311	2	PP	6,096,563	548
PSDC	173,109	1	PL	5,017,166	380
PSL	121,102	0	PV	1,367,330	55
			PC do B	889,065	10

Source: *O Estado de São Paulo*, 11 February 2004, Supreme Electoral Court.

two principal axes around which the government and opposition coalitions are structured. While the PT emerged as the biggest vote-getter, the PSDB was the most competitive, in terms of the number and importance of the municipalities it won, especially in terms of the overall population it now governs. The municipal election reversed the PT's aspirations of becoming a hegemonic party, increased the opposition's bargaining power, and improved the standing of parties such as the PPS and PDT which are government allies, but are nonetheless critical of the government's performance.

Table 8.2: ***2004 Municipal electoral results***

Party	Number of voters	Percent
PSDB	25.6 million	21
PT	17.0 million	14
PMDB	16.9 million	14
PFL	15.5 million	13

The 2004 election results are likely to reinvigorate opposition parties, in the municipalities as well as in Congress, as well as forcing a review of the executive branch's strategy. Furthermore, the opposition's significant growth in the more developed regions of the country, especially the South and Southeast, and the PT's growth in the Northeast, reversed previous trends.[17]

The explanations for the new balance of power are various, and go beyond the previously mentioned time-lapse between growth and its effects on employment and real incomes. The PT's initial political endowments were gradually eroded throughout 2004, in part because of the scale of the party's political ambitions. This oversized ambition led the PT to tactical mistakes, such as requiring allied parties to accept PT mayoral candidates (in the campaign, 66 percent of allied candidates were from the PT) and failing to accept local electoral coalitions with parties in the government alliance. These mistakes tended to revive the PT's old image as a party hostile to coalition.

Another contribution to the electoral results came from a series of events that eroded the PT's image as being 'exceptional' within the Brazilian party system, as well as a number of events that suggested a clear authoritarian streak. Four overall trends were visible in this regard and were heavily covered by the media. First, the staffing of state companies and state banks with party members, in combination with the adoption of various clientelistic criteria for nominating allies to government positions, with an eye to maintaining a Congressional majority. Second, widespread frustration with the party's weak social policy performance (precisely the area which had the greatest symbolic weight for the government's legitimation), combined with evidence that programs such as 'Zero Hunger' and 'First Job' were more marketing themes than programs in their own right.[18] Third, efforts that were authoritarian and corporatist in nature, seeking to discipline the most vocal sectors of the press and artists through proposed projects such as a Federal Journalism Council and ANCINAVE, a regulatory agency for the movie and audiovisual industry. In both cases, the government was forced to retreat in the face of widespread opposition. Fourth, a series of scandals beginning in February 2004 that involved political advisors and the directors of publicly owned banks, evidence of conflicts of interest, and press reports of the difficulty some members of the government faced in separating the public and private spheres of their lives.

The political effect of these trends on the better informed members of the electorate, and above all, on the political centre and the middle class recently conquered by Lula and the PT, was clearly seen in the more developed regions and those in which the media is most independent. Understanding the depth of this reversal in expectations, especially among the most influential segments of the electorate and businessmen in the productive sector, is fundamental if we are to analyse the prospects for 2005 and 2006 with a view to the possibility of a convergence between financial credibility and political legitimacy (and its possible trade-offs). The likelihood of the government undertaking an effective course correction depends largely on a correct evaluation of expectations. The argument here is that the negative political impact of the PT's governmental performance and evidence of a clear performance deficit on social policy – a deficit of policy formulation and management in 2004 – should not be judged solely on the basis of the clientelistic practices common in Brazil and other emerging countries. Instead, it must be judged by four performance criteria that influence the electorate's preferences, in light of the legitimation criteria that brought PT to power.

First: the contrast between the actual practices of the PT as a governing party and its long-term image, constructed over 25 years as an opposition party and as a paladin of ethics and of social equity. This apparent contrast is reinforced by the shortage of competent staff to formulate and administer policy at state banks, state-owned companies and in social policy, in sharp contrast to the image of technical competence the party projected in the 2002 electoral campaign as it sought to overcome middle class and elite 'prejudices'.[19] Second: the contrast between the rhetoric about the 'malignant legacy' inherited from the Cardoso government, and the Lula government's continuation not only of economic policies inherited from Cardoso, but also of the only effective income transfer program, Bolsa-Familia, which is no more than an aggregration of programs conceived under Cardoso.[20] Third: the deliberate de-institutionalization of the party system, seen in the PT's unprecedented efforts to encourage party switching in Congress, even as it seeks to preserve party unity.[21] Fourth: and most important, an imbalance between two aspects of economic policy is increasingly visible to the middle class and businesspeople in the non-finance sector of the economy (industry and agriculture). While the government is undertaking severe orthodox monetary and fiscal policies – with signs of overkill – centred around rigid Central Bank inflation targets as well as the systematic increase in the tax burden on the formal economic sector, there has been no political resolve to discipline current government spending, which increased significantly between 2004 and 2005. Needless to say, this is unorthodox in light of the fiscal conditions. It also highlights a marked disparity in terms of accountability between municipalities and state governments which are governed by the Fiscal Responsibility Law, and the permissiveness of the federal government's spending. One of the principle causes of this disparity is the fact that the federal budget approved by Congress is not mandatory – that is, it only authorizes spending items, and stands few chances of being closely followed by the executive branch, which is eager not to rein in its budgetary discretion.

The limits to the convergence of financial credibility and political legitimacy

The Brazilian experience provides evidence of a series of limitations on the convergence between the long-term objectives of financial credibility and political legitimacy. The first and most controversial limitation is of a technical order, and has to do with the diagnosis and prescription for short-term economic policy: despite having reined in inflation, to what measure are conditions for sustainable growth being created? There is little doubt that the government of Lula da Silva will report GDP growth of over 5 percent in 2004 and something around 3.3 percent in 2005. The question of sustainable growth, however, remains unresolved, even though the government's capacity to deliver this sustainable growth is essential to its legitimation, and will be critical to securing Lula's re-election.

There are growing doubts about external vulnerability, the difficulties of raising investment rates, and the fiscal regime. There is a growing dependency on external capital for balance of payments financing; in spite of excellent export performance, the relationship of exports to foreign debt has not yet reached levels that will safeguard the country against volatility. The attractiveness of Brazil to financial flows is due in part to international liquidity derived from low interest rates in the United States, Europe and Japan, and in part to the comparative rigidity of domestic monetary policy. However, in light of the high interest rates set by the Central Bank of Brazil, the debt–GDP ratio – the main criteria of performance (and of solvency) in the eyes of the market – remains high (even though it is declining). The fiscal results, for their part, are largely the result of the *ad hoc* management of revenues by the Federal Revenue Service, which have guaranteed an increase in tax collection without any sign of a proportionate effort on the other side towards cutting expenditure. The tax 'reform', accomplished at the end of 2003 was not a true reform, but merely a reiteration of the fiscal policy of the previous government. This led to a soaring increase in tax-like 'contributions' (a device used to circumvent the constitutional obligation to transfer a high proportion of tax revenues to states and municipalities), and the extension of the central government's ability to withhold a portion of revenue transfers to sub-national governments. On the fiscal front, however, tax collection is on the increase as a consequence both of improved growth and the more than proportionate increase in tax collection.

There was much to celebrate in 2004 – and possibly will also be in 2005 – but it is worth recognizing that the bonanza on the global stage may not continue. On a positive note, the Lula administration has delivered high growth, whose effects on formal employment and income levels is beginning to show through in the government's recovering poll results. In addition, the Brazilian economy has been propped up by the performance of the export sector of the economy, which has not traditionally been at the heart of Brazil's economic expansion. The positive effects of this export-led growth include rising production and employment levels as well as better capital flows, and suggest a structural shift in the behavior of domestic businesses and the country's participation in the global market.[22]

Nonetheless, this performance depended on a framework that has been under construction on two foundations for over a decade. The first was the cumulative effect of trade liberalization, economic stabilization, and a renewed conception of the role of the state (privatization, regulation, civil service organization, decentralization, and state–society partnerships). It also includes great advances in the fiscal arena, such as the Fiscal Responsibility Law, and changes in the exchange rate and monetary regimes, thanks to the adoption of a floating exchange rate and of inflation targeting, in the wake of the 1999 devaluation. The second foundation was the restructuring undertaken in the private sector, which has also been underway for a long time, both in agriculture, which today has the most productive agro-industry in the world, and in manufacturing, which has seen increased productivity and reorganized itself domestically before turning to global markets beginning in 1999.

Furthermore, there are signs that development of this framework is being interrupted, if not undermined, by the continued review of the role of the state and the fiscal discipline of the federal government. The liberal microeconomic agenda espoused by the Finance Ministry is far from being achieved, in particular the elements which are most critical to increasing the rate of public investment and attracting private capital. The Finance Ministry has not managed to overcome the setbacks suffered as a result of the *dirigiste* approach which has consumed the regulatory agencies and the executive branch's political operations. It also has not managed to reverse the use of partisan criteria in filling key government positions. Meanwhile, the federal government's fiscal discipline is limited to the activities of the Federal Revenue Service, while personnel expenditures have risen alarmingly in recent months. A symptom of the deep distortion of the system is the fact that the federal government collects revenue amounting to 27.5 percent of GDP, but its investments total only 0.5 percent of GDP. The newest political and economic challenge is to carry out a fiscal adjustment without further increasing the tax burden, currently at 37 percent, and do so in a manner that penalizes production and consumption less.

In sum, the Lula government has been working on these issues from two angles: it has an eye on the financial market, even as it seeks to attract Esse setor do governo, heavyweight allies to its congressional coalition, and in particular, to gain the support of parties with large electoral machines that will be indispensable in the 2006 elections, such as the PMDB. The main problem is the solution adopted by the PT to overcome the gap between the content of macroeconomic policy and its political and social support. There is a clearly apparent inconsistency between the strengthening of macroeconomic policy on orthodox lines (consolidated by the renewal of the agreement with the IMF), and microeconomic policies that affect the conditions for investment. The Lula government has had the most lacklustre performance in the area of microeconomics, above all of infrastructure development, in large part because the political and technical teams in this area are those with the strongest interventionist tendencies. The replacement of the leadership of the BNDES national development bank in the wake of the 2004 elections shows that the government is aware of the limitations that group was setting on the country's main state investment bank, as well as being a clear victory by Finance Minister Palocci over the statist group within the government.

Two other limitations exist regarding the political strategy of the PT: its electoral calculations and its long-term relationships with other parties. In terms of its electoral strategy, the outcome of the 2004 elections has prompted Lula and the PT leadership to adopt new guidelines that will restrain party members' enthusiasm for local-level party alliances in 2006. Meanwhile, the intensity of internal competition within the party, especially over the nominations for governorships in the 2006 elections, will play directly into the dispute over the economic policy agenda. Judging by the agenda set by the Ministry of Finance, 2005 would be the year of Central Bank autonomy. Although this proposal has the support of the opposition parties, it remains a sensitive theme for the PT congressional delegation, which has been lukewarm.

The main limit to the convergence of credibility and legitimacy in the long term is the prevalence of short-term political calculations by government strategists regarding the relationship between the PT and other parties. There has been a reversal of the trend seen throughout the 1990s, during which the Brazilian political party system was decanted into five or six major parties, as a result of the PT's need to build a parliamentary majority out of a fragmentary coalition. The upshot is that the government has built a coalition quickly on the basis of favours (even before the PMDB was formally included) for the approval of reforms. With incentives from the presidential palace, this process resulted in intense inter-party migration. The large opposition parties were significantly reduced – the PFL elected 84 deputies and can now count upon only 65, and the PSDB, which elected 70 deputies, today has some 52 congressional representatives. There are two parties allied to the government which were previously of little significance, but whose rolls jumped from 26 deputies each to 55 and 42 respectively.

Conclusion

This chapter has discussed possible consequences of the entrance of a party such as the PT into the credibility game. Brazil and Lula's government are enjoying the fruits of past and present policies on the macroeconomic front, but the prospects for sustainable growth are not yet clear. At the same time, the hybrid character of the PT government leads us to re-evaluate two questions. First, the considerable degree of political discretionality that is needed to bridge the enormous chasm between the content of economic policies required to sustain financial credibility and the preferences of the electorate, as well as of the party's own supporters (in particular if the international situation should worsen, that is, under conditions of greater economic uncertainty). Second, the amount of time necessary to reduce the gap in legitimacy is much greater than that required for adjusting to market humours, given the firepower of international capital markets, which remain alert to Brazil's solvency conditions.

Notes

1 "For it is worth noting that in a democracy most of the conditions that are of great interest to citizens (e.g. those who can voice their opinions or own resources) are not a potential object of the collective decision making of even vast majorities because they are constitutionally entrenched. As a consequence of both rights and procedures being thus guaranteed as well as supposedly implemented through the day-to-day operation of the judicial system, *democracies make for a non-violent, limited, and civilized character of political conflict and incremental change.*" C. Offe, 'A atual transição da historia e algumas opções básicas para as instituições da sociedade', in L.C. Bresser Pereira, J. Wilheim and L. Sola, eds., *Sociedade e estado em transformação*, São Paulo: Editora UNESP, 1998

2 Ibid.

3 In the second round Lula's adversary, Senator Serra, obtained 33,370,739 votes – 38.73 percent of the valid votes, while blank and annulled votes totalled 3,772,138. The number of PT parliamentary seats jumped to 92, making it the largest party in the Chamber of Deputies.

4 Lula da Silva took office with 83.6 percent of public approval, and his government began with a negative evaluation of only 2.3 percent, as well as the high expectation of complying with the promises made during the electoral campaign, around 64 percent during March 2003.

5 Right from the start Roseana Sarney was far from being her party's preferred official candidate for the presidency. At the polls her performance ended in a turnabout in the electoral strategy of her very own party. In reality, the PFL polls held to discover voter intentions had pointed to the candidate's profile as symbolizing changes. The gamble by the PFL strategists on a woman, the governor of one of the poorest northeast states, and the daughter of ex-president José Sarney, was, above all, looking to increase the PFL's bargaining power in negotiations with the PSDB party for electoral alliances that would come later.

6 The PPS party is a modernized form of the Brazilian communist party that emerged in the post-Cold War era. Ciro Gomes had run as a candidate in the presidential election of 1998.

7 Data from I. Goldfajn, 'The Brazilian crisis, the role of the IMF and democratic governability', Paper presented in the Assamblea del Club de Madrid, Madrid, Spain, 1–2

November 2003. See also J.R. Mendonça de Barros, M. Baer and C. Pio, 'Brazil and the IMF: virtues and limits of the 2002 agreement', Paper presented in the Assamblea del Club de Madrid, Madrid, Spain, 1–2 November 2003.

8 See chapter by Santiso in this volume.

9 As well as the negative image of bankers in general, and of foreign banks in particular, the Bank of Boston had been one of the principle targets of the public diatribes of PT senator Aloísio Mercadante when the devaluation of the Real occurred in 1999: he accused the bank (and the government) of having benefited from insider information.

10 For an analysis of the trajectory of the PT, see Leoncio Martins Rodrigues, *Partidos, ideologia e composição social: um estudo das bancadas partidárias na Câmara dos Deputados*, São Paulo: Edusp, 2002.

11 For an analysis of the current economic policy, based on recent experience, see B. Sallum Jr. and E. Kugelmas, 'O modo Lula de governar', in B. Sallum Jr., ed., *Brasil e Argentina hoje: política e economia*, São Paulo: Edusc, 2004. For a discussion on the risks of 'Mexicanization', equating the anti-democratic potential of the PT to that of the Mexican PRI, see articles on the website www.primeiraleitura.com.br.

12 For an analytically in-depth account of this problem consult Malloy, J. and Catherine Conaghan, *Unsettling Statecraft, Neoliberalism in the Andes*, Pittsburgh: Pittsburgh University Press, 1998.

13 Constitutional Amendment Project No. 40, to Article 92 of the Brazilian Constitution.

14 Observe the similar experience in Bolivia during the 1980s, described by Malloy and Connaghan, op. cit.

15 This strategy seeks to enlist new party members, use income transfer programs and the 'Zero Hunger' program to increase the PT's electoral popularity, and incorporate new organized interest groups such as the Movement of the Roofless and the Movement of the Universityless (modelled on the Movement of the Landless, or MST).

16 The Lula da Silva government's commitment to a primary fiscal surplus of 4.25 percent of GDP (higher than the level set in the IMF agreement or the Cardoso government's 3.5 percent surplus), in conjunction with a strict monetary policy that imposed high real interest rates and a considerable fiscal burden, appeared to many critics as a classic example of overkill in the name of recovering credibility.

17 In addition to losing its command of important capitals in the South and Southeast (including São Paulo and Porto Alegre), the PT faced important defeats in Rio de Janeiro and in middle-sized cities in these regions. The one exception was the capital of Minas Gerais, Belo Horizonte.

18 The 'First Job' program only managed to meet 1 percent of its target. The resettlement of landless peasants was far below the declared targets, although in this case the government continues to guarantee a significant transfer of resources to the primary organization in this area (the MST, associated with the PT) and to block efforts for the MST to account for the origin and use of its revenues.

19 See Sallum Jr. and Kugelmas, op. cit., on the reversal of general expectations among opinion leaders.

20 See S. Draibe, 'Políticas sociais no governo Fernando Henrique Cardoso', in 'Dossiê do segundo governo Fernando Henrique Cardoso', *Tempo Social*, 6/2, 15–30, and the extremely constructive interview by Paes de Barros in 'Miséria Zero, deve ser a próxima etapa', *O Estado de São Paulo*, 16 January 2005. Paes de Barros, one of the most important poverty specialists in Brazil, suggests transforming the Bolsa Familia into an effective substitute for the Zero Hunger program, and criticizes the deliberate confusion of hunger and poverty.

21 Although the PT is not the first to exploit the vulnerability of the Brazilian party system, it has gone beyond the efforts of past governments. Not only is the scale of the effort much broader, but the double standard is remarkable, since the PT will not allow party switchers to join its party. The PT's membership in Congress increased by only one deputy under this

government. See interview by PT Federal Deputy Paulo Delgado of Minas Gerais justifying this policy in 'O Congresso não é um clube social', *O Valor*, 12 January 2005.

22 This argument is supported by J.R. Mendonça de Barros, 'Mudança estrutural e desenvolvimento', presentation at joint seminar of the Instituto Sergio Motta and the Instituto Fernando Henrique Cardoso, 29 November 2004, accessible at www.ism.org.br, link 'Quinta Semana Sérgio Motta'.

Chapter 9

Wall Street and emerging democracies: financial markets and the Brazilian presidential elections

Javier Santiso

'Ama a incerteza e seras democratico'
Adam Przeworski

IN A BRIEF but stimulating essay, Paul Krugman criticised the double standards enforced by financial markets. Simply put, policies that would be regarded as completely unsustainable and perverse at home are often advocated for emerging market economies. An example that Krugman mentions is Brazil, a country that during the summer of 1998 was suffering an economic slowdown when the collapse of Russia triggered a speculative attack on the Brazilian currency, the real. Once again, the loss of confidence accelerated the deterioration when markets decided that Brazil had become a bad risk and that its problems lay in large budget deficits. In order to restore confidence, the government pursued an extremely tight monetary and fiscal policy that set the country towards an eonomic downturn the following year. Why did Brazil pursue a policy that breaks with the Keynesian compact used in the OECD heartland under such circumstances? Part of the answer lies, as Krugman states, in "the double standard and the perceived need to win market confidence at all cost".[1]

But these events also occurred at a specific political moment: in October 1998, when Brazil held presidential elections. Economic weaknesses and uncertainties therefore colluded with endogenous political ones. Brazilian financial crises, like those experienced in Mexico and Argentina, tend to be synchronized with major political events such as elections. In 1998, the Brazilian presidential elections opened a window of uncertainty in an economic context that was already frightening for investors. Financial markets became extremely risk averse to the Brazilian democratic game, the outcome being perceived as uncertain because of possible risks and setbacks for economic liberalization if Cardoso were to lose the race. The nervousness of financial markets was also apparent during the 2002 Brazilian presidential campaign. Brazilian fundamentals presented vulnerabilities, one of them being the debt burden.[2] However, they were not shaky. The trigger for a crisis appeared to be the forthcoming elections and change of government. Once again, with elections approaching, exchange rates, spreads and interest rates moved with impressive speed and oscillations.[3] The EMBI spread, for example, which measures the difference between the yield on dollar-denominated bonds issued by the Brazilian government and corresponding ones issued by the US Treasury, captured this volatility. At the beginning of 2002, the Brazilian EMBI spread was around 700 bps (basis points); by the October election it reached an impressive peak of 2,400 bps, falling gradually by the spring of 2003 under 1,000 bps and reaching 750 bps once again by year-end.[4] This episode once again invites the question about the political preferences of financial markets: are financial markets politically correct?

This chapter focuses on the interactions between politics and finance in emerging economies stressing the case of Brazilian presidential elections. More precisely, we will underline how Wall Street (i.e. financial markets) incorporates and reacts to major Latin American political and democratic events such as presidential elections. As a case study, the 2002 Brazilian presidential elections are a starting point, after having analysed, in a first approximation, the market preferences of political regimes through the indexes. The second section presents an empirical study of Wall Street analysts' perceptions of a major political occurrence, the presidential elections in Brazil. The empirical analysis is based on the production output and reports of Wall Street investment firms during the year 2002, focusing on the top fixed income teams of Wall Street, as ranked by Institutional Investors, Bloomberg and Latin Finance in their league tables.[5] Finally, in the third and last section, economic and financial data of previous Brazilian election years is used to view the events in historical perspective.

Political regimes and finance markets: an index game approach

It seems, in a first analysis that markets tend to be very sensitive to democratic uncertainty. That does not mean that financial markets have preferences for non-democratic regimes. In fact, we know very little about their political preferences. One way would be to look at the composition of indexes used by investors for their asset allocation. There has been an explosion in the number of indices. Barclays Global Investors, one of the world's leading asset managers, used by the beginning of the twenty-first century more than two hundred indices in managing its index funds. MSCI (Morgan Stanley Capital International, the world's biggest index company) says it has a total of 11,000 indexes of one sort or another. Accurate data on the size of the index industry is however hard to pin down. MSCI estimates that by 2001 there was about US$3,500 billion of assets benchmarked against its indexes, while FTSE, another leading indexer, offered a ballpark figure of US$2,500 billion for its own products.[6]

Focusing on the leading indexes used by portfolio investors could, however, give a useful tool to approximate the political preferences of financial markets. If we focused on the leading fixed income and equity emerging and global markets indexes, we could risk a tentative answer to the above question. For the data on political regimes we used the classification and data developed by Michael Coppedge in 2003, the *Polyarchy Scale 2000*, an eleven-point scale measuring thresholds of polyarchy for sixty selected countries (for some of the countries not included we complete the data). Four variables were considered: free and fair elections; freedom of organization; freedom of expression; and availability of alternative sources of information (full polyarchies have a score of zero). We used also the Polity IV and Polyarchy datasets, the two most widely used measures of democracy. Largely based on the ground breaking work of Ted Gurr, these datasets evaluate the degree of democratization of a state by codifying four institutional dimensions with the objective of placing political regimes along a democracy – autocracy continuum. The index it generates is a combination of a democracy scale (political participation, competition, openness, and constraints on chief executives) and an autocracy scale (lack of competition, regulations of political participation, lack of competitiveness, and lack of constraints), each composed of four categories. The Polity dataset was originally constructed to test the durability of states.[7] Tatu Vanhanen's Polyarchy dataset covers 187 countries over the period 1810 to 1998.[8] Vanhanen's index of democracy offers a measure of the quality of democracy assessing the degree of participation (measured by the percentage of voters as per the voting-age population) and competition (assessed by the relative weight of the ruling party), largely based on the classical Dahl concept of polyarchy.[9]

For the indexes coverage, data from major indexers is being used here. For fixed income emerging markets, JP Morgan constructs that which is most used. The indexes are constructed using a peculiar weighting scheme and have a specific instrument and country coverage. These indexes are designed as market benchmarks, reporting the returns investors could have made by investing in different portfolios of emerging markets assets. In emerging bond markets the dominant indexes are those developed by JP Morgan. The first was the EMBI, developed at the beginning of the 1990s. JP Morgan later issued new indices: the EMBI+; the EMBI Global; and the EMBI Global constrained. According to JP Morgan, in the following decade fund managers began to prefer a more diversified benchmark and by the end of 2003 the leading index according to JP Morgan client survey was the EMBIG Diversified (adopted by nearly 40 percent of the asset managers that answered), against 32.5 percent that preferred the EMBI+ and 28 percent the EMBI Global. The four indexes have similar objectives, as they are all indicators of benchmark returns, but they differ in the class of assets included, the pool of issuing countries and the weights given to them. The narrowest one is the EMBI covering only sovereign bonds issued by eleven countries. In comparison, the EMBI Global has a broader coverage (27 countries) and a wider class of assets.

In 2000, the EMBI, which focuses exclusively on Brady bonds, attached the greatest weight to Latin American countries, all of them polyarchies emerging from authoritarian regimes that were in power until the 1980s. For years Latin American bonds formed the core of the emerging market universe. In 2000 only four of the EMBI countries were outside Latin America, Nigeria being the only one notorious non-polyarchy. In this index, Latin America had a weight of nearly 84 percent by the beginning of 2000 (much more than the 52 percent in the EMBI Global Constrained). If the other (larger) indices are also analysed, to include 27 countries, all but three (Nigeria, Ivory Coast and China) registered polyarchy scores below five. In other words, 90 percent of the countries included in the EMBI Global Diversified are democracies. Half of the countries have levels of polyarchy comparable to major OECD countries. Based on this first approximation, one can hardly argue that financial markets investors (in fact fixed income asset managers) are politically incorrect, that is that they tend to prefer non-democratic regimes to democratic ones. In fact, it is rather the contrary: the ones that follow the indexes at least tend to invest their assets in full (or nearly full) polyarchies.

If the indexes are taken into account, country weights and the expansion of the indexes during the 2000s (more countries have been added) the 'democratic preference'of financial markets remains and still looks massive. By the end of 2001, also as a consequence of default and collapse in Argentina, the country coverage of the EMBI+ was enlarged. Ukraine, Qatar, Colombia, Philippines, South Korea and Turkey joined the club. This enlargement deteriorated the ratio of polyarchies versus non-polyarchies but only marginally. If we rank Ukraine and Qatar above a score of 5, there are still only 3 out of 17 countries that are not polyarchies in this index and they represented less than 3.5 percent of the weightings in the EMBI+. By mid-2003, the EMBI+ covered nineteen countries, the EMBI Global and the EMBI Global Diversified 31. For all of these indexes Mexico, a democratic country, was the largest country covered with respective weights of 21 percent, 19 percent and 11.5 percent.[10]

However, the EMBI+ remained quite concentrated on three major issuers, all of them more or less consolidated polyarchies, Brazil, Mexico and Russia making up more than 60 percent of the index. This concentration and the wishes of investors to reduce their exposure to Latin American credits, largely as a result of the Argentina default, accelerated the development of other indexes like the EMBI Global Constrained Index, now called the EMBI Global Diversified. In 2003, this index counted 32 countries and according to JP Morgan by the same year fund managers using EMBI Global and the EMBI Global Diversified already reached more than 60 percent. In 2002 and 2003, the EMBI Global and the EMBI Global Diversified had 33 countries, some of them notorious non-polyarchies like China and Nigeria, others like Algeria, Pakistan, Egypt, Tunisia and Morocco that could at the time hardly be defined as full democracies. The expansion base of the emerging markets indexes universe was clearly not totally politically correct. However the weights of all non-polyarchies countries included were marginal. By mid-2002, Brazil, Mexico and Russia were still the largest country weights in the index, accounting for more than 50 percent (see Table 9.2). For nearly all the non-polyarchies included in the index, their country weight was less than 1 percent for each one. The only two above a 1 percent weight were China and Nigeria with nearly 2 percent each.

Financial markets and elections: the Brazilian 2002 Odyssey

If we take a look at the EMBI indexes, used by fixed income asset managers and produced by JP Morgan, most of the countries listed are democratic regimes. The same is true for equity indexes, mainly the ones produced by MSCI for emerging markets. Financial markets seem to be rather politically correct. However the question of political regime preferences of financial markets can be complexified. Another way to look at the political preferences of financial markets is to focus on the concept of uncertainty and the core definition of democracy.

As stressed by Przeworski, one of the characteristic features of democracy is precisely that outcomes appear uncertain. In a democracy, the results of an election or the parliamentary outcome of a proposed reform is always an open and uncertain issue.[11] Therefore, electoral competition, collective choices and preferences crystallised during reform processes, are all part of the usual life of a democracy and at the same time, boosters of uncertainty to which financial markets tend to be very sensitive. Dictatorships also generate uncertainty but in a very different manner. In a dictatorship first there are no elections and therefore we do not have the uncertainty linked to electoral competition. Secondly, in a dictatorship the political outcomes are only deduced from the preferences of one sole actor. In a democracy, in contrast, they derive from the conflicting preferences and rules of multiple arbitrages, actors and institutions. Under a dictatorship, there is an omniscient observer and an absolute ruler, who is certain about the outcomes. "Under democracy", as stressed by Przeworski, "there is no such actor. Hence the difference in uncertainty is conditional in the following sense: in an authoritarian system it is certain that political outcomes will not include those adverse to the will of the power apparatus, whereas in a democracy there is no group whose preferences and resources can predict outcomes with near uncertainty." The difference between democracy and dictatorship is not therefore absolute but rather conditional uncertainty. "The point is that under a democracy no one can be certain that their interests will ultimately triumph. Capitalists do not always win conflicts which are processed in a democratic manner."[12]

Another characteristic of democracy is its temporal dimension. As underlined by Juan Linz, democracy is a government pro-tempore.[13] Governments are chosen for a fixed term limit, they have therefore limited time horizons. Their longevity is bounded by democratic institutions. In contrast, autocrats' horizons have longer time frames. They can stay in power as long as historical and biological conditions permit. Investors can, however, face great uncertainties within an autocracy but in a different recurrent manner than that they face in democracies. Subjects in an autocracy always face what financial markets call 'political risk', i.e. some risk of expropriation by *le fait du prince*, some risk that their capital will be confiscated, their loans repudiated. This risk reduces the amount of savings and investments even when autocrats are forward-looking and with long temporal horizons.[14] Limited executives tend to be associated with stronger property rights. Olson et al. showed that there is a strong relationship between the length of time a democratic system has lasted and the security of property rights.[15] They also found that the longer the tenure of an individual autocrat is positively correlated with better property and contract rights. What seems to matter is either institutional stability or individual stability, lasting temporal horizons of institutions and lasting temporal horizons of individuals. The shorter the time horizon of the ruler, the greater their incentives to behave as a kleptocrat or cartelocrat.[16] In order to have fiscal and financial institutions developing, the key is that ruler's hand must be voluntary tied, that is to have "political institutions that force governments with limited time horizons to behave as if they have infinite time horizons".[17]

Elections, government formation or dissolution, removals, legislative decision-making are inherent to democratic games but remain unpredictable. It seems that financial markets also behave quite nervously when faced with regular democratic events such as elections in emerging countries. The monitoring of politics by financial markets tends to intensify during election periods in a dramatic way even for small emerging economies such as Central American ones.[18] Financial operators have intensively analysed the coverage of political issues during the meltdown of Argentina by the end of 2001 and the collapse that followed as clear evidence of political governance, representation and legitimacy crisis.[19] In the same way that Mexico's 1994 elections and the 1995 'Tequila crisis' has caught the attention of analysts, in 1997, market instability reached South Korea during its presidential election year.[20]

Election years are particularly viewed as critical junctures from a financial investors' point of view, owing to the density of reports incorporating political dimensions, within the financial industry, causing uncertainty to jump to unprecedented levels. In fact when the behaviour of financial variables during election years in emerging markets is examined more closely, these events are associated with great volatility. Bussière and Mulder found (for 22 emerging countries between the 1994 and 1997 period associated with the 'Tequila' and Asian crises), that elections and political volatility are significantly related to currency crises while coalition stability is not.[21] Uncertain electoral results tend to make it difficult for forward-looking financial market actors to predict economic conditions under the forthcoming government whose policy preferences remain, if not uncertain, under scrutiny and suspicion. Elections are also associated with lower ratings published by agencies and with greater frequency of sovereign rating downgrades and with higher pre-election spreads versus post-election spreads. Steven Block and Paul Vaaler analysed both trends for developing countries holding presidential elections between 1987 and 1999, their results clearly suggesting that at least two key actors in financial markets, agencies and bondholders, viewing routine democratic events such as elections negatively.[22] Of the 64 agency downgrades in their sample of emerging markets, thirty occur during their election year. Of these thirty downgrades, 26 occurred within the six months prior to the election. Regarding bondholders they tend to demand higher risk premiums as compensation for the pre-election uncertainty and risk. With elections approaching and incumbent's intentions with regard policies more and more revealed, bondholders seem to give back and risk premiums decline. Interestingly, bond spreads gradually decline in the run-up to elections and more dramatically, when concerns about intentions, behaviours and policies by the incumbents decrease. From an empirical point of view, it seems that for sovereigns issuing bonds during the six months previous to an election is a costly exercise that might be avoided (even when it remains possible – which is not often the case). Symmetrically, there might be after elections a rally that could benefit the sovereign with the burst of the pre-election 'spreads bubble'.

The 2002 Brazilian presidential election was, from this point of view, a paradigmatic case study. The Brazilian episode underlined that financial turbulences are contingent, neither inevitable, nor preordained, but rather involving countries that enter a risky zone, causing a speculative tunnel effect, where the government lacks the political and economic capacity to curb market perceptions in order to fend off financial pressure. In this critical juncture, as stressed by Eichengreen, "if investor sentiment turns against the country, for whatever reason, the government of a country with heavy financial burden or a weak economy may be unable to sustain the harsh policies of austerity needed to deflect mounting pressures. If, on the other hand, market sentiment remains favourable, the same economic and financial fundamentals will be sustainable, and no crisis will result."[23] It is therefore central, to the understanding of the dynamics of financial turbulences, to focus on these market sentiments, in other words to analyse how Wall Street cognitive regimes change regarding a country. The purpose of this chapter is precisely to show these changing perceptions in Brazil during 2002.

It is important, however, to stress that during 2002, behind the election issue, economic fundamentals also worried investors. More precisely, and contrasting with previous crises in emerging markets, rather than concerns over the exchange rate, investors were focused on debt dynamics. Since 1999 Brazil has adopted a floating exchange rate regime, and the most recent round of financial market turbulence has concerned fiscal sustainability rather than the sustainability of a fixed exchange rate. During the period covered by the present essay there was a major change in the Brazilian macroeconomic framework, a period therefore during which investors' concerns pre-1999 were likely to be very different from those experienced post-1999. In the same way, it's also important to stress that what is referred to as 'Wall Street' is not at all a uniform 'epistemic community', investors and analysts views being plural. The concerns of equity investors and investors in debt (government bonds) are also likely to have not been perfectly coincident. Post-1999 – and particularly during the 2002 elections – it was the possibility of a government default on its debt that loomed largest.

That said, it is also important to bear in mind, in order to understand investors and analysts nervousness, that Brazil is by far the largest Latin American economy, with some 40 percent of the region's output. From a financial perspective, it is also a major equity and bond market for international investors. By the beginning of 2002, the country's sound economic track record was praised by almost everybody from New York to London, and from Washington to São Paulo. Brokers' reports were stressing the substantial decoupling of the Argentine and Brazilian economies, for example pointing to the weak trade links existing between the two countries and low Brazilian banking exposure to Argentina. Investment banks and brokers reports lauded Brazilian economics and politicians, and some analysts underlining Brazil potentials: "global decoupling seems to gain ground", wrote a bullish strategist, "funds are flowing to emerging markets, but have not reached Brazil; Brazil could now be the last diversification play".[24] Others stressed the decoupling process between Brazil and its troubled neighbour: "the correlation between daily returns on Argentina and Brazil in the EMBI+, which stood at very high levels between 1995 and 2000, dropped to 0.8 in the summer of 2001 when deposits withdrawals accelerated in Argentina, and slumped to 0.15 in November 2001 when Argentina's default was announced."[25]

The celebration of Brazil culminated in March 2002 during the annual meeting of the Inter-American Development Bank held in Fortaleza. At the time, Arminio Fraga, a major analyst and player in the market confidence game, appointed as Central Bank governor in 1999, after a brilliant career in Wall Street at Salomon Brothers and Soros Fund Management, was elected "Man of the Year" by *Latin Finance* magazine for being "the man who saved Brazil". Particularly emblematic of the mood at the time with regard to Latin American emerging markets, was the Merrill Lynch report and summary conclusions of the IADB meetings. As did many of its competitors, Merrill Lynch organized for its clients a conference in Fortaleza attended by IMF personnel, portfolio managers, US Treasury representatives and other officials. "The mood in Fortaleza", concluded the firm's emerging markets debt strategist, "was generally upbeat. In contrast to a year ago in Santiago de Chile, there was no major crisis in the making, such as was the case with Argentina back then. Indeed, one of the more remarkable market, economic, and political developments over the past year has been how little regional contagion has been triggered by the Argentine crisis. [...] The principal focus at the meetings was the Brazilian election, and participants appeared to be reassured that despite a volatile period ahead, a candidate from the government coalition is still the most likely successor to President Cardoso."[26]

But by late April, the Brazilian currency suddenly slumped and the risk premium on the country's bonds soared, putting them on a similar level to Nigeria's. The reason for such a sudden and quick fall from stability was that in October 2002, Brazil faced a major presidential election. By March, political polls started to be published and were extensively incorporated by major Wall Street brokers. Investors abhor uncertainty. From this point of view, the 2002 presidential elections created a major issue, and given that Fernando Henrique Cardoso, who since 1995 contributed to modernize the Brazilian government and economy, was unable to compete to his own succession, he left the options open to three major contenders: two leftist candidates, Luiz Inácio Lula da Silva and Ciro Gomes, and José Serra (who was favoured by Cardoso, the incumbent president).[27] The first two candidates mentioned have spoken in the past of debt restructuring. At the time (and sadly for Brazil) the market sensitivity regarding the debt issue was extreme due to the fact that Argentina had defaulted on its public debt by the end of 2001, just a few months before. In addition, some analysts had it in mind that past presidential elections in Brazil had also led to a costly devaluation that almost destroyed the economy. Between April and July 2002, when investors started to worry that one of the leftist candidates might win, anxiety translated into financial variables. By July, spreads levels jumped above 2,000 bps and the currency sank to over R$3.5 to the dollar, from a previous level of R$2.30 at the beginning of the year.

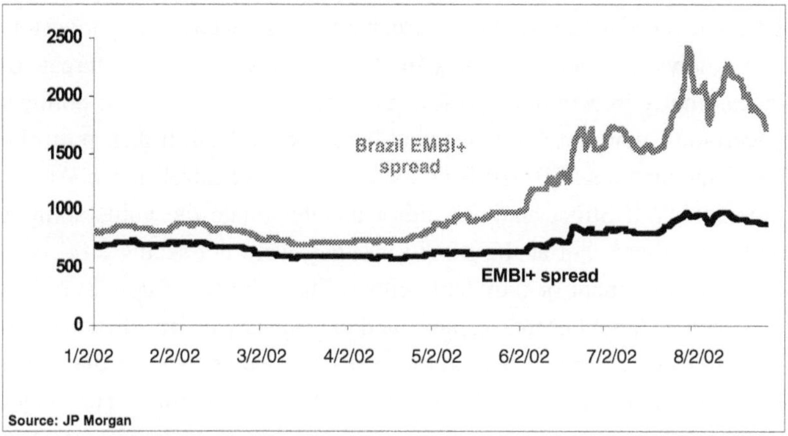

Fig. 9.1 ***Brazilian and emerging bond spreads***

By the beginning of May a few brokers started to publish more cautious reports renewing attention to the role of political factors. Later, during the month, nearly all Wall Street firms started to crunch numbers to foresee the sustainability of Brazilian debt dynamics. Brazilian public debt presents, in fact, a very unusual case amongst emerging markets which consists of its high sensitivity to financial variables. Brazil's debt was at that time 80 percent indexed to either domestic interest rates or to currency exchange levels. Models were used in order to find which primary fiscal surplus was required to stabilize the debt-to-GDP ratio, using stress case scenarios for the major variables affecting debt dynamics, which consists of real interest rates, exchange rate, GDP growth and the amount of net contingent liabilities.[28]

The change to a more cautious tone regarding Brazil was mainly triggered by opinion polls showing support for Lula da Silva, the candidate of the left-leaning Workers' Party (PT).[29] As underlined by Walter Molano from BCP Securities, in a report towards the end of May entitled "Da Lula Monster", "there seems to be a sense of panic as economic agents realise that Lula will win the elections. The behaviour by the multinationals seems to be the mirror of what is happening in the bond market. It is too bad that Brazil will not get the benefit of the doubt."[30] The cautious stance on Brazil was also exacerbated by a much more risk-averse global financial environment for emerging markets because of uncertainties regarding the recovery of the United States economy. But in the case of Brazil, politics accentuated the risk aversion. Lula's advance in the polls was perceived as a growing risk by investors and analysts, since it represented a perceived serious threat of discontinuity in economic policy. As a result of the increased political uncertainty, many of the investment banks began to shift their portfolio recommendations of Brazil from overweight to a neutral stance. At that moment, Wall Street analysts didn't underestimate the vulnerabilities and risks ahead, but at the same time they were not seeing a crisis in Brazil as imminent or inevitable either. The rollover of domestic debt was seen as large but manageable, and the capacity of Brazilian government to meet its foreign obligations was regarded as stronger than what the spreads on foreign obligations assumed at the time. The major concern was, in fact, the presence of an increasing impact on debt dynamics caused by a prolonged investor confidence risk aversion regarding Brazil.[31] A Brazilian crisis was not seen as a most-likely-scenario by Wall Street analysts who still envisaged a happy ending in October.

Table 9.1 ***Wall Street strategists's recommendations on Brazil bond debt 2002***

	Rating Change	*Date*
ABNAmro	Neutral from Overweight	May 1st
Goldman Sachs	Neutral from Overweight	May 1st
Santander Investments	Neutral from Overweight	May 3rd
Deutsche Bank	Neutral from Overweight	May 9th
JP Morgan Chase	1st reduction of Overweight	June 4th
	2nd reduction of Overweight	July 1st
	Overweight to Marketweight	July 22nd
	Moved to Underweight	December 9th
BCP Securities	Sell	August 8th
Morgan Stanley	Downgrade to Underperform	August 12th
Salomon Smith Barney	Changes in marcoeconomic forecast	August 20th
UBS Warburg	Increased Overweight	August 30th
Bear Stearns	Cuts to Underweight	September 19th
Merrill Lynch	Moved to Underweight	September 25th
Goldman Sachs	Moved to Underweight	September 27th
Merrill Lynch	Moved back to Marketweight	October 4th

Source: Based on JBIC and Wall Street investment banks reports, 2002.

Extensive and very complete political analysis started to be published. For example, in a detailed report, BBVA (Banco Bilbao Viscaya Argentaria) economic research team in Brazil analysed the PT's economic program.[32] JP Morgan published a complete guide to the Brazilian candidates, political parties and timetables.[33] Polls were analysed closely by all Wall Street firms, some focusing on the data releases, others on television as a crucial determinant of voter intentions for the presidential elections. On 8 May, UBS Warburg, for example, devoted a complete report to analyse the impact of free television time on the presidential race.[34] Other firms created specific tools for political dynamics: Goldman Sachs created a "Lulameter", a model that tried to quantify the probability of Lula victory that was priced in by currency markets.[35]

Because of their creative tools – and above all because of their negative conclusions regarding Brazil perspectives – some firms faced inside turbulence. For example, on 3 May the Santander Central Hispano New York research department downgraded Brazilian bonds to neutral from heavy weighting, citing the country's sluggish economy and political

Table 9.2 ***Countries that traded north of 2,000 bps***

EMBIG Countries which traded above 2,000 bps spreads and defaulted

	Days Above 2,000 bps Before Default	*Default Date*
Argentina	38	December 2001
Russia	40	October 1998
Ivory Coast	2	March 2000
Ecuador	163	September 1999

EMBIG Countries which traded above 2,000 bps spreads and avoided default

	Days Above 2,000 bps	*Period*
Mexico	8	March 1995
Venezuela	94	Spring 95, Aug 98
Bulgaria	32	Summer 94, Spring 95
Algeria	10	April 1999
Nigeria	308	1994–95, 2000
Pakistan	5	September 2000
Ukraine	97	June 2002, Spring 01
Brazil	35	June 2002–October 2002

Source: Own estimations for Brazil; and JP Morgan Chase, Emerging Markets Outlook, August 2, 2002.

risk ahead of the October presidential election. In Brazil, officials publicly disagreed with the downgrade and the bank, which had deep business interests in the country, moved towards firing the twelve-member sovereign research team. In the end, the bank, concerned about damaging its credibility on Wall Street, decided not to fire its analysts, and the unit was asked to no longer share its recommendations with the press. This episode underlines some of the reasons for rigid downgrades within the financial industry, which most of them related to the relations between the brokers sales side of research and business, and other units of investment banks.[36] Several other investment banks (including Merrill Lynch, ABN-Amro, and Morgan Stanley) also downgraded Brazil. By the beginning of July, JP Morgan Chase strategists implemented a second reduction of the overweighted recommendation for Brazil.[37] A month later, the firm analysts started to ask how long could Brazil sustain levels of spreads above 2,000 bps without defaulting. Based on an historical analysis, the quantitative team found eleven examples where this occurred. The results were however inconclusive as several countries sustained these spreads at these levels for a period of time, and in the end avoided default. Of the eleven countries, four defaulted (Argentina, Ecuador, Russia and the Ivory Coast), two completed distressed debt exchanges (Pakistan and Ukraine) and five others (Algeria, Bulgaria, Mexico, Nigeria and Venezuela) traded higher than 2,000 bps without defaulting. Research at BBVA estimates that C-bonds traded higher than 2,000 bps during 35 days.

By the beginning of August, even more bullish analysts of Brazil started to call urgently for caution. The data was suggesting a sudden stop to capital flow with portfolio investors lowering their Brazilian exposure, sharp cuts in credit lines, as financial institutions were accelerating their reduction of exposure, and capital outflows accelerating in July (US$1.1 billion in capital outflows by the non-resident CC-5 accounts, which represents twice as much as the previous month). By mid-July, Barclays Capital strategists were stressing the many differences between Argentina and Brazil, seeing Brazil as "moderate positive play".[38] A few weeks later, after the Brazilian spreads overshot above 2,000 bps and the real slump above 3.5 to the dollar, Barclays Capital reported, "the trigger for all crises is now underway" while public domestic debt restructuring and private exterior debt default probabilities during the next three to six months were raised respectively to 45 percent and 35 percent.[39] In fact, at that time, the elections were no longer the sole and unique factor behind Wall Street perceptions of Brazilian risks.

By the beginning of August a well-known and respected Wall Street analyst took a more radical position, simply advising his clients to end any Brazilian exposure: "It is time to get out", wrote Walter Molano. "The outcome in Brazil does not depend on who wins the elections (…) Over the past year, Brazil's debt to GDP ratio exploded almost 20 percent as it went to 58 percent from 49 percent. In 2003, more than 90 percent of the amortizing domestic debt will be indexed to interest rates or the dollar. Therefore, the incoming administration will need to restore investor confidence quickly in order to stabilize the exchange rate and interest rates. However, investors always need time to become comfortable with the new administration, even if it is Serra. It will be much worse if it is Ciro Gomes or Lula. Therefore, the odds are stacked against Brazil."[40]

On the 7 August, the confidence game was continuing with a new player. Brazil reached an agreement with the International Monetary

Fund (IMF) on a US$30 billion loan to help restore investor confidence to the country's battered financial markets. As Ilan Goldfajn, then deputy governor for economic policy at the Central Bank of Brazil, noted: "Brazilian presidential candidates were at the centre of the IMF agreement and the resolution of the crisis. The IMF agreement signed in September 2002 was based on the agreement between major political candidates to maintain the backbone of economic policy based on fiscal responsibility, respect for existing contracts (including public and external debt, but also the IMF agreement itself), and monetary policy based on inflation targeting and floating exchange rate regime. There was no signed agreement by the candidates. However the candidates' public statements were essential to reach an agreement with the IMF."[41]

The IMF agreement worked as a 'pre-commitment', a signal to financial markets scared by the increasing perception that a political change would result from the elections with major consequences for future policies. It helped to reduce uncertainties in the electoral period, even if they were not totally dissipated, and confirmed two lessons for policy makers, Godfajn had stressed: that it was important to decouple economic and political costs of adjustments, to avoid concentrating both at one point in time; it was also essential to build rules and institutions that worked as stabilizers able to smooth political transitions and generate consensus for future reforms (even if the help of an 'external' institution is necessary such as the IMF).

Markets were already pricing the announcement, rallying strongly in anticipation of the deal. Some leading economists were asking for it.[42] The exchange rate slumped from its high (3.46 real to the United States dollar by the end of July to 3.01 real to the dollar, just the day before the announcement) and the country's risk premium, as measured by bond yields over the United States treasuries, plunged under the 2,000 bps, tightening by more than 500 bps in a few days. The magnitude of the swings also indicated the financial impact of the confidence game and volatile sentiments. Most analysts and fund managers supported the agreement. "This generous agreement", concluded a Wall Street strategist, "combined with O'Neill's trip to the region and final passage of trade promotion authority this week, creates a potentially significant positive shock for Latin America."[43] Business therefore could be maintained, the IMF keeping alive Brazil as a 'buy opportunity'. Confidence was further boosted when the main candidates also supported the agreement. In one day, the Brazilian real rose by more than 5 percent against the dollar, breaking the R$3 barrier for the first time since the end of July. Throughout the world, companies with large exposures to Brazil and Latin America experienced dramatic increases in their stock prices with, for example, the Spanish equity market closing 5 percent higher.

The confidence game, however, was seen to be one of timing; if the size of the loan (US$30 billion) was impressive, and much larger than the one expected by the market, 80 percent would be released in 2003, after Brazil's new administration was due to take office in January 2003. Clearly then, the IMF's vote of confidence was a cautious one, another key player within the confidence game. In the end, the IMF agreement was a boost. "The IMF agreement could be the way to give some assurance to the market that sensible policies should be in place in 2003 (maybe beyond), regardless of who was in charge by that time."[44]

BCP Securities' Walter Molano was even more sanguine. He suggested that the IMF package was a win-win solution for the US Treasury and the State Department for their Latin America policy and, above all, for the Cardoso administration, allowing the Brazilian president and his economic team, praised by the IMF and the international community, "to finish their term in office without suffering the embarrassment of a default or an economic collapse". But, in the end, the IMF's 'new money' was modest and left the problems unresolved: "it is time", concluded Molano, "to leave the party. Take the opportunity that there is a bid for Brazilian paper and look for the door."[45] Eichengreen insisted at the time that it was geopolitics not economics that drove the decision and above all stressed that the "real danger" was no longer Brazilian elections, but the global economic climate in 2003: "the crisis will reemerge, and unless the IMF and the United States government are prepared to provide yet another mega-package, which is unlikely, Brazil will be forced to default and restructure its debt."[46]

In August, several leading economists criticized the IMF bailout for a lack of clarity.[47] Others openly pledged that "options such as an orderly restructuring of Brazil's nearly US$250 billion debt must be considered with due speed, otherwise a default is likely to occur soon".[48] "The IMF", wrote a senior fellow of the Washington-based Institute of International Economics, "must put debt restructuring at the heart of its conditions for financial assistance".[49] In fact, the financial market's euphoria towards the IMF rescue package was short lived. After the initial rally, bond interest rates settled once again at levels incompatible with long-term solvency. Once again risk premium on Brazil's government bonds rose while the Brazilian currency soon fell back to, as before, below three reís to the dollar. On 12 August, a major Wall Street investment bank, Morgan Stanley, published a bearish report on Brazil, downgrading the country to 'underperform', stressing that it would be hard for Brazil, even with the rescue package, to enter a virtuous circle. This move was synchronized with other portfolio recommendations to 'underperform' positions in nearly all South American credits.[50] By the end of August, another leading Wall Street investment bank, Salomon Smith Barney, changed its 2003 Brazilian macroeconomic forecast, reducing GDP growth, increasing inflation and currency depreciation, the base case scenario calling for an opposition victory in the October elections.[51]

Later, Brazilian authorities repeated the gestures to rally confidence. By the end of August, Arminio Fraga met with a group of market analysts in New York to reassure their confidence.[52] During the first weeks of September, as polls drove concerns of a Lula victory in the first round of the presidential elections, Finance Minister Pedro Malan and Central Bank governor Arminio Fraga once again toured Europe to reanimate investors. Brazil included an upward adjustment in its primary surplus target for 2002, Serra rose in the polls and trade and current account data remained positive. However, investment banks remained sceptical[53] and leading international banks continued to seek to reduce their Brazilian exposure, despite the public commitment that was made in New York in August. Citigroup, in particular, while maintaining a pledge to local officials to keep trade lines open, continued to reduce lending exposure as reported by Bloomberg (Citigroup reported US$9.3 billion in outstanding cross-border claims for Brazil on 30 June, compared to US$11.4 billion on 31 March). By September, the loss of confidence had become generalized in the cognitive regime of Wall Street operators. For Goldman Sachs – another operator that still believed in mid-September 2002 that analysts declared prematurely that Brazil was on an unsustainable debt path – the answer was also a confidence shock: "whoever wins will have to appoint a strong economic team, deepen fiscal adjustment, and implement structural reforms to reduce the public debt ratio gap and restore growth."[54]

Opinion polls were confirming financial markets' fears of a widening gap between the candidates, with Lula moving above 40 percent of voting preferences while Serra's ratings remained unchanged. Arminio Fraga and Ilán Goldfajn, respectively governor of the Central Bank and its deputy governor for economic policy, tried to calm investors' concerns over debt levels with an article in a leading confidence game arena, the *Financial Times*.[55] But Brazil's appeal to financial operators fell on deaf ears. Once again, just a few days later, Brazilian spreads crossed the 2,000 bps barrier while the currency depreciated to a low record. By the end of September, as the Brazilian currency was tumbling and risk premiums were rising, emerging markets debt research teams of both Merrill Lynch and Goldman Sachs joined the 'underweight' shifting recommendations.[56] As the IMF/World Bank meetings approached, proposals to manage debt crises proliferated in the international financial community such as editorials from Guillermo Ortiz, governor of the central bank of Mexico[57] and Josef Ackerman, the chairman of Deutsche Bank.[58] After the meetings, the loss of confidence was even higher. Walter Molano was particularly sanguine describing the IMF–World Bank Monster's Ball Annual Meetings in these terms: "a gallow's humor permeated the Fall Meetings, as investors, government officials and future ex-Ministers gathered for what seemed to be the last hurrah of the emerging markets." Meanwhile, "the fair weather friends on the sell-side (i.e. Wall Street analysts) abandoned Brazil at its darkest moment'.[59] At Bear Stearns, another leading Wall Street firm, the return from Washington was also gloomy as the sovereign debt restructuring mechanism (SDRM) discussions retained most of the attention, suggesting that Brazil's next president could be tempted to implement it. "But what about Lula ? Lula might be a policy maker who would use this policy instrument (SDRM). Under this scenario, investors might be even more nervous than they already are."[60]

By the beginning of October, the political coverage of Brazilian elections among Wall Street firms intensified. Meanwhile Pimco, manager of the biggest emerging market bond fund (US$7 billion of developing nation bonds in various funds), assured that Brazil would never default on its debt. "Brazil has the willingness and ability to make its debt payments", said El-Erian, Pimco's fund manager, to Bloomberg. "Those who are betting on a Brazil default are likely to lose. We're bullish on Brazil because it is a good buy at these levels." On 4 October 2002, Pimco managers declared that they were adding to the roughly US$1 billion of the country's sovereign bonds they owned on June 30 2002.

Pimco's confidence that Latin America's biggest country would not default on US$300 billion in public debt stood in marked contrast to other Brazilian bond investors as shown by an investor poll undertaken by JP Morgan by the end of September. As underlined by Bloomberg, Pimco bought Brazilian bonds in the first three months of the year, just before the country's currency and bonds started to slide in line with polls showing Lula was increasing his lead.

Wall Street 'mea culpa' and its love affair with Lula

After thirteen years and four attempts, on 27 October 2002 Luiz Inácio Lula da Silva became Brazil's president-elect. With 61.3 percent of the vote, Lula's victory gave power to the Workers' Party (PT), Latin America's largest party of the left. The victory was possible because the PT had moved to the centre of the political spectrum.[61] In 2003, Lula won another victory: he gained the confidence of financial markets which had started to regard the pragmatic approach of his administration as credible. Lula's election was soon accompanied by a wave of optimism. The real rebounded and spreads on Brazilian bonds plummeted. Market sentiment started to improve and bond spreads began compressing 500 bps. By mid-November 2002, the Brazilian real rallied almost 10 percent from its level of a month earlier, and the Brazilian EMBI tightened 30 percent since the end of September. An economic 'market friendly' team – in the precise sense of commitment to fiscal and monetary stability – was by this time perceived as helping bridge the gap between Lula and the markets. Lula and financial markets were enjoying a honeymoon – or as one observer commented, a "Lula de Mel".[62] But reports suggested that the romance would be short-lived as most Wall Street firms maintained their cautious stance, pointing to fiscal weaknesses, soaring domestic debt, high interest rates, poor growth and rising inflation.[63] On 9 December 2002, JP Morgan moved to 'underweight' its recommendation on Brazil.[64] Based on a detailed analysis of the economic situation, the report concluded that Brazil would not experience a 'quick fix', with domestic debt dynamics remaining a chronic and challenging problem, and advocating for a fiscal anchoring and a deeper fiscal adjustment in order to restore solvency and confidence. However on 6 March 2003, the same JP Morgan raised its Brazilian debt recommendation from 'underweight' to 'neutral', citing President Lula da Silva's pledge to control spending.

Wall Street firms flocked to Brazilian upgrades. One of the first to move was Barclays Capital: on 19 December 2003 the broker's emerging markets strategists changed their cautious stance on Brazil to a positive stance reiterated in the following reports of 2003.[65] The impulse for this change of attitude was a virtuous circle of an appreciating real, pushing inflation down and helping to improve Brazil's debt dynamics. A few weeks later other strategists and analysts followed, with BCP Securities stressing in its January 2003 regional update that Latin American bonds were poised to be the best performers in 2003 and that Brazil was the top pick for the year.[66] Others like Goldman Sachs, raised their recommendation on Brazil to 'overweight'. "It is funny", remarked Alex Schwartazmann, one of the most respected Brazil-based economists, "how people can change their opinion (sometimes from black to white) so quickly. Last year, in the midst of severe financial turbulence in Brazil, top advisors foretold that the country had entered an explosive debt path, often citing resemblance to the Argentine crisis. Today, these same analysts have largely abandoned their apocalyptic beliefs, for debt to GDP ratio continues to fall fast with the helping hand of higher inflation."[67]

Many other banks similarly radically altered their stance, amid the rush to raise the recommendation on Brazilian debt after Lula restated his commitments to cap spending on civil service pensions and streamline the tax system. Walter Molano had warned about these shifting loyalties, commenting in the month of the election, "don't think for a second that the Street won't try to do a makeover on Lula once the elections are over. It will only take a few crab puffs, glasses of cabernet and bars of nice jazz to make Lula appear like the Latin American version of Milton Friedman."[68] In the meantime, between the elections and the Wall Street upgrades, Brazilian officials also raised the promises of further highly rewarding deals: "The Brazilian Central Bank announced that it planned to issue USD 4 billion in new international bonds during 2003. This would make Brazil the biggest bond issuer in Latin America, and probably in all the emerging markets. The bond sales could represent as much as US$20 million in fees for investment banks. Given that bonuses were heavily hit in 2003, many analysts could be hoping that Brazil's return to markets could improve their own financial outlook for the year."[69]

The change of opinion on Wall Street was motivated mainly by measures implemented by Lula's administration to place the (perceived) right people at the Ministry of Finance and at the Central Bank. Lula appointed Henrique Meirelles, a former international banking chief for Bank of Boston, as Central Bank governor and Antonio Palocci, a physician, long time Workers' Party member and respected economist, as finance minister. As stressed by Molano, large Wall Street firms started to publish glossy reports changing their views on Brazil, asking for forgiveness for having given such negative outlooks on a Brazil run by Lula, now confident that "the strong rally in Brazilian bond prices, compiled with the possibility that Brazil could become one of the best new issuance candidates in the near future, is creating direct and indirect pressure from the capital markets desks to induce analysts to change their views on Brazil".[70] The news that Brazil aimed to sell US$4 billion in bonds to refinance debt was "officially filtered" by Bloomberg on 5 February. In fact rumours were already spreading around Wall Street emerging markets fixed income desks which had been hard-hit by the low levels of bond issuance in 2002 and low levels of fees. On 17 January 2003 Morgan Stanley's quarterly emerging market report, in which estimations of potential issues for 2003 were released, the Brazilian issue of US$4 billion was mentioned. It is also interesting to note that, along with Turkey's estimated US$4.5 billion bond issues, the Brazilian was the largest for 2003. The total bond issues in emerging markets had reached US$23 billion, with Brazil therefore representing some one-fifths of the possible total for Wall Street fixed income emerging markets teams.[71] The same day, CSFB published a report arguing for optimism on Brazil (even if vulnerabilities like stress remained), that the orthodox profile of the new administration's economic program, and the appointments made, removed concerns about possible extreme scenarios.[72]

Less than a month later, nearly all major Wall Street firms upgraded their recommendations on Brazil. Some, however, had been positive during 2002, such as UBS Warburg and CSFB which had remained cautiously positive all year. By early 2003, UBS Warburg revised its economic forecasts for Brazil anticipating a stronger currency, lower interest rates and lower inflation, the revision being mainly driven by better than anticipated local fundamentals.[73] Others, like Lehman Brothers, stressed by mid-December 2002 when to 'overweight' Brazil was one of the major timing trades issues for 2003 and that "if Brazil stabilizes, and we think it will, the emerging market crisis should not appear, the asset class should rally, and the Russia to Brazil trade should be investor's gambit in a less risk averse credit environment".[74] Merrill

Lynch at the start of the year indicated that the view on the Brazilian economy was constructive and supportive, based on a backdrop of global risk aversion, adequate implementation of macroeconomic policies and "political conditions that allow the formation of an adequate majority in Congress towards governability and the pursuit of structural reforms".[75] The positive views were reiterated the following months with upgrades of growth and of foreign accounts.[76] Goldman Sachs insisted on the upside potential by early January stating that the macroeconomic outlook for Brazil has improved and that the "combination of the extraordinary political capital gained by Lula and PT in the elections and the resolve by Palocci and team to do the right macroeconomic things could surprise on the upside".[77]

CSFB, a leading Wall Street firm with a strong fixed income Brazil-based research team, also adopted an overweight position in Brazilian bonds from January 2003. By that time, reports were cautiously optimistic although some doubts remained about the economic model that would be followed by Brazil's new government. Speeches of Lula's chief of staff, José Dirceu, and the planning minister, Guido Mantega, were carefully analysed. Other inaugural speeches, also closely monitored, acted as "important confidence boosters", confirming the strong commitment to fiscal austerity and monetary orthodoxy. As stressed in the CSFB report in January 2003,

> the appointment in December of Antonio Palocci (from the moderate wing of the PT party) as Finance Minister and Henrique Meirelles (an experienced banker) as Central Bank governor were important indications that the PT administration would follow a moderate line. We have also been encouraged by the appointments of advisors to Palloci and Meirelles, neither of whom has a strong technical background in the design of macro-policies. Fraga's advisors were kept on as directors of the Central Bank, and fiscally conservative economists have been appointed to the Ministry of Finance (Joaquim Levy and Marcos Lisboa were appointed as Secretary of the Treasury and Secretary of Economic Policy respectively). This lends support to the view that the Cardoso-administration's responsible fiscal and monetary policies will remain in place.[78]

The confidence game could continue, supported by these key appointments.

In a period of less than six months, Brazilian spreads moved from more than 2,400 bps to less than 800 bps. The real stabilized below three reals per dollar. Lula started his period in office as the most popular president in Brazilian history. The monitoring of the markets started to shift towards balance of payments improvements, debt ratios and inflation stabilization. For most analysts, the legacy of dramatic overshooting of the Brazilian real and debt dynamics in 2002 was merely an old story. Some worries focused on inflation because Brazil missed its inflation target in 2002 for the second year in a row and was expected to do so again in 2003.[79] The interest rate hikes of the new administration in January and February were rewarded by market participants boosting their confidence in the orthodox stance of Lula's government against inflation. By the beginning of April, the Lula da Silva government won passage through Congress of financial sector reform legislation and the amendment to Article 192 of the constitution cleared the way for potential Central Bank autonomy. The ample legislative victory (the vote was 442 to 13 in the lower house) was underlined by Wall Street and was the occasion of detailed reports on political dynamics[80] and celebration of the passage of C-Bonds spreads to less than 1,000 bps, back to the levels of early 2002.[81]

Tax and pension reforms became central points of attention.[82] The ambitious measures proposed by Lula (reigning in the burgeoning social security deficit and rewriting the growth-stifling tax code) were in fact unfinished business of Cardoso's two administrations. The attention of markets to the political reforming process is another example of the interactions between temporal financial horizons and political temporal horizons. In Brazil, as in many emerging countries, reforming the constitution or making major reforms are lengthy processes. On average, for example, reforms under Cardoso's first mandate took eight months to be approved, the length of the processes reaching thirty months for administrative reform and 44 months for social security reform.

To analysts, the deficit of the pension system remained one of the most important sources of Brazilian fiscal imbalances with official figures putting the deficit at 5.4 percent of GDP in 2002.[83] The reform agenda, congressional activity and the creation of committees to discuss reforms, negotiations between the government and the opposition PMDB as to whether it would join the ruling coalition, micro political events, all came under close Wall Street scrutiny.[84]

Table 9.3 ***Brazil reform scorecard in April 2003 according to Merrill Lynch***

Reform	*Change*	*Recent Developments*	*Quality Score (1)*	*Progress Score*	*Reform Score*
Social Security	Neutral	Presentation 16–17 April	2.5	2.5	5.0
Tax Reform	Neutral	Presentation 16–17 April	2.5	2.5	5.0
Central Bank Autonomy	Positive	Final vote expected by mid-April	4.0	1.5	5.5
Bankrupcy Law	Neutral	Already in Congress	3.0	3.0	6.0
Reform Agenda Composite Score (2)			2.7	2.5	5.2

Source: Merrill Lynch, April 2003.
Notes:
(1): The scorecard summarizes the Progress Score, which range a higher score in a scale from 0 to 5 to a reform the closer it is to being approved, and the Quality Score, also evaluated on a scale from 0 to 5 and with higher points the closer the reform's current form is to a first best reform.
(2) Reform Agenda Composite Score gives the weighted score of the reforms as per the following weights: social security 50%, tax 25%, bankrupcy 15%, and Central Bank Autonomy 10%.

Citigroup issued a tentative timetable comparing timelines for the social security reform.[85] After a visit to Brazil, in mid-June 2003 Citigroup economists confirmed their positive views both on improving macroeconomics and the outlook for economic reform.[86] Merrill Lynch, another leading Wall Street broker, started producing reports on the major components of the reform agenda, descriptions of objectives, procedural requirements and potential impacts of the reform, giving views on the likely timing and outcome of voting in Congress for each step of the reform process. By early April, Merrill Lynch analysts introduced a detailed reform 'scorecard' that was updated regularly as a tool to monitor progress of the reforms.[87] Goldman Sachs issued its own schedule of reforms considering that the macroeconomic policies of the Lula administration were heading in the right direction and offering also a tentative schedule for the structural reforms.[88] When the Lula administration gave

Table 9.4 ***Brazil reform scorecard in December 2003 according to Merrill Lynch***

Reform	*Change*	*Recent Developments*	*Quality Score (1)*	*Progress Score*	*Reform Score*
Social Security	Positive	Approved by the Senate 2nd round	3.5	5	8.5
Tax Reform	Positive	Approved by the Sentate 1st round	2	4.8	6.8
Central Bank Autonomy	Neutral	Complementary Law expected in 2004	4.0	2	6
Bankrupcy Law	Neutral	Approved by Lower House (next Senate)	3.0	4	7
Reform Agenda Composite Score (2)			3.1	4.5	7.6

Source: Merrill Lynch, December 2003.
Notes:
(1): The scorecard summarizes the Progress Score, which range a higher score in a scale from 0 to 5 to a reform the closer it is to being approved, and the Quality Score, also evaluated on a scale from 0 to 5 and with higher points the closer the reform's current form is to a first best reform.
(2) Reform Agenda Composite Score gives the weighted score of the reforms as per the following weights: social security 50%, tax 25%, bankrupcy 15%, and Central Bank Autonomy 10%.

signs in July of making controversial concessions to the judiciary on social security reform, Goldman Sachs underlined that this could trigger "an adverse reaction from financial markets and opposition from the economic team and state governors".[89]

Lula, however, quickly reached agreements and secured votes in the Congress. In August, social security reform passed its first votes on the floor of the lower house. In September, the tax reform also passed its two votes on the floor of the lower house. Both victories were welcomed by Wall Street.[90] Firms such as Crédit Suisse First Boston further increased their overweight recommendation for Brazil due to good short-term prospects,[91] while the wave of optimism in Brazilian financial markets continued to sustain the upside trend in the stock market. Constitutional reforms to streamline an unwieldy tax system and cut unsustainable social security benefits were applauded by investors and helped to improve

Brazil's credit risk standing. Spreads improved yet again and the exchange rate remained stable despite the slowing of the economy that was technically now in recession. When Brazilian officials arrived in Dubai for the IMF/World Bank annual meeting, both Central Bank of Brazil governor Enrique Meirelles and finance secretary Antonio Palocci participated in several of the investment banks' forums (Citigroup, JP Morgan, Deutsche Bank and CSFB) to deliver the 'good news': fiscal orthodoxy with a primary target of 4.25 percent of GDP would help to maintain inflation under control and push down the debt/GDP ratio; the monetary easing cycle started in July would continue, in order to recover growth for 2004, a major trade surplus would be enjoyed by Brazil and the congressional agenda would continue with the soon to be expected approval of the social security and tax reforms.[92] (In practice, the results for 2004 were even more positive for foreign investors than Palocci had predicted.)

In fact, the reform process was passing through Congress at high speed and by mid-December 2003 the bulk of reforms were approved while Brazilian spreads reached levels below 500 bps, their lowest level in five years. In less than a year, Lula's administration passed a reform that had failed several times during the Cardoso government, the victim of complex political games.[93]

But the speed of the success had costs. By mid-December 2003, the PT expelled four of its legislators for having voted against the bill to trim the pensions of public workers (a measure to contain Brazil's debt), alienating left-wing members of the PT and many within the working class. The episode was another example of the tensions created by the increasingly pragmatic approach of Lula's governments. Throughout 2003, the government implemented policies aiming to convince sceptical investors that Brazil would be fiscally responsible to avoid debt default and high inflation. The government's economic policy conducted by Palocci had been an anathema to the left: fiscal austerity, high interest rates to contain inflation, a new agreement with the IMF and pension reform. In financial terms, the government's orthodox policy paid off in capital markets, so achieving one of its targets: reversing financiers' 2002 avoidance of Brazil. By 2003, Brazil had become the darling of Wall Street investors.

By the end of 2003, Wall Street firms were virtually unanimous regarding their Brazilian outlook. Merrill Lynch's recommendation was positive, while Deutsche Bank's fixed income research team similarly pushed its investment recommendation on Brazil to overweight, placing Brazil at the top of its list of 2004 recommendations.[94] For JP Morgan, Barclays Capital and UBS, Brazil remained the largest overweight external debt recommendation and favoured bet in external debt markets, and Santander Central Hispano and CSFB also improved their 2004 Brazilian outlook.[95] Goldman Sachs insistence that the stabilization program anchored on stringent financial policies was bearing fruit and the macroeconomic outlook remained favourable. Led by a Brazilian-born economist, Paulo Leme, the global emerging markets research nevertheless insisted on several long-term vulnerabilities. Reforms were viewed in a positive way but its economic benefits (for example, social security reform in terms of reducing the net value of the social security deficit) were perceived as small compared to the political costs (i.e. the increase in the social security deficit estimated around 0.5 percent of GDP in 2004 was expected to be larger than the projected savings from the reform).[96] In the medium term, however, several vulnerabilities were identified. These included the debt dynamics problem (which was postponed but not resolved), the crowding out of the private sector by the public sector, the lack of trade openness and trade integration strategies, the low levels of savings and investment ratios that jeopardized the growth potential of the country, and last but not least the need for microeconomic reforms and deregulation.

As stressed by Morgan Stanley's fixed income research team, Brazil's debt situation had, by the end of 2003, moved off Wall Street analysts' radar screen. "It is remarkable", noted Morgan Stanley economists in a year-end report, "how little is written nowadays on Brazil's debt situation. Just one year ago, investors focused almost exclusively on debt-sustainability models, which were proffered as evidence that default or capital controls were inevitable. We objected to the 'inevitability' thesis, but still spent the bulk of our time working through the vulnerability posed both by Brazil's domestic and external public debt, as well as the risks arising from the amortization of private external debt. In contrast today most of the focus from Brazil watchers is on the timing, the breadth and the sustainability of the Brazilian economy. After a zero growth in 2003, all watchers focused their attention on 2004 GDP growth."[97] Brazil's rate cutting cycle, starting in July, was aimed at pushing the country out of recession. With the reforms approved, Brazil was ready for a consolidation of a virtuous cycle.

These supportive and positive Wall Street fixed income research views were also helped by the expected Brazilian issues programmed for 2004, the largest issue in emerging markets, apart from those of Poland and Turkey. A detailed analysis of the positions recommended by a leading broker in fixed income markets underlines that there is no strong positive bias (i.e. overweight-neutral recommendations): if both overweight and neutral recommendations for 2004 are taken into account, they totalled eighteen countries (from a list of 33). A closer view shows however that four biggest weights in emerging markets portfolios (Russia and Brazil, each with portfolio weights of over 20 percent, Mexico with around 16 percent and Turkey with 6 percent – they simply totalled more than 60 percent of the weights) were all with positive overweight recommendations. Poland and Hungary were clearly among the leaders in terms of bond issuance programmed for 2004 but their portfolio weights were zero for each one. The picture is very different for a country such as Brazil: it was not only one of the largest expected 2004 issuers, but a heavyweight in emerging markets portfolios (the same applies to Turkey and Mexico, the two other leading overweighted issuers).

In 2003, Brazil became the most important bet for emerging markets watchers and investors. During that year emerging debt markets experienced a tremendous boom. The global appetite for risk, the excess of liquidity in an international low rates environment and the search for yields, pushed the asset class in a booming trend. In equity markets, the story has been simply more impressive. In 2003, riskier assets, such as emerging markets, tended to outperform with the FTSE emerging markets index up about 65 percent (while the Lehman Brothers emerging bond index was up about a 'mere' 30 percent), with four countries seeing a doubling of indices in dollar terms. The Brazilian stock market was one of the rising stars, bouncing back with a gain of nearly 100 percent and, for most of the equity research teams, remaining the favourite Latin American market for 2004.[98]

In bond markets, the rally became generalized. Given the appetite and demand for emerging bond products, emerging market debt issues jumped to nearly US$90 billion in 2003, compared to a mere US$50 billion in 2002. According to the United States research firm EmergingPortfolio.com, emerging bond market bonds drew a record of US$3.3 billion in net investments in 2003, almost double the US$1.7

billion of the previous year. Returns on emerging markets dollar debt – measured by JP Morgan's EMBI+ index – reached 30 percent as yield spreads fell to historical lows. Latin America became the best performing region, reaching returns as high as 35 percent, while Asia lagged below 15 percent. These levels of returns are in any case well above the average returns reached from 1970 to 2000, about 9 percent per annum[99] and well above in 2003 of any other asset class (the average annualized return of the EMBI+ asset class is above the S&P or US Treasuries developed markets instruments during 1994–2003.

In 2003 Brazil impressively led returns in emerging markets: over 50 percent spread changes in emerging markets asset class was driven by Brazil's performance. The same country that in 2002 was in default became, just one year later, one of the best performers in emerging markets. Bullish views on Brazil spread all around Wall Street, the contagion being massive in the so-called 'buy side' industry. To make the right (or wrong) 'call' on Brazil was the issue of the year for the industry's asset class. As stressed by global emerging markets strategists, "a bullish Brazil view if both the key foundation of our market call is it's main risk. Among the 22 sovereigns we currently cover, we only have four overweights – Brazil, Colombia, Peru and Ivory Coast – which is low by historical standards."[100]

Brazilian elections and financial markets: a case study in historical perspective

Wall Street views on Brazil during the months immediately before and after the 2002 presidential election underline that financial markets' opinions are quite dynamic, if not volatile. The political transition has led to an extreme level of uncertainty and, afterwards, to a significant rally. The dispersion of opinions, while important, and thus reflecting diversity within the industry, narrowed with the approaching elections and caused uncertainty to rise with rising intentions for the vote for Lula since April and the unexpected rise of a third candidate, Ciro Gomes, in the July opinion polls. Brazil is a compelling example of political influence on markets in Latin America.[101] The worsening of financial markets in Brazil was not, however, exclusive to the 2002 electoral year. Political uncertainty has always had a considerable influence on financial variables in Brazil.

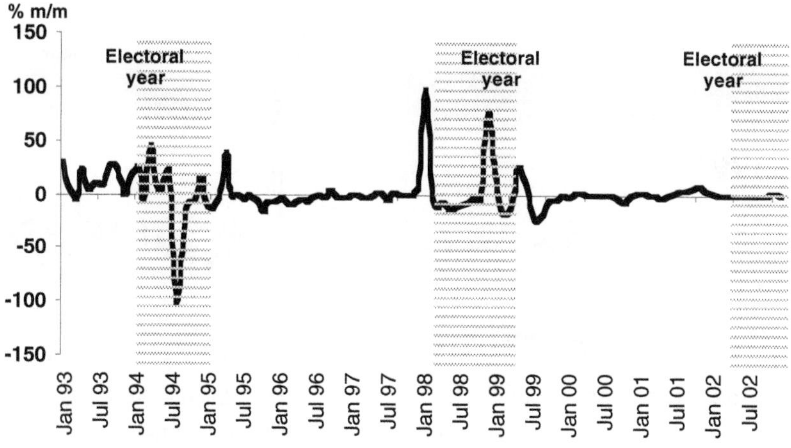

Figure 9.2 ***SELIC volatility***

Source: Bloomberg.

To understand this, the years in which the last three Brazilian presidential elections took place – 1994, 1998 and 2002 – will be considered with two motives. First, the holding of elections always unleashes political uncertainty. This uncertainty is accentuated in emerging markets given that the new leaders have less economic policy margin. The second motive is specific to Brazil. In the three electoral years being considered, similar opinion polls materialized that indicated an intention to Lula, seizing opportunities to remove the incumbent coalitions from power (as represented by Cardoso in 1994 and 1998 and by Serra in 2002).

Opinion poll ratings for Lula serve as an indicator of political uncertainty. Observing the graph, it is possible to appreciate that these electoral years are similar in terms of political uncertainty and timing. For three years Lula started to improve in the opinion polls in April (1994, 1998 and 2002) reaching a high in June, to fall progressively until the elections in October. The only difference between these years is that in 1994 and 2002 Lula held first place in opinion polls for some time, while in 1998 he was not able to achieve this (according to the June polls, he was virtually tied with Cardoso). Nevertheless, the fact that in 1998 Lula also had a significant number of intended voters, this gave him a real possibility of winning, and the resulting political uncertainty was not so different from those of the other two electoral years.

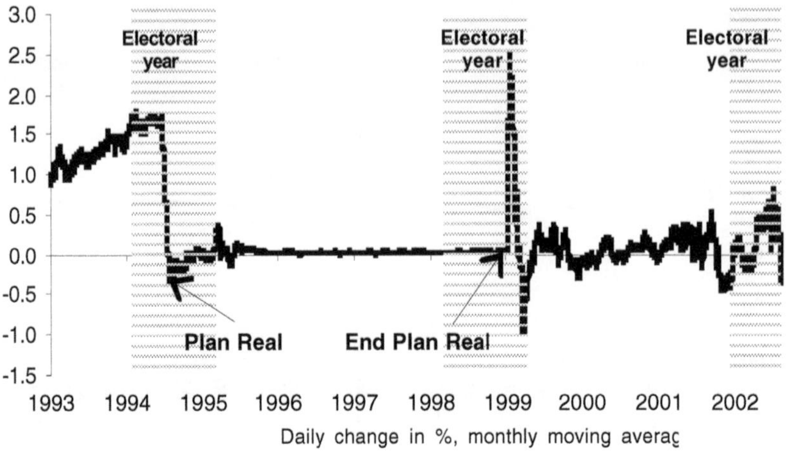

Figure 9.3 ***Real/Dollar volatility***

Source: Bloomberg.

To confirm whether political uncertainty has an impact on financial variables in Brazil, the behaviour of domestic short-term interest rates is analysed, using the SELIC (overnight interest) rate, the real/dollar exchange rate and the long-term interest rates of the external public debt (represented by the Brazilian bond spread). First, domestic short-term interest rates and the real/dollar exchange rate will be examined. In the graphs, the high volatility of these variables in the electoral years are visible.

It goes without saying, however, that the behaviour of these variables is interrelated and affected by foreign shocks, as could be the case for the Asian crisis in 1997, or the Russian crisis in 1998. Likewise, the domestic interest rates and the exchange rate are seriously affected by economic policy decisions, such as the implementation of the Real Plan in July 1994, an anchor for the exchange rate implemented to control inflation, or such as the devaluation of the real in January 1999. These decisions, as mentioned at the beginning of this chapter, are influenced in part by the timing of the political cycle, and make the analysis of the separate impact of electoral uncertainty on these two financial variables difficult. So, the profile of the exchange rate during the last three electoral years presents two abrupt movements associated with the beginning and the end of the Real Plan in July 1994 and in January 1999, respectively. Logically, during the application of the Real Plan, during which time the

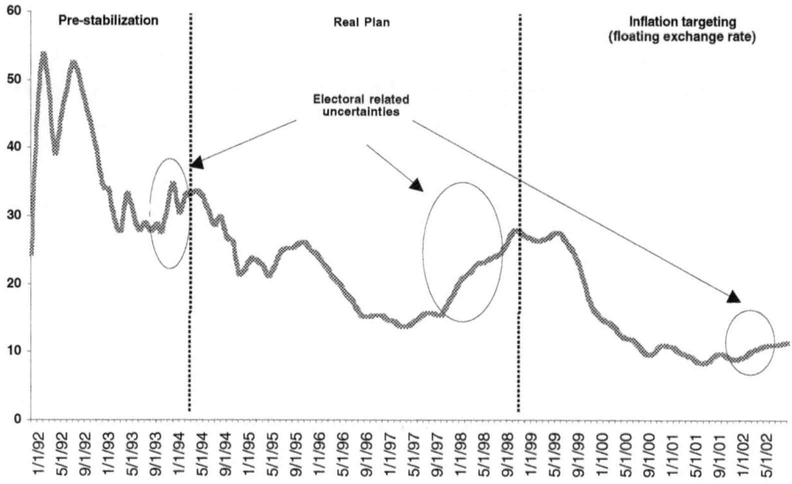

Figure 9.4 ***Real interest rates, 1992–2002***

Source: Banco central do Brazil, IBGE.

electoral year of 1998 is included, the exchange rate was allowed to fluctuate within a narrow band, whose limits could be adjusted. That impeded brusque variations of the exchange rate. What can be recognized is that in the first half of the years 1994 and 2002, there is a gradual increase of the depreciation of the Brazilian real, parallel to an increase in the electoral uncertainty associated to the improvement of Lula in the opinion polls.

With respect to domestic short-term interest rates (with this chapter using the SELIC rate – the Central Bank of Brazil's overnight interest rate), one can also observe the existence of peaks in the electoral years of 1994 and 1998. Once again, it is sufficient to recall that part of the volatility of interest rates is also due to external factors, such as, fundamentally the Russian crisis in August 1998, and, in fact, it is difficult to know in which way the national electoral uncertainty is responsible for financial volatility. The increased stability of the SELIC rate in the year 2002 is related to the current exchange rate regime in use in Brazil. When exchange rate systems are fixed or semi-fixed, as the one existing in Brazil up until the beginning of 1999, the adjustment as a result of any internal or external shock came from the side of the interest rates and real variables of the economy. In the current situation, the exchange rate is the variable that is responsible for absorbing any internal or external shock, which reduces the impact on interest rates and economic activity. This means that a strong increase in foreign exchange volatility is consistent with the stability of the SELIC that was observed in 2002. Furthermore, and irrespective of the foreign exchange system in use, what can be observed in the first half of the last electoral years, are increases in real interest rates, which are a product of the higher profitability demanded by the investors, to compensate the increase in the premium risk associated with the possibility of the victory of an opposition candidate in the presidential elections.

In sum, during the electoral years of 1994, 1998 and 2002 one can observe higher volatility in the exchange rate and in the SELIC as well as increases in real interest rates. This is a consequence not only of the uncertainty associated with the evolution of the electoral polls, but also of the fact that the exchange rate and interest rates are interrelated and conditioned by economic policy decisions, such as the Real Plan, which in turn are influenced by the electoral calendar and the volatility associated with political uncertainty. Likewise, the financial volatility seen in the last three electoral years, at times was originated by external factors like the crises that have occurred in other emerging markets.

In an attempt to eliminate the factors that limit the observation of the impact of political uncertainty in financial markets we used the long-term external interest rates. For that purpose we used the spread of the Brazilian debt over the US bonds in the EMBI (in 1994 and 1998) and EMBI+ (in 2002) indexes of emerging bonds of JP Morgan. This single variable synthesizes, day by day, what investors think about the state of the economy. This spread, the Emerging Market Bond Index (EMBI), is the difference between the yield on a dollar-denominated bond issued by the Brazilian government and a corresponding one issued by the US Treasury. It is thus a measure of financial markets' assessment of the probability whether Brazil might default or not on its debt obligations.

Among the drivers of the EMBI are international factors. As for other Latin American countries, one of the main determinants of Brazilian spreads is United States monetary policy and United States interest rates in particular.[102] Guillermo Calvo has made in particular a strong case for the importance of worldwide effects such as the ENRON one in 2002, that is United States corporate bonds and US Treasuries, in order to explain the Brazilian component of the EMBI spread.[103] In fact, during 2002, the correlation between the EMBI Brazil and the United States corporate spread has been mostly driven by coincidence of three events during the first quarter of the year, two of them global and one local: the jump in United States corporate spreads associated with the collapse of ENRON and the increasing risk aversion worldwide (measured in emerging markets by the increase of the EMBI spread), and the rise of political uncertainty in Brazil. However, after Spring 2002, the correlation between the EMBI Brazil and the United States Corporate spreads has been much weaker than in the previous instances. The trigger of the spreads' movements appears to be much more local and linked, in particular, to the forthcoming elections[104] and the nervousness with debt dynamics.[105]

Unlike the domestic short-term interest rates, the spread of the Brazilian bonds is not influenced by the exchange rate system because they are foreign currency debt. Nevertheless, the Brazilian debt spread over the United States can be increased by external shocks like an increase in the risk aversion of the international investors or a financial crisis in another emerging country that reduces, through the so-called 'herd instinct', the attractiveness of the whole emerging debt. To isolate this from external shocks we used the spread between Brazilian bonds over the whole emerging bonds integrated in the EMBI+ index. An increase of the spread between the Brazilian debt and the group of emerging countries can, therefore, not be attributed to a higher risk aversion on behalf of foreign investors, nor to the 'herd effect' associated with the crisis of one of these countries, given that in these two situations, the deterioration would be similar for all of these emerging bonds, and so the Brazilian spread over the emerging bonds should not change significantly. Therefore, the causes of an hypothetical increase of the spread of Brazil over the emerging bonds would be fundamentally domestic. In this case, the political variables hold a prevailing role, given that not only do they influence the 'ability to pay' the debt, derived from an increase in the profitability demanded at moments of uncertainty, but also the 'willingness to pay', associated with the electoral victory of one of the candidates.

Thus, in the search for a more effective indicator that shows the influence of Brazilian presidential elections on financial markets, we studied the correlation between political uncertainty, represented by the support for Lula in opinion polls, and the sovereign risk, represented by the evolution of the spread of Brazil external bonds over the whole emerging countries within the EMBI (in 1994 and 1998) and EMBI+ (in 2002) indexes.[106]

Upon observing the three graphs corresponding to each of the three last electoral years, a certain 'seasonality'can be observed with regard to the movement of the spread of Brazil compared to the ensemble of emerging bonds. So, up until March in each of these three years, the relative spread of Brazil over the emerging bonds slightly narrows. This coincides with either the absence of even electoral opinion polls, as was the case in 1994, or with a slight decline in Lula's chances of being elected, from the popularity polls, as was the case in 1998 and 2002. From March on, a relative deterioration of the Brazilian debt occurred in each of the three years, which could be related to either the beginning of the electoral polls in 1994, which showed considerable popularity for Lula, 35 percent, or to the fact that he had the majority of support in the opinion polls in 1998 and 2002. The relative deterioration of the Brazilian debt reached its maximum in May and June of 1994 and 1998, when Lula reached his high point in the opinion polls. From this moment on in 1994, support for Lula consistently dropped away, with some ups and downs in September/October 1998 as the relative spread in Brazil improved. Although the emerging debt volatility was increased by the Russian crisis of August 1998, this factor did not change the fact that in the months prior to the October presidential elections, the relative spread in Brazil was still affected by the opinion polls.

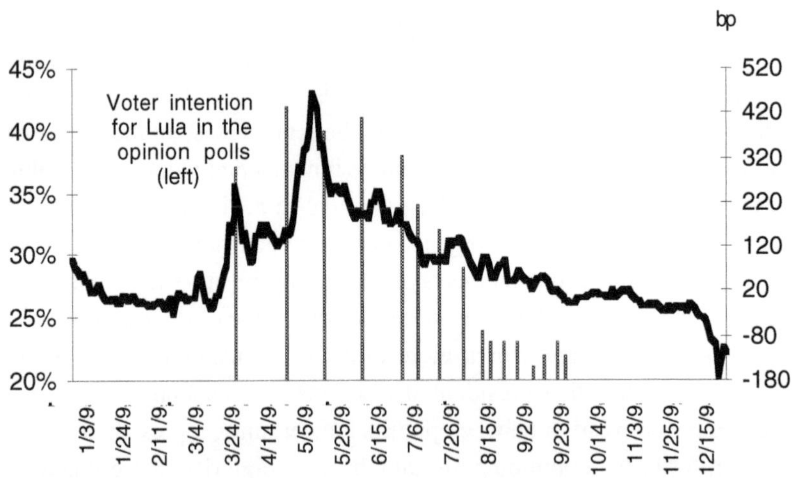

Figure 9.5 ***Spread Brazil–emerging countries and electoral polls, 1994***

Source: Datafolha, JP Morgan.

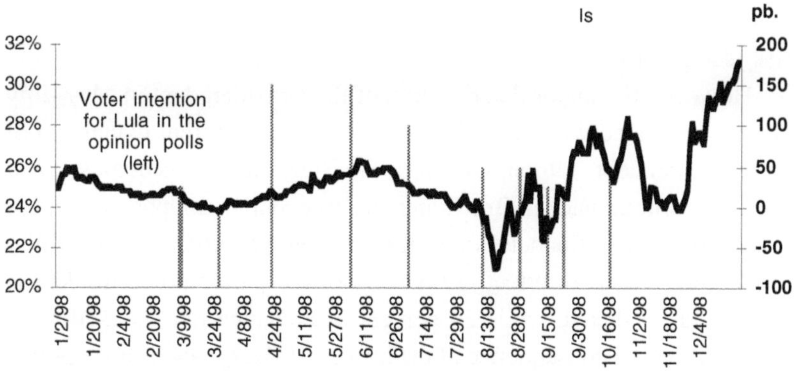

Figure 9.6 ***Spread Brazil–emerging countries and electoral polls, 1998***

Source: Datafolha, JP Morgan.

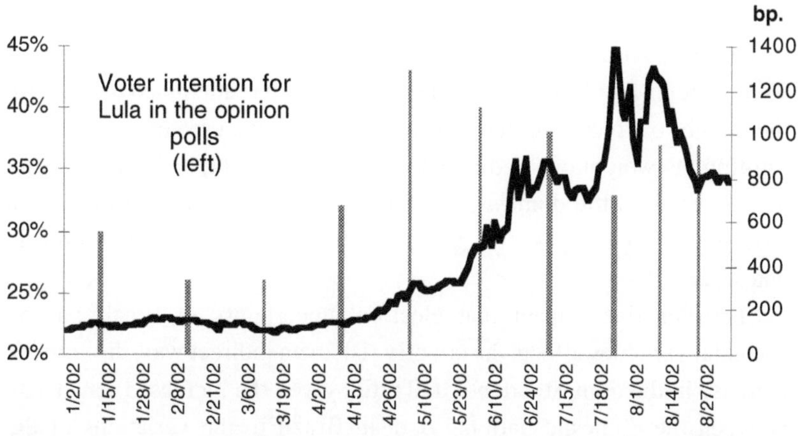

Figure 9.7 ***Spread Brazil–emerging countries and electoral polls, 2002***

Source: Datafolha, JP Morgan.

Opinion polls registered a similar evolution in 2002 to those in the two previous presidential election years mentioned, with a progressive decline in Lula's popularity ratings in the polls in May–June. Nonetheless, from that point on, there is a decoupling between our electoral uncertainty index and the relative spread of Brazil. There are two reasons that can explain this occurrence, and in both cases, the political factor plays a revealing role. The first explanation is the appearance of a new candidate, Ciro Gomes, who had a more heterodox programme to that of Lula. There was not a similar occurrence in either 1994 or 1998, which helps to explain the relative deterioration in 2002 of Brazilian sovereign risk (see graph).

However, the major deterioration of the Brazilian debt in May–July can be associated with other factors, such as the inherent dynamism of the Brazilian debt. Although most of the Brazilian debt is domestic and therefore denominated in Brazilian reals, its peculiar composition makes it very sensitive to financial variables, and consequently, to the volatility of electoral years. In effect, 50 percent of the public domestic debt is interest rate indexed, while 30 percent is exchange rate indexed. This composition is a consequence of the history of Brazil, and is not a policy decision of the Brazilian authorities. If Brazil could borrow at fixed rates and at long-term maturity dates, they would do it. As can be observed in the graph, the Brazilian government was only able to borrow at fixed rates, with a weight of the mentioned debt over the total domestic debt of about 40 to 60 percent, when the Brazilian exchange rate system was fixed or semi-fixed. With a floating real, Brazil has attempted to increase the weight of fixed rate debt but the markets have created an obstacle, limiting the weight of fixed rate debt of the total debt, to 10–15 percent. Moreover, the little domestic debt that Brazil has been able to set at a fixed rate over the past few years has been with short-term maturing dates.

The negative impact that electoral uncertainty in Brazil has on financial variables affects the country risk in an indirect way, through the increase in the domestic debt/GDP ratio, given the increased sensitivity between the domestic national debt in Brazil to the variations of the

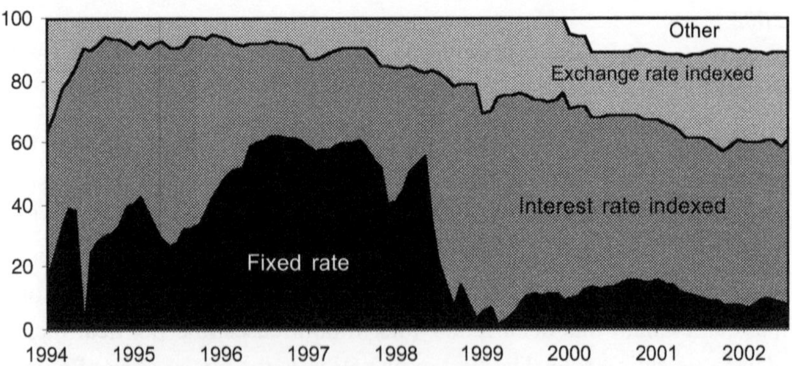

Figure 9.8 ***Domestic public debt composition***

Source: Banco Central do Brazil.

interest and exchange rates. In addition, the increase in the Brazilian spread during 2002 can be related not only to the fear of a change in the 'willingness' to pay back domestic debt associated with the growing possibility of victory of one of the opposition candidates (Lula da Silva or Ciro Gomes) in the presidential elections, but also to the deterioration of the 'ability to pay', associated to the considerable influence of financial variables on the increment that can be witnessed in the domestic debt/GDP ratio. One can appreciate that behind both explanations lie political factors and not a fundamental change in the Brazilian economy.

Given this exception explaining the apparent disassociation between the popularity vote for Lula and the Brazil–emerging debt spread came about in 2002, the influence of political uncertainty on the Brazilian spread will be quantified. To do this, the correlations in the electoral periods of 1994, 1998 and 2002 were calculated, defined as the time periods that mediate between the appearance of the first electoral polls and the last, between the Lula popularity vote in each of the polls and the mean of the relative Brazilian spread over the group of emerging countries in the subsequent period. The result is illustrated in Table 9.5. In the three years, a high and positive correlation can be observed between the electoral uncertainty and the risk premium that investors demand for the Brazilian debt. This electoral year has been subdivided into two periods in order to exclude the months of June, July and August when a disassociation between Lula's popularity vote and the Brazilian

Table 9.5 ***Cross-correlation between the Brazil–emerging debt spread and popularity vote for Lula***

1994	
April–October	0.92
1998	
March–September	0.68
2002 (Lula)	
January–August	0.54
January–May	0.98
2002 (Lula + Ciro)	
January–August	0.88
January–May	0.97

Significance level: 0.50 (1994); 0.63 (1998); 0.60 (2002)

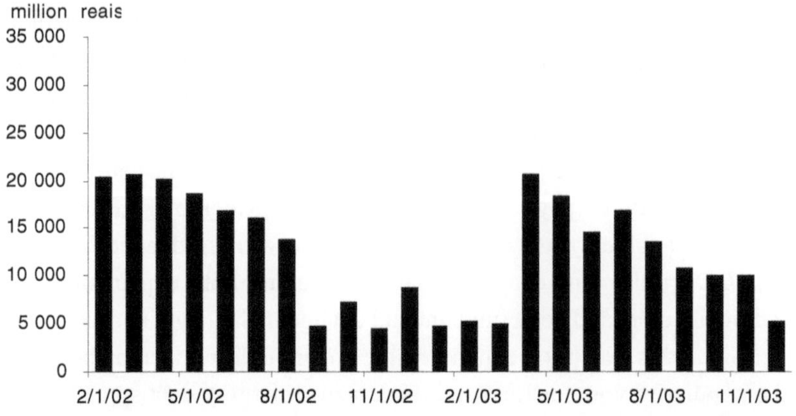

Figure 9.9 ***Amortization profile of domestic public debt (Jan. 2002)***

Source: Banco Central do Brazil.

relative spread occurred, which in turn, can also be explained by political factors mentioned previously. If we were to add the popularity vote of Ciro Gomes to that of Lula da Silva, as a measure of political risk, the correlation with the relative spread of Brazil is very high not only in the period between January and May (0.97) but also in the whole period (0.88).

The Brazilian authorities, aware of the above situation, were conscious of the impact that electoral uncertainty could have on financial markets in this year. In an attempt to prepare for uncertainty, they built a very

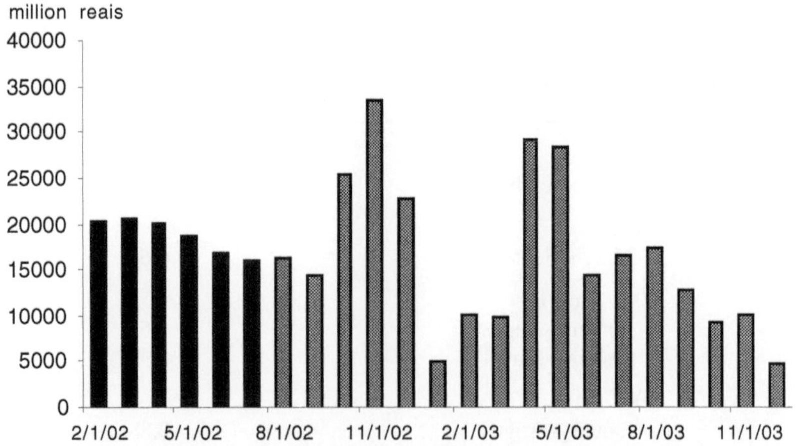

Figure 9.10 ***Amortization profile of domestic public debt (June 2002)***

Source: Banco Central do Brazil.

accommodating amortization profile of domestic public debt around the holding of the elections in October and in the subsequent months (see graph). This breathing room aspired to limit the impact of the elections on the Brazilian debt.

The progressive increase of political uncertainty, along with Lula's stable position leading the opinion polls and the large increase in Ciro Gomes' ratings, completely distorted the amortization profile designed by the Brazilian authorities at the beginning of the year. The breathing room, created by Brazilian leaders, was thus transformed under the pressure of the market, into a much more abrupt situation with significant peaks. The market did not accept bonds with maturing dates longer than the duration of the current government of Cardoso, because it discounted that the possibility of a victory of government with lower 'willingness to pay' is high. One must bear in mind that even though presidential elections are held in October, the change in government does not take place until December, during which time the government was obliged to basically emit domestic debt with amortization dates prior to the end of 2002.

Conclusion

Both the number of crises in emerging markets and the number of publications on the subject have increased.[107] Moreover, developments have been made toward understanding the interactions between financial markets and politics. These interactions are at the very heart of the definition of an 'emerging market', which involve countries where political uncertainty is a major outcome for economic stability and financial operators. Employing empirical evidence, this chapter sought to contribute arguments to underline the close interactions between financial markets and politics. The specific case study of Brazil, analysed through the perceptions of Wall Street analysts and a quantitative economic historical perspective, shows that these ties are strong for emerging markets.[108] More precisely, a possible definition of emerging markets might be the intricate link between political uncertainty and financial volatility, i.e. what could be called the economic fog of democratic uncertainty. In developed countries, political outcomes such as presidential elections are not perceived, from a financial market point of view, to be such critical junctures as they are in developing countries. As this chapter suggests, the outcome of elections in emerging markets matters to a much greater degree than in industrialized countries. Further research would be needed in order to understand why precisely the outcome of elections in emerging economies assumes this level of importance. One possible answer may be provided in recent economic studies that emphasize that the existence of strong institutions dominates other factors in explaining why countries are economically successful. According to Calvo and Mishkin, the choice of monetary regime, for example, maybe matters less than the creation of good monetary, fiscal and financial institutions.[109] Central Banks should be independent in more than name. In theory, the Argentine Central Bank appeared more independent than Canada's; yet Argentina, not Canada, replaced a well respected central bank governor with a servile government appointee in 2001, the year the country defaulted on its debt.

Indeed, some would argue that democratic forms of government are more likely to deliver stable institutions over time than autocratic governments.[110] The question of instability and uncertainty might in fact be central to understanding the intricate links between financial markets and politics in emerging economies. More precisely, financial instability, financial markets' overreactions during electoral processes, might be explained rather by uncertainty regarding institutional stability and continuity rather than uncertainty linked to democracy itself. In other words, instability in emerging markets derives not from the democratic process itself but from the background of institutional weakness. Where institutions are weak, and consequently the government's ability to honour its promises over time are called into question, the identity of the winning candidate becomes much more important to investors than in countries with strong institutions. To put the point another way, in countries with strong institutions the government's ability to honour its commitments is not primarily dependent on the identity of office-holders. Whether George W. Bush or Al Gore had won the United States presidential election 2000, either new government would have met its obligations to holders of T-bonds. The fact, however, in Brazil is that the outcome of the election did (or was perceived as) making a difference. Some preliminary findings related to institutional weakness suggest such a link. A recent research underlined precisely that lack of transparency and institutional weakness affect international portfolio investments. Not only do international funds invest less in less transparent countries but herding behaviour among funds tends also to be more prevalent in less transparent countries.[111]

If institutions matter, history also seems to be relevant. In particular, past economic episodes and behaviour affect the day-to-day dynamics in financial markets. The analyses of Wall Street reports confirm that analysts pay attention to the past. Instead of lacking memory, they tend to look for comparisons, across space but also backward, across time. In a stimulating paper, Reinhart, Rogoff and Savastano insisted on the importance of historical legacies: debt intolerance is linked to the phenomenon of serial default.[112] Defaults and restructurings since 1970 in emerging countries tend to take place in countries with ratios of external debt to GDP below 60 percent and in some cases (13 percent of episodes) defaults even occurred despite debt being less than 40 percent of GDP, levels that would seem quite manageable by OECD countries' standards.

Countries with a long history of debt defaults tend to suffer more from debt intolerance. Brazil is a clear example of a serial defaulter: over the period from 1824 to 2003, Brazil was either in default or undergoing restructuring a quarter of the time. The Argentine situation was similar to that of Brazil, whereas Venezuela and Colombia were in default or undergoing restructuring for almost 40 percent of the time since independence, and Mexico for almost half the same period. Having a long-term record of debt is therefore of no help to Brazil, which has defaulted seven times on its external debt over a period of 175 years; during the same period, Argentina defaulted four times, Venezuela nine times and Turkey six times. Serial defaulters tend to register higher risk premiums and their ratings tend to be worse than those of emerging markets non-defaulters or those of industrial countries.

There is, however, no debt curse. A country can escape from debt intolerance and serial defaults: Spain for example, defaulted thirteen times on its debt from the sixteenth through the nineteenth centuries (the first one was recorded in 1557 and the last one in 1882); France defaulted eight times between 1550 and 1800. Comparing the nineteenth and twentieth centuries, one observes that the frequency of Latin American defaults decreased. Between 1820 and 1914 (i.e. during the first era of globalization), a total of 77 governments defaulted on their debt, of which 58 of these governments were Latin American. Between 1914 and 1931, the total of sovereign defaults reached 21, including thirteen Latin

American. Between 1820 and 1940, Mexico and Honduras, for example, were on average in default 57 percent and 79 percent of the years respectively, considerably more than either Brazil (17 percent) or Uruguay (12 percent).[113]

At a more fundamental level, market reactions to the 2002 Brazilian presidential elections encouraged reflection on democracy and financial markets. Georges Soros, a leading voice in global finance and chair of Soros Fund Management, noted: "admittedly, Brazil is going to elect a president who the financial markets do not like; but if international financial markets take precedence over the democratic process, there is something wrong with the system."[114] In a Wall Street report, analysts underlined this point: "we believe that investors can't rightfully ask presidential contenders to state everything they intend to do when and if elected. Trying to figure out what to believe and what not to believe from any presidential candidate is extremely difficult and sometimes unfair to them. Our opinion is that investors should wait for the political dust to settle on what the next elected president intends to do."[115] Kenneth Maxwell, from the Council on Foreign Relations, put it in an even more sanguine way: "Wall Street analysts and IMF bureaucrats should leave Brazilian politics to its 115m voters and stop confusing fact and fantasy."[116]

The problem lies precisely in the fact that financial markets are a forward-looking world where anticipations and what Hirschman once called the political economy of impatience are central. Therefore financial and political temporalities can be conflicting: with presidential elections on the horizon what happens is a narrowing of all temporal horizons in the very short term. Financial anticipations enter in resonance with political elections by definition dominated by uncertainty. In the Brazilian case, the uncertainty was on the rising probability of a Lula victory, that is, in the end, the rising probability of an anti-establishment vote. At a more fundamental level it opens the question of financial markets tolerance for electoral uncertainty in emerging democracies, that is in the end, if we accept Przeworski's definition of democracy (i.e. a regime whose essence is the institutionalization of uncertainty, locked in electoral outcomes[117]), the political preferences of financial markets.

More empirical research would be needed to explore the intricate links between financial markets and politics. It could be interesting, for example, to examine if there is a 'democratic premium' in financial markets. In other words, do financial markets give a positive premium to democracies or, on the contrary, democratic elections in emerging countries, because they bring uncertainty, are systematically correlated with financial volatility, rising risk premiums and exchange rate ups and downs? The analysis here of Brazilian presidential elections invites empirical research of a larger sample of countries (for example, to include 21 emerging countries of the JP Morgan EMBI+ Index). It seems important to focus on country case studies and specific development as the distinctions between political regimes and the levels of consolidation of emerging democracies can play in favour of more or less stability. Some countries with less consolidated democratic institutions, more opaque policy processes and where the risks of a democratic reversal is more likely, can suffer more from financial volatility.[118] At the same time the implementation of democratic institutions and their consolidation does not eliminate political uncertainty and financial volatility. Some of the most routine democratic politics such as elections can translate into extreme financial volatility. As our empirical analysis suggests, the globalization of financial markets is not without costs on emerging democracies: there is no free lunch, not even for young democracies.

Regarding creditworthiness, recent research underlined that there is a lack of 'democratic advantage'. This is because even if democracies are supposed to pay lower interest rates than authoritarian regimes, given that they are more capable of making credible commitments to repay their debts, the evidence shows that this expectation is unfounded. Empirical economic historical research, using a large sample of data on sovereign loans for 132 countries during the period of 1970 to 1990, suggests not only that dictatorships were less likely to reschedule their debts but also that the major source of better borrowing conditions for emerging democracies was due to the behaviour of multilateral agencies that tend to bail out democracies rather than enhance the capacity of these emerging democracies to make credible commitments.[119] In other words, democracies do not pay higher rates (associated with the fact that they are more likely to reschedule their debts than dictatorships) because they have an 'exogenous' advantage as some lenders, such as multilateral institutions, are willing to help them because of their political regime. A closer view at emerging markets fund managers' political preferences or democratic premium would be, from this point of view, interesting to develop in order to catch, corroborate on or, to the contrary, falsify the idea that democracy and markets go hand in hand. In the same line of ideas, a comparative economic historical perspective could bring useful insights in order to foresee the intricate links between emerging democracies, i.e. the expansion of universal vote, and financial markets during the twenty-first century.

More socio-economic research would also be needed to link faces and names to this confidence game. Apart from the importance of abstract numbers and figures, men and women interact with financial markets. The Brazilian case underlines how trust (and mistrust) are embodied by individuals. Pedro Malan (the Brazilian finance minister) and Arminio Fraga (Brazil's Central Bank governor) have both been key players, the financial markets' and IMF's favourite sons. Wall Street, the US Treasury and Washington-based multilateral organizations were happy dealing with them, an asset not enjoyed by either Lula da Silva or Ciro Gomes. Both Malan and Fraga are comfortable in the world of financial markets and international policy makers. They speak the same language of orthodox economics, both are US-educated, and both moved in the same circles as IMF officials and Wall Street players. Fraga was a former fund manager for Soros, while Malan has been an executive director of the World Bank. It would be interesting, as alluded to by Barro and Lee, to test the intricate links between finance and politics, by examining the backgrounds of officials in finance ministries and central banks in emerging countries.[120] This would probably confirm the suspicion that, over the past decade, a distinct 'pedigree' has become a necessary but insufficient condition to play the 'confidence game'. A United States academic background and connections with Washington and New York circles (or their European equivalents) might be essential for finance officials within emerging market governments.

José Serra shared this pedigree, Lula da Silva and Ciro Gomes did not, according to the perceptions of financial markets. Quite simply, Lula had neither a doctorate nor a background familiar to the IMF. Instead he began his working life as a shoe-shine boy before becoming a mechanic and eventually the leader of the São Paulo metal workers' union, from which position he fought in the 1970s against the military regime. Lula's victory can also be considered as an (exceptional) victory of democracy and social mobility in a country known for its social inequality. It is also a victory in the world's fourth biggest democracy, as Lula won by the ample margin of 53 million to 33 million votes.[121]

However, in a globalized (financial) world, winning an election in your home country is not enough. For the rest of his mandate, Lula's challenge will be to restore and maintain financial confidence. A few days before the second round elections, a fund manager simply explained in the *Financial Times*, "what Lula must do to save Brazil" (i.e. to win Wall Street confidence), suggesting a set of four political economic reforms, strategic appointments and close collaboration with international financial institutions.[122] Whether this advice was in fact heard, it was, in effect, heeded, with appointments of private bankers to key functions, such as Meirelles (formerly of the Bank of Boston) as the new Central Bank governor in 2003 and Alex Schwartsmann (a respected chief economist and former employee of Unibanco) as the head of international affairs.

The tremendous ability of the Lula administration to win votes of confidence of financial markets was confirmed in 2003. By the end of the year, the nightmares of 2002 were forgotten. Lula, feared by the markets as a 'Monster', had been transformed. In less than twelve months, Lula reversed the expectations of investors. The administration's economic orthodoxy pleasantly surprised Wall Street. Tight fiscal and monetary policies brought inflation under control and sent financial markets soaring. Investors who bet on Brazil saw a stunning 130 percent return in dollar terms on the Brazilian stock exchange, the Brazilian real stabilized while Lula, in spite of the dismal economic performance (Brazil ended the year with nearly zero growth) and a series of unpopular austerity measures, has managed to maintain an enviable poll rating of nearly 70 percent, a record in Brazil after a year in office.

In April 2003, Walter Molano, the Wall Street analyst, confessed that just a year before, "I forecasted that Brazil would be in midst of a default by this time. Obviously, I was wrong. However things also changed. Lula won the elections." Most importantly, Lula's victory in 2002 was an important milestone for Brazil. "Presidential elections are moments of great uncertainty", explained Molano. "However Brazil's election of an openly leftist government was a key test. Investors were terrorized about the possibility of a PT government. Furthermore, investors knew the current leadership would probably remain in power for the next eight years creating the time horizon needed to make new fixed investments."[123] The 2002 election and its aftermath removed an important element of uncertainty that clouded the horizon: the victory of a left-wing candidate in Brazil was not equivalent to economic irresponsibility and chaos, as shown by the experience of pro-market policies implemented in 2003.

Lula regained the confidence of the markets. However, his experience also reveals the narrow band where governments are able to move. Disillusionment set-in amongst his left-wing supporters. More than half of the population by the end of 2003 believed that the president had not even begun to fulfil his campaign pledges, above all that of creating more jobs. Furthermore, inflation remained high, eroding the average purchasing power of Brazilians by roughly 15 percent in 2003. Most of the policies implemented were sound and, in a positive way, one can look at financial markets as forces helping the 'limited rationality' of Ulysses (i.e. Governments) to move away from the songs of the Sirens (that is, the macroeconomics of populism described by Dornbusch and Edwards[124]). However, it raised a fundamental question regarding the links between democracy and markets. As stressed by Laurence Whitehead, "democracy persists, in the sense that Argentines, Bolivians, Haitians, and the rest can periodically choose their national authorities through competitive electoral contests. But once ensconced in their offices those national authorities have little – or perhaps – no say in the economic and social outcomes of most interest to their votes."[125] The Brazilian experience of Lula, with a mix of social policies and economic orthodoxy, will be important in this way: to underline the margin to manoeuvre allowed to governments of developing countries.

Lula's experience suggests that Wall Street's aversion to outsiders requires orthodoxy to gain the confidence of financial markets. Presidential races are not only national races, involving citizens, the media, candidates and so on. Presidential candidates also have to win the confidence game – that is, the vote of confidence of the financial markets. On the 5 August 2002, Lula visited the Bovespa, Sao Paulo stock exchange. Lula was the first presidential candidate in 113 years to visit Bovespa, an act calculated to alter his image, having chosen as his presidential running-mate a former chairman of the exchange. By 19 August 2002, Lula and Gomes met Cardoso in a symbolic move to agree on basic economics and to try and boost confidence. Once elected, Lula multiplied the 'market-friendly' signals towards Wall Street in order to win their confidence. The difficulty of the exercise lies in the asymmetric temporalities between markets and democracies. Financial markets are governed by short-term economic and financial rationality, while the dynamics of political interactions are complicated by the lengthy temporalities of legislators, bargaining games and search of consensus that are at the heart of democratic engineering. Elected politicians and financial operators do not share the same temporal cognitive regimes, the interactions between both worlds being, "complicated by the extreme slowness of reaction times in the realm of national political leadership, as compared to the almost instantaneous speed of adjustment in currency and money markets".[126]

The political economy of financial markets could bring useful insights to understand this confidence game dynamic of international finance and, in particular, of financial crisis. The ups and downs of financial variables can be explained by economic fundamentals. But part of the story behind emerging market financial crises is of self-fulfilling prophecies, risk-seeking and risk-aversion and changing perceptions, that loans, symbolics, money lending or political gestures try to curb. Another part of the story, as has been stressed, lies in the intricate links between politics and finance, between individual and institutional interactions and macroeconomics and financial variables. In the end, the name of the game in emerging markets is confidence, trust and mistrust.

Notes

1 See Paul Krugman, 'The confidence game', in Paul Krugman, *The Return of Depression Economics*, London: Penguin, 2000, pp. 102–17.

2 On Brazilian debt history see Eliana Cardoso and Rudiger Dornbusch, 'Brazilian debt crises: past and present', in Barry Eichengreen and Peter Lindert, eds., *The International Debt Crisis in Historical Perspective*, Cambridge, MA: MIT Press, 1989, pp. 106–39.

3 For a model and an analysis capturing the features of the debt crises of the Brazilian type, see Assaf Razin and Efraim Sadka, 'A Brazilian-type debt crisis: simple analytics', *NBER Working Paper*, no. 9606, April 2003.

4 In the case of Brazil volatility spread significant impacts on many financial variables (such as domestic interest rates and the exchange rate) and, because of debt indexed mechanisms, these exchange and interest rate fluctuations induced corresponding fluctuations in the ratio of public debt to GDP. For a detailed analysis of these dynamics, see Carlo Favero and Francesco Giavazzi, 'Targeting inflation when debt risk premia are high: lessons from Brazil', *IGIER Universita Bocconi Working Paper*, Milan, May 2003.

5 According to Bloomberg's survey on emerging market bond underwriting, in 2002, the ranking was the following one: 1) Salomon Smith Barney (US$10 billion of bonds placed for emerging markets borrowers during the year); 2) JP Morgan (US$8.6 billion); 3) Morgan Stanley (US$5.7 billion); 4) CSFB (US$5 billion); 5) UBS Warburg (US$ 3.1 billion); 6) Deutsche Bank (US$ 3 billion).

6 According to Barclays Global Investors, independent surveys estimated that MSCI's international equity indexes had a roughly 90 percent market share in the US and over 60 percent in continental Europe.

7 See Ted Gurr, 'Persistence and change in political systems 1800–1971', *American Political Science Review*, 68 (1974), 1482–1504; Ted Gurr, K. Jaggers and W.H. Moore,

'The transformation of the western state: the growth of democracy, autocracy, and state power since 1800', *Studies in Comparative International Development*, 25 (1990), 73–108; K. Jaggers, K. and T. Gurr, 'Tracking democracy's third wave with the Polity III data', *Journal of Peace Research*, 32 (1995), 469–82.

8 Tatu Vanhanen, 'A new dataset for measuring democracy 1810–1998', *Journal of Peace Research*, 37/2 (2000), 251–65. Vanhanen's index of democracy is a continuum while the Polity project adopts a scalar approach. They reflect a growing concern to better capture the nature of political regimes in the grey area between liberal democracies and overt autocracies. Consequently, however, they are also marked by problems of measurement and accuracy, as they are largely based on subjective measurements.

9 Robert Dahl, *Polyarchy: Participation and Opposition*, New Haven, CT: Yale University Press, 1971.

10 For a detailed analysis see Jonathan Bayliss, *Emerging Markets as an Asset Class*, New York: JP Morgan Emerging Markets Research, September 2003.

11 See in particular Adam Przeworski, *Democracy and the Market. Political and Economic Reforms in Eastern Europe and Latin America*, Cambridge: Cambridge University Press, 1991, pp. 40–50.

12 See Adam Przeworski, 'Democracy as a contingent outcome of conflicts', in Jon Elster and Rune Slagstad, eds., *Constitutionalism and Democracy. Studies in Rationality and Social Change*, Cambridge: Cambridge University Press, 1988, pp. 59–80.

13 See Juan Linz, 'Les contraintes temporelles de la démocratie', in Javier Santiso, ed., *A la Recherche de la Démocratie. Mélanges Offerts à Guy Hermet*, Paris: Karthala, 2002, pp. 13–41; and Juan Linz and Yossi Shain, eds., *Between States: Interim Governments and Democratic Transitions*, Cambridge: Cambridge University Press, 1995.

14 See Mancur Olson, 'Time, takings and individual rights', in Olson, *Power and Prosperity*, New York: Basic Books, 2000, pp. 25–43.

15 Christopher Clague, Philipp Keefer, Stephen Knack and Mancur Olson, 'Property rights in autocracies and democracies', *Journal of Economic Growth*, 1/2 (1996), 243–76.

16 See these intricate links not only in Olson's already mentioned works but also Chapter 5 of Douglass North, *Structure and Change in Economic History*, New York: Norton, 1981.

17 See Stephen Haber, Douglass North and Barry Weingast, 'Political institutions and financial systems: theory and history – a precis', Stanford University, February 2003 (unpublished). For a country case study on the intricate links between the structure and performance of financial markets and society's underlying political institutions see the historical study examining two extreme cases, the United States and Mexico during the period 1790–1914, Stephen Haber, Armando Razo and Noel Maurer, *The Politics of Property Rights: Political Instability, Credible Commitments, and Economic Growth in Mexico, 1876–1929*, Cambridge, MA: Cambridge University Press, 2003; and Noel Maurer, *The Power and the Profits: the Mexican Financial System, 1876–1932*, Stanford, CA: Stanford University Press, 2003.

18 See for example full dedicated reports such as the ones produced by Bear Stearns, 'Election update: Central America and the Caribbean', New York, Bear Stearns Emerging Markets Sovereign Research, 10 July 2003.

19 See, for example, the reports produced by JP Morgan Chase (27 and 31 December 2001); 'Argentina: the "model" – not just the peg – suffers', JP Morgan, Economic Research.

20 See for a comparison between political cycles and financial crises in Mexico and South Korea, Michele Chang, 'Reading the news: elections, institutions and market speculation in Mexico and Korea', Colgate University Department of Political Science, paper presented at the 2002 Annual Meeting of the American Political Science Association, Boston, MA.

21 Matthieu Bussière and Christian Mulder, 'Political instability and economic vulnerability', *International Journal of Finance and Economics*, 5 (2000), 309–30.

22 Steven A. Block and Paul M. Vaaler, 'The price of democracy: sovereign risk ratings, bond

spreads and political business cycles in developing countries', *Journal of International Money and Finance*, 23/6 (2004), 917–46.

23 Barry Eichengreen, 'Predicting and preventing financial crises: where do we stand? What have we learned?', University of California at Berkeley, prepared for the Kiel Week Annual Conference, 2002.

24 'Brazil: why is this emerging market not like the others?', Morgan Stanley, Latin America Equity Research Strategy, 25 February 2002.

25 For a balanced assessment of Brazilian economic weaknesses and risks, see 'Brazil: volatility or fragility in 2002?', Crédit Agricole Indosuez, Global Economic Markets Strategy, 25 February 2002, pp. 15–20.

26 'What we learned at Fortaleza and beyond', Merrill Lynch, 19 March 2002.

27 See their respective websites: www.lula.org.br and www.cirogomes.com.br.

28 See, for example, 'Brazil: On the edge', Deutsche Bank, Global Markets Research, Emerging Markets, 24 May 2002; and 'Brazil: fiscal shocks as the cure for a confidence crisis', Goldman Sachs, Latin America Economic Analyst, 28 June 2002. Some did it before but the series of simulation, realized were mainly to stress the Brazilian capacity to manage turbulences as, for example underlined in a report stressing that 'there is a very ample room for the real to weaken in 2002 before dynamics could become unstable', see 'The many dynamics of public debt', Merrill Lynch, Fixed Income Strategy, 13 February 2002.

29 See the website of the Workers' Party: www.pt.org.br.

30 Walter Molano, 'Da Lula monster', BCP Securities, 24 May 2002.

31 See 'Terminal do Brazil?', CDC Ixis, Flash Marchés Emergents, n° 2002-10, 17 June 2002.

32 'No free Lunch: Lula in the sky with diamonds', BBA Creditanstalt Economic Research on Brazil, 13 May 2002. For a closer analysis of political data, see 'No free lunch: lies, damn lies, and statistics', BBA Economic Research, 19 July 2002. See also 'Brazilian election countdown: Serra's chance increase', Trip notes, Bear Stearns, Emerging Markets Sovereign Debt Strategy, 25 June 2002; for an extensive analysis of Brazilian presidential candidates' economic platforms, 'Stress testing the candidates's economic programs', Merrill Lynch, Latam Macro Insights, 30 August 2002; and on a specific candidate, 'Ciro Gomes: a candidate in transition', Salomon Smith Barney, Economic and Market Analysis, 23 August 2002.

33 'Brazil: a guide to the October elections', JP Morgan Chase, Emerging Markets Research, May 17, 2002.

34 'Brazil – TV time match', UBS Warburg, 8 May 2002. See also Citigroup, Salomon Smith Barney, May 2002. 'Overview: The Brazilian presidential campaign', in Citigroup, Latin American Economic Perspectives, Citigroup, Economic & Market Strategy Analysis: 3-12; and 'Brazil: 'til debt do us part', Morgan Stanley, Fixed Income Research Latin America, 19 July 2002.

35 See 'The Lulameter in GS', Emerging Markets Strategy, Goldman Sachs, 6 June 2002.

36 L. Boni and K. Womack, 'Wall Street's credibility problem: misaligned incentives and dubious fixes?', *Brookings-Wharton Papers in Financial Services*, December 2002.

37 See for an extensive analysis of the situation at the time, 'Special report: Brazil's economy and the upcoming election', JP Morgan Chase, 5 July 2002.

38 'The emerging call: market drivers. Why Brazil is different from Argentina', Barclays Capital, Emerging Markets Strategy Americas, 19 July 2002.

39 'The emerging views', Barclays Capital, Emerging Markets Strategy Americas, 1 August 2002.

40 Walter Molano, 'Brazil: Last chance to get out', BCP Securities, 5 August 2002.

41 Ilan Goldfajn, 'The Brazilian crisis, the role of the IMF and democratic governability', Catholic University of Rio de Janeiro, Working Paper, October 2003 (unpublished).

42 S. Edwards, 'Brazil's only hope of avoiding collapse', *Financial Times*, 4 August 2002.

43 'The Brazil IMF package – what does it mean for emerging markets?', Bear Stearns, Emerging Markets Sovereign Debt Research, 8 August 2002.

44 'No free lunch: getting by with a little help of our friends', BBA Economic Research: 2, 7 August 2002.

45 BCP Securities, 8 August 2002.

46 B. Eichengreen, 'A temporary respite for Brazil', University of California, Berkley, 9 August 2002, p. 5, available at http://elsa.berkeley.edu/users/eichengr/website.htm.

47 R. Hausmann, 'Baffled by Brazil', *Financial Times*, 14 August 2002.

48 P. Desai, 'Brazil's options for the here and now', *Financial Times,* 19 August 2002.

49 M. Goldstein. 'Brazil's unwatched borrowing', *Financial Times*, 27 August 2002. For closer analysis of the IMF agreement, see M. Goldstein, 'Debt sustainability, Brazil and the IMF', *Institute of International Economics*, Working Paper WP03-1, 2003.

50 'Bearish on Brazil. Model portfolio update', Morgan Stanley, Global Fixed Income Research, 12 August 2002.

51 'Brazil, Economic and Country Market Analysis', Salomon Smith Barney, 20 August 2002.

52 'Arminio Fraga meeting highlights', Salomon Smith Barney, Economic and Market Analysis, 26 August 2002.

53 See for example, 'Still Brazil', Morgan Stanley, Fixed Income Research, EMD Focus, 6 September 2002. Others were however more bullish on the near-term outlook for Brazil stressing the improvements (growing trade surplus and lower current account deficits), insisting however that 'an upside for Brazilian financial assets largely depends on the new president appointing a strong economic team and implementing economic policies to reduce the debt to GDP ratio'. See Goldman Sachs (September 6th 2002). An update on Brazil and Mexico, Goldman Sachs, Latin America Economic Analyst.

54 See 'A look at Brazil, oil, and Colombia', Goldman Sachs Latin America Economic Analyst, 20 September 2002.

55 Arminio Fraga and Ilán Goldfajn, *Financial Times*, 18 September 2002.

56 Emerging Markets Daily, Merrill Lynch Emerging Markets, 25 September 2002. A few days later, just before the 6 October 2002 Brazilian elections, Merrill Lynch issued a new report upgrading this time Brazilian bonds. Emerging Markets Debt Monthly, Merrill Lynch Emerging Markets, 4 October 2002.

57 G. Ortiz, 'Solving debt crises', *Financial Times*, 20 September 2002.

58 J. Ackerman, 'There is a better way to manage debt crises', *Financial Times*, 26 September 2002.

59 'Overview: Monster's Ball', BCP Securities Latin American Adviser, 1 October 2002.

60 'Some impressions from the World Bank/IMF Annual Meetings', Bear Stearns Sovereign Latin America Update, Emerging Markets Sovereign Debt Research, 1 October 2002.

61 On the transformation of the PT, see David Samuels, 'From socialism to social democracy: party organization and the transformation of the Workers' Party Brazil', University of Minnesota, Department of Political Science, January 2003 (unpublished).

62 'Lula de Mel', Merrill Lynch, Emerging Markets Debt Monthly, 1 November 2002.

63 'Brazil: Three months that could make or break the Lula government', JP Morgan Emerging Markets Research, Emerging Markets Today, 28 October 2002; 'Brazil: Towards a definition', Lehman Brothers Global Economics, Latin America Weekly, 1 November 2002; 'Focus: is the pressure on Brazil's real and bonds over?', Barclays Capital, Emerging Markets Strategy, The Emerging Call, 28 October 2002.

64 'Brazil: There is no quick fix. Position for enduring volatility', JP Morgan Chase Emerging Markets Research, 9 December 2002; and 'Brazil: watch for disappointment as the time comes to act on benign rhetoric', JP Morgan Chase Emerging Markets Research, 3 December 2002.

65 'Focus: Brazil – the right start and the virtuous cycle', New York, Barclays Capital Emerging Call, 9 January 2003; and Barclays Capital Emerging Call, 19 December 2002.

66 Walter Molano, 'Overview: regional update', Greenwich, CT, BCP Securities Latin America Adviser, 22 January 2003.
67 'Where's the blow out ?', São Paulo, Unibanco Research, 31 January 2003.
68 Walter Molano, 'Plate tectonics', BCP Securities Latin American Adviser, New York, 8 October 2002.
69 Walter Molano, 'What is a smoking gun?', BCP Securities Latin American Adviser, New York, 6 February 2003.
70 Walter Molano, 'Do Mea Culpa', BCP Securities Latin American Adviser, New York, 5 February 2003.
71 'Emerging Markets Debt Perspectives: a look at opportunities in emerging markets debt, first quarter 2003', New York, Morgan Stanley Fixed Income Research Sovereigns, 17 January 2003.
72 'Lula's government: a good start, but still with big medium-term challenges', New York, Crédit Suisse First Boston, CSFB Fixed Income Emerging Markets Research, 5 February 2003.
73 'Brazil: Forecast Update', New York, UBS Investment Research, 17 January 2003.
74 2003 Strategy Outlook, New York, Lehman Brothers Emerging Markets Strategy, 13 December 2003.
75 'Brazil: credibility and a better world?', New York, Merrill Lynch Emerging Market Debt Monthly, 10 January 2003.
76 'Brazil: Happiness beyond carnival', New York, Merrill Lynch Latam Macro Insights Equity Strategy, 21 March 2003.
77 'Brazil: sell on speculation, buy on the news', New York, Goldman Sachs Latin America Economic Analyst, 10 January 2003.
78 Debt trading monthly, New York, London and São Paulo, CSFB Emerging Markets Fixed Income Research, 17 January 2003, p. 28.
79 'Brazil: cleaning up after the FX shock', New York, Morgan Stanley Latin America Fixed Income Research, March 25 2003. See also Agnès Belaisch, 'Exchange rate pass-through in Brazil', IMF Working Papers, no. 141, July 2003.
80 'Brazil: Off to a good start', São Paulo, Salomon Smith Barney Citigroup, Economic and Market Analysis, 4 April 2003.
81 'Less than 1,000 points on Brazil', New York, Goldman Sachs Latin America Economic Analyst, 3 April 2003.
82 See for example 'Focus: Brazil's congressional agenda gains more focus', New York, Barclays Capital Research Emerging Call, 11 April 2003.
83 See for example, 'Brazil: The outlook for social security reform. So much owed to so many by so few', São Paulo and New York, JP Morgan Emerging Markets Research, 24 February 2003. For analysis of Brazilian pension system see Marcos Bonturi, 'The Brazilian pension system: recent reforms and challenges ahead', OECD Economics Department Working Paper, n° 340, August 2002.
84 'Focus: Brazil's new social security reform proposal', New York, Barclays Capital Research Emerging Call, 28 February 2003; a few days later another report on the issue, 'Focus: Brazil's congressional agenda after the Carnaval', New York, Barclays Capital Emerging Call, 6 March 2003.
85 'Brazil: social security reform', São Paulo, Citigroup Emerging Markets Latin America, 6 June 2003.
86 'Brazil trip report', New York, Citigroup Economic and Market Analysis, 17 June 2003.
87 'Brazil: The busy agenda ahead', Merrill Lynch Latam Macro Insights, 11 April 2003; 'Brazil: Tax reform and scorecard update', Emerging Markets Daily, New York, Merrill Lynch Emerging Markets, 10 November 2003, pp. 12–13; and for the scorecard update, 'Brazil: Tax reform and scorecard update', in Merrill Lynch, Emerging Markets Daily, New York, Merrill Lynch Emerging Markets, 15 December 2003, p. 15.
88 'Focus: Brazil – It is now time for reforms', New York, Goldman Sachs Latin America Economic Analyst, 7 March 2003.

89 'Focus: Brazil. Reforms experience first challenge in Congress', Goldman Sachs, 17 July 2003.

90 Emerging Markets Economics Daily, New York and São Paulo, CSFB Fixed Income Research, 4 September 2003; Global Emerging Markets Daily, UBS Investment Research, Stamford, 5 September 2003.

91 'Debt trading monthly: reigning in some risk', New York, CSFB Emerging Markets Fixed Income Research, 19 September 2003. In July 2003, Brazil was already CSFB's largest overweight recommendation in emerging markets, the fixed income research team seeing the country as the most attractive combination of valuations and fundamentals, see Debt trading monthly, New York, London and São Paulo, CSFB Emerging Markets Fixed Income Research, 18 July 2003. CSFB initiated a small overweight recommendation on Brazilian bonds by the beginning of January 2003, see Debt trading monthly, New York, London and São Paulo, CSFB Emerging Markets Fixed Income Research, 17 January 2003.

92 See the Dubai reports of CSFB's Issuer Investor Forum, Emerging Markets Economics Daily, New York, London and São Paulo, CSFB Emerging Markets Fixed Income Research, 23 September 2003.

93 On Brazilian legislative dynamics during the Cardoso years, see David Samuels, *Ambition, Federalism and Legislative Politics*, Cambridge, MA: Cambridge University Press, 2003.

94 '2004 Emerging Markets Outlook: Searching for value', New York and London, Deutsche Bank Global Emerging Markets Research, 15 December 2003.

95 Emerging Market Outlook, New York, JP Morgan Emerging Markets Strategy, 7 November 2003; Emerging Market Debt Strategy Perspectives, Stamford, UBS Global Economic and Strategy Research, October 2003; Global Emerging Market Drivers Outlook for 2004, New York, Barclays Capital Research, Global Emerging Markets Strategy, 16 December 2003; Strictly Macro, New York, SCH Emerging Markets Economic Research, Santander Central Hispano, 13 November 2003; Latin America Outlook: Q1 2004, New York and São Paulo, CSFB Fixed Income Emerging Markets Research, 19 December 2003.

96 'Focus: Brazil – setting the agenda for 2004 and beyond', in Goldman Sachs, Latin America Economic Analyst, New York, Goldman Sachs, 21 November 2003.

97 'Brazil country update: Agora é growth', Morgan Stanley Fixed Income Research, 20 October 2003.

98 See for example 'Top picks 2004: Brazil should continue to lead the way', New York, São Paulo, Mexico and Madrid, BBVA Latin America Equity Strategy, 11 December 2003.

99 C. Klingen, B. Weder and J. Zettelmeyer, 'How private creditors fared in emerging debt markets, 1970–2000', IMF, mimeo, June 2003.

100 'Got Brazil?', New York, Morgan Stanley Global Fixed Income Research, 22 August 2003.

101 J. Frieden and E. Stein, *The currency game: exchange rate politics in Latin America*. Baltimore: Johns Hopkins University Press, 2001.

102 B. Eichengreen and A. Mody, 'What explains changing spreads on emerging market debt?' in S. Edwards, ed., *Capital Flows and the Emerging Countries: Theory, Evidence, and Controversies*, Chicago and London: University of Chicago Press, 2000, pp. 107–134; Vivek Arora and Martin Cerisola, 'How does U.S. monetary policy influence sovereign spreads in emerging markets?' IMF Staff Papers, Volume 48, No. 3; S. Herrera and G. Perry, 'Determinants of Latin spreads in the new economy era: the role of US interest rates and other external variables', *The World Bank*, 2002, mimeo (unpublished).

103 G. Calvo, 'Explaining sudden stop, growth collapse and BOP crisis', May 2002, *Mundell-Fleming Lecture*, IMF, forthcoming in *IMF Staff Papers*.

104 C. Favero and F. Giavazzi, 'Targeting inflation when debt and risk premia are high: lessons from Brazil', *IGIER, Universita Bocconi*, May 2003, unpublished.

105 C. Favero and F. Giavazzi, 'Why are Brazilian interest rates so high?', *IGIER, Universita Bocconi*, 2002, unpublished.

106 Note that Brazil is included in all EMBI and EMBI+ indexes.

107 Barry Eichengreen, *Capital Flows and Crises*, Cambridge, MA: MIT Press, 2003; S. Edwards and J. Frankel, eds., *Preventing Currency Crises in Emerging Markets*, Chicago: University of Chicago Press, 2002; and M. Dooley and J. Frankel, eds., *Managing Currency Crises in Emerging Markets*, Chicago: University of Chicago Press, 2002.
108 Roberto Chang, 'Financial crises and political crises', Rutgers University, Department of Economics, September 2002.
109 G. Calvo and F. Mishkin, 'The mirage of exchange rate regimes for emerging market countries', NBER Working Paper, no. 9808, June 2003.
110 Mancur Olson, *Power and Prosperity: Outgrowing Communist and Capitalist Dictatorships*, New York: Basic Books, 2000; and Javier Santiso, 'Corporate governance and political governance: multinationals, portfolio investors and institutions in emerging markets', prepared for the OECD Development Centre, 2002.
111 G. Gelos and S. Wei, 'Transparency and international investor behavior', NBER Working Paper, no. 9260, October 2002.
112 C. Reinhart, K. Rogoff and M. Savastano, 'Addicted to dollars', NBER Working Papers, no. 10015, August 2003.
113 For a detailed economic history of defaults and capital flows in Latin America, see Michael Tomz, *Sovereign Debt and International Cooperation*, Cambridge: Cambridge University Press, 2003; Alan Taylor, 'Foreign capital Latin America in the nineteenth and twentieth centuries', NBER Working Paper Series, no. 9580, March 2003; and on Mexico, see Michael Costeloe, *Bonds and Bondholders: British Investors and Mexico's Foreign Debt, 1824-1888*, London and New York, Praeger, 2003.
114 George Soros, 'Don't blame Brazil', *Financial Times*, 13 August 2002.
115 'Inside Brazil', New York, Morgan Stanley Latin America Fixed Income Research, 12 August 2002.
116 Kenneth Maxwell, 'Lula falls foul of a foreign fantasy', *Financial Times*, 27 September 2002.
117 Adam Przeworski, Democracy and the Market: Political and Economic Reforms in Eastern Europe and Latin America, Cambridge, MA: Cambridge University Press, 1991.
118 See the Indonesia case study in J. Hays, J. Freeman and H. Nesseth, 'Democratization and globalization in emerging market countries: an econometric study', *2001 Annual Meeting of the American Political Science Association*, San Francisco, 30 August–2 September 2001.
119 S. Saiegh, 'Is there a democratic advantage? Assessing the role of political institutions in sovereign borrowing', *2001 Annual Meeting of the American Political Science Association*, San Francisco, 30 August–2 September 2001.
120 R. Barro and J.W. Lee, 'IMF programs: who is chosen and what are the effects?', Harvard University, Working Paper, April 2002.
121 Lula's electoral victory was the largest since Ronald Reagan achieved 54.5 million votes in the United States' 1984 presidential election.
122 M. El-Erian, 'What Lula must do to save Brazil', *Financial Times*, 23 October 2002.
123 Walter Molano, 'Brazil: is it for real?', Greenwich, CT, BCP Securities Latin American Adviser, 15 April 2003.
124 Rudiger Dornbusch, ed., *The Macroeconomics of Populism in Latin America*, Chicago: University of Chicago Press, 1991.
125 Laurence Whitehead, 'Democratization with the benefit of hindsight: the changing international components', paper pesented at the *XIX World Congress of the International Political Science Association*, Durban, South Africa, 30 June–4 July 2003.
126 Laurence Whitehead, Chapter 1 in this volume. For a detailed analysis of the interactions between state and financial market temporalities see Javier Santiso, 'Wall Street and the Mexican Crisis: A temporal analysis of emerging markets', International Political Science Review, vol. 20, n° 1, January 1999, pp. 49–73.

Chapter 10

From the economics of politics to the politics of monetary policy in Brazil

Kurt von Mettenheim

THE TITLE OF this chapter paraphrases a landmark essay by Giovanni Sartori that was published over thirty years ago. Entitled 'From the sociology of politics to a political sociology',[1] Sartori's argument was that sociologists tended to underestimate the autonomy of politics. His targets – Parsonian sociology and Marxist reductionism – may no longer be practised today, but the core problem he discussed remains. Political phenomena remain fair prey for misguided explanations by scholars working in neighboring disciplines, especially those from sociology and economics. The empirical focus of this chapter is the politics of money, credit, central banking and democracy in Brazil. However, the broader theoretical goal is to counter the reduction of politics to either a sticky source of macroeconomic irrationality or the foreseeable result of microeconomic rational choice. By examining the advances of central banking *after* price stability in 1994 and the continued importance of federal government banks in Brazil, the aim here is to clarify the eminently political character of financial statecraft and monetary policy in new democracies.

Political science shares the concerns of economists about monetary policy – the deepening of markets for money and credit, and their impact on economic growth, inflation, employment, income, and other economic variables. However, the primary concern of political science remains elsewhere. The focus in this chapter, and volume, is on 'statecraft', that is to say the gradual construction of institutions capable of exercising increased monetary authority in new democracies as a political process. The impact of monetary policies on state–society relations and the prospects for social inclusion in the new context of price stability and democracy in Brazil since 1994 are also concerns. A central argument in this chapter is that causal claims about the primordial necessity of central bank independence and the need to isolate policy-makers from electoral cycles and other political and social pressures are flawed, especially in Brazil and other new democracies in developing countries. Unfortunately, to the extent that politics is considered at all by economists, the relation between politics and monetary policy is generally perverse: politics is seen to steer government credit and money policies off a correct course, fuel inflation, and exacerbate macroeconomic disequilibria.[2] The gradual construction of monetary authority since price stability in 1994 suggests a more positive-sum relation between politics, monetary policy, and central banking.

This chapter is organized as follows. Review of the fundamentally different schools of new-institutionalism across the social sciences frames this study to clarify how politics differs from economics and sociology. Discussion of recent economic and political trends in Brazil follows, especially the character of advances in central banking and the new division of financial labour that has emerged in the Brazilian financial system after a decade of price stability, liberalization, and privatization (1994–2004). Contrary to the expectations of neoliberal theory (and its critics), two phenomena suggest that central banking and political economy have taken a somewhat different path in Brazil. The first apparent anomaly is that the causal direction between price stability and independent central banking assumed by economists and neoliberal theory was precisely the reverse: advances in central banking in Brazil occurred *after* heterodox policies ended inertial inflation during 1993–94. The second anomaly is that, after a decade of price stability and financial liberalization, the three largest banks in Brazil remain government owned and run financial institutions. In sum, this chapter reviews the development of central banking since 1994, compares the evolution of domestic, foreign, and government banks during the last decade, and argues that new monetary policies of social inclusion are needed for political development and Brazilian democracy.

Divergent new-institutionalisms in economics, politics and sociology

Before focusing on specific debates about central banking and recent trends in the Brazilian financial system, a few general observations about the study of institutions in the social sciences are in order. These comments are necessary to clarify the wide variety of neo- or new-institutionalisms in the disciplines of economics, sociology and political science. The focus here on democracy, statecraft, and central banking involves a fundamentally different approach than either equilibrium models in economics or the largely organizational concerns in sociology.[3] Unlike new-institutionalisms in economics that customarily date to Douglas North's *Institutions, Institutional Change, and Economic Performance*, political science works within a fundamentally different tradition that dates from March and Olsen's 'New institutionalism: organizational factors in political life'.[4] March and Olsen's article coincided with renewed debate about parliamentary and presidential government in post-transition contexts and quickly involved a variety of historical and institutional analyses across several sub-fields of political science.[5] Comparative political analysts have developed considerable understanding of the consequences of instructional design in post-transition contexts for governance, legitimacy and democracy. But rather than bold causal claims about the virtues and vices of formal typologies of forms of government or other abstract institutional attributes, the methodological message is that understanding political institutions requires more focused analysis of common problems and differences across regional and national contexts.[6]

This is a fundamental difference between economics and politics. Political institutions *do not* reflect some point of formal equilibrium. Consequently, instead of interpreting institutions as a supposed outcome of interests or rational actions, the interest here in the specific context and path-dependent trajectory of central banking and the place of government banks in the new division of financial labour that are critical for both monetary authority and democracy in Brazil. Understanding the construction of monetary authority since transition from military rule in 1985 and price stability in 1994 implies a genetic explanation for monetary policies and their relation with a variety of economic reforms pursued by Brazilian governments while exiting from authoritarian rule. A genetic and developmental analysis of central banking in Brazil is incompatible with perspectives and theories from economics that describe institutions as a state of equilibrium.[7]

This divide between political science and economics is deep. Indeed, founding works in political science focus on the core difference between politics and markets precisely in these terms: Politics means disequilibria.[8]

Pearson cites Riker's argument that: "… politics is *the* dismal science because we have learned from it that there are no fundamental equilibria to predict."[9] If Riker's assertion that no fundamental equilibria exist in politics is correct (and here it is believed that it is), then it follows that core assumptions of economic theory about individual preferences, collective action, firms and consumers that presuppose equilibrium do not apply to many central questions in political science, especially those concerned with the origin and development of institutions. This seems to be an insurmountable barrier between the disciplines of economics and political science and grounds to adopt a more open, empirical, and contextual analysis of recent advances in central banking since price stability in Brazil.[10]

Some political scientists have attempted to skirt this fundamental problem by arguing that actors use institutions to solve coordination problems. From this perspective, new institutional procedures and organizations can be understood to the extent that actors converge on a set of institutions to solve coordination problems typical of collective action.[11] Once institutions become established, they become autonomous or, as Carey argues: "institutional equilibria are sticky, even in the face of changes in the surrounding political environment."[12] But, once again, theories and language from economics appear to interfere with analysis of phenomena not amenable to assumptions about equilibrium.

The origin and evolution of institutions must be understood through the analysis of social and political context. Research on advanced economies does suggest that effective monetary policy and central banking have to do with intervening variables of politics such as business–labour relations and the partisan composition of governments.[13] However, empirical comparison of governments according to standard typologies such as minority/majority, multi-party/two-party, short-lived/longstanding suggest that different forms of government fail to provide significant explanation for the success or failure of monetary policy. Like past studies of political institutions, these recent findings suggest that causal relations are more complex, more contextually specific, and more path dependent than ones that appear in cross-sectional aggregate comparison of countries. Moreover, the abandonment by Germany and France of fiscal and monetary targets set in the European Community Stability and Growth Pact during 2003 suggests serious misgivings both with monetarist theories about the preconditions for growth and the virtues of independent central banking.[14]

Instead of formal typologies and causal relations, contextual and historical analysis is required to understand the construction of central banking. In this respect, Polanyi's analysis of the development of central banking in European and North American history is surely relevant to current debates in new democracies. Polanyi argued that central banking emerged as part of a regulatory wave in Europe after 1870 that reflected the reaction of financiers against the classic doctrines of economic liberalism – especially belief in equilibria and self-regulating markets. Given that unemployment, class conflict, exchange devaluation, imperialist rivalries, and protectionism predominated in Europe after the 1873 depression, the core assumptions of economic liberalism about the gold standard, domestic banking, and credit markets had to be revised. Polanyi argues that central banks were designed throughout Europe and North America to centralize and regulate exchange markets, provide clearer references for interest rates, avert the impact of recessions on firms, and reverse the persistent disinflation caused by a fixed exchange rate. Polanyi's description of central banking as part of a self-protective movement against the doctrine of self-regulating markets and equilibria provides a strong justification for a more open-ended analysis of experiences in new democracies such as Brazil.

Study of central banking in Brazil is also important to counter generalizations based on perceptions about poor monetary policy in the country's past. Analyses of monetary policy in Brazil and Latin America often emphasize mismanagement and underdevelopment. For Dornbusch, lax monetary policy was at the centre of the vicious cycles of populist policy in the region that involved the monetarization of fiscal excess, high inflation, and severe disequilibria.[15] The recent Brazilian experience is, therefore, a critical case for monetary policy and central banking. The sheer size of domestic and foreign shocks to the Brazilian economy has long made policy decisions exceedingly difficult, with tough trade-offs between almost equally perverse outcomes amidst dismal economic and social indicators being the reality. That central banking has advanced under democratic politics since price stability in 1994 provides a compelling opportunity to re-examine core ideas about politics, economics, and broaden questions of citizenship and social inclusion.

However, before turning to recent events, review of neo-institutionalisms would be incomplete without at least brief reference to sociology.[16] The variety of perspectives that can be described as neo-institutionalism in sociology is beyond the scope of this chapter. Two common concerns in sociology and politics deserve mention: a focus on leadership and patterns of popular participation. Pierson notes that neo-institutionalist sociology today emphasizes matters long at the heart of political science such as the role of political entrepreneurs or "skilled social actors" in triggering reforms and "the contribution of previously marginalized actors in modifying institutional arrangements".[17] In this respect, recent sociology focuses on central problems both about how institutions change and, more importantly, the inclusion of social groups and classes in political institutions. This concern has been at the centre of politics and sociology since 'political development' studies during the 1960s and 1970s.[18] Classic works of political sociology include Moore's *Social Origins of Dictatorship and Democracy*,[19] Skocpol's *States and Social Revolutions*,[20] Luebbert's *Liberalism, Fascism, or Social Democracy*,[21] and the Colliers' *Shaping the Political Arena*.[22] Mahoney and Reuschemeyer, Thelen, and Pierson and Skocpol provide recent reviews of this tradition described as historical institutionalism.[23]

In sum, political sociology focuses on the inclusion and/or exclusion of social classes during economic development and social modernization. From this perspective, the central question about monetary policy in Brazil has to do with the distributive impact of policies on social classes and groups, and the prospects for inclusion and citizenship. Democratic theorists such as Dahl and Sartori, and comparative political scientists such as Lipset, Rokkan, Linz, Huntington, Tilly and many others attempted to understand how social classes are incorporated into political institutions during modernization. Although often perceived as conservative, elite oriented, and dated, the concept of political development draws attention to the still unfinished business of popular incorporation in Brazil. It is precisely the dramatic distribution of Brazilians in terms of IBGE social classes – more simply the persistence of poverty – that suggests the importance of price stability, government banks, and sound central banking for income distribution and social inclusion in Brazilian democracy. Leaving normative questions aside, a political sociology approach focuses on the reality that social classes C, D and E form an immense majority of Brazilian voters. This chapter suggests that federal banks and new monetary policies may be the most efficient mechanisms to allocate resources and incorporate voters into the new markets and institutions of Brazilian democracy.

This focus also implies that domestic matters provide far more opportunities for policies of redistribution and popular credit than generally acknowledged among analysts of political economy who tend to emphasize international constraints. While much ado is made of globalization, external shocks, and constraints from abroad, the theory of *inertial inflation* produced more political capital, presidential popularity, and the allocation of resources to lower classes than any social policy since the transition from authoritarian rule. In this respect, the theory of inertial inflation remains a conceptual landmark and lesson worthy of emulation because Brazilian (and Latin American) economists rejected orthodox monetary policies and developed theories able to *reduce inflation while redistributing income to the poor.*

The set of economic policies pursued by the Brazilian government since 1999 also reinforces the argument that domestic policies matter. Since adoption of a flexible foreign currency exchange rate regime in January 1999 and inflation targeting soon thereafter, external shocks have been buffered to a greater degree. Under the fixed currency exchange regime from 1994–99, the Brazilian government was forced to react to international currency crises by dramatically increasing domestic interest rates. Since 1999, external shocks to the Brazilian economy have been absorbed primarily through market driven currency exchange devaluation. This shift thereby increases the opportunities for domestic credit policies including popular savings and credit programs that may bring previously excluded Brazilians into the formal economy. To better assess these opportunities, review of monetary policy and bank change in Brazil since 1994 is in order.

A reverse causal order: from price stability to central banking in Brazil

The Brazilian experience suggests that causal claims about correlations between central bank independence and economic performance are seriously flawed, and that the political and economic conditions for the construction of monetary authority are necessarily more complex and open ended in developing economies such as Brazil. The content of debates among economists suggests that the insistence on formal central bank independence is very out of place in new democracies such as Brazil.[24] While central bank independence correlates with a variety of positive economic indicators in advanced economies, this does little to provide causal explanations relevant for understanding how to develop central banking in emerging markets that often lack the virtual cycles and positive causal relations typical of advanced economies.

The reality that central banking advanced after price stability in Brazil is counter-intuitive. Since Alesina reported correlations between central bank independence, lower inflation, and higher levels of economic growth,[25] many economists and political scientists have argued that a strong causal relation exists.[26] Economists argue that central bank independence (from the executive and party politics) can reduce inflationary expectations and wage demands by labour and other organized groups. Once again, from this perspective, politics threatens correct monetary policy due to either electoral cycles that fuel inflation or excessive government spending that slows economic growth. Globalization is also seen as further constraining governments and increasing the stakes for the delegation of monetary authority to build and sustain the confidence of markets.[27] Central bank independence is interpreted as both emerging from and legitimizing a type of contract whereby governments are induced to accept delegation of monetary policy in return for better economic performance.[28] Policies of inflation targeting increase the importance of this contract by concentrating the attention of investors, consumers, and international finance on matters of monetary policy and central banking.

Johnson argues that independent central banks emerged quickly in the post-communist world because of a transnational epistemic community that shared both a neoliberal ideology and sufficient material resources to guide the creation of these institutions.[29] For Johnson, this process created new institutions but dramatically reduced policy autonomy and sovereignty throughout Eastern Europe. The importance of epistemic communities counters theories that see central bank independence as an inevitable consequence of globalization, or as simply being imposed by international financial institutions or actors such as the IMF or the US. In the Brazilian case, a tempered and reluctant support for central bank autonomy seems to have emerged among political elites across a variety of political ideologies, a realism that coexists with support for other issues such as government banking that belie traditional policies of neoliberalism.

Arguments about the virtues of central bank independence must also be qualified in the Brazilian case for several reasons. First, rather than the imposition of orthodoxy, the trajectory of monetary policy in Brazil involves heterodox policies of inertial inflation that were used to reduce high and persistent inflation. Second, the successful reduction of inflation, while redistributing wealth to the poor, provided the political impetus and legitimation for statecraft during the transition to democracy, both in terms of economic policies and in terms of party-electoral realignment. The dramatic distributive effects under the first three years of the Real Plan not only projected Fernando Henrique Cardoso from the finance ministry to the presidency, but it also cemented a coalition government with broad popularity among voters. Armijo argues that this link is causal: that the end of military rule and the transition to mass democracy made price stability possible.[30]

The virtues of muddling through: from the gradualism of the Real Plan to the construction of central banking in Brazil

After five years of policy drift, failed packages, and record inflation under the caretaker presidency of Jose Sarney from 1985–90 and the false heroics of Fernando Collor de Mello from 1990–92, the virtues of muddling through permitted Fernando Henrique Cardoso not only to reduce inflation without orthodox austerity, but also to set post-transition politics in Brazil on a new footing. Contrary to those seeking broad constitutional reform or economic policy-packages (whether neoliberal or heterodox), and contrary to zero-sum conceptions that set democratization against sound economic policy, the successes of economic policy in this new democracy have been based on muddling through. The failure of seven economic packages from 1985–93 to reduce inflation, adjust the economy, and provide sustainable growth suggests that centralized policy-making by technocratic teams of economists in executive offices failed to secure the political conditions for policy implementation. All seven economic packages that preceded the Real Plan were designed in secret and announced unexpectedly to shock inflationary expectations, freeze prices and wages, and confront forces in financial and currency exchange markets.

The success of gradual, inclusive, and transparent approach used to implement the Real Plan suggests the virtues of muddling through. Upon his nomination to the finance ministry in May 1993, Cardoso sought to assure business leaders and the public that their lives and investments would no longer be submitted to policy packages that tend to radically alter prices, incomes, savings, currency exchange rates, and investment returns. Instead, Cardoso adopted a gradualist approach focusing on fiscal reform, monetary restraint, and the need for more transparent public view of the economic policy process. Repeated ministerial appearances in the media assured Brazilians that inflation was high but stable, that the government was not going to freeze wages and prices or confiscate savings, that draconian adjustment policies would be averted. In retrospect, the achievements of Cardoso as finance minister appear piecemeal, even minor if compared to the dramatic economic packages preceding his tenure.

Focusing the attention of investors and the public on a single government index against inflation permitted Cardoso and his economic team to gradually ratchet down inflationary expectations by setting and subsequently meeting realistic fiscal and monetary performance targets. After six months of gradually shifting market expectations, Cardoso was able to accompany the announcement in May 1994 that an indexed instrument (UVR) would serve as reference to launch a new currency on 1 July (made by his successor at the Ministry of Finance). Once again, policy measures were publicized well ahead of time rather than attempting to shock inflation out of the economy by unexpectedly unveiling secret economic packages. The stabilization of the new currency, the real, during 1994 symbolized the success of this gradualist approach in reducing inflation and projected Cardoso into the presidential race.

The popular appeal of Cardoso was based on the significant redistribution of wealth to poor Brazilians produced by the end of high inflation. Contrary to the accepted trade-off between inflation and income in monetary theory, inflation fell during the first six months after the plan (June–December 1994) while real wages increased an estimated 20 percent. Furthermore, contrary to the tendency of monetary policies to impact lower income groups, the real income of poor Brazilians increased an estimated 50 percent during this period because inflation no longer eroded salaries (while policies sought to secure the prices of subsistence goods).[31] Given the reluctant consensus throughout advanced economies about the necessity of incurring high social costs during economic adjustment, the Brazilian experience of reducing inflation while positively redistributing wealth is a notable achievement.

Understanding how the Franco and Cardoso administrations reduced inflation without imposing austerity or recession requires recognition of the specific context and causes of inflation in Brazil. Theories of inertial inflation identified the indexation of prices, wages, and financial instruments as the most important independent cause of very high but rarely hyperinflation throughout Latin America during the 1980s.[32] The reality is that, since the mid-1970s, Brazilian business, finance, and asset-holders had shifted to instruments indexed against inflation. Consequently, higher levels of inflation no longer affected business, finance, and asset-holders in ways expected by traditional economic theory. Instead, the persistent erosion of real wages during the 1980s and early 1990s was functional in the short-term because it transferred wealth away from wage and salary earners and toward asset holders.[33] While theories of inertial inflation correctly identified causes, the implementation of packages designed to correct this indexation of the economy failed to keep inflation down because of an exclusive policy-making style and the lack of political negotiations to buttress plans for fiscal and monetary reform able to sustain growth.

Statecraft: the construction of monetary authority *after* price stability

From 1985 through 1994, central bank officials were forced to react to radically shifting economic circumstances during a sequence of policy packages. The need to participate in the design and implementation of anti-inflation plans required close collaboration among a small group of economists across a variety of ministries and agencies. After price stability in 1994, the Central Bank of Brazil developed new, more specialized functions, agencies, and policies more traditionally associated with bank supervision, money management and interest rate policies. This shift suggests the gradual construction of monetary authority in the wake of price stability. Although a series of severe external and internal shocks wracked the Brazilian economy from 1994 through 2002, price stability brought new horizons for the gradual development of central banking in Brazil. The stabilization of the Brazilian economy permitted the development of a variety of new initiatives such as setting bank capital and risk requirements under the Basel II accord, the creation of greater regulatory capacity over banks and credit risk, depositor insurance, mechanisms for warning and intervention, dialogue with dealers and market makers of government debt and foreign currency exchange, and other matters traditionally pursued by central banks such as money management and inflation targeting. Since the mid-1990s, a variety of gradual institutional reforms have been pursued to provide earlier warnings to anticipate banking problems and policy instruments able to ensure market-driven solutions to problems.

This gradual shift from reactive policies and informal collaboration in a core economic team to more specialized functions of monetary policy can be seen in terms of the recent organizational evolution of the Central Bank of Brazil. Before price stability in 1994, the Central Bank functioned with a comparatively small, centralized staff that attempted to coordinate macroeconomic policies during the implementation of economic packages designed to reduce inflation. The succession of plans from the Cruzado (1986), Bresser (1987), Verão (1989), Collor I (1990), and Collor II (1992) required broad measures to meet monetary, fiscal, and currency targets set in plans. In organizational terms, the Central Bank of Brazil suffered during this period from a severe lack of trained staff, poor information technology, and a low ability to monitor money supplies and market trends. Instead of monitoring banks, money, credit, and currency exchange markets, Central Bank staff were forced to react to crises once they had escalated. This implied adopting more invasive policies such as direct intervention into markets and the liquidation of failed banks rather than anticipating and solving problems through market solutions.

As noted by Sola and Marques in Chapter 6 of this volume, Provisional decree 1.182 of November 1995 (voted into law in March 1995) expanded the prerogatives of the Central Bank to audit financial institutions and pursue preventative policies focusing on market operations and capital requirements. This new framework for central banking permitted the infusion of capital, the transfer or acquisition of shares by the central bank, or the reorganization of financial institutions through merger or acquisition instead of simple government intervention based on legislation dating from the Vargas regime and 1930s. This shift from reacting to dramatic macroeconomic events through gross interventions to more advanced policies of central banking continued with the publication in 1997 by the Central Bank of Brazil of new *Core Principles for Effective Bank Supervision.* Based on the principles for banking prudence and risk management proposed by the Bank for International Settlements, the Central Bank designed new capital reserve requirements and reporting standards for the risk of bank portfolios, developed new measures to induce banks to respect these requirements, and trained and equipped staff capable of auditing and supervising bank and credit risk.

The Central Bank also created a new Centre for Credit Risk in 1997, charged to create a new data base on domestic credit risk requiring financial institutions detail information on loans over R$5,000. The centre replaced the use of two categories with both qualitative evaluation and indexes expanded (in 1999) to nine levels of credit risk, ranging from 'AA' to 'H'. Data on credit and bank risk have been placed online for consultation by credit institutions since 2000. Over 874,000 credit risk consultations were made during first semester 2001, increasing to over five million consultations during first semester 2002.

Instead of a small nucleus of economists reacting to dramatic macroeconomic change through informal collaboration with personnel from other economic ministries and agencies, the Central Bank now retains a large staff to supervise credit institutions. Since 1994, the Central Bank has computerized procedures for legal appeals, created databases of housing loans and consortium lending, introduced a new payments system for daily electronic clearing of financial transfers, and new market mechanisms for reserves and foreign currency trading. Sola and Marques also note the importance of a new federal deposit insurance fund that guaranteed personal bank deposits up to R$20,000 financed by a quarter percent monthly contribution from deposits. The creation of federal government deposit insurance was an important development that increased confidence in the banking system and reduced the need for ad-hoc interventions by the central bank.

In sum, before 1994, the Central Bank was called on to accompany and react to fundamental changes in domestic liquidity and banking caused by the dramatic changes during volatile and high inflation, indexation, and policy packages. Since price stability in 1994, the development of a variety of measures to manage credit risk, supervise banks, and increase the transparency of markets suggests that the Central Bank of

Brazil has shifted away from crisis management and focused on more specialized matters traditionally associated with money management.

Liberalization, privatization and bank change, 1994–2002

In mid-1995, the presidency and finance ministry announced new policies for the financial sector involving both the privatization of state government banks and permission for foreign banks to participate in auctions. These measures departed sharply from the national-developmentalist tradition and required approval of constitutional amendments by three-fifths of the votes in both chambers of congress.[34] As noted by Sola and Marques in Chapter 6, the Central Bank of Brazil assumed control of the Banco Econômico (August 1995), the eighth largest private domestic bank, and Banco Nacional (November 1995), the sixth largest private domestic bank. By making it apparent that financial institutions faced problems adjusting to the new context of price stability, these bank failures quickened the pace and broadened support for preparation of bank reorganization legislation (completed in November 1995).

The government also created new legislation designed to facilitate the acquisition of troubled banks by other financial institutions as an intermediate step before acquisition by the government. This legislation replaced bank intervention rules in place since the 1930s that relied on simple decrees by the executive. The new PROER regulations called for the separation of the problematic assets and liabilities from the bank in question and the sale of the rest of the financial institution to another private or public bank, with federal funds provided in terms of treasury

Table 10.1: ***Private bank failures and interventions***

Bank interventions	*Buyer*
Banco Econômico	Excel e Caixa Econômica Federal*
Banco Nacional	Unibanco
Banco Mercantil de Pernambuco	Rural
Banco Banorte	Bandeirantes
Banco Bamerindus	HSBC, Caixa,** Banco do Brasil (BB)

Source: Central Bank of Brazil, Dept. of Bank Operations.
* 7/1994 to 5/1997; ** real-estate portfolio only.

bills or other government entities to reduce the direct cost of interventions.

Price stability produced problems for private banks, but federal government policies toward state government banks were more dramatic. The program of incentives to reduce the state government public sector in banking activities (PROES) involved the intervention, sale, or reorganization of 28 banks. By 2000, only two state government banks remained solvent in terms of government rules for intervention (See Appendix 1). Sola and Marques describe the politics in late 1994 surrounding the intervention into the São Paulo and Rio de Janeiro state banks. Provisional decree 1.514 of August 1996 defined the terms for federal government intervention into the remaining state banks. State governments choosing to participate in the PROES program were offered new credit lines for the expenses incurred in either a) intervention and reorganization of state banks into development agencies, or b) their sale at auction, or c) required their transfer to federal government control. Federal government funds were offered to cover up to 50 percent of the cost to reorganize state government banks, at (subsidized) 6 percent annual interest rates over thirty years with payment caps in terms of a percentage of state government receipts.

The reorganization of federal government banks

Although many regard the 1990s as a period of neoliberalism in Brazil and abroad, the reality in the early twenty-first century is that the three largest banks in Brazil remain federal government institutions. After more than a decade of liberalization, privatization, foreign financial investment, and regulatory reforms designed to bring Brazilian banks within Basel II Accord guidelines (and tougher central bank guidelines), the federal government retains considerable initiative in terms of finance, money, and credit policies through three large financial institutions. Considered separately, each federal government bank has an essential place in the economy. The Banco do Brasil (BB) acts as the primary agent of agricultural credit and development, while also focusing on international commerce and export programs. The Banco Nacional de Desenvolvimento Econômico e Social (BNDES) provides long-term credit to economic sectors seen as critical by the federal government for economic and social development. During the 1990s, the BNDES also coordinated the federal government program of privatization and remains a major provider of export financing and agent for new development strategies. The Federal Savings Bank, Caixa Econômica Federal (CAIXA), traditionally focused on urban development, sanitation and housing, the transfer of government benefits and such as pensions, unemployment funds, and has shifted toward both investment banking and popular credit. Finally, Banco do Nordeste (BNB) and Banco da Amazonia (Basa) remain central agents of regional development. Taken as a whole, these publicly owned financial institutions provide large levers over the Brazilian economy at significant odds with the global shift away from government allocation of resources in favour of markets.

Until recently, many economists in international financial institutions argued that privatization is the only solution for government banks.[35] Review of private and public banking in Brazil since price stability in 1994 suggests that claims about dysfunctional moral risk, poor performance, and financial repression involving government banks are overstated. On the contrary, trends since 1994 in Brazil suggest that privatization of state (but not federal) banks, the influx of foreign banks, and the capitalization and reform of federal government banks have created a new distribution of financial labour and positive sum allocation of credit. The shape of banking in Brazil today belies expectations of neoliberalism, fails to confirm fears of neo-imperial domination, and differs from past experiences of state-led developmentalism. This section reviews developments in banking, credit, and monetary policies since price stability in 1994 that suggest the contours of this new division of financial labour.

Comparison of public and private banks suggests that federal government banks provide no greater credit risk than private domestic or foreign banks currently operating in the country (see Appendix 2).[36] Although these are rough comparisons, the data is slighted against government banks because of the additional costs incurred from the administration of federal government programs. For example, the Federal Savings Bank, CAIXA, serves as principal executor of a wide variety of government services such as FGTS, PIS/PASEP, unemployment funds, grants and loans for education, and the new 'citizenship card'. The bank is also contracted to accumulate data for the federal government through the CNIS (Cadastro Nacional de Informacões Sociais, National Registry of Social Information) and CAGED (Cadastro Geral de Empregados e Desempregados, National Registry of Employment and Unemployment).

These and other administrative responsibilities mandated by the federal government present a unique set of opportunities, risks, and costs for the bank. Furthermore, while much ado is made about the extent of non-performing housing loans at the CAIXA, the majority of these loans originated when the bank was forced to acquire the BNH (Banco Nacional de Habitação, National Housing Bank) when liquidated in 1986.

The recent performance of Brazilian federal government banks counters critics of government banking in economics, political economy, and international finance that see these institutions as just another example of bad banks led by bureaucrats. Brief review of policies pursued by the federal government to reduce credit risk, improve ratings, capitalize, and reorganize government banks suggests that these institutions remain a viable part of the Brazilian financial system and political economy. In 1995, the federal government initiated review of the Banco do Brasil, recognizing the poor quality of portfolios that mixed problematic loans alongside sound credit and consumer deposits. In 1993, the Banco do Brasil received R$8 billion in capital from the government in the form of treasury notes. In 1999, a central bank audit revealed the need for further provisions and suggested that broader reform of federal government banks be undertaken. This led to the commission of a study by the Finance Ministry, public hearing during 2000, and the June 2001 plan to capitalize and reorganize federal financial institutions.

The June 2001 reforms of federal government banks transferred problematic portfolios to a new financial institution under the Treasury (Emgea), exchanged assets with low liquidity and low interest rates for more liquid instruments paying market interest rates, and increased capital in three of the four federal government banks. The cost of this program is estimated at R$12.18 billion for treasury during 2001, while an additional R$62.4 billion of bonds were issued to cover shifting assets from the banks to the treasury. Capitalization brought Brazilian federal banks within Basel Accord capital requirements as well as Central Bank of Brazil resolution 2.682/99 that set additional guidelines for provisions against credit risk. The Ministry of Finance also set new guidelines for reforms that attempted to guarantee the continuity of these institutions as agents for the implementation of federal government policies while ensuring against the recurrence of large liabilities. The balance sheets of these banks since 2001 suggest that profits, capital risk, asset quality, and performance of federal government banks have remained at par or indeed above benchmark private and foreign banks in Brazil.

Another assumption of this chapter should be made clear: that federal government banks differ from state government banks, the latter being the focus of sustained criticism from a variety of political, economic, and fiscal perspectives.[37] While the perverse behaviour of state banks has been widely documented, scholars have also emphasized the reality that discipline, supervision, refinancing, privatization, and political-financial reform have come 'from the top down'. The Central Bank of Brazil and other ministries and federal government agencies responsible for fiscal, monetary, budget, and banking policies have introduced a series of reforms that have altered the domestic financial system and federal banks. Federal banks are also different than state banks because federal politics differs from politics within states. Unlike state governments, the Brazilian federal government faces external realities. Federal politics is also more contested, involves more actors, draws more media attention, and has been in the forefront of financial reforms.

In terms of political sociology the question is whether federal banks can channel credit and savings to those left behind during Brazilian development. Critics of government banking and intervention should be considered carefully.[38] In the past, especially under military rule, abuses involving big business and middle classes tied to political machines often predominated. Nonetheless, in the new context since 1994 marked by democracy, price stability, and advances in bank supervision and credit monitoring, these matters appear different. Small loans to popular sectors differ in terms of risk (both default and moral) from state banking practices in the past involving the capture of these institutions by middle class groups, political machines, and big business. Commercial and non-profit banking find that higher default rates in popular credit are more than compensated by greater profit margins and the greater pulverization of risk across a greater number of clients. Although further analysis will be needed, this appears to have considerable implications for the political sociology of federal banking. Programs of popular credit are more viable and less prone to risks of default than the traditional program lending and subsidized middle class housing loans that have haunted federal bank balance sheets.

Comparing the cost of saving private, state government and federal government banks after price stability in 1994 is also in order. Data from the Ministry of Finance and Central Bank of Brazil, and comparative studies suggest that the total fiscal cost of bank interventions and privatizations through 2001 is estimated to have reached approximately 8 to 9 percent of the Brazilian GDP. Although expensive, this cost remains considerably below the average cost of domestic banking crises in developing countries during the 1980s and 1990s (approximately 17 percent of GDP). The cost of the three banking programs in Brazil from 1994 through 2001 (16 percent) also sum to over the average cost of banking crises in advanced economies (12 percent of GDP).[39] The impact of the PROER designed to rescue private banks was 0.88 percent of GDP, the PROES designed to privatize and/or reorganize state government banks totalled 5.68 percent of GDP, while the reorganization of federal government banks summed to over 8 percent of GDP by July 2002.

The new division of financial labour in Brazil

During the 1990s, financial liberalization, privatization and bank reform reduced the presence of state government banks, increased the importance of foreign financial institutions, recast the role of federal government banks, and encouraged the creation of new institutions responsible for micro- and small-credit operations. Capital flight, global risk aversion, and fear of political discontinuity reduced portfolio investment in Brazil through mutual funds and financial investments from 2001 through 2003. Nonetheless, trends during the 1990s appear to have fundamentally altered the relation between public, private, and foreign finance in Brazil. The end of high inflation, the liberalization of the economy, and the sequence of economic reforms implemented during the 1990s led to the expansion of domestic savings from 34 percent of GDP in 1995 to over 48 percent of GDP in 2002. Furthermore, the allocation of resources through mutual funds accounts for this increase. The value of mutual funds in Brazil increased from 11.6 percent of GDP in 1995 to over 27 percent of GDP in 2002, while the value of bank deposits remained stable at just over 20 percent of GDP.

Bank change during the 1990s also involved significant internationalization. After 1994, foreign banks entered the Brazilian market through purchase of state government banks in privatization auctions and through mergers and acquisitions. Inflows of foreign direct investment

Table10.2: ***Types of savings, percent of GDP***

	1995	*1996*	*1997*	*1998*	*1999*	*2000*	*2001*	*2002*
Mutual Funds	11.6	16.3	16.2	17.1	24.2	28.2	30.2	27.6
Savings Accounts	9.8	9.2	11.1	11.8	11.5	10.3	10.0	10.6
Time Deposits	12.6	10.3	10.0	9.7	9.8	8.3	9.1	10.2
Total	34.0	35.8	37.3	38.5	45.6	46.8	49.3	48.4

Source: Central Bank of Brazil, *Financial Stability Report* (2003).

into the financial sector totalled US$19.8 billion, or 15 percent of total direct foreign investment from 1994–2002. The first wave of bank change after price stability in 1994 involved federal government intervention into state government banks, 17 of which were privatized. The second more gradual shift during the late 1990s was the increase of mergers and acquisitions; many led by foreign banks seeking to enter the Brazilian market.

The consequences of these two waves of change were to consolidate the federal government's role in banking, while dramatically reducing the traditional national-developmental role of state banks and increasing the presence of foreign banks in the Brazilian financial system. It is of note that both these cycles occurred under a fixed foreign currency exchange regime and overvalued real during 1994–99, a reality that produced serious capital losses for foreign banks once the flexible exchange rate regime (adopted in January 1999) led to the devaluation of the real from approximately 1/1 against the United States dollar to approximately 3/1 by 2002.

Although theories of governments as grabbing hand and commanding heights set public and private sector inexorably against once another, empirical comparison of private, foreign, and government banks suggests that a new, more positive sum, division of financial labour has emerged in Brazil since price stability in 1994. Most state government

Table 10.3: ***Bank privatizations, mergers and acquisitions, 1994–2002***

	94	*95*	*96*	*97*	*98*	*99*	*00*	*01*	*02*
Gov. Interventions	10	18	5	10	6	1	2	4	1
Mergers and Acq.'s	0	1	8	6	11	2	10	3	5

Source: Central Bank of Brazil, *Financial Stability Report* (2003).

Table 10.4: ***Bank capital, government, domestic, and foreign, 1994–2002***

	1994	*1995*	*1996*	*1997*	*1998*	*1999*	*2000*	*2001*	*2002*
Government	34.3	36.8	33.5	32.8	27.2	26.5	19.8	16.5	16.4
Domestic	56.1	49.9	56.1	52.7	50.6	47.6	51.3	52.1	50.4
Foreign	9.6	13.3	10.4	14.5	22.2	25.9	28.9	31.4	33.2
Total	100.0	100.0	100.0	100.0	100.0	100.0	100.0	100.0	100.0

Source: Central Bank of Brazil, *Financial Stability Report* (2003)

banks were privatized during the 1990s. However, the federal government retains control of three of the largest financial institutions in Brazil, while foreign banks and non-bank cooperatives and credit organizations have increased their presence in the Brazilian financial system. Data on bank capital, assets, and credit confirm the new structure of the Brazilian financial system. First, in terms of total bank capital, the decline of government banks from over 34 percent of total capital in 1994 to 16 percent of total bank capital in 2002 reflects the privatization of state government banks and the reorganization of federal government bank portfolios. Indeed, the proportion of domestic private bank capital remained relatively stable, declining from approximately 56 percent of total in 1994 to 50 percent of total in 2002, while foreign banks increased the proportion of domestic bank capital from under ten (9.6) percent in 1994 to over 33 percent in 2002.

This new division of financial labour can also be seen in the shifting number of financial institutions, government and private. The total number of banks in Brazil has decreased from 246 in 1994 to 171 in 2002.[40] The total number of private banks has decreased from 214 to 157, reflecting a decline of 176 domestic banks in 1994 to 92 domestic banks in 2002, while the number of foreign banks increased from 38 to

Table 10.5: ***Number of banks, government, private, and foreign, 1994–2002***

	1994	*1995*	*1996*	*1997*	*1998*	*1999*	*2000*	*2001*	*2002*
Government	32	32	32	27	23	19	19	16	14
Domestic	176	173	159	145	122	108	107	96	92
Foreign	38	37	40	45	58	67	69	70	65
Total	246	242	231	217	203	194	195	182	171

Source: Central Bank of Brazil, *Financial Stability Report* (2003).

Table 10.6: ***Bank credit, government, domestic and foreign, 1994–2002***

Bank credit	*1994*	*1995*	*1996*	*1997*	*1998*	*1999*	*2000*	*2001*	*2002*
Government	59.3	62.3	58.4	52.6	53.7	48.0	39.6	25.2	28.1
Domestic	35.5	32.0	32.9	35.6	31.3	32.0	34.9	42.8	41.3
Foreign	5.2	5.7	8.7	11.8	15.0	20.0	25.5	32.0	30.6
Total	100.0	100.0	100.0	100.0	100.0	100.0	100.0	100.0	100.0

Source: Central Bank of Brazil, *Financial Stability Report* (2003).

65. The total number of government banks decreased considerably from 32 in 1994 to 14 in 2002, reflecting the privatization of state government banks discussed above. No federal financial institution was scheduled for privatization during the 1990s and none are currently slated for sale by the Lula da Silva administration. The consolidation of a new Brazilian banking system since price stability, financial liberalization, and modernization coincided during the 1990s thus appears to involve a select number of large federal government banks, an expanded presence of foreign banks, and a variety of new cooperatives and other credit institutions.

Supply of credit also reflects this shift from public to private lenders, with the market share of government bank loans declining from 59 percent of total domestic credit in 1994 to 28 percent in 2002. Meanwhile, private credit increased from 40 percent of domestic credit in 1994 to over 70 percent in 2002, with foreign banks increasing their share of domestic credit market from 5.2 percent in 1994 to 30.6 percent in 2002.

The cycle of bank privatizations, reorganizations, acquisitions, and mergers that followed reforms and legislative changes during the 1990s was largely completed as of 2001. Indeed, the federal government capitalization reform of federal government banks in June 2001 provides the last of a series of bank reforms required to adjust financial institutions to the end of high inflation and the new regulatory framework embodied by the capital guidelines of the Basel Accord. Since 2001, the evidence suggests that public banks have stabilized in terms of credit, deposits, capital, and other indicators of bank credit risk and prudence. Indeed, given the concentration of foreign and private bank capital in government paper, their respective risk ratings summarized in the Basel index is often inferior to Basel index levels reported by Brazilian federal government banks.

Comparison of the credit profile of government, domestic, foreign,

Table 10.7: ***Size of loans by type of financial institution, 2002***

	Government		*Domestic*		*Foreign*		*Non-Bank*	
Loans	*June*	*Dec*	*June*	*Dec*	*June*	*Dec*	*June*	*Dec*
< 5k	11.4	11.7	14.6	14.5	12.4	12.5	23.1	24.9
5–50k	23.4	21.2	14.9	14.6	21.9	19.3	28.7	33.1
50–500k	12.3	12.2	11.6	11.9	10.5	11.5	20.5	16.3
500k–1m	2.3	2.3	3.5	3.6	2.7	2.9	5.0	4.1
1m–5m	5.0	4.8	10.7	11.1	10.0	10.3	10.1	9.3
5–10m	2.7	2.6	5.8	6.0	7.0	6.4	3.3	3.8
10–20m	3.1	3.1	6.5	6.4	8.0	7.8	2.1	2.4
20–50m	5.7	5.3	9.6	9.6	12.7	12.6	2.8	2.5
> 50m	34.1	37.0	22.7	22.3	15.0	16.7	4.2	3.8

Source: Central Bank of Brazil, *Financial Stability Report* (2003).

and non-bank financial institutions also indicates a new division of financial labour in Brazil. Data from 2002 suggests that government banks tend to concentrate at the top and bottom of the credit market, in other words specializing in large and small loans. In comparison, private domestic and foreign banks tend to specialize in intermediate levels of credits. Non-bank financial institutions such as cooperatives tend to specialize in the concession of smaller credits.

In sum, data on the Brazilian financial system since 1994 suggest that a new division of labour has emerged involving domestic private, federal government, foreign, and non-profit financial institutions. Privatization of state government banks, liberalization of financial regulations, and new incentives for foreign financial investment are important developments that drove change in Brazilian banking. However, far from a linear shift toward commercial banking and private capital along the lines of neoliberal theory, the reorganization of federal government banks and their continued centrality in Brazilian development suggests a different course. And far from the nationalist and state-led development practices involving rent seeking and capture of credit programs, clientelism, corporatism, and favouritism, new popular credit and incomes policies practised by the Brazilian government through public banks appear to provide new examples of positive-sum relations between public and private finance, credit, money, and politics.

New monetary policy and democratization

The path of bank change in Brazil since 1994 suggests that monetary policies may be shifted toward a fundamentally new direction that accelerates social inclusion and economic development by basing policies on core concepts of social justice and citizenship as much as market equilibrium and property rights. Recent proposals by political theorists such as stakeholding and basic income programs suggest that, while respecting economic constraints on the pace of change, the realities of credit risk, and other matters at the heart of monetary theory, basic income policies may be compatible not only with monetary theory but also with expanded notions of democracy and social justice. Pateman and Barry argue that recent political theory and comparative political analysis lack a broader view of possibilities for citizenship and democratization through basic incomes policies.[41] This analysis of central banking in Brazil and other new democracies concurs in this respect: Debates about monetary policy and politics need a broader theoretical and programmatic horizon. If the theory and analysis of democratization is to accompany political and economic change and provide viable policy alternatives capable of deepening citizenship, institutions and markets, then core ideas about the credit channel, monetary policy, property rights, income distribution, and economic adjustment and growth need to be reassessed.

Debates about stake holding and basic income are especially relevant to discussion of democracy in Brazil after transition from military rule. Given the dramatic levels of social exclusion and income inequality in Brazil, more dramatic measures capable of creating wealth, channelling resources, and providing substance to citizenship and liberty are required. Ackerman and Alstott argue that a one-time payment of US$80,000 at 21 years of age would provide a profound increase in the patriotism and economic role of individuals, increasing the stake that individuals have in the economy.[42] Van Partij also argues for basic income and grants to deepen the freedom of individuals while averting the creation of disequilibria in terms of monetary theory and economic development.

It is argued by Pateman that a basic income would have a profound influence not only on the economy but also on citizenship and democracy.[43] While these matters cross a variety of disciplines, theoretical perspectives, and complex conceptual and empirical matters, the broader sense of the social sciences is that current debate is far too constrained. Basic income policies imply reconsideration of the constraints on change, one that integrates advances in monetary economics involving the credit channel that makes adjustment both more precise and more humane, and concerns in political theory and public policy about social justice, relief of poverty, equality of opportunity, the flexibility of labour markets, and individual freedom. Instead of partitioning democratization studies from discussions in political theory and economics, this chapter suggests that the sequence of reforms involving liberalization, privatization, and increasing transparency in Brazilian central banking sets the stage for new monetary policies of social inclusion much more than past paradigms would have expected. Given the creation of new social policies in Brazil that include basic grants for mothers and children in school, and the reality of databases in government banks, agencies, and ministries, the expansion of existing grants to broader guarantees of basic income seems compelling in terms of social justice, viable in terms of economic theory, and essential in terms of political socialization and citizenship. If statecraft shall continue to deepen the attachment of Brazilians to the institutions of democracy and markets, then more dramatic policies of money, credit, and income will be necessary. Waiting for higher levels of undirected economic growth to resolve the legacies of social exclusion and political underdevelopment is not realistic.

Conclusion

This chapter has sought to broaden the view of banking and monetary policy in Brazil since price stability in 1994 to explore general themes about central banking in new democracies. As the volume goes to press in October 2005, legislation designed to formalize central bank independence has been taken off the immediate agenda of the PT coalition government under Lula da Silva. This confirms the reality that the Central Bank of Brazil lacks formal independence set by law. Instead, the construction of more effective central banking and increased monetary authority has occurred in Brazil without definition of operational or constitutional central bank autonomy. Instead, a new, somewhat reluctant, but nonetheless solid consensus appears to have emerged in Brazilian politics that monetary policies must be entrusted to technical authorities. This sober conclusion is based on recognition of past mistakes that contributed to the breakdown of democracy in 1964 and witness of further financial abuses under military rule and the political vacuum of prolonged transition. The severity of financial crisis in neighbouring Argentina reinforced this reluctant consensus among Brazilian politicians. Surveys of political elites suggest that a sober realization that government policies must respect market constraints. For perhaps the first time in Brazilian history, policy involving the domestic money supply, foreign currency exchange markets, interest rate policies, hard currency reserves, credit risk, and prudent banking principles have been delegated to specialist subsecretaries in the Central Bank of Brazil, Treasury, and Ministry of Finance.

In this respect, recent developments suggest a gradual separation and specialization of institutions responsible for monetary policies in the federal government. Since the late 1980s and early 1990s, a fundamental shift has occurred away from the need for a select nucleus of economists responsible for quickly adapting policies to volatile change under high inflation and repeated attempts to de-index financial instruments. Since price stability in 1994, the trend toward specialization and differentiation is unmistakable. Instead of centralizing a variety of decisions and reacting to circumstances by attempting to coordinate a wide variety of monetary, fiscal, tax, finance, and bank lending policies, central bank officials increasingly delegate decisions to specialized departments in the attempt to monitor markets, regulate banks, and anticipate crises rather than react to events. This specialization and differentiation of central banking in Brazil suggests both the opportunities for statecraft during the first decade of price stability in the country and the importance of the separation of powers in Brazilian political institutions. Indeed, scholars of Brazilian politics have emphasized the simultaneous empowerment of legislative, judiciary, and executive since the 1988 Constitution. Review of monetary policy and central banking suggests that congressional oversight, judicial review, and executive capacity appear to involve an increasingly complex, positive-sum policy process involving all branches of government.

Debates about the primordial necessity of central bank independence as a condition for price stability and economic growth fail to capture this causal sequence. In Chapter 3, Mailson de Nóbrega and Loyola place the development of central banking in broader historical perspective. Nonetheless, the pace of change accelerated during the 1990s. And far from an example of orthodoxy, advances in monetary and fiscal policy began with very heterodox measures designed to end inertial inflation. Furthermore, anti-inflation policies gained political legitimacy because de-indexation dramatically shifted income to those previously without indexed assets (the poor). This causal sequence suggests that context-specific policies and path dependent sequences for the creation of new central bank capacities are at the heart of creating monetary authority in a developing economy. In a broader sense, insistence on formal central bank independence appears to be another mistaken agenda of liberal reformism that seeks to impose institutions (such as parliamentary government, party discipline, a district electoral systems, or a long list of economic policies deemed as necessary conditions for growth). Theories that elevate the correlation between independent central banking and economic indicators such as lower inflation and higher growth presuppose the existence of deep markets, effective regulatory agencies, and a variety of economic indicators that embody advanced market economies and old democracies. If policy-makers simply transplant central bank independence to developing economies where parameters for monetary policy fluctuate dramatically, then, paraphrasing Merton, one can expect unexpected consequences.

Perhaps the most paradoxical finding of this chapter is the importance of federal government banks. Liberalization, privatization, and a wave of foreign financial investment have reshaped Brazilian banking. However, far from confirming neoliberal assumptions about the superiority of foreign banks or similar fears of Brazilians about imperialist domination, this chapter provides evidence that bank change in Brazil differed in important respects. From 1994 through 2002, President Cardoso's government privatized state government banks and encouraged foreign banks to invest in the country. However, the Cardoso administration also capitalized federal government banks and challenged these institutions to develop new business plans. Far from simply neoliberal, an important consequence of 'Toucan' reforms under Cardoso and his finance minister, Pedro Malan, is that the Brazilian federal government still retains control and ownership of the three largest financial institutions in the country. And far from the financial black holes associated with government banking in the past, rating agencies and Basel II measures of capital risk suggest that these institutions are as sound as the best private domestic and foreign banks operating in Brazil.

Price stability and democratization in Brazil have provided significant opportunities for economic, social, and political development. Nonetheless, in comparative perspective, Brazilian credit markets remain markedly underdeveloped. While the volume of credit in developed economies often exceeds 100 percent of the gross domestic product, credit in Brazil remains below one-third of the country's GDP. This suggests that the development of banking, finance and credit remain central challenges for Brazil's new democracy. The contributions to this volume suggest that the dramatic events of transition from military rule, a full decade of price stability amidst a seemingly endless sequence of financial crises since 1994, and an equally unprecedented change of government from Fernando Henrique Cardoso's PSDB coalition to Lula da Silva's PT-led coalition in 2003 sum to place central banking and democracy in Brazil on a new footing. Given the gradual construction of central banking and monetary authority during this turbulent and tested decade, the prospects for social inclusion today (especially through federal government banks) are now both considerable and considerably different. These differences suggest that the politics of democracy and central banking in Brazil today differ markedly from past experiences, whether with welfare states in Europe, market driven growth and inclusion in the US, or past experiences with national populism and state-led developmentalism in Brazil and Latin America.

These differences also suggest that central banking in new democracies requires statecraft – the gradual construction of institutions through politics – rather than the simple imposition of orthodoxies or reforms from abroad. Scholars, policy makers and markets now appear to agree that considerable progress has been made in Brazil during the last decade in terms of liberalization, privatization, macroeconomic adjustment, and a variety of fiscal, administrative, and monetary reforms. However, far from confirming the correct adoption of policies from abroad, or now providing models for emulation by other developing nations, it is essential to recognize that advances in central banking occurred in Brazil through a tempered realism about the need to reconcile democratization and monetary authority. Brazil is not a model. Since price stability in 1994, the costs of adjustment to economic shocks from abroad and at home have been high and the legacies of underdevelopment are still cruel. Nonetheless, the cumulative impact of reforms has made the Brazilian economy more resistant to the crises and dramatic reversals that have marked emerging economies and new democracies. This chapter suggests that federal government banks and new monetary policies of social inclusion may further transform what has traditionally been seen as a zero-sum relation into a more positive-sum cycle capable of reinforcing property rights, prudent banking, economic development, and citizenship, deepening both financial markets and democracy.

Notes

1 Giovanni Sartori, 'From the sociology of politics to a political sociology', in S.M. Lipset, ed., *Politics and the Social Sciences*, Oxford: Oxford University Press, 1969.

Appendix 1: ***25 largest banks in Brazil, year-end 2003***

Bank	*Assets*	*Credit*	*Deposits*	*LqA*	*LVG*	*EFC*	*ROA*
Banco do Brasil*	230.1	65.6	110.0	12.2	17.9	0.73	19.5
Bradesco	176.0	42.1	58.0	13.6	11.9	0.64	16.8
BNDES*	151.9	37.8	1.5	12.8	na	na	12.3
Caixa Econômica*	150.5	21.8	81.0	5.7	25.0	0.59	28.0
Itau	118.7	35.5	36.7	12.9	8.1	0.48	16.6
Unibanco	69.6	23.4	25.3	7.9	7.72	0.54	13.1
Santander	58.9	13.1	18.0	7.9	6.37	0.56	21.3
ABN Amro	55.4	21.5	26.7	7.1	6.76	0.67	15.9
Safra	32.9	11.6	8.6	3.0	9.8	0.39	20.1
Nossa Caixa**	27.5	3.4	18.9	1.8	14.1	0.54	24.6
HSBC	10.1	26.2	10.3	15.1	1.9	12.8	0.80
Votorantim	24.9	4.0	8.8	2.3	9.4	0.22	26.4
BankBoston	19.4	6.6	3.3	2.5	6.6	0.47	19.7
Citibank	19.2	4.6	2.2	2.0	8.2	0.91	4.6
Banrisul**	11.7	3.7	7.5	0.8	13.6	0.55	35.5
Pactual	6.7	0.1	1.0	0.5	11.1	0.18	33.0
Santos	6.2	2.2	1.7	0.5	10.2	0.63	20.1
JP Morgan	6.2	0.2	1.2	1.5	4.4	0.16	23.7
Rural	6.0	3.0	3.5	0.6	8.2	0.64	17.3
Alfa	6.0	3.1	1.4	1.0	5.0	0.38	11.5
Fibra	5.7	0.6	0.9	0.4	12.8	0.31	21.8
Deutche	4.4	0.9	0.8	0.2	16.8	0.40	–13.9
Mercantil do Brasil	4.3	1.7	2.4	0.4	0.8	0.90	8.8
BicBanco	4.1	2.2	1.8	0.3	10.5	0.49	20.2
BBM	4.1	0.4	1.0	0.3	11.8	0.28	33.6
BESC**	3.5	0.3	1.7	0.2	19.6	0.93	6.2

Source: *Conjuntura Econômica*, May 2004, p. 28.
Notes: DEP = Deposits, LQA = Liquid Assets, LVG = Leverage, EFC = Efficiency, ROA = Return on Assets;
* Federal government banks;
* State government banks.

Appendix 2: *State government banks assumed by federal government*

Banacre, Banco do Estado do Acre S.A.
Banap, Banco do Estado do Amapá S.A.
Bandern, Banco do Estado do Rio Grande do Norte S.A.
BDRN, Banco de Desenvolvimento do Estado do Rio Grande do Norte S.A.
Bemat, Banco do Estado do Mato Grosso S.A
Beron, Banco do Estado de Rondônia S.A.
Minascaixa, Caixa Econômica do Estado de Minas Gerais
Produban, Banco do Estado de Alagoas S.A.
Baner Banco do Estado de Roraima S.A. (liquidated)

Privatizations of state government banks by state governments
Bandepe, Banco do Estado de Pernambuco S.A.
Baneb, Bancoc do Estado de Bahia S.A.
Banerj, Banco do Estado de Rio de Janeiro S.A.
Banestado, Banco do Estado de Paraná S.A.
Bemge, Banco do Estado de Minas Gerais, S.A.
Credireal Banco de Crédito Real de Minas Gerais S.A.
Paraiban Banco do Estado da Paraíba S.A

Privatizations of state government banks by federal government
Banespa, Banco do Estado de São Paulo S.A.
BEA, Banco do Estado de Amazonas S.A.
BEC, Banco do Estado de Ceará S.A.
BEG, Banco do Estado de Goiás S.A.
BEM, Banco do Estado de Maranhão S.A.
BEP, Banco do Estado de Piaui S.A.
BESC, Banco do Estado de Santa Catarina S.A.

Reorganized State Government Banks
Banese, Banco do Estado de Sergipe S.A.
Banestes, Banco do Estado de Espírito Santo S.A.
Banpará, Banco do Estado de Para S.A.
Banrisul Banco do Estado do Rio Grande do Sul S.A.
NCNB, Nossa Caixa Nossa Banco S.A.

State Government Banks outside of Proes
Bandes, Banco de Desenvolvimento de Espírito Santo S.A.
BRB, Banco Regional de Brasília S.A.

2 For a review of central banking, see Alan S. Blinder, *Central Banking in Theory and Practice*, Cambridge: MIT Press, 1998, John. T. Wooley, 'The politics of monetary policy: a critical review', *Journal of Public Policy*, 14 (1994) 57–85, and James Forder, 'Some methodological issues in the statutory characterisation of central banks', *Western European Politics*, 24/1 (2001), 202–16.

3 For an overview of institutionalisms, see: Peter Hall and Rosemary Taylor, 'Political science and the three new institutionalisms', *Political Studies*, 44 (1996), 936–57.

4 Douglas C. North, *Institutions, Institutional Change, and Economic Performance*, Cambridge: Cambridge University Press, 1990; James March and Johan Olsen, 'New institutionalism: organizational factors in political life', *American Political Science Review*, vol. 78 (1984), 724–49; James March and Johan Olson, *Rediscovering Institutions: The Organizational Basis of Politics*, New York: Free Press, 1989. See also: Bert Rockman and Kent Weaver, eds., *Do Institutions Matter?* Washington, DC: Brookings Institution, 1993.

5 For an overview, see: Paul Pierson and Theda Skocpol, 'Historical institutionalism in contemporary political science', in Ira Katznelson et al., eds., *The State of the Discipline*. New York: W.W. Norton, 2002.

6 On the importance of regional and national contexts for the comparative analysis of political institutions, see: Kurt von Mettenheim, ed., *Presidential Institutions and Democratic Politics: Comparing Regional and National Contexts*, Baltimore: Johns Hopkins University Press, 1997 and Rockman and Weaver, op. cit.

7 This distinction between equilibria and origins and trajectories has been widely adopted by political scientists. See: Robert Bates, et al, 'The politics of interpretation: rationality, culture, and transition', *Politics and Society*, 26/4 (1998); Barry Weingast, 'Rational choice institutionalism', in Ira Katznelson et al., eds., *The State of the Discipline*, New York: W.W. Norton, 2002, pp. 660–92; John Carey, 'Parchment, equilibria, and institutions', *Comparative Political Studies*, 33/6–7 (2000), 735–61.

8 Nonetheless, rational choice perspectives have emphasized the equilibria effects of institutions, often citing Riker's argument that institutions tend to provide stability because they solve certain cycles endemic to collective choice processes. See: William Riker, 'Implications from the disequilibrium of majority rule for the study of institutions', *American Political Science Review*, 74 (1980), 432–46.

9 William Riker, op. cit., p. 443.

10 See: Joseph Colomer, 'Disequilibrium institutions and pluralist democracy', *Journal of Theoretical Politics*, 13/ 3 (2001), 235–47.

11 Carey, op. cit., and Randall L. Calvert, 'Rational actors, equilibrium, and social institutions', in Jack Knght and Itai Sened, eds., *Explaining Social Institutions*, Ann Arbor, MI: University of Michigan Press, 1995, pp. 57–93; Gary Miller, 'Rational choice and dysfunctional instutions', *Governance*, 13/4 (2000), 535–47.

12 Carey, op. cit., p. 754.

13 See: Douglas Hibbs, 'Political parties and macroeconomic policy', *American Political Science Review*, 71 (1977), 1467–87; Christopher Way, 'Central banks, partisan politics, and macroeonomic outcomes', *Comparative Political Studies*, 33 (2000), 196–224; Hall and Soskice, op. cit.; Herbert Kitschelt, et al., eds., *Continuity and Change in Contemporary Capitalism*. Cambridge: Cambridge University Press, 1999; Gosta Esping-Anderson, *Three Worlds of Welfare Capitalism*, Princeton, NJ: Princeton University Press, 1990; Evelyn Huber and John Stevens, *Development and Crisis of the Welfare State*, Chicago: University of Chicago Press, 2001; and Paul Pierson, *The New Politics of the Welfare State*, Oxford: University of Oxford Press, 2001.

14 William H. Buiter, 'Two naked emperors? Concern about the stability and growth pact and second thoughts about central bank independence', Institute for Fiscal Studies Annual Lecture, London, 2001, www.nber.org/~wbuiter/ifs.

15 Rudiger Dornbusch, *The Macroeconomics of Populism in Latin America*, Chicago:

University of Chicago Press, 1991; and Carlos G. Langoni, et al., eds., *The Quest for Monetary Stability*, Washington, DC: DA Publishing (FGV), 1996.

16 See: Ronald L. Jepperson, 'The development and application of sociological institutionalism', RSC no. 1001/5, European Forum Series, European University Institute, 2001.

17 Pierson, 2002, op. cit., p. 9.

18 A classic work remains Samuel Huntington, *Political Order in Changing Societies*, New Haven: Yale University Press, 1968. For an overview see: Robert Packenham, *Liberal America and the Third World*, Princeton: Princeton University Press, 1973.

19 Barrington Moore, *The Social Origins of Dictatorship and Democracy*, Boston: Beacon Press, 1966.

20 Theda Skocpol, *States and Social Revolutions*, Cambridge: Cambridge University Press, 1978.

21 Gregory Luebbert, *Liberalism, Fascism, or Social Democracy: Social Classes and the Political Origins of Regimes in Interwar Europe*, New York: Oxford University Press, 1991.

22 Ruth B. Collier and David Collier, *Shaping the Political Arena*, Princeton, NJ: Princeton University Press, 1991.

23 Thelen, op. cit.; James Mahoney and Dieter Reuschemeyer, eds., *Comparative Historical Analysis in the Social Sciences*, Cambridge: Cambridge University Press, 2003; Paul Pierson and Theda Skocpol. 'Historical institutionalism in contemporary political science', in Katznelson and Milner, eds., op. cit., pp. 693–721.

24 On the general problem of central banking in new democracies, see: Laurence Whitehead, ed., *Emerging Market Democracies: East Asia and Latin America*, Baltimore: Johns Hopkins University Press, 2002.

25 See: Alberto Alesina and Nouriel Roubini, with Gerald D. Cohen, *Political Cycles and the Macroeconomy*, Cambridge, MA: MIT Press, 1997.

26 Alex Cukierman, et al., *Measuring Central Bank Independence and its Effect on Policy Outcomes*, San Francisco, CA: ICS Press, 1994; Alex Cukierman and Francesco Lippi, 'Central bank independence, centralization of wage bargaining, inflation, and unemployment: theory and some evidence', *European Economic Review*, 43 (1999), 1395–434; Alex Cukierman, *Central Bank Strategy, Credibility, and Independence*, Cambridge: MIT Press, 1992; and Robert Barro, *Determinants of Economic Growth: A Cross Country Comparison*, Cambridge: Cambridge University Press, 1977.

27 William R. Clark and Mark Hallerberg, 'Mobile capital, domestic institutions, and electorally induced monetary and fiscal policy', *American Political Science Review*, 94 (2000), 323–46; and Geoffrey Garret, *Partisan Politics in the Global Economy*, Cambridge: Cambridge University Press, 1998.

28 Carl Walsh, 'Optimal contracts for central bankers', *American Economic Review*, 85 (1995), 150–68; Kenneth Rogoff, 'The optimal degree of commitment to and intermediate monetary target', *Quarterly Journal of Economics*, 100, November (1985), 1169–90; and Henrik Jensen, 'The credibility of optimal monetary delegation', *American Economic Review*, 87 (1997), 911–20.

29 Juliet Johnson, 'Financial globalization and national sovereignty', paper presented at the Annual Meeting of the American Political Science Association, Boston, September 2002.

30 Leslie E. Armijo, ed., *Debating the Global Financial Architecture*, Albany, NY: SUNY Press, 2002.

31 Estimates from the Fundação Instituto de Pesquisas Economicas da Universidade de São Paulo and DIEESE (Departamento Intersindical de Estatistica e Estudos Socioeconomicos) reported in *Folha de São Paulo*, 26 March 1995, Section 2, p. 5.

32 Luiz C. Bresser Pereira and Yoshiaki Nakano, *The Theory of Inertial Inflation*, Boulder, CO: Lynne Rienner, 1987.

33 On what Brazilian scholars have described as an inflationary coalition during the 1980s, see: Lourdes Sola, ed., *Estado, mercado e democracia: política e economia comparadas*,

São Paulo: Paz e Terra, 1993.

34 See trajectories of laws EM/MF 89 of 7 March (1995) and EM/MF 311 of 23 August (1995).

35 For a more balanced discussion, see: Gerard Caprio, et al., eds., *The Future of State-Owned Financial Institutions: Policy and Practice*, Washington, DC: Brookings Institution Press, 2005.

36 Central Bank of Brazil reports data on the Basel index of government, domestic private, and foreign banks operating in the country since 2001. During the four semesters measured by Central Bank risk analysts, domestic and government banks consistently rank better on Basel index than foreign banks. See: Central Bank of Brazil, *Financial Stability Report, 2003*, Brasília: Brazilian Government Publications.

37 On state government bank privatizations, see: Harry M. Makler, 'Bank transformation and privatisation in Brazil: financial federalism and some lessons about bank privatization', *The Quarterly Review of Economics and Finance*, 40/1 (2000); and Sérgio Werlang and Armínio Fraga, 'Os bancos estadiais e o descontrole fiscal: alguns aspectos', *Revista Brasileira de Economia*, 49/2 (1995), 165–75.

38 Rafael La Porta, Florencio Lopez-de-Silanes and Andrei Shleifer, 'Government ownership of banks', National Bureau of Economics Research Working Paper No. 7620, 2000; Andrei Schleifer and Robert W. Vishny, *The Grabbing Hand: Government Pathologies and Their Cures*, Cambridge, MA: Harvard University Press, 1999.

39 On the cost of banking crises, see: Liliana Rojas-Suarez and Steven Weisbrod, *Banking Crises in Latin America: Experience and Issues*, Washington, DC: Inter-American Development Bank, 1995.

41 Carole Pateman, 'Freedom and democratization: why basic income is to be preferred to basic capital', in Kieth Dowding, et al., eds., *The Ethics of Stakeholding*, London: Palgrove, 2002; Brian Barry, 'Real freedom and basic income', *The Journal of Political Philosophy*, 4 (1996), 242–76. On Brazilian programs, see: Eduardo M. Suplicy, 'Renda básica: a resposta está sendo soprado pelo vento', *Brazilian Journal of Political Economy*, 23, 2/90, 47–62.

42 Bruce A. Ackerman and Anne Alstott, *The Stakeholder Society*, New Haven, CT and London: Yale University Press.

43 Carole Pateman, 'Democratizing citizenship: some advantages of basic income', in Erik O. Wright, ed., *Redesigning Distribution*, London: Verso, forthcoming, 2005.

Postscript

Laurence Whitehead and Lourdes Sola

THIS BOOK GOES to press in October 2005, at a time when the Brazilian economy is undergoing a vigorous recovery from the financial crisis of 2002, and after Luiz Inácio Lula da Silva's Workers' Party (PT) administration has enjoyed a powerful three year rerating of private investor confidence. The government's macro-economic policies have been surprisingly orthodox, and it has succeeded in introducing a significant number of legislative reforms that are viewed as 'market-friendly'. But at the time of writing the Lula administration is rocked by scandals initiated by the alleged bribery of congressmen belonging to junior partners of the PT led coalition. There is increasing evidence that members of the government kitchen cabinet, (who had been the architects of the PT's successful electoral strategy in 2002), played a leading role in building up an extensive network of party and business interests that obtained huge transfers from state enterprises, public banks and pension funds. As the three congressional committees of enquiry have discovered as they pursued their investigations, the scale of the emerging corruption has proved much greater than initially anticipated. It includes fiscal evasion, money laundering, illegal remittances by PT governed municipalities, and widespread collusion between public enterprises and private sector-firms and small banks.

Although the political fallout has become increasingly severe, so far financial markets have reacted calmly. This will prove a major inflexion point in terms of the electoral prospects for 2006 and of the worsening conditions of governance for the next months. The risks are high, on both fronts, but not so much because the members of the ruling party (who are urging a return to more traditional left-wing policies) are likely to gain the upper hand. At most it seems they may be able to split the PT – but only in that event are they likely to be relegated to the opposition. It is more that the current crisis underscores the risks associated with a break in market confidence. This could arise if guidelines of economic policies were to change dramatically or if a populist candidate becomes competitive, although neither of these outcomes is currently rated as probable. For now most analysts anticipate a continuation of favourable economic trends during 2005. However, the re-election of Lula da Silva for a second term in 2006 – a prospect viewed as probable only three months ago – is now considered a less viable electoral outcome by most political analysts. Polls continue to show that candidates are increasingly competitive from the opposition parties (in particular the PSDB) that are traditionally committed to responsible macroeconomic policies and market friendly reforms. Among the reforms in place for this year is a new bankruptcy law that will make it easier for creditors to secure their claims against insolvent debtors. But there is no longer any early prospect of a law to reinforce the autonomy of the Central Bank of Brazil. The Lula administration had already lost the initiative in this area (with its loss of control in Congress at the beginning of 2005) before this scandal broke.

Inevitably, therefore, market sentiment is also subject to countercurrents and areas of anxiety. According to some critics, macroeconomic orthodoxy is offset by countervailing tendencies to favour interventionism and overregulation in sectoral markets. A more diffuse anxiety reflects the fear that – as in the past – the current cyclical upsurge may once again presage a further shock and abrupt reversal, perhaps occasioned by a setback to the Chinese economy (from which so much stimulus has been derived over the past couple of years), or by renewed turbulence in world financial markets (given the growing imbalances in the United States economy). On the domestic side, however, inflationary tendencies have been curbed, thanks to the rigid inflation target practised by the Central Bank – a trend reinforced by the perhaps excessive strength of the Brazilian real against the US dollar. Concern with inflation in 2004 explains why the Central Bank had embarked on a new round of tightening of interest rates that remain extraordinarily high in real terms, among the highest in the world. This trend will be reversed as inflationary pressures are choked back, but only in the last quarter of this year and then very slowly, despite the effectiveness of the monetary policy.

Issues concerning the legal and political accountability of Central Bank directors are yet to be fully resolved in Brazil, as in other emerging market democracies. Thus, at the beginning of the current year accusations of tax evasion forced the resignation of one member of the monetary policy committee; as only the supreme court can consider lawsuits against cabinet ministers, Lula da Silva's administration was prompted to extend 'cabinet status' to all Central Bank presidents as the 1988 constitution shelters the incumbent Central Bank president from legal challenge.

At a more structural level, some influential Brazilian policymakers have singled out 'jurisdictional uncertainty' as a possible distinguishing feature explaining why anything more than the most short-term voluntary lending in domestic currency remains unavailable even to the highest quality of borrowers (including the federal government). They argue that this exceptional deficit in the structure of Brazilian financial intermediation renders monetary policy unusually ineffective, misallocates domestic investment, distorts the tax system, and renders the country excessively dependent on volatile international capital markets. Although they can envisage a theoretically preferable market-clearing alternative financial system, they recognize that there is no simple and safe path from the present structure to their desired substitute.[1] This analysis is not consensual, however. Other influential policymakers, who played a leading role in the stabilization effort of 1993–94 and in initiating market-friendly reforms, point to another source of anxiety. They claim that the Central Bank's inflexible commitment to a given (too low) inflation target, set for a definite (too short) time span has underestimated the fiscal damage and the reduction of investment incentives arising from the consequent imposition of a prolonged exposure to unnecessarily and exceptionally high real short-term interest rates. These critics of rigid inflation targeting are not to be confused with the traditional economic populists who still populate the political scene, but who lack much prospect of exercising sustained economic influence. They accept the need for severe monetary tightening to cope with inflationary shocks (such as the 1999 devaluation). But they argue that in current circumstances, with a much improved balance of payments point (including a trade surplus and a rising inflow of foreign direct investment), together with a substantial fall in the ratio of government debt to GDP (from a high of 63 percent to a more manageable 51 percent) such extreme monetary restraint inflicts unnecessary losses on the real economy. A more gradualist strategy of disinflation could therefore stabilize monetary expectations without crippling essential investment and thereby storing up future bottlenecks to sustained growth. There is perhaps a parallel here with Alan Greenspan's recent resistance to the idea of rigid inflation targeting at the US Federal Reserve. "Discretion" may sometimes be needed to supplement "rules" when navigating through an unpredictable and globalized financial system.[2]

There is an evident political undercurrent to these two criticisms of Brazil's current monetary policy. The jurisdictional uncertainty argument points towards the need for further pro-market reforms, whereas the call for more gradualism in the monetary field attracts the support of state interventionists. But at the technical level these two criticisms are far from being straight alternatives. To the contrary, it could perfectly well be argued that excessive rigidity in monetary policy is in part both a reaction to jurisdictional uncertainty and also in part a cause of damage to the 'real' side of the economy that in turn tends to generate further jurisdictional uncertainty.

Both these political anxieties and these technical disagreements reinforce the judgement that Brazil remains some way distant from the consolidation of an institutionally stable and intellectually consensual system of monetary authority. It would certainly be premature to assume that the country has yet got securely on track to 'lock in' financial stability with an autonomous and depoliticized central bank guaranteeing conventional technical management in terms convergent with liberal market-centred bank systems abroad. From the standpoint of this volume, the cumulative institutional reforms of the past decade still leave much scope for further experimentation, and for a range of non-standard outcomes. Three points, in particular, are worth underlining here: 1) the persistence of significant further risks of financial instability derived from Brazil's location in a far from stable international monetary order; 2) the significance of Brazil's experience for other emerging market democracies – not so much as a 'deviant case', but rather as an illuminating and relevant experiment in 'statecrafting', and 3) the vital need for analysis and policy prescription in such cases to be grounded in a contextual analyses of feasible routes to more robust and effective monetary institutions, not just abstract deductions from idealized (and perhaps unattainable) end-states.

On the first point, in November 2004, Kenneth Rogoff, a former head of research at the International Monetary Fund (IMF), stated publicly that it was "time to think about the next debt crisis". He began by observing that over the past two centuries, "Turkey has defaulted six times, Brazil seven times, Mexico eight times, and Venezuela nine times". Rogoff noted that some argue "[h]aving more flexible exchange rate systems, combined with improved policies – notably in Brazil and Turkey – insulated the world against a replay of the global debt crises of the past twenty years". In response, Rogoff acknowledges that this is a possibility, but pointed out that "it is surprisingly easy to think of five or six solid reasons why problems could arise over the next few years". These are the usual reasons – high public debt, volatile commodity prices, rising international interest rates, a possible abrupt fall in United States demand for imports, and the 'shock' effects of some catastrophic event such as a major terrorist event.[3] With similar reasoning, the International Development Bank's (IDB) 2005 report on economic and social progress in Latin America reviewed all banking crises around the world between 1974 and 2003:

> Compared with other regions, Latin America ranks highest in terms of the average number of crises per country, as well as for the recurrence of banking crises ... In Latin America, 35 per cent of countries have experienced recurrent crises, almost three times higher than in any other region. These results are striking and indicative of how much remains to be done to achieve banking stability in the region. This pattern of recurrent banking crises is particularly worrisome because ... on average fiscal costs have been greater then 20 per cent of GDP for Latin American countries, and about a third more than the average for other emerging markets.[4]

Indeed the same report also estimated that "entering a financial crises reduces annual long-term growth by approximately one percentage point, indicating that these episodes can be traumatic in the longer term as well".[5]

On the second point, both of the above quoted sources bracket Brazil with other emerging market democracies, rather than treating the country as unique, or even a statistical outlier. In fact a paired comparison of monetary instability would probably show that, even now, Brazil is somewhat more stable than Turkey, despite the Central Bank of the Republic of Turkey and its monetary authorities having been made formally independent following a major banking scandal in 2003. With Turkish inflation not yet quite down to single digits (which it has not been since 1972) and with interest rates lower than Brazil's, the discipline of the IMF's latest stand-by agreement with Turkey may pull the emerging democracy towards convergence with standard international market practices.[6] Turning to Latin America, according to the latest "effective creditor rights" index published by the IDB, Brazil ranks well ahead of the regional average, and far ahead of both Mexico and Argentina.[7] The fiscal cost of the 1994–96 bank rescue episode was the third lowest of the thirteen episodes studied by the IDB.[8] As discussed above in Chapter 6, between 1995 and 1999 an *ex-ante* safety net was introduced which strengthened the banking system at a reasonable cost, thereby enabling Brazil to absorb the shocks of 1999 and 2002 with less disruption than in the other Latin American and east Asian emerging markets. The financial dollarization that so preoccupies the IDB in chapter four of its latest report does not represent the same dangers in Brazil where severe restrictions on onshore dollar deposits mean that in 2001 its banking system was by far the least dollarized of all the fourteen Latin American republics under consideration.[9] This underscores our twin arguments that incrementalism can pay off, and that context specific analysis is crucial.

As discussed in Chapter 10 of this volume, Brazil has a strong tradition of reliance on state banking, institutions that fell out of favour with the Washington-based custodians of financial orthodoxy in the 1990s. But chapter 11 of the IDB report finds that existing evidence on the negative role of state-owned banks is "not as strong as previously thought" and it is even possible that public banks "do not amplify" but, if anything, "smooth", credit cycles.[10] In summary, although Brazil's institutional choices in the banking sector undoubtedly involve severe trade-offs, and contain significant risks, it is far from clear that they are less appropriate, or more destabilizing, than the arrangements now prevalent in most other emerging market democracies. There are constructive lessons to be learnt (in both directions) by comparing Brazil's trajectory of financial institution-building with that of its neighbours. Instead of imposing a single 'one size fits all' orthodox blueprint it may be more realistic, and less socially costly, to encourage intelligent and open-minded 'statecrafting' an area of activity where Brazil has much to teach as well as to learn.

Finally, therefore, the third observation concerns the benefits of situating policy recommendations in a country-specific and historically grounded context. This may be especially important for large, proud, and autonomous democracies (such as those of Brazil, India and South Africa) which have no realistic prospect of submerging themselves in over-arching regional integration projects such as the Eurozone. In such contexts reformers need to start from what already exists in workable form, and to pay close attention to path dependence and the interaction of the various possible components of reform in a financial system. It is significant that even the Brazilian analysts who are most dissatisfied with their country's existing monetary inheritance end on a note of caution:

> It is easy to think of scenarios in which the unwinding of policies may backfire ... Jurisdictional uncertainty has deep institutional roots in the executive, the legislative, and the judiciary branches of the state. If property rights were to be violated in the process of dismantling these distortions, for instance, it would be very hard to convince agents that the problem of jurisdictional uncertainty is being tackled appropriately. In particular, a big bang approach could be dangerous. As jurisdictional uncertainty is the result of history, restoring confidence in the jurisdiction is perforce a long road ... it seems that a step-by-step approach, with well-defined criteria for moving from one state to the next, is the best way to go.[11]

In our parlance, this is the case for statecrafting. Within this framework it is not self-evident that the granting of full and formal autonomy to the Central Bank of Brazil is necessarily the best next step.[12] If the co-operation of Congress and the political parties may be required in order to redress an existing bias against creditors; if the post-1999 exchange rate regime (inflation targeting and 'dirty' floating) remains in place and dollarization is not permitted in the domestic market; if external shocks are still capable of precipitating monetary and fiscal crises; if income, asset, and regional inequalities remain at the threshold of social tolerance; and if a new democracy requires reassurance that the public can exercise some influence over previous bastions of authoritarian privilege; then there could be higher priorities for reform than the establishment of a central bank narrowly focused on the achievement of only one low inflation goal. After all, somewhere in the emerging institutional structure it will be necessary for policymakers to coordinate monetary and fiscal policy; to improve bank supervision (including the oversight of state banks); and to determine exchange rate policy as well as to set interest rates. A professional, responsible and credible central bank is certainly an integral part of such a system, and Brazil has already made substantial progress in that direction. Is such progress more likely to be reinforced, or jeopardized, by legally enshrining one rigid set of obligations, (and thus exempting the Central Bank from other functions it has hitherto been accustomed to performing)? The answer depends not just on the content of this one reform measure, viewed in isolation, but on how it will interact with other equally critical reforms in related areas.

The latest IDB report aims to promote deep and stable bank lending without excessive dependence on foreign currency, through appropriate policy reforms. In principle, such policies include the introduction of credible central bank independence and monetary regimes aimed at stabilizing inflation, for example through inflation targeting. However, even if this were the right way to go, it may be difficult for countries to credibly maintain such policies given the magnitude of capital account reversals and the effects of sudden stops. These events may force countries to abandon inflation pegs or to endogenize monetary policy, either because of fiscal dominance when governments go bankrupt or because of banking system "bailouts".[13] Faced with such problems, emerging market democracies need to craft monetary institutional arrangements that are both responsible and flexible. It is no easy task simultaneously 1) to build *and* 2) to retain *and* 3) to generate financial market credibility, while also retaining the discretionality required to cope with systemic risks, and generating the political legitimacy required for democratic consent. Even long-established democracies struggle to strike the right balance here, as demonstrated by the current crisis in Italy. The emergence that the governor of the Banca d'Italia (Italy's central bank) is legally unmovable, even when exposed to public embarrassment, and also that the privatization of the country's state banks has turned them into majority shareholders in the entity supposed to regulate them, confirms that it is not only developing countries that can face problems of legitimation in the area of monetary authority. The European Central Bank is also not immune to such questioning.[14] So, as the Brazilians attempt to statecraft their own monetary authority, they should be guided by pragmatism and a realistic attention to their specific national realities rather than by institutional dogma or market fundamentalism.

Notes

1 Persio Arida, Edmar Lisboa Bacha and André Lara-Resende, 'Credit, interest, and jurisdictional uncertainty: conjectures on the case of Brazil', in F. Giavazzi and I. Goldfajn, eds., *Inflation Targeting and Debt: The Case of Brazil*, Cambridge, MA: MIT Press, forthcoming.
2 Andrew Balls, 'Greenspan's record: an activist unafraid to depart from the rules', *Financial Times* (London), 22 August 2005.
3 'Kenneth S. Rogoff argues that while it may be too soon to be overly worried about debt crisis, problems could arise', *The Banker*, 1 November 2004.
4 International Development Bank (IDB), *Unlocking Credit: The Quest for Deep and Stable Bank Lending*, Washington: Johns Hopkins University Press, 2004, p. 30.
5 Ibid, p. 32.
6 In December 2004 the Central Bank of the Republic of Turkey cut its overnight interest rate to 18 percent, while Brazil raised the SELIC to 17¾ percent. In January 2005 six zeros was cut off the Turkish lira, and the Turkish Monetary Policy Committee started to meet regularly to set interest rates. Inflation targeting will be formally introduced in 2006.
7 *Unlocking Credit*, op. cit., p. 24.
8 Ibid., p. 31.
9 Ibid., Table 4.5, p. 52. In 2001 only about 10 percent of Brazil's total bank deposits were in dollars, all offshore.
10 Ibid, pp. 21–2.
11 "Credits, interest, and jurisdictional uncertainty", op. cit., final remarks.
12 The Bank of England was granted full independence in 1997 and this is often regarded as a precedent for others. But the task of strengthening monetary authority in Britain is only indirectly relevant to the tasks faced in Brazil. In any case, it should be recalled that as a counterpart to the granting of independence, the Bank was stripped of its responsibilities of banking supervision (some regard this as a delayed reaction to its failure over the BCCI affair). And also, the British move was a reaction to the country's humiliating 1992 departure from the European Exchange Rate Mechanism (ERM) and must be seen in the context of Britain's reluctance to subordinate its monetary policy to the new European Central Bank. Brazilian policy makers should take this context into account before concluding that what seems to have worked in Britain must also be best for Brazil. Nor should they assume that there is only one 'best practice' model of central banking that applies throughout all time and space. There has certainly been an international process of convergence around some core principles, but this falls well short of one size fits all. See, for example, Laurence Whitehead 'Models of central banking: how much convergence in neo-democracies?', paper presented at the IPSA Conference, Durban, South Africa, July 2003.
13 *Unlocking Credit*, op. cit., p. 47.
14 See, for example, Jeffrey Kishor Kulkarni, 'Central bank independence as ideology: disinflation, dissimulation and labour market deregulation', DPhil in Politics, University of Oxford University, 2005. As further examples, the Swiss electorate is grappling with the question of how to allocate the proceeds of gold sales from its central bank; while the Bank of England is simulating crisis management strategies to cope with a possible terrorist attack on the City of London.

Bibliography

Abreu, Marcelo P., ed. (1990). *Ordem do progresso: cem anos de política econômica republicana, 1889–1989.* Rio de Janeiro: Campus

Ackerman, Bruce and Anne Alstott (1999), *The Stakeholder Society.* New Haven, CT: Yale University Press

Aghion, Philippe et al. (2000). 'A simple model of monetary policy and currency crises', *European Economic Review*, Vol. 44, pp. 728–38

Alesina, Alberto (1988). 'Macroeconomics and politics', in Stanley Fischer, ed., *NBER Macroeconomics Annual.* Chicago, IL: University of Chicago Press

Alesina, Alberto and Allan Drazen (1991). 'Why are stabilizations delayed?', *American Economic Review*, Vol. 81, no. 5, December, pp. 1170–88

Alesina, Alberto and Lawrence Summers (1993). 'Central bank independence and macro-economic performance: some comparative evidence', *Journal of Money, Credit, and Banking*, Vol. 25, no. 2

Alesina, Alberto et al. (1997). *Political Cycles and the Macroeconomy.* Cambridge, MA: MIT Press

Alexander, Gerard (2001). 'Institutions, path dependence, and democratic consolidation', *Journal of Theoretical Politics*, Vol. 13, no. 3, pp. 240–70

Amann, Edmund and Werner Baer (2000). 'The illusion of stability: the Brazilian economy under Cardoso', *World Development*, Vol. 28, no. 10, pp. 1805–19

Ames, Barry (1987). *Political Survival: Politicians and Public Policy in Latin America.* Berkeley: University of California Press

Ames, Barry (2001). *The Deadlock of Democracy in Brazil.* Ann Arbor, MI: University of Michigan Press

Andrews, David (1994). 'Capital mobility and state autonomy: toward a structural theory of international monetary relations', *International Studies Quarterly*, Vol. 38, no. 2, pp. 193–218

Armijo, Leslie E. (1996). 'Inflation and insouciance: the peculiar Brazilian game', *Latin American Research Review*, Vol. 31, no. 3, pp. 7–46

Armijo, Leslie E., ed. (2002). *Debating the Global Financial Architecture.* Albany, NY: SUNY Press

Baer, Mônica (1986). *A internacionalização financeira no Brasil.* Petrópolis, Vozes

Baer, Werner (1991). 'Social aspects of Latin American inflation', *Quarterly Review of Economics and Finance*, Vol. 31, no. 3, pp. 45–57

Baer, Werner (1995). *The Brazilian Economy: Growth and Development*, 4th edn., New York: Praeger

Baer, Werner and Paul Beckerman (1980). 'The trouble with index-linking: reflections on the Brazilian experience', *World Development*, Vol. 8, no. 9

Barro, Robert (1977). *Determinants of Economic Growth: A Cross Country Comparison.* Cambridge: Cambridge University Press

Barro, Robert and David B. Gordon (1983). 'Rules, discretion, and reputation in a model of monetary policy', *Journal of Monetary Economics*, Vol. 12, no. 1

Barros, Ricardo P. et al. (1996). 'Pobreza e inflação no Brasil: uma análise agregada', in IPEA (Instituto de Pesquisa Econômica Aplicada), ed., *A economia brasileira em perspectiva – 1996*, Vol. 2, Rio de Janeiro: IPEA, pp. 401–20

Barry, Brian (1996). 'Real freedom and basic income', *The Journal of Political Philosophy*, Vol. 4, pp. 242–76

Bates, Robert H. (1989). *Beyond the Miracle of the Market: The Political Economy of Agrarian Development in Kenya.* Cambridge: Cambridge University Press

Berger, Suzanne and Ronald Dore, eds. (1996). *National Diversity and Global Capitalism.* Ithaca, NY: Cornell University Press

Bernhard, William (1998). 'A political explanation of variations in central bank independence', *American Political Science Review*, Vol. 92, no. 2

Bernhard, William and David Leblang (1999). 'Democratic institutions and exchange rate commitments', *International Organization*, Vol. 51, no. 1

Bernhard, William et al. (2002). 'The political economy of monetary institutions', *International Organization*, Vol. 56, no. 4

Blinder, Alan S. (1998). *Central banking in theory and practice.* Cambridge, MA: MIT Press

Block, Steven A. and Paul M. Vaaler (2004) 'The price of democracy: sovereign risk ratings, bond spreads and political business cycles in developing countries', *Journal of International Money and Finance*, 23/6

Boylan, Delia, M. (2001). *Defusing Democracy: Central Bank Autonomy and the Transition from Authoritarian Rule.* Ann Arbor, MI: Michigan University Press

Bresser-Pereira, Luiz C. (1984). *Development and Crisis in Brazil, 1930–1983.* Boulder, CO: Westview Press

Bresser-Pereira, Luiz C. (1996). *Economic Crisis and Reform of the State.* Boulder, CO: Lynne Rienner

Bresser-Pereira, Luiz C. and Yoshiaki Nakano (1987). *The Theory of Inertial Inflation.* Boulder, CO: Lynne Rienner

Buiter, William H. (2001). 'Two naked emperors? Concern about the stability and growth pact and second thoughts about central bank independence', Institute for Fiscal Studies Annual Lecture, available at: http://www.nber.org/~wbuiter/ifs

Bulhões, Octávio G. (1990). 'Depoimento. Programa de história oral', CPDOC/FGV, Editora FGV, Rio de Janeiro

Calogeras, J.G. (1910). *La politique monétaire du Brésil.* Rio de Janeiro: Editora Nacional

Calvert, Randall L. (1995). 'Rational actors, equilibrium, and social institutions', in Jack Knight and Itai Sened, eds., *Explaining Social Institutions.* Ann Arbor, MI: University of Michigan Press, pp. 57–93

Campos, Roberto (1997). *A lanterna na popa – Memórias.* Ed. Topbooks, Rio de Janeiro

Capie, Forrest et al. (1994). *The Future of Central Banking*. Cambridge: Cambridge University Press

Caprio, Gerard et al., eds. (2005). *The Future of State-Owned Financial Institutions: Policy and Practice*. Washington, DC: Brookings Institution Press

Cardoso, Eliana (2000). 'Brazil's currency crisis: the shift from an exchange rate anchor to a flexible regime', in Carol Wise and Riordan Roett, eds., *Exchange Rate Policies in Latin America*. Washington, DC: Brookings Institution

Cardoso, Fernando H. (1979). 'On the characterization of authoritarian regimes in Latin America', in David Collier, ed., *The New Authoritarianism in Latin America*. Princeton, NJ: Princeton University Press

Carneiro Netto, Dioníso D. and Armínio Fraga Neto (1984). 'Variáveis de credito e endoginidade da oferta de moeda no Brasil', *Pesquisa e Planejamento Econômico*, Vol. 14, no. 1

Carneiro Netto, Dionísio D. et al. (1993). 'Strengthening the financial sector in the Brazilian economy', Discussion Paper, PUC-RJ Economics Department, no. 307

Clark, William R. (2003). *Capitalism, not Globalism: Capital Mobility, Central Bank Independence and the Political Control of the Economy*. Ann Arbor, MI: University of Michigan Press

Clark, William R. and Mark Hallerberg (2000). 'Mobile capital, domestic institutions, and electorally induced monetary and fiscal policy', *American Political Science Review*, Vol. 94, pp. 323–46

Clemens, Elizabeth and James Cook (1999). 'Politics and institutionalism: explaining durability and change', *Annual Review of Sociology*, Vol. 25, pp. 441–66

Cohen, Benjamin (1996). 'Phoenix risen: the resurrection of global finance', *World Politics*, Vol. 48

Cohen, Benjamin (1998). *The Geography of Money*. Ithaca, NY: Cornell University Press

Collier, Ruth B. and David Collier (1991). *Shaping the Political Arena: Critical Junctures, the Labor Movement, and Regime Dynamics in Latin America*. Princeton, NJ: Princeton University Press

Colomer, Joseph (2001). 'Disequilibrium institutions and pluralist democracy', *Journal of Theoretical Politics*, Vol. 13, no. 3, pp. 235–47

Cuckierman, Alex. (1992). *Central Bank Strategy, Credibility, and Independence*. Cambridge, MA: MIT Press

Cuckierman, Alex and Francesco Lippi (1999). 'Central bank independence, centralization of wage bargaining, inflation, and unemployment: theory and some evidence', *European Economic Review*, Vol. 43, pp. 1395–434

Dahl, Robert (1971). *Polyarchy*. New Haven, CT: Yale University Press

Dornbusch, Rudiger, ed. (1991). *The Macroeconomics of Populism in Latin America*. Chicago, IL: University of Chicago Press

Dornbusch, Rudiger (1997). 'Brazil's incomplete stabilization and reform', *Brookings Papers on Economic Activity*, no. 1

Dornbusch, Rudiger and Alejandro Reynoso (1989). 'Fatores financeiros do desenvolvimento econômico', *Revista Brasileira de Economia*, Vol. 43, no. 4

Easterly, William and Stanley Fischer (1999). 'Inflation and the poor', Paper presented to the World Bank Conference on Development and the Poor

Edwards, Sabastian, ed. (2000). *Capital Flows and the Emerging Economies: Theory, Evidence, and Controversies*. Chicago, IL: University of Chicago Press

Eichengreen, Barry (1992). *Golden Fetters: The Gold Standard and the Great Depression, 1918–1939.* Oxford: Oxford University Press

Eichengreen, Barry (1998). *Globalizing Capital: A History of the International Monetary System.* Princeton, NJ: Princeton University Press

Eichengreen, Barry (2002) 'Predicting and preventing financial crises: where do we stand? What have we learned?', University of California at Berkeley, prepared for the Kiel Week Annual Conference, Germany 24–25, available at elsa.berkeley.edu/users/eichengr/website.htm

Fischer, Stanley (1986). *Indexing, Inflation, and Economic Policy.* Cambridge, MA: MIT Press

Fishlow, Albert (1973). 'Some reflections on post-1964 Brazilian economic policy', in A. Stepan, ed., *Authoritarian Brazil: Origins, Policies, and Future.* New Haven, CT: Yale University Press

Ford, A.G. (1962). *The Gold Standard, 1880–1914, Britain and Argentina.* Oxford: Oxford University Press

Forder, James (1998). 'Central bank independence – conceptual clarifications and interim assessment', Oxford Economic Papers, no. 50, pp. 307–34

Forder, James (2001). 'Some methodological issues in the statutory characterisation of central banks', *Western European Politics*, Vol. 24, no. 1, pp. 202–16

França, Paulo (1986). 'A "conta-movimento" entre o Banco Central e o Banco do Brasil', *Conjuntura Econômica*, Vol. 40, no. 3

Franco, Gustavo (2000). *O desafio brasileiro: ensaios sobre desenvolvimento, globalização e moeda.* São Paulo: Editora 34

Franzese, Robert Jr. (1999). 'Partially independent central banks, politically responsive governments, and inflation', *American Journal of Political Science*, Vol. 43, no. 3

Freeman, John, M. (2002). 'Competing commitments: technocracy and democracy in the design of monetary institutions', *International Organization*, Vol. 56, no. 4

Friedman, Jeffrey (1991). 'Invested interests: the politics of national economic policies in a world of global finance', *International Organization*, Vol. 45, no. 4, pp. 524–41

Friedman, Milton, ed. (1956). *Studies in the Quantity Theory of Money.* Chicago, IL: University of Chicago Press

Fry, Maxwell J. (1998). *Money, Interest, and Banking in Economic Development.* Baltimore, MD: Johns Hopkins University Press

Furtado, Celso (1959). *The Economic Growth of Brazil: A Survey from Colonial to Modern Times.* Berkeley, CA: University of California Press

Garrett, Geoffrey (1998). *Partisan Politics in the Global Economy.* Cambridge: Cambridge University Press

Gasiorowski, Mark J. (2000). 'Democracy and macroeconomic performance in under-developed countries: an empirical analysis', *Comparative Political Studies*, Vol. 33, no. 3, pp. 319–49

Geddes, Barbara (1994). *The Politicians' Dilemma: Reforming the State in Latin America.* Berkeley, CA: University of California Press

Gerschenkron, Alexander (1962). *Economic Backwardness in Historical Perspective.* Cambridge, MA: Harvard University Press

Goertzel, Ted (1999). *Fernando Henrique Cardoso: Reinventing Democracy in Brazil.* Boulder, CO: Lynne Rienner

Goldsmith, Raymond (1969). *Financial Structure and Development*. New Haven, CT: Yale University Press

Goodman, John B. (1992). *Monetary Sovereignty: The Politics of Central Banking in Western Europe*. Ithaca, NY: Cornell University Press

Gourevitch, Peter (1993). 'Democracy and economic policy: elective affinities and circumstantial conjunctures', *World Development*, Vol. 21, no. 8, pp. 1271–81

Gouvêa, Gilda P. (1994). *Burocracia e elites burocráticas no Brasil*. São Paulo: Ed. Paulicéia

Grilli, Vittorio et al. (1991). 'Political and monetary institutions and public financial policies in the industrial countries', *Economic Policy*, Vol. 13, pp. 341–92

Gudin, Eugênio (1956). *Inflação, crédito e desenvolvimento*. Rio de Janeiro: Agir

Gudin, Eugênio (1956). *Princípios de economia monetária*. Rio de Janeiro: Civilização Brasileira

Haddad, Claudio (1978). *Crescimento do produto real no Brasil, 1900–1947*. Rio de Janeiro, Fundação Getulio Vargas

Haddad, Claudio (1982). *As operações com títulos públicos federais e a execução da política monetária*. São Paulo: Adeval

Haggard, Stephan et al., eds. (1993). *The Politics of Finance in Developing Countries*. Ithaca, NY: Cornell University Press

Haggard, Stephan and Robert Kaufman (1995). *The Political Economy of Democratic Transitions*. Princeton, NJ: Princeton University Press

Hagopian, Frances (1996). *Traditional Politics and Regime Change in Brazil*. Cambridge: Cambridge University Press

Hall, Peter and Rosemary Taylor (1996). 'Political science and the three new institutionalisms', *Political Studies*, Vol. 44, pp. 936–57

Hall, Peter and David Soskice, eds. (2001). *Varieties of Capitalism: The Institutional Foundations of Comparative Advantage*. Oxford: Oxford University Press

Hall, Rodney B. (2003). 'The discursive demolition of the Asian development model', *International Studies Quarterly*, Vol. 47, no. 1

Hellman, Thomas et al. (2000). 'Liberalization, moral hazard in banking, and prudential regulation: are capital requirements enough?' *American Economic Review*, Vol. 90, no. 1, pp. 147–64

Hibbs, Douglas (1977). 'Political parties and macroeconomic policy', *American Political Science Review*, Vol. 71, pp. 1467–87

Hirschman, Albert O. (1961). 'Ideologies of development in Latin America', in *Latin American Issues: Essays and Comments*. New York: The Twentieth Century Fund

Hirschman, Albert O. (1981). 'The social and political matrix of inflation: elaborations on the Latin American experience', in A.O. Hirschman, *Essays in Trespassing: Economics to Politics and Beyond*. Cambridge: Cambridge University Press

Holt, Robert and John E. Turner (1966). *The Political Bases of Economic Development: An Exploration in Comparative Political Analysis*. Princeton, NJ: D Van Nostrand

Huntington, Samuel (1968). *Political Order in Changing Societies*. New Haven, CT: Yale University Press

Iverson, Torben et al., eds. (2000). *Unions, Employers, and Central Banks: Macroeconomic Coordination and Institutional Change in Social Market Economies*. Cambridge: Cambridge University Press

Jenkins, Rob (1999). *Democratic Politics and Economic Reform in India.* Cambridge: Cambridge University Press

Jensen, Henrik (1997). 'The Credibility of Optimal Monetary Delegation', *American Economic Review*, Vol. 87, pp. 911–20

Johnson, Juliet (2002). 'Financial globalization and national sovereignty', Paper presented at the Annual Meeting of the American Political Science Association, Boston

Kahler, Miles, ed. (1998). *Capital Flows and Financial Crises.* Ithaca, NY: Cornell University Press

Kearney, Christine A. (2001). 'The comparative influence of neoliberal Ideas: economic culture and stabilization in Brazil', PhD dissertation, Brown University, Department of Political Science

Kindleberger, Charles (1978). *Manias, Panics, and Crashes: A History of Financial Crises.* New York: Basic Books

Kirschner, Jonathan (1995). *Currency and Coercion.* Princeton, NJ: Princeton University Press

Kitschelt, Herbert et al., eds. (1999). *Continuity and Change in Contemporary Capitalism.* Cambridge: Cambridge University Press

Kreps, David (1990). *A Course in Microeconomic Theory.* New York: Harvester-Wheatsheaf

Kydland, Finn E. and Edward C. Prescott (1977). 'Rules rather than discretion: the inconsistency of optional plans', *Journal of Political Economy*, Vol. 85, no. 3

La Porta, Rafael et al. (2000). 'Government ownership of banks', National Bureau of Economics Research Working Paper Nº 7620

Langoni, Carlos G. et al., eds. (1996). *The Quest for Monetary Stability.* Washington, DC: DA Publishing and Fundação Getulio Vargas

Leblang, David (1999). 'Democratic political institutions and exchange rate commitments in the developing world', *International Studies Quarterly*, Vol. 43, no. 4

Lees, Francis A. et al. (1990). *Banking and Financial Deepening in Brazil.* New York: MacMillan

Leff, Nathaniel H. (1968). *Economic Policy Making and Development in Brazil, 1947–1964.* New York: Wiley

Lessa, Carlos (1963). *Quinze anos de política econômica*, mimeo (Rio de Janeiro: Centro de Desenvolvimento Econômico, CEPAL/BNDE)

Lindblom, Charles E. (1959). 'The science of muddling through', *Public Administration Review*, Vol. 19, no. 2

Lohmann, Susanne (1992) 'Optional commitment in monetary policy: credibility versus flexibility', *American Economic Review*, Vol. 82, no. 1

Lohmann, Susanne (1998). 'Federalism and central bank independence', *World Politics*, Vol. 50

Lopreato, Francisco L.C. (1992). 'Crise de financiamento dos governos estaduais (1980–1988)'. Doctoral dissertation, UNICAMP, 1992

Loureiro, Maria R. (1997). *50 anos de ciência econômica no Brasil: pensamento, instituições, depoimentos.* São Paulo: Fipe/Vozes

Luebbert, Gregory (1991). *Liberalism, Fascism, or Social Democracy: Social Classes and the Political Origins of Regimes in Interwar Europe.* Oxford: Oxford University Press

Lukauskas, Arvid and Susan Minushkin (2000), 'Explaining styles of financial market opening in Chile, Mexico, S. Korea, and Turkey', *International Studies Quarterly*, Vol. 44, no. 4, pp. 695–723

Magalhães, Augusto F.R. (1971). *Os bancos centrais e sua função reguladora da moeda e crédito*. Rio de Janeiro: A Casa do Livro

Mahoney, Robert and Dieter Reuschemeyer, eds. (2003). *Comparative Historical Analysis in the Social Sciences*. Cambridge: Cambridge University Press

Mainwaring, Scott P. (1999). *Rethinking Political Systems in the Third Wave of Democratization: The Case of Brazil*. Stanford, CA: Stanford University Press

Makler, Harry M. (2000). 'Bank transformation and privatisation in Brazil: financial federalism and some lessons about bank privatization', *The Quarterly Review of Economics and Finance*, Vol. 40, no. 1

Malan, Pedro S. (2001). 'Sumoc', *Dicionário histórico bibliográfico brasileiro*. Editora FGV, Rio de Janeiro (2ª edição).

Maloy, James and Catherine Conaghan (1994). *Unsettling Statecraft: Democracy and Neoliberalism in the Andes*. Pittsburgh, PA: University of Pittsburgh Press

Mangabeira, João (1943). *Rui o estadista da República*. Rio de Janeiro: José Olympio

Manley, J. (1971). *The Politics of Finance*. Boston: Little Brown

March, James and Johan Olsen (1984). 'New Institutionalism: organizational factors in political life', *American Political Science Review*, Vol. 78, pp. 724–49

March, James and Johan Olsen (1989). *Rediscovering Institutions: The Organizational Basis of Politics*. New York: Free Press

Martinez, Juan and Javier Santiso (2003). 'Financial markets and politics: the confidence game in Latin América emerging market economies', *International Political Science Review*, Vol. 24, no. 3, pp. 365–95

Martins Rodrigues, Leôncio (2002). *Partidos, ideologia e composição social: um estudo das bancadas partidárias na Câmara dos Deputados*. São Paulo: Edusp

Matos Dias, J.L. and Maria B. Levy (2001). 'Banco Central do Brasil', *Dicionário histórico bibliográfico brasileiro*. Editora FGV, Rio de Janeiro, 2ª edição

Maurer, Noel (2002). *The Power and the Money: The Mexican Financial System, 1876–1932*. Stanford, CA: Stanford University Press

Maxfield, Sylvia (1998). *Gatekeepers of Growth: The International Political Economy of Central Banking in Developing Countries*. Princeton, NJ: Princeton University Press

McCallum, Bennet (1995). 'Two falacies concerning central bank independence', *American Economic Review Papers and Proceedings*, Vol. 85

Mendonça de Barros, José R. et al. (2003). 'Brazil and the IMF: virtues and limits of the 2002 agreement', Paper presented to the Madrid Club, Madrid Spain, November 1–2

Milesi-Ferretti, Gian M. (1995). 'The disadvantage of tying their hands: on the political economy of policy commitments', *Economic Journal*, Vol. 105

Miller, Gary (2000). 'Rational choice and dysfunctional instutions', *Governance*, Vol. 13, no. 4, pp. 535–47

Montero, Alfred P. (2000). 'Devolving democracy? Political decentralization and the new Brazilian federalism', in Peter R. Kingstone and Timothy J. Power, eds., *Democratic Brazil: Actors, Institutions, and Processes*. Pittsburgh, PA: University of Pittsburgh Press

Moore, Barrington (1966). *The Social Origins of Dictatorship and Democracy*. Boston, MA: Beacon Press

Moser, Peter (1999). 'Checks and balances and the supply of central bank independence', *European Economic Review*, Vol. 43

Mostajo, Rossana (2000). 'Gasto social y distribución des ingreso: caracterización e impacto redistributivo en paises seleccionados de América Latina y el Caribe', ECLAC Serie Reformas Económicas, no. 69, Santiago, Chile: United Nations Economic Commission on Latin America and the Caribbean

Neri, Marcelo and Claudio Considera (1996). 'Cresimento, desigualidade e pobreza: o impacto da estabilização', in IPEA (Instituto de Pesquisa Econômica Aplicada), ed., *A Economia Brasileira em Perspectiva-1996*, Vol. 1, Rio de Janeiro: IPEA, pp. 49–82

Ness, Walter L. (1994). 'Bank stability in economic instability', Paper presented at the XVIII International Congress of the Latin American Studies Association, Atlanta, Georgia, March

Nóbrega, Mailson F. (1985). *Desafios da política agrícola*. Ed. Gazeta Mercantil, São Paulo

Nogueira, Dênio (1993). *Depoimento*. Rio de Janeiro: Programa de História Oral do CPDOC/ FGV, Editora FGV

Nordhaus, William, D. (1975). 'The political business cycle', *Review of Economic Studies*, Vol. 42, no. 2

Oatley, Thomas and Robert Nabors (1998). 'Market failure, wealth transfers, and the Basle Accord', *International Organization*, Vol. 52, no. 1, pp. 35–54

O'Donnell, Guillermo A. (1973). *Modernization and Bureaucratic-Authoritarianism: Studies in South American Politics*. Berkeley, CA: Institute of International Studies, University of California

Packenham, Robert (1973). *Liberal America and the Third World*. Princeton: Princeton University Press

Paes, Julieda P.P. (1996). 'Bancos estaduais, "criação" de moeda e ciclo político'. Master's dissertation, EAESP-FGV, São Paulo

Pelaez, Carlos M. and Wilson Suzigan (1976). *História monetária do Brasil: análise da política, comportamento e instituições monetárias*. Rio de Janeiro: IPEA/INPES

Pérez, Sofia A. (1998). 'Systemic explanations, divergent outcomes: the politics of financial liberation in France and Spain', *International Studies Quarterly*, Vol. 42, pp. 755–84

Pierson, Paul (2001). *The New Politics of the Welfare State*. Oxford: Oxford University Press

Pierson, Paul (2003). 'Politics in time: history, institutions, and political analysis', Harvard University, manuscript

Pierson, Paul and Theda Skocpol (2002). 'Historical institutionalism in contemporary political science', in Ira Katznelson et al., eds., *The State of the Discipline*. New York: W.W. Norton

Pierson, Paul and Shannon O. Trowbridge (2002). 'Asset specificity and institutional development', Paper presented to the Annual Meeting of the American Political Science Association

Pivetti, Massimo (1991). *An Essay on Money and Distribution*. London: Macmillan

Polanyi, Karl (1944). *The Great Transformation: The Political and Economic Origins of Our Time*. New York: Rinehart and Co.

Posen, Adam (1995). 'Declarations are not enough: financial sector sources of central bank independence', NBER Macroeconomic Annual, Vol. 10

Powell, Walter and Paul DiMaggio, eds. (1991). *The New Institutionalism in Organizational Analysis*. Chicago, IL: University of Chicago Press

Przeworski, Adam (1991). *Democracy and the Market: Political and Economic Reforms in Eastern Europe and Latin America*. Cambridge: Cambridge University Press

Putnam, Robert (1969). *The Comparative Study of Political Elites*. New York: Prentice Hall

Reid, Michael (1999). 'Brazil: the disorders of progress', *The Economist*, 27 March, Brazil Survey pp. 1–18

Riker, William (1980). 'Implications from the disequilibrium of majority rule for the study of institutions', *American Political Science Review*, Vol. 74, pp. 432–46

Roberts, Richard and David Kynaston (1995). *The Bank of England: Money, Power, and Influence, 1694–1994*. Oxford: University of Oxford Press

Rockman, Bert and Kent Weaver, eds. (1993). *Do Institututions Matter?* Washington, DC: Brookings Institution

Rogers, Colin (1989). *Money, Interest, and Capital: A Study in the Foundations of Monetary Theory*. Cambridge: Cambridge University Press

Rogoff, Kenneth (1985). 'The optimal degree of commitment to an intermediate monetary target', *Quarterly Journal of Economics*, Vol. 100, pp. 1169–90

Sallum Jr, Brasilio, ed. (2004). *Brasil e Argentina hoje: política e economia*. São Paulo: Edusp

Samuels, David (2001). 'The Cardoso administration and "predatory" federalism in Brazil', University of Minnesota: Department of Political Science, memo

Samuels, David (2003). 'Fiscal straightjacket: the politics of macroeconomic reform in Brazil, 1995–2002', Paper presented at the Meeting of the Latin American Studies Association, Dallas, Texas

Santos, José Maria (1930). *A política geral do Brasil*. São Paulo: J. Magalhães

Scharpf, Fritz (1991). *Crisis and Choice in European Social Democracy*. Ithaca, NY: Cornell University Press

Schleifer, Andrei and Robert W. Vishny (1999). *The Grabbing Hand: Government Pathologies and Their Cures*. Cambridge, MA: Harvard University Press

Schmitter, Philippe C. (1976). *Interest Conflict and Political Change in Brazil*. Stanford, CA: Stanford University Press

Schumpeter, Joseph (1912). *The Theory of Economic Development*. Harvard University Press

Shapiro, Helen (1991). 'The public–private interface: Brazil's business–government relations in historical perspective, 1950–1990', mimeo, Harvard Business School

Singer, André (1999). *Esquerda e direita no eleitorado brasileiro*. São Paulo: Editora 34

Sinn, Hans W. (1999). *The German State Banks*. Cheltenham: Edward Elgar

Skocpol, Theda (1978). *States and Social Revolutions*. Cambridge: Cambridge University Press

Smith, William et al., eds. (1994). *Latin American Political Economy in the Age of Neoliberal Reforms*. New Brunswick, NJ: Transaction

Sobel, Andrew (1999). *State Institutions, Private Incentives, Global Capital*. Ann Arbor, MI: University of Michigan Press

Sochaczewski, Antônio C. (2001). 'Sistema financeiro', *Dicionário histórico bibliográfico brasileiro*. Editora FGV, Rio de Janeiro (2ª edição)

Sola, Lourdes, ed. (1993). *Estado, mercado e democracia: política e economia comparadas*. São Paulo: Paz e Terra

Sola, Lourdes (1995). 'Estado, regime fiscal e ordem monetária: qual estado?', in Lourdes Sola and Leda M. Paulani, eds. *Lições da década de 80*. São Paulo, Brazil: Editora da Universidade de São Paulo (EDUSP)

Sola, Lourdes, Laurence Whitehead and Eduardo Kugelmas, eds. (2002). *Banco Central: autoridade política e democratiziçao – un equilíbrio delicado*. Rio de Janeiro: Fundaçao Getulio Vargas

Spiller, Pable E.S. and Mariano Tommasi (2003). 'Political institutions, policy making processes, and policy outcomes: an intertemporal transaction framework', Inter-American Development Bank, manuscript

Steinmo, Sven et al., eds. (1991) *Structuring Politics: Historical Institutionalism in Comparative Analysis*. Cambridge: Cambridge University Press

Syvrud, Donald E. (1974). *Foundations of Brazilian Economic Growth*, Stanford, CA: Hoover Institution Press, Stanford University

Tavares, Martus A.R. and Nelson Carvalheiro (1985). *O setor bancário brasileiro: alguns aspectos do crescimento e da concentração*. São Paulo: IPE/EDUSP

Ter-Minassian, T. et al. (1998). 'Brazil: recent economic developments', IMF Staff Country Report 98/24

Teurissen, Jan J. and Age Akkerman (2003). *The Crisis That Was Not Prevented: Lessons for Argentina, the IMF, and Globalisation*. The Hague: FONDAD

The Economist (2003). 'A cruel sea of capital', Survey, 3 May

Thelen, Kathleen (1999). 'Historical institutionalism and comparative politics', *Annual Review of Political Science*, Vol. 2, pp. 369–404

Tsebelis, George (1995). 'Veto players and institutional analysis', *Governance*, Vol. 13, no. 4, pp. 441–74

Tyler, William (1983). *The Brazilian Industrial Economy*. Lexington, MA: Lexington Books

Van Parijs, Philippe (1995). *Real Freedom for All: What (if Anything) Can Justify Capitalism?* Oxford: University of Oxford Press

Viana, Maria A (1987). *A administração do milagre: o conselho monetário nacional, 1964–1974*. Petropolis: Vozes

Viera, D.T. (1962). *Evolução do sistema monetário brasileiro*. São Paulo: Gráfica da FFCL

Walsh, Carl (1995). 'Optimal contracts for central bankers', *American Economic Review*, Vol. 85

Way, Christopher (2000). 'Central banks, partisan politics, and macroeconomic outcomes', *Comparative Political Studies*, Vol. 33, pp. 196–224

Weingast, Barry (2002). 'Rational choice institutionalism', in Ira Katznelson et al., eds., *The State of the Discipline*. New York: W.W. Norton, pp. 660–92

Welch, John H. (1993). *Capital Markets in the Development Process: The Case of Brazil*. Pittsburgh, PA: University of Pittsburgh Press

Werlang, Sérgio and Armínio Fraga (1995). 'Os bancos estadiais e o descontrole fiscal: alguns aspectos', *Revista Brasileira de Economia*, Vol. 49, no. 2, pp. 165–75

Weyland, Kurt (1996). *Democracy without Equity: Failures of Reform in Brazil*. Pittsburgh, PA: University of Pittsburgh Press

Weyland, Kurt (1999). 'Neoliberal populism in Latin America and eastern Europe', *Comparative Politics*, Vol. 31, no. 4, pp. 379–402

Weyland, Kurt (2000). 'The Brazilian state in the new democracy', in Peter R. Kingstone and Timothy J. Power, eds., *Democratic Brazil: Actors, Institutions, and Processes*. Pittsburgh, PA: University of Pittsburgh Press

Weyland, Kurt (2002). *The Politics of Market Reform in Fragile Democracies: Argentina, Brazil, Peru, and Venezuela*. Princeton, NJ: Princeton University Press

Whitehead, Laurence (1990). 'Political explanations of macroecnomics management: a survey', *World Development*, Vol. 18, no. 8

Whitehead, Laurence (2002). 'How much convergence in central banking?' Nuffield College, manuscript

Whitehead, Laurence, ed. (2002). *Emerging Market Democracies: East Asia/Latin America*. Johns Hopkins University Press

Willis, Eliza J. (1986). 'The state as banker: the expansion of the public sector in Brazil'. PhD dissertation, University of Texas, Dept. of Political Science

Woolley, John T. (1984). *Monetary Politics: The Federal Reserve and the Politics of Monetary Policy*, Cambridge: Cambridge University Press

Wooley, John. T. (1994). 'The politics of monetary policy: a critical review', *Journal of Public Policy*, Vol. 14, pp. 57–85

Zini, Alvaro A. Jr. (1992). 'Monetary reform, state intervention, and the Collor Plan', in Alvaro A. Zini, ed., *The Market and the State in Economic Development in the 1990s*. Oxford: Elsevier Science Publishers B.V.

Zysman, John (1983). *Governm ents, Markets, and Growth Financial Systems and the Politics of Industrial Change*. Ithaca, NY: Cornell University Press